Xcogitate

An Introduction to the Examined Life
2nd Edition

David G. Payne, Ph.D.

ISBN 978-1492235477

To Lo,
who found me.

"Tell me one last thing," said Harry, "Is this real? Or has this been happening inside my head?" ...
"Of course it is happening inside your head, Harry, but why on earth should that mean that it is not real?"

- Harry Potter and the Deathly Hallows

Table of Contents

Preface   ix
  Part 1: Foundations
    1. The Basics   3
    2. Consciousness   21
    3. Operating Systems   47
    4. Theorizing   75
    5. Conceptual Schemes   103
    6. Extending Our Conceptual Schemes   123
  Part 2: Explications
    7. Truth   151
    8. Our Knowledge   171
    9. Certainty   199
    10. Coherence   223
  Part 3: Applications
    11. Determinism   243
    12. God   267
    13. Self   293
    14. Morality   321
    15. Extending Coherence   349
    Afterward   375

Illustration Credits   381
References   383
Index   387

Preface

● ●

Suppose someone recommends a good book, say, Joseph Conrad's novella, The Heart of Darkness. You sit down one night and begin to read. You like the characters, enjoy the story, and, when you put it down, you feel satisfied—like after a good meal. But what if, while reading, you begin to notice more than just a good story. Perhaps you begin to see some of the characters as typifying the way people go through life, and you thus begin noticing similar details throughout, and then you begin to wonder if maybe Conrad doesn't have more on his mind than merely telling a story; maybe he's trying to say something about life and how we approach it. This is a different approach to a book. Instead of reading the story and enjoying it like a good meal, you transcend the story, the plot line, and think about what it means. You reflect upon the story. The person who reads Conrad's book in this way gets more from the book than the person who reads it as merely a good story. I am making no judgment about a person being a better person or the book being a better book for having done this. These are simply two different approaches. Two people read the same book, both enjoy the story, but one gets more from it than the other—from the same story!

Life is a multi-layered book. Some approach it like the first reader. They enjoy the characters they meet, find the plot interesting, and never think anything more. There is something delightfully childlike about this approach. Others live like the second reader. They see more going on, different levels of characterization, symbols, themes, connections. Same world; different pleasures. Let me say again, I am not claiming one approach is *inherently* better than the other, but I do think something is lost if we don't experience both, and the only way to choose between two options is to try both and then decide. This is my challenge to you: try the reflective approach to life. If you don't like it, you certainly don't have to continue. There are no judgments attached if you decide you don't. Think of this as an opportunity to add new tiers of pleasure to your life.

❧

Almost everyone can benefit from at least some exposure to philosophy. A philosopher is not necessarily someone who teaches philosophy or who has a degree in philosophy. You are a philosopher if you reflect carefully upon your life and make choices based upon these reflections. You are a philosopher if you strive to rise above the value systems others are constantly trying to impose upon you. Being philosophical is an attitude toward the world which we need not learn in class or from books; it is a way of approaching life—one I think is valuable because of what it can do for you. You, of course, may not be philosophical at all, but that's okay, too. To say the unexamined life is not worth living (as Plato once did) is much too harsh. Many will be happier not examining their lives, but this is for them to find out for themselves, which is what this text is designed to do—find out how far down the rabbit hole you might want to go.

We live in a world infinite in its potential for surprise. All too many people all too much of the time are all too certain of their own view of the world, and their certainty enslaves them within a box that blinds them to the wondrous sights awaiting them beyond the boundaries of their beliefs. The emphasis throughout this book will be on connections; the connections between the parts of an atom, between the parts of a cell, the connection of cells to our bodies and our selves, the connections between neurons, between people, groups, nations, the universe and beyond. Deep connections can only be discovered by means of reflection. The more you reflect on yourself and reality the more connections you will be exposed to, and connections are the very essence of life, love and meaning.

The beauty of the philosophical enterprise is that if at any time the going gets too tough, you can always conveniently forget what you once saw and return to your prior prereflective state with no regrets. I hope this won't happen. I point this out so you can proceed without trepidation, for there is danger ahead—danger that many of your cherished beliefs may fall by the wayside. Indeed, the very concept of a cherished belief may have to go. If this talk does not deter, let us begin; let us examine our beliefs, asking why we believe them, where they came from, and whether or not they are worth keeping. It is this task I hope to help you perform, for this, I think, is the beginning of wisdom.

I wrote this text because there seems to be a paucity of philosophy books written for the general public—books that talk about truth and morality and how we know what we know. There are many wonderful books on these subjects, but none seems to take the larger "big-history" kind of approach, and it is only by taking this approach that one can begin to see the multifarious connectedness of the world in all its glory. The critics will complain that by taking this approach we miss the trees for the forest, and this is true; but we need to at least consider this perspective if we want to appreciate the larger connections in life.

Introductory philosophy texts seem to be written for those who want to major in philosophy. In twenty years of teaching introduction to philosophy classes only maybe a half dozen of my students have gone on to study philosophy proper, which means I should not be pretending to prepare people for a life in academic philosophy. Most people take a philosophy class simply because the topic interests them. I hope, if this is your reason, you will not be disappointed. I have tried to dispense with philosophical jargon and to keep the topics simple, but this was not an easy task, and I hope it did not muddle instead of make clear. There's a reason philosophers talk in convoluted language; they are looking at ordinary topics from an extraordinary vantage point, but it's easy to get carried away. I have tried to find a happy medium.

The text is divided into three main sections. The first, foundations, lays down the basis for all that is to come. Here we have to talk about neurology, for the way our brain works determines how we see the world. All of the information we become conscious of is processed information—we are never conscious of raw data. This immediately gives rise to a problem: what is the world like before our perception of it is processed? We will answer this question, but first we will have to introduce the major thesis of the book: we are theorizing beings to the core. This is how we get about in the world—we theorize. Thus, we will spend some time on the concept of a theory and how this applies to our lives.

The second main section, explications, delves more deeply into some major philosophical concepts: truth, knowledge and certainty. We will discuss these in light of what we have learned about theorizing. The difficulty in simplifying some complex material in this section has led to a methodological dilemma. I have dealt with this by explaining certain concepts like truth in their common sense fashion at first and later developing a more sophisticated position. I hope this is not confusing. If you make it through this section, there is smooth sailing ahead, for section three, applications, merely applies what we have learned from the previous two sections. Hopefully, these chapters will deepen your understanding of the concepts we have explicated in the previous sections.

I have said that the overall theme is one of connections. This is inextricably intertwined with another, which I have referred to by means of the anchor metaphor: we humans have a penchant for intellectual anchors. We like to fasten our beliefs to something solid, objective and unchanging. This is understandable, but can be stultifying. Thus my theme: unhitch yourself, float free. Ironically, once we cut our anchors to unchanging objective realities, the connections we have become more important. If this makes no sense, then continue on: we have miles to go before we sleep.

Part 1: Foundations

1. The Basics

· ·

Bring on the wonder,
bring on the song;
we've kept you down deep
in our souls for too long...
- Susan Enan

SYNOPSIS

(1) We are thrown into this world blind and helpless. Knowledge of our surroundings is a necessary condition of our survival. (2) Maslow's hierarchy is insufficient for describing this, but he is correct in his claim that we want more than mere survival. What we want in life is what I will refer to as well-being. An attempt at defining this. (3) A digression on increments. The world is complex. The more we know, the more we know we don't know, and the less likely we are to make black and white distinctions. (4) Achieving well-being involves coming to understand not only our own self, but also our relationship to the world and other people. The relationships between these are complex and can easily become obstacles to our well-being. (5) Philosophical reflection is what helps us overcome these obstacles, but it can be overdone. A distinction is made between levels of reflection and reduction. (6) As we reflect, and knowledge of the complexity of our situation grows, we will notice an increasing number of connections to different aspects of reality. These connections are what give meaning to our lives. (7) Chapter Summary.

CHAPTER OBJECTIVES

- to emphasize the importance of thinking reflectively about your life
- to make you aware of the fundamental problems of knowledge inherent within life

§1 THE FOG OF LIFE

I f you've ever dabbled in computer games you may be familiar with a feature called the discovery option. When this is turned on, you begin as the only light spot in an otherwise darkened world. You know the location of neither resources nor rivals, and to discover these you must wander, widening your light patch as you go. This is an apt metaphor to describe humans on several levels: both individual and species. Our situation may be likened to what von Clausewitz called the fog of war. As he describes it:

> The great uncertainty of all data in war is a peculiar difficulty, because all action must, to a certain extent, be planned in a mere twilight, which in addition not infrequently—like the effect of a fog or moonshine—gives to things exaggerated dimensions and unnatural appearance. (2.2.24)

Might we not call this instead, the fog of life? We humans crawl forth into this world blind, entirely dependent on others, mastering the art of living by using both our innate tools and good tricks[1] passed down from others. We are lost within a forest dark, and gradually expand our familiar territory by pushing the perimeter of the unknown, as armies of old used picket lines, feeling our way tentatively into *terra incognita*, blundering into the unexpected. Expanding the metaphor of blindness to the species, we note that evolution itself proceeds in the same way—blind to the future needs of the species it spawns. How to proceed, then? Two important questions arise immediately:

1. Where are we going?
2. How do we get there?

The dark forest in which we are lost is our life, which is an epic journey, a quest. We have goals: to be happy, to be fulfilled, but what do these terms mean? This is

---

[1] A good trick is an evolutionary trait (biological or cultural) or adaptation that leads to a cas-ᶜading series of consequences that improve an organism's ability to get by in the world. There are also bad tricks. In biology these are usually naturally selected out, but in culture they may persist, for example, the habit of drinking alcohol to excess. The phrase was coined by Daniel Dennett (1996).

the first question. The second is obviously dependent upon the first. Do we wander blindly, hoping to happen across a path or are there preferred routes? Many, maybe most, never take the time to think carefully about these fundamental issues. Sartre speaks of this way of living in his novel, *Nausea*:

> They have dragged out their life in stupor and semi-sleep, they have married hastily, out of impatience, they have made children at random. They have met other men in cafes, at weddings and funerals. Sometimes, caught in the tide, they have struggled against it without understanding what was happening to them. All that has happened around them has eluded them… And then, around forty, they christen their small obstinacies and a few proverbs with the name of experience, they begin to simulate slot machines: put a coin in the left hand slot and you get tales wrapped in silver paper, put a coin in the slot on the right and you get precious bits of advice that stick to your teeth like caramels. (68)

This is what happens when we proceed unthinking through life, wandering without a plan. But this is the only life we have! To ensure it is well-lived, we must think about how to proceed through it. We need to know where we are going; we need to have a life-plan, because by doing so we establish how to have a meaningful life. We need a map, and the beauty of being human is that, at least in part, we get to participate in our own cartographic enterprise. Certain features will appear on everyone's map; these we can use for general orientation, but where we want to go and how we get there may vary significantly from person to person. Death, for instance, as the end of our journey, is on everyone's map, but what after that? And what before?

In order to construct a useful map we must first know something about ourselves as humans, and this search will lead to deeper questions—how do we know where we want to go? What is knowledge? Who are we? These are proper philosophical questions that must be explored, and these are the questions we must address. Consider the following thought experiment:

> Suppose you awaken one day to find you have been chosen as the subject of a lifelong cosmic experiment. You are wrenched rudely from your life, placed in a rocket and blasted into space, all with minimal explanation. Your only instructions are to explore the universe. You are told only that your personal spacecraft has cutting edge technological abilities: it can travel faster than light and has an endless fuel supply, so distant stars and galaxies are easily reached; it can adjust to various environments, translate complex languages, sense many different modalities on various spectrums; and it has extensive defensive capabilities, including weapons and cloaking devices—or at least, so you've been told. You find yourself staring at an amazing array of instruments, but you have no clue what they mean or how to use them. When you look around the spacecraft you find wondrous gadgets, contraptions, instruments, weapons and wardrobes, and there, on a small table you find a large, densely written manuscript entitled "Operating Manual," within which is a detailed explanation of how to use every feature of your craft. You scan a few lines, but the book is hard to read—complex and demanding—so you put it aside and never look at it again, preferring instead to fly your rig by the seat of your pants, a come-what-may attitude

that has always served you well in the past. Thus you kick back, bring up one of the endless pulp novels stored in your spacecraft's database, and wait for the adventure to begin.

An implausible allegory, but one which illustrates my point. We are all on an exciting adventure, wrenched rudely from the womb, placed in an intricately complex craft (our body), controlled by sophisticated software (our brain), moving through a hostile environment (the world). Yet most people know little about the conglomeration of cells which make up their body, much less about the world beyond them, and, even more odd, don't seem to care. Until something goes wrong they live their lives in a blissful haze, and even then might defer knowing to experts who can treat their ailments and instruct them how to avoid future tribulations. They know even less about that neuronic mass they think of as their control center, the brain. They know they want to be happy, but they don't know how to achieve this.

§2 *What We Want*

Abraham Maslow is famous for his ideas on human needs, capturing some basic truths within his hierarchical structure (Figure 1–1). Less well known is his idea of a second hierarchy intimately related to the first, a hierarchy of knowledge. In order to achieve the various levels of the hierarchy of needs we must learn about our world, ourselves, and others. The problem with Maslow's approach is the hierarchy itself, for it implies the first level is a necessary condition for reaching the second, and so forth, while life is never so simplistic. Instead, we find multitudes of interrelationships between the various levels. A further criticism concerns the goal of self-actualization as the highest level of achievement. This has been criticized as

Figure 1–1
Maslow's hierarchy of needs, a much-used, but still useful diagram that illustrates how one set of needs functions as a precondition for reaching others. Despite its flaws, it still reminds us there is a basic order of operations on our quest for fulfillment.

ethnocentric, as a particularly Western goal. We need a more general goal, a goal all people everywhere strive for. The danger in stating such a goal is triviality, for it may be so broad as to be vacuous, but we will deem the danger worthwhile and claim that what we humans want, in general, is some degree of happiness. In this I follow Jeremy Bentham (1748-1832), who held that, at base, all of our actions, goals, deliberations and moral rules are the result of our "sovereign masters," pain and pleasure.

> They govern us in all we do, in all we say, in all we think: every effort we can make to throw off our subjection, will serve but to demonstrate and confirm it. In words a man may pretend to abjure their empire: but in reality he will remain subject to it all the while. (Bentham 14)

This goal of happiness is spoken of in different ways, but it is not the mere titillation of a dopamine drip from our brain's reward system, not the satiation of a gourmet meal or the pleasure of winning a competition or an award, but rather a comprehensive contentment I will refer to as well-being. We might define this loosely as follows:

Well-Being: a reflective state of contentment with our present condition and expected future.

By a "reflective" state of contentment I mean more than mere contentment. A well-fed canine basking in the warmth of the fireplace at its master's feet may be content, but not in the sense we mean, for it does not contemplate its life as a person and project this into the future. This kind of projection implies the ability, not merely to experience, but to reflect upon our experience. (We will discuss this distinction in more detail in the next chapter.)

The reference to the "expected future" is the desire for a lasting state of happiness. Fleeting happiness is fine while it lasts, but, as the ancient Stoics argued, knowing our present happiness is fleeting immediately lowers the level of that happiness because we dread its coming to an end. In order to achieve long term well-being, we must understand more fully what it is we are seeking. Knowing our goal gives us a standard by which to judge our progress; otherwise, we are running a race, unaware of the location of the finish line. When we reflect on what we want out of life, we usually have a vague idea of what is important to us. This is a value judgment which is then used as a standard to measure our progress. For example, once we know what goals we are striving for we might judge certain activities (say, smoking cigarettes, using heroin, driving recklessly, having unprotected sex) detrimental to achieving them. Our actions should then conform to our judgment.

We assume a connection between our deliberations concerning our goals (no matter how trivial) and our actions. This simple assumption is based on two others, both of which will have to be discussed in more detail later. First, that the world is rational, which means that our deliberations can change the world in predictable ways. We are continually making probability calculations about the future, and when these probabilities are high enough so that we are convinced of the consequences, we act accordingly. This is what we mean when we say we are rational. For example, most cigarette smokers know there is a significant correlation between smoking and cancer, but they are not necessarily irrational when they continue to smoke. They make, and continually revisit and revise, probability calculations concerning the impact of this information on their own health, weighing these against the pleasures of smoking. If, for whatever reason, they become certain smoking is harming them, they will act accordingly to eliminate the threat. If they want to live a long and happy life and they are absolutely convinced smoking will interfere with this goal, they would be irrational to continue smoking. (We will examine the force of certainty on our actions in chapter 9.) The second presupposition behind our actions is that we are free in some sense, that our actions really do change our future. Fatalism denies this, but it is impossible to be a practicing fatalist and remain a rational human. Most people only resort to fatalism as a flickering hindsight to console themselves about events over which they had no control. (We will examine free will and determinism in chapter 11.)

Once we have added the reflective component to well-being we run into difficulties. The psychologist Robert Biswar-Diener interviewed sex workers in Calcutta and found they were (on average) "more satisfied than dissatisfied," (Haidt 104) and even prisoners in Nazi ghettos and concentration camps often found a certain contentment within their situation. Could these individuals, in the midst of their suffering, really experience well-being? Isn't their state too temporary, too fleeting to warrant the appellation? There are two schools of thought on this matter. On the one hand, the ancient Stoics and many modern day Buddhists believe even a prisoner under torture can be content, while on the other, most ancient Greeks would agree with Sophocles, who said, "call no man happy until the day he dies," believing severe misfortune will necessarily interfere with your well-being. This latter school would say a better way to characterize the sex-workers and concentration camp inmates is that they were able to find "moments of contentment" in an otherwise horrible environment. Which school of thought is preferable? Before answering this question we must digress.

§3 INCREMENTAL INVESTIGATIONS

Once upon a summer drive my wife pointed to some huge boulders on the side of the road with the comment, "Look at the size of those stones!" "Stones?" I replied. "Those aren't stones. Those are boulders." This led to a (still) continuing debate on the incremental nature of reality, for she immediately challenged me to define the difference between pebbles, rocks, stones and boulders. My definition was based on the ability to throw them and inflict harm. Even a child can throw a pebble and not hurt anyone; stones, too, are easy to heft, but can hurt; rocks take two hands to lift and will incur serious damage; and boulders can't be lifted at all by mere humans.

> **TAXONOMY**
> A clasification of objects or organisms into groups based upon their presumed similarities of structure or relationships.

Today, whenever a conversation arises in which rocks are involved, we look at each other and smile, agreeing to disagree on the intricacies of rock taxonomy.

This is how we humans think about the world. We classify things by means of concepts, which are abstractions upon objects in the world. 'Rock,' for example, is an abstraction that covers a multitude of different objects. Problems arise when we assume our concepts necessarily correspond to real delineations in the world. Reality is analog; our brains are digital processors.[2]

The continuum is a device particularly useful for illustrating analog features. Figure 1–2(a), for instance, illustrates gradations of shading from black to grey. As we move from left to right on the continuum, black slowly fades to grey, but where, exactly, on the continuum, does the change occur? It's impossible to say, but we humans need answers, so we stipulate an arbitrary line at which point everything to the left is some shade of black while everything to the right is some shade of grey. This is an interesting technique, because the more we know about a situation the less likely we are to find a decisively rational spot on a continuum.[3] For instance, suppose we are only able to distinguish six different gradations, as in Figure 1–2(b). If this were so, we might not have a problem drawing our line on the continuum distinguishing the two. But suppose we can distinguish over one hundred different shades? or one thousand? By multiplying the choices, the differences between the shades becomes almost imperceptible, which makes distinguishing between them impossible. In Figure 1–3(a), for example, there are three different colors, all of which I would consider black, but at some point, there will be a discernible difference, maybe not between any two adjacent colors, but overall. Where the three colors in Figure 1–3(a) are adjacent on the grey scale, the three in Figure 1–3(b) are separated by ten (arbitrary) gradations.

This is important, for it seems to indicate that the more information we have the more difficult it is to distinguish where one color starts and the other stops. One of the functions of technology is to extend our senses, allowing us to make finer and finer discriminations, which in turn destroys our ability to make precise categorical distinctions. Most of the fine distinctions we are so comfortable with are arbitrary, including the pebble-stone-boulder distinctions indicated in Figure 1–4. We humans have the tendency to turn arbitrary distinctions into real distinctions, that is, distinctions actually existing in the world. I will refer to this tendency throughout this text as the rock-pebble fallacy.

The question that led to this digression was how to fit the hard cases into our definition of well-being. To side with either the Stoics and Buddhists or with Sophocles would be to make an arbitrary distinction where none is needed. What we have learned from the above digression is that life is not always so cleanly divisible. Our answer, then, is to accept both as possibilities and build our own continuum of contentment. We will allow there are those who could experience contentment even in extreme situations. Most of us are not so sagacious, but we, too, should be allowed to call ourselves content.

---

[2] This doesn't mean our concepts never correspond. Money and speed limits are examples of socially constructed conventions, but all our concepts need not be. As Pinker says (2003), "If it walks like a duck and quacks like a duck, it probably is a duck. If it's a duck, it's likely to swim, fly, have a back off which water rolls, and contain meat that's tasty when wrapped in a pancake with scallions and hoisin sauce." (203) That is, there probably really are ducks which correspond to our concept 'duck.'

[3] This becomes important in practical issues. For example, within the abortion debate, there are those who want to use conception as the point when the organism takes on a right to life. This assumes there is a moment of conception, but the more we know about the process of fertilization the more we realize this is a vast oversimplification. So also in legal issues, as when we set an age of accountability.

Black   Grey

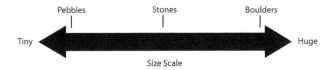

Figure 1–2
A gray-scale continuum illustrating how our arbitrary divisions affect our perception. In (a) the gradations are minute, so that there is a continuous shading, while (b) uses larger divisions resulting in a less continuous shading.

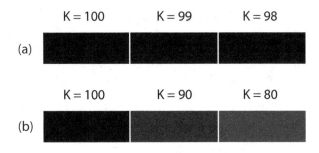

FIGURE 1–3
Various arbitrary gradations on the greyscale. Using the K-scale, (a) shows three gradations separated by only one point. The resulting colors are identical to the human eye; while if we separate the gradations by ten points we can easily discern the differences.

FIGURE 1–4
A continuum illustrating the arbitrary size distinctions we might use to distinguish between pebbles, stones and boulders.

§4   THE CONDITIONS OF OUR WELL-BEING

What are the general conditions of well-being for us ordinary mortals? What do we minimally need in order to achieve this? Maslow is surely correct in identifying a few fundamental physiological needs as necessary. We must, for instance, procure a sufficient amount of food and shelter in the short term, which means we must have some minimal knowledge of our surroundings. This is not to say we need a well-built house and three square meals. Without the minimal conditions of food

On the Definition of a Planet

When the ancients looked into the night sky they noticed that a few of the heavenly bodies (seven of them) were different from the rest. These seven changed their position relative to the background stars. These "wanderers" (which is what the word 'planet' originally meant), were thus distinguished from stars, which moved together as a group. The seven planets were: Mercury, Venus, Mars, Jupiter, Saturn, the Sun and the Moon. The Earth was thought to be the center of the universe, which is why the Sun and Moon were both considered planets and the Earth was not. The designation was simple, based on what humans could see with the unaided eye—if its movement was not in tune with the background stars it was a planet. This changed with the Copernican Revolution, in which the Sun was seen to be fixed with the Earth and other planets orbiting it. Now the Earth became a planet, the Sun was dropped, as was the Moon (a moon orbits a planet, but is not itself a planet). Technology (the telescope) changed the grouping once again: Uranus, which is technically visible to the naked eye, was discovered in 1781, Neptune in 1846 and Pluto in 1930. The definition of 'planet' was intuitively simple throughout the years: big, round, and orbits the Sun. But trouble was brewing. In 1831, Guiseppe Piazzi had discovered Ceres, an orbiting body with an equatorial radius of approximately 500 kilometers located between Mars and Jupiter (in what we now call the Asteroid Belt). Though classified for a while as the eighth planet, the "big" condition eventually won the day and Ceres was demoted to asteroid status. When Pluto was discovered (mean radius: 1153 km), the same "big" condition made it the ninth planet. Then, in 2005, Eris was discovered. With a mean radius of c. 1300 km, and 27% more massive than Pluto, it became a candidate for the tenth planet. But with discoveries of bodies rivaling the size of Pluto accumulating, the concept of Planet itself was in need of a makeover, and in 2006, the International Astronomical Union formulated a new definition containing three conditions. An object is a planet if and only if it: 1) orbits the Sun; 2) has achieved hydrostatic equilibrium; and 3) has cleared its orbit of smaller debris. The "big" condition is still here—hydrostatic equilibrium is a function of gravity, which is a function of mass, and gravity is responsible for helping clear the orbit of smaller debris. Hydrostatic equilibrium is achieved when the internal pull of gravity is sufficient to overcome the structural integrity of an object (the result of this equilibrium is the roundness of a planet), so really the third condition is the true addition to "big." But the third is sufficient to disallow both Pluto and Ceres from the sisterhood of the planets, for neither has cleared its orbit (especially Ceres). So, both were relegated to the demeaning status of "dwarf planet." The debate was officially settled (arbitrarily of course), and only temporarily, no doubt, for technology never sleeps. It's probably only a matter of time until the third condition comes under scrutiny. As we see more clearly what lies in the orbits of objects we will have to define more precisely what it means to "clear an orbit." And so goes the neverending story...

and shelter humans will die. Also, most of us, in order to achieve well-being have to know our state of affairs is secure. It's not enough to be well-fed and housed now if we know we will be out on the street in a week or a month. A prima facie test of your well-being is to ask: "What changes would I make in my life right now if I could?" If your answer contains significant life changes, you have not yet arrived, for well-being, in its highest manifestation, is a state in which you would change nothing.

Figure 1–5 shows the relationship between the three major factors we have to deal with in our lives: self, world, and others. These are mutually interconnected. As we consider each, we are always led back to the others.

SELF

You must learn who you are. This involves thinking about your self. Who are you? Who is this thinking thing that refers to itself as "I"? What is your relation to your memories? Is this all you are? Neuro-scientists tell us the brain is composed of modules, each of which processes certain parts of our experiences. But if this is so, how do we have what seems to be a unified experience? a central experiencer? This is known as the binding problem in neurology. We must understand our own human role in experiencing the world in order to understand our relation to the world and others. We will begin this investigation in the next chapter.

THE WORLD

This begins as a problem of knowledge: how do we come to know anything outside of our own experience? The more we know, the more there is to know, and information about the world seems deeper than our resources to obtain it. As we mine the bowels of the cosmos for its truths we falsify past truths, though we would

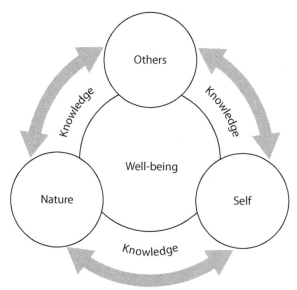

Figure 1–5
The well-being triad. Knowledge of self, others and nature is necessary in order to achieve well-being. These aspects are all interrelated in complex ways.

never have reached the present truths without those past ones. This should give us pause, for it at least hints at the possibility that many propositions we now think true will one day be proved false.

OTHER PEOPLE

We are social beings. We cannot survive alone. Taken in its broadest sense, this is what we call a deep truth, for it is true not only on the human level, but on all levels of existence. Interactions between systems make things what they are, from atoms to galaxies. Particularly in the world of living organisms, symbiosis, defined broadly as mutual system-dependence, is always necessary. We humans could not have survived either as a species or as individuals without others. We are social creatures and construct our own arbitrary social systems (language is the most fundamental of these) to facilitate living together. An investigation into these systems shows the distinctions made within them do not precisely map the world, for we impose our concepts upon the world, which, in turn, is more complex than we would make it out to be. (The very concept of a system itself, whether it be solar or social, is arbitrary.) The result is that our concepts, even when precisely defined, tend to blur together when applied to the world. Incremental investigation speaks to the complexity of our world.

We are thus led back to self and the world, for no one really knows all they think they know. This is true on several levels. First, it follows from the complexity of the world, but on a deeper level, it follows from the fact that the very mechanisms we use to make judgments about the world (our cognitive processes) may be flawed. We are not designed to find truth, only to survive, and our survival abilities evolved in hunter-gatherer times. Unless we have special training in reasoning, math, and probability theory, we will be drawing flawed conclusions (those not in our best interest). This is why education is so important.

This ignorance claim includes you! And to make matters worse, it includes not only what you (and others) think about the world and other people, but what you think about yourself. Your self-images (including those you project to others) may very well be fabrications. We are a part of the complexity we are trying to understand.

Even if our tools were optimal, we would still be in trouble. You may remember Robinson Crusoe, the sole survivor of a shipwreck on a remote island. Robinson was extremely resourceful and made himself comfortable—there were no dangerous beasts on the island and plenty of food and other resources. Though he missed human interaction, he was content... until the day he saw a human footprint in the sand. This footprint implied the existence of another human on the island, and therein lay the problem, for humans have intentions that run contrary to each other, and these intentions are inscrutable.

If this is true, then we must take to heart that "everybody lies," especially if we broaden the concept of lying to include the unintentional passing on of falsehoods as truths, but it is also true in its stricter definition of intentionally passing on falsehoods. We need other people to help us fulfill our life-quest, yet they, too, have a life-quest to fulfill which, to them, is more important than ours. Given any two people and a relatively scarce resource necessary for the fulfillment of the life-quests of both: who gets the resource? We are faced, then, with a quest, the success of which depends on having the help of other people. But we can't always trust other people because, even if they have our best interests at heart, they could be leading us astray.

§5 Levels of Reflection

I have defined the philosophical enterprise of examining our lives in terms of reflection. Ignorance is not necessarily bliss. We need knowledge of our world and knowledge of and from other people in order to get by. Furthermore, we are not like dogs or cats or cows; we are more reflective, and it is our amazing reflective abilities that give us the capacity for achieving well-being. Reflection is not enough, but it does stack the deck in our favor, lessening the impact of the slings and arrows of outrageous fortune upon our lives. Still, we should avoid over-thinking to the extent that it hampers our ability to make decisions, or causes us to become depressed by focusing too much upon past mistakes.

On a more theoretical level, this is the problem of trying to explain the world in terms of abstractions. Abstracting too much causes people to lose sight of the details that are important for understanding every day life. The opposite problem arises when we get too immersed in the details. When this happens we say a person can't see the forest for the trees. There is a place for such extreme detail. The problem lies in thinking that the same explanatory methods are valid on all levels of reflection. This is the problem of reduction.

There are good and bad reductionist positions. On one hand, we use reduction to explain basic facts about our life. These are the taxonomic structures referred to above that allow us to talk about objects. In identifying an animal as, say, a cow, we have reduced the entity to a stereotype. We have not fully appreciated the complexity of the thing. This is why the word 'stereotype' is often used in a pejorative sense—it fails to treat humans as individuals. And yet, such reductions are necessary. We can explain a vast amount of things in terms of our concepts.

Steven Pinker says (2003), "Reductionism, like cholesterol, comes in good and bad forms." (69) The bad, or greedy, form of reductionism tries to reduce everything to its smallest component. We can reduce a human to its molecular structure, since, after all, everything is composed of molecules and their interactions. There is nothing wrong with this reduction per se, until we assume we can explain the same sorts of thing by resorting to molecular interactions that we can in talking about concrete humans. We can, in theory, explain our entire life as the result of molecular interactions, but what we would lose in such an explanation would be all the hopes, wants, desires, and meanings that make us what we are. The good form of reductionism avoids this error, helping to explain the causal links in one field with the smaller components in its own without feeling the need to replace the one with the other. The sign of a greedy reductionist is the use of the phrase "nothing but," as in "the mind is nothing but neurons firing in the brain." A statement like this fails to take account of emergent systems in which the whole is more than its parts.

Somewhere between the two extremes lies the mean to strive for with respect to reflection. We should appreciate all levels of complexity, but not make the mistake of thinking that every level has equal explanatory ability.

§6 CONNECTIONS

The deeper we explore any field, the more we reflect, the more complex our information concerning that field becomes. The more we know about the complexities, the more connections we will begin to see, not only to other aspects within the field itself, but to other fields. For example, suppose you decide you want to study history. You engage in this endeavor, but you immediately realize you have to make a choice. You could write a history of the universe, but in order to do so you would have to deal in very large concepts which would mean acquiring a vast amount of knowledge concerning science and mathematics. So maybe you limit your area of expertise to U.S. history, but even here the amount of data is imposing, so you limit your area even more, maybe to the civil war era or the colonial era. Even these are vast, which will mean overlooking a lot of information. This aside, once you start your research you might realize you can't really understand history unless you understand the thoughts behind those who are influential in historical decisions. This would entail knowledge of philosophy, psychology, neurology, sociology, biology, chemistry—the list is endless. All of these are complications which arise from the fact that everything is connected.

Connections are all important in our examination of our lives as well, and we will continually be referencing to these connections, for within them lie the meanings of our lives. The brain, for example, is a map. In fact, the brain is mapping itself continually in neuronic traces, drawing and redrawing our perceptual worlds. We must understand the importance of this. First, consider memory. Our lives depend on our memory, which is a map drawn through our brain, connecting the dots of past perceptions. When I perceive a situation, sitting here in my chair, typing, drinking coffee, the visual representation is stored in one part of my brain, the aural in another, the warmth of the room in another, the taste of the coffee in another, the emotional content in another, the spatial relations of objects in another, the tactile sense of my fingers on the keyboard in another, and on and on, little bits of information scattered across a vast countryside filled with like bits. These are not stored as photographs which tell the true tale of the way of the world, but are my interpretations of these events, and when I remember them tomorrow, an evanescent trace will connect these disparate areas and bring them together—not all of them, for some will have evaporated, but what remains will be reconnected and passed through yet another filter of subjective awareness before a mental picture is assembled artistically and I "remember" sitting here yesterday as I am today.

Memories, in this sense, are imprints from the past, and this is only our reflective memory. Our non-reflective memories include those that condition us to act in various ways. And if this is our definition of non-reflective memory, then it seems our DNA itself must be included as a memory, for our connections go beyond the internal connections of our mind. We are connected to other people, places, things (though ultimately these connections depend mostly upon memory as well). But how are our social connections to be separated from what we are? If our genotype is a kind of memory, giving rise to our phenotype, where do we draw the line on what we call our phenotype? Phenotypic traits are usually cited as skin and eye color, body height, and personality, but why not include behavior as well? (Dawkins 1999) The beaver builds a lodge and a dam because he is programmed to do so by his genes. His dam, then, is as much a part of his phenotype as his fur and flat tail. And us? Our behavior, too, is our own extended phenotype. Our cognitive processing of the world is such an extension, as are our mating rituals, our social behavior, and our desire for well-being, with its corresponding quest for meaning. If we include cognitive behavior, then our ideas, when made public, become connection points for other individuals, extending our phenotype into culture.

Willard Quine (1964) once referred to human life-paths on earth as "a couple of serpentine stere-years somewhere-when in past and future space-time." (193) I love this image. A stere is a cubic meter, so this gives us a picture of our lives as three dimensional cubic-tubes on maps, moving through time, intersecting with the lives of others, sometimes briefly, crossing paths, sometimes with more duration; and sometimes from the union of two stere-years new paths are created and begin their own paths, continuing on after their ancestors have faded. We can plot these three dimensional life-paths on a two dimensional map, though they must be severely delimited (fictional worlds are more delicately populated than real worlds, and so more easily traced); but even a cursory attempt yields an amazingly complex array of connections. (I would like to see a human phenome project, where everyone's extended phenotype was mapped. These could then be superimposed on others.) This is what people do when they trace their ancestry. This is important for some people, for it grounds them in history as a person in the same way that photographs and friendships ground others.

We are also connected to other animals, though our relations are too far distant to warrant care (like that second cousin of your great uncle you barely knew). But we could plot a connection nonetheless, and connections, well, *connect*. This gives us an entirely new map, or maybe a continuation of our ancestral map into the past. We no more sprung from apes than you sprung from your Uncle John.

> **GENOTYPE**
> The genetic constitution of an organism.
>
> **PHENOTYPE**
> The observable characteristics of an organism, resulting from genetics plus environment.

We have a common ancestor, and this links us, however grudgingly, giving us ape memories we cannot dismiss. Understanding we are so connected to other organisms is like finding a box of old photographs in your grandmother's attic. It gives us a deeper appreciation of who we are; it places us in the context of the world we live in.

And what of non-living things? We are connected to them as well. Not only are we the stuff of stars, formed from chemicals created in star cores and spewed into the universe at large by supernova explosions, we humans can also imbue inanimate objects with meaning. They can become touchstones for us; places which give rise to memories of a past important because it is ours. These things or places may become sacred to varying degrees. To return to a place you remember, a place of your childhood perhaps, is to revisit the past. When you stand where you stood as a child, you make yourself more real, and if, by chance, your name is etched in a tree or a sidewalk, so much the better. Leave evidences of your being on this earth, for yourself and for others. These kinds of experiences place you more firmly in time. They are bittersweet, reminding you of your past, but also of your mortality and the inexorable passing of time.

Other inanimate objects are more mundane, but all have a history. Even those that don't function as a touchstone to our own past have stories intertwined within the history of others. The chair I am sitting in, a gift from a dear person now dead, was made by other hands, dear to others, each with lives of hardship and joy. Even mass-produced objects were designed and made by humans with lives as complex as our own, and their products, in our life, constitute yet another fleeting connection on the overlapping maps of our extended phenotypes.

§7 CHAPTER SUMMARY

We have seen that there are obstacles in our path to knowledge of self, world and others. Later chapters will illuminate even more obstacles. Skepticism is a philosophical position that claims we cannot know anything, and, taking the above points into account, it may seem we are heading that way, but this is not so. A thorough understanding of ourselves and our processing powers will help us in our quest for methods to overcome these obstacles, while awareness of their difficulty will caution us not to accept easy solutions. We may have to rearrange and redefine some of our conceptions concerning truth, knowledge, and even ourselves, but what we gain in the process will make this well worth the sacrifice.

It would be nice to leap into a discussion of truth, but we must do some groundwork first. Truth is derived from a linguistic cloud floating over the world of humans. A true sentence says something about the way the world is. But the only way we can know the world is through our senses. So before we look at truth we must examine the cognitive faculties that allow us to experience the world, what I call our operating system. As the operating system of a computer controls how input is handled, so also our cognitive operating system controls and interprets the information from the world that enters into our consciousness. Consciousness is the screen upon which the results of our excogitations are projected, so before we can talk about what is projected we should look at the screen itself. This, then, is where we will begin our exploration.

NOTES / QUESTIONS

2. Consciousness

. . . .

When Tallahassee goes Hulk on a zombie, he sets the standard for "not to be fucked with."

—Columbus, Zombieland

SYNOPSIS

In the first chapter we spoke of the importance of reflection for attaining well-being. In this chapter I want to explore the concept of reflection by distinguishing different levels of awareness. (1) There are certain problems of consciousness the solution to which are beyond the scope of this work. (2) The concept of "zombie" is used to explore the various levels of consciousness. In this sense a zombie is a limiting factor. We know we aren't zombies, so what exactly do we have that they do not? (3) The most basic attribute to consider is life itself, which, it seems, a zombie must possess. (4) Three levels of awareness are considered in order. Here we deal with the first level: sentience—an attribute possessed by all living things (unless kept alive artificially). (5) The second level of monitoring is core consciousness or sensation—the ability to feel. (6) The highest level of monitoring is self-consciousness. This attribute, in its most sophisticated form, is what eventually distinguishes us humans from all other animals. Only humans have the capability of attaining the highest levels of self-consciousness. (7) Both the benefits and the detriments of self-consciousness are discussed. (8) Having discussed the various levels of awareness, we now take a final look at zombies. (9) The brain's amazing powers give rise to a problem: how do we know what parts of our experience (and the world) are produced by the brain? We will address this question in the chapters that follow. (10) Chapter Summary.

CHAPTER OBJECTIVES

- to define more precisely the terms sensation, consciousness, and self-consciousness and how these are applied to different organisms.
- to understand the fundamental truth that all our experiences are ultimately the result of unconscious brain processes.
- to appreciate the claim that the world, as it appears to us, is, in a sense, a hallucination.
- to introduce the concept of reification.
- to understand why the world is not necessarily the way it appears to us in every day life.

§1 INTRODUCTION

The topic of consciousness is fraught with confusion. The very term itself can be applied to everything from mere sentience (bacteria are conscious of danger or of a food source) to explicit self-consciousness (I am now thinking about how I think). We will handle this by distinguishing between three levels of awareness: 1) Sentience, the ability to sense the environment without being conscious of it; 2) consciousness, sensing the environment with feelings attached (sensations), but no concept of their belonging to you as someone distinct; and 3) self-consciousness, when you become explicitly aware of your sensations, or aware of your awareness. This last level is what we referred to in the previous chapter by the term 'reflection.' Each of these levels will be explored below in §4-§6.

Another problem arises when we try to describe exactly how consciousness happens. We can only speak in vagaries here, for no one really knows. There is talk of the mappings of the brain, of sensory pathways, feedback loops and privileged standpoints, but all of this is metaphorical. When it comes to how the brain allows us to feel pain or emotions or see images, much less make obscure memories connect to these, no one knows. Some scientists and philosophers believe this information is not only unknown but unknowable, lying forever beyond our grasp by its very nature. I am not among them. We will see that the graveyard of history is littered with the corpses of claims that various aspects of reality are, in essence, unknowable, and that have since become perfectly clear.

The third problem of consciousness is the question of location—the NCC or neural correlates to consciousness. We know that consciousness is a function of brain processes, but present research seems to indicate there is no one site within the brain which gives rise to consciousness. Rather, it seems, there are many sites which, when working together, spontaneously give rise to consciousness as an emergent behavior. In neuroscience this is known as the binding problem. Each of us feels we are a single entity, so how do all the various brain activities meld into this one thing? Here again, we will not attempt a solution. We know there are diverse regions of the nervous system that make up consciousness; we also know that these are somehow unified. We need not know more for our purposes.

I am also not going to address the nature of the self in this chapter, but will return to this topic later in chapter 13. A general examination of consciousness in what follows will clarify the use of some terminology as well as introduce many of the concepts with which we will be dealing throughout the rest of this book.

§2 ZOMBIES

Zombies are everywhere—well, everywhere in books, movies and video games—but are there any real zombies? Zombies usually spread their zombie-ness via biting, but is this vindictive behavior or are they simply hungry? That is, does the disease instill within its host a desire to spread? Or does it merely wipe out their consciousness? Whichever it is, we know it is important to avoid them in order to avoid becoming infected. That said, the most dangerous zombie would be one which appears exactly like other humans—no drooling, snorting, or staggering. Most zombie movies allow for telltales such as the vacant stare or a lack of emotion, for without these we would be helpless before them, and they would inevitably spread throughout the world. But wait… How do you know the person next to you on the bus or in the next room isn't a zombie of this sort? For that matter, how do you know your spouse or your mother isn't? I want to focus on this, for I think a serious search for zombies will help us understand more about what we are.

We should first determine exactly what a zombie is, and then look for one, but I'm going to purposefully leave the definition vague, for there are zombies and then there are zombies. There are the horrible mindless creatures of the *28 Days Later/Resident Evil* variety who simply want to kill anything that moves, or there are the urbane zombies of *The Invasion/Invasion of the Body Snatchers* ilk, infected humans who simply want to make you like them—beings completely devoid of emotion. In some ways these latter zombies are more frightening. They might even use reason to try to reassure you that the world will be a better place without emotion.

The best place to start is with ourselves, since we know we aren't zombies, then we can determine what must be lacking in order to be classified as a zombie. In essence, our search is an examination of human consciousness, a vastly complex subject which we will only treat in a topical fashion, starting at a the most basic level, life, and working our way toward our own explicit self-consciousness.

§3 LIFE

Are zombies dead or alive? I think we can safely say they are alive, though a little reflection may begin to make you wonder (after all, they are often referred to as the "living dead"). What is the distinction between the living and the dead? Scientists and philosophers have spent much time and effort trying to give necessary and sufficient conditions for what constitutes life, but doing so may be just another example of our procrustean penchant for precise categorizing (the pebble-rock fallacy). The truth is, the non-living shade into the living without black and white simplicity (Figure 2–1). Aristotle was already aware of this more than two thousand years ago:

FIGURE 2–1

The Life Continuum. On the left are obviously non-living things, on the right obviously living. The difficulties arise with those things existing near the center.

Nature proceeds little by little from things lifeless to animal life in such a way that it is impossible to determine the exact line of demarcation. (History of Animals, 8,I,588b4)

Most thinkers consider some kind of homeostasis as necessary for life, that is, some internal processing that allows an organism to stand alone against the universe, generate its own energy and replicate. The virus is often cited as an organism that fails this test. A virus can replicate, but only by invading a host cell and usurping its reproductive machinery. A virus has no inner life of its own, no metabolism. In short, a virus is to cells what a zombie is to humans. Both are machinelike mimics of their prey, mere shells.

And yet there are other organisms, unquestionably alive, which also have this limitation—*rickettsiaa* and *chlamydia* are bacteria that reproduce only within a host. They do have their own internal metabolic generators, though, so maybe this is the difference. There is also the interesting case of the prion, an infectious agent (leading to mad cow disease in cattle and Creutzfeldt-Jakob disease in humans) which is nothing more than a misfolded protein. The prion, though, can propagate without any nucleic acids (RNA, DNA). It does this by inducing properly folded proteins to misfold. These misfolded proteins then accumulate within a cell, eventually breaking it down. There is no cure for a prion infection.[1]

We have to be careful using the concept of dependence to exclude organisms from our life-concept, for all organisms are dependent upon other organisms to some extent. Cows are a good example, for without their host bacteria, living in a specially designed stomach compartment, or rumen, they could not digest their food, and would be unable to replicate. And how is this different from us humans? We have billions of bacteria throughout our bodies with which we have developed a symbiotic relationship and without which we could not survive.

We could be cell-snobs, and exclude viruses from the category of the living by fiat, or maybe we should instead admit we are dealing with a pebble-rock situation and grudgingly allow them membership in the club of the living—maybe as proto-living organisms if nothing else. The problem is: if we admit viruses, don't we have to allow sophisticated machines as well? The line must be drawn somewhere, but be assured that wherever it is drawn, it will be arbitrary.

We know when something is dead. In order to be dead, a thing must, at some time, have been alive. A rock is not dead, for it was never alive. If you've ever

---

[1] Note that replication cannot be necessary for defining life. Mules (a cross between a horse and a donkey) cannot reproduce, yet no one doubts they are alive.

watched an animal die, the difference between the two states is obvious. Your pet, who was once jumping around with a stick in his mouth wanting to play, is now an unmoving lump of matter lying before you. But what is it to die? The individual cells within a living thing begin to die when they no longer produce enough energy to maintain integrity against the outside world, and the breakdown of the parts leads eventually to a breakdown of the whole. Integrity is important: it is captured in the notion of homeostasis as a thermodynamic equilibrium, that is, the ability to produce enough energy to maintain a barrier between the organism and the outside world—an outside world which is deadly if it breaks your boundaries. Death occurs when this barrier can no longer be maintained, and entropy (previously kept precariously at bay) takes over, and we begin to dissolve. Our barriers collapse, we lose our individuality and become one with the world once again. This isn't a pleasant thought. Disembowelment comes to mind. Homeostasis fails, but chemistry continues; the laws of physics rule and to dust we do return.

We will return to equilibrium, integrity, and metabolism in chapter 15, but I should note that the previous paragraph, and talk of individual integrity in general, glosses, and thus distorts to some extent, the true picture. This is yet another example of how we use our categories to break the world into explainable pieces and yet by doing so, by abstracting, we miss important details. Inherent within metabolism is the expulsion of waste products according to the laws of thermodynamics. The waste of one organism is the fodder of others (do we not breathe the excretions of plants?). Everything is connected. As Lynn Margulis (2000) points out:

> Most writers of biology texts imply that an organism exists apart from its environment, and that the environment is mostly a static, non-living backdrop. Organic beings and environment, however, interweave. Soil, for example, is not unalive. It is a mixture of broken rock, pollen, fungal filaments, cilliate cysts, bacterial spores, nematodes, and other microscopic animals and their parts. (20)

We're not going to solve the problem of life, but luckily we don't have to. We know we are alive and that, despite the appellation "living dead," so are zombies. In other words life is a necessary condition for being a zombie.

§4 LEVEL I: SENTIENCE

All living things (and some non-living things) have the capability of sensing (and responding to) their environment. We will call this sentience, which, in its most basic form, is what allows an organism to find food and escape predators. Bacteria are sentient; so are beetles, mosquitoes, mushrooms, trees, cows, monkeys and humans. (Of course, so are cameras and robots, which is why we can't take this to be a defining feature of the unequivocal living.) Zombies, too, are sentient; their eyes and ears work at least, which is why we must hide from them, but now things are getting interesting, for maybe this is all a zombie is—sentient, but nothing else. We can examine the human members of the class of sentient creatures in order to determine what we mean by 'zombie,' for we know we non-zombies are more than merely sentient. We know we have a more zestful outlook than a bacteria, but what does this mean?

It's complicated. There are many different schemata we could invoke to show what we humans have that bacteria don't, but I'm going to use a tripartite division in which I distinguish between sentience, sensation (consciousness) and self-consciousness. Sensation presupposes sentience while self-consciousness presupposes sensation. We could thus generate another continuum, shown in Figure 2–2, that would indicate the three major categories.

Consciousness Continuum

FIGURE 2–2

A full spectrum consciousness continuum. Consciousness proper (as we are defining it) begins with sensation. The grey areas denote the fact that we may not be able to make hard distinctions between the various gradations.

I want to approach this from a different tack, though. Let's suppose we have invented a zombie detector, which is also a consciousness detector: this is an instrument that measures the above-mentioned aspects of our mental life and gives a readout in three numbers. Each number can range from zero to nine with zero being the lowest and nine the highest. We could connect our detector to anything whatsoever and find out what sort of mental life, if any, it possesses. So, if you measured yourself as a test case the detector should read: 999 (as indicated in Figure 2–3). The first meter is a measure of your sentience; the second of your sensation; the third of your self-consciousness. If you attached this detector to a rock it would read 000. These two readings (000 and 999) give us the extremes of a continuum containing all living things. What lies in between? Where do zombies fall? Do we

Consciousness Detector

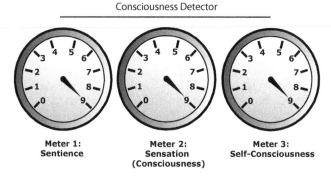

FIGURE 2–3

Consciousness meter, showing readings consistent with being connected to a normally functioning human.

ourselves sometimes measure less than 999? Before we answer these questions we must explain in more detail what the second and third meter readings indicate. But first a few side issues.

All zombies are brain-damaged humans, but all brain-damaged humans are not zombies. Because damage is often limited to very specific areas of the brain, other functions may be normal. This is even true of the vaunted cerebral cortex.[2] This means we might possibly get an anomalous reading of 909, for example, on our zombie detector. A zombie could never have a reading of nine on the third meter. In general, for any of the three meters on our consciousness detector, no meter should read higher than the meter to its left. Cases in which this general rule is broken may result in partial zombies or temporary zombies. Consider Jason:

> Because of damage to the anterior cingulate cortex in the front of his brain, Jason couldn't walk, talk, or initiate actions. His sleep-wake cycle was normal but he was bedridden. When awake he seemed alert and conscious... He sometimes had a slight "ouch" withdrawal in response to pain, but not consistently. He could move his eyes, often swiveling them around to follow people. Yet he couldn't recognize anyone—not even his parent or siblings. He could not talk or comprehend speech, nor could he interact with people meaningfully. (Ramanchandran 2011: 245)

Jason doesn't sound like an unusual neurological case; he's maybe a notch above a vegetative state, but there's more:

> ... if his father, Mr. Murdoch, phoned him from next door, Jason suddenly became alert and talkative, recognizing his dad and engaging him in conversation. That is until Mr. Murdoch went back into the room. Then Jason lapsed back into his semiconscious "zombie" state. (245)

Jason can make sensory representations of the world (he is sentient), but because of his brain damage, these are not pushed up for higher visual processing.[3] If his anterior cingulate had been massively damaged, nothing would be pushed up, but in Jason's case the damage was very specific and the auditory channels escaped unscathed.

Antonio Damasio (2010) describes another patient who would occasionally experience periods of diminished consciousness.

> In the middle of our conversation, the patient stopped talking and in fact suspended moving altogether. His face lost expression, and his open eyes looked past me, at the wall behind. He remained motionless for several seconds. He did not fall from his chair, or fall asleep, or convulse, or twitch. When I spoke his name, there was no reply. When he began to move again, ever so little, he smacked his lips. His eyes shifted about and seemed to focus momentarily on a coffee cup on the table between us. It was empty, but still he picked it up and attempted to drink from it. I spoke to him again

---

[2] There is a condition in which children are born with intact brain-stem structures but no cerebral cortex, thalamus and basal ganglia, and yet manifest mindful behavior—more so than, say, humans in a vegetative state. (see Damasio:2010 80f)

[3] Jason's condition is known as telephone syndrome.

and again, but he did not reply. I asked him what was going on, and he did not reply. His face still had no expression, and he did not look at me. I called his name, and he did not reply. Finally he rose to his feet, turned around, and walked slowly to the door. I called him again. He stopped and looked at me, and a perplexed expression came to his face. I called him again, and he said, "What?" (163-64)

This patient had experienced a kind of epileptic seizure called an absence seizure. He was there one moment and gone the next, only to return again after a time. Neither of these patients are true zombies; they merely have zombie moments (or

---

OBSERVING THE BRAIN'S ACTIVITY

The different methods utilized by neuroscientists to measure brain activity can be categorized in terms of their ability to capture action sequences within the brain. Static methods are like photographs; they record a single moment. Intermediate dynamic methods can record a progression of brain events over time, but cannot capture high speed events. Dynamic methods can capture extremely high speed events. There is a trade-off for this ability, however, for though dynamic methods can capture high-speed events, they cannot specify location as precisely as the slower methods. In practice, several different methods should be used in conjunction to obtain the best results. (see Nunez 2010: 89f.)

Static:
1) CT (computed tomography)
2) MRI (magnetic resonance imaging): better contrast in picturing soft tissue

Intermediate dynamic: Excellent spatial resolution, poor temporal resolution
1) fMRI (*funct*ional magnetic resonance imaging) - measures changes in blood oxygen level in the brain.
2) PET (positron emission tomography) - measures local metabolic activity

Dynamic: (millisecond time scales, faster than the speed of thought)
1) EEG (electroencephalography) - poor spatial, excellent temporal (better for measuring the cortical surface)
2) MEG (magnetoencephalography) - measures magnetic fields 2-3 centimeters above the scalp produced by synaptic currents (better for measuring activity in cortical folds)

One other measurement technique is the Galvanic Skin Response (GSR) or Skin Conductance Response (SCR). When you encounter an evocative stimulus, the brain generates a response, and prepares itself for further response (fight, flight, and so on).

A mildly, moderately, or profoundly emotional experience elicits a mild, moderate, or profound autonomic reaction, respectively. And part of these continuous autonomic reactions to experience is microsweating: Your whole body, including your palms, becomes damper or dryer in proportion to any upticks or downticks in your level of emotion arousal at any given moment. (Ramachandran 2011: 70)

An ohmmeter can measure the moment by moment fluctuations in this galvanic skin response, thus giving scientists a reliable guide to your emotional state (more reliable than verbal testimony which could be censored by the subject).

---

non-zombie moments). But then, don't we all? What about those times when you are driving to work, performing a complex routine of steering, braking, acceleration, when suddenly you awaken, having been oblivious of your maneuvering through traffic, stop lights and all the other minutia of driving? Or when you are awakened from a deep sleep and slowly orient yourself to the world?

This refers us to other limits of conscious behavior, namely, comas and vegetative states. Comas, states in which there is no brain activity—no telltale EEG—are not zombie states, for zombies (for the most part, we are assuming) can function like normal humans and thus must at least register brain activity. People in vegetative states also cannot be considered zombies, for although they do register brain activity (and fMRI readings indicate many are aware, on some level, of questions being asked of them even though they give no external manifestation of this awareness) we are never fooled. They do not walk the halls and impress us with their casual banter and debonair attitude. We can say, then, that sentience is necessary for zombiehood since zombies must sense their environment in order to fool, infect or feed upon us. But we also see that sentience is not unique, for it is necessary for all life not artificially maintained.

§5 LEVEL II: SENSATION (CONSCIOUS MIND)

We will arbitrarily proclaim creatures with sensation to be conscious. Sensation is sentience-plus-something-more; it is sentience pushed up for higher processing. An amoeba might register on the first meter of our zombie detector (200? 800?), but it will never register on the second meter, for a reading on the second meter depends upon neurons. The *sentient* creature responds to its environment (via reflex), but it does not *feel* the environment impinge upon it. The *sensate* creature feels, and neurons make this possible. Neurons form a processing level one step up from sentience; they map the stimuli coming in from both body and environment, which allows for more precise responses to such stimuli. Figure 2–4 gives a representation of the difference between sentience and sensation.

We can imagine our amoeba responding to a heat stimulus and taking action accordingly—moving either toward or away from the heat—but the amoeba has no sensation of hotness. Feelings, the hotness of heat, the painfulness of pain, the redness of red, are conscious reactions to stimulations. Most humans live in a continuous stream of sensations. Being human is like sitting in a river as it flows around us: we are awash in reds, blues, greens, bright light, fog, dampness, cold, dull aches, sharp pains, contentments, sugary sweetness, music, traffic noises, bird songs, whiffs of rotting vegetables, perfumes, hints of garlic, the feel of corduroy or silk. These swirl around us in a wondrous mix we almost always take for granted. Our lives would be impoverished if we lost the sensations from even one of our senses—and yet it could, and does happen. Blindness and deafness come to mind as examples of losing our ability to sense, but these rude incapacitations do not capture the subtlety of the distinction. Blindness takes away sensation, but it also takes away visual sentience.

To capture the more subtle variances involved, consider the neurological condition (usually resulting from a stroke) known as blindsight in which those afflicted

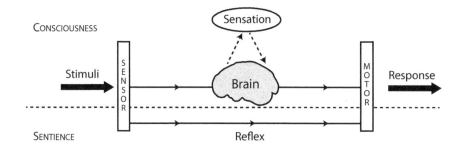

FIGURE 2–4

A representation of the difference between pure sentience and consciousness. A merely sentient creature does not possess neurons—sense signals go straight to the motor response. Creatures with consciousness run their sentient processes through the brain, which sends them directly to the motor response without further processing.

have no visual sensation of the world, yet behave as if they can see. The explanation of this lies in the fact that there are two neural pathways from our senses to our brain, one ancient, one more recent. Consider visual sensations. Blindsight results when the primary visual cortex within the occipital lobe is damaged, leaving other areas intact. Information is still transmitted from the retina, but only to the subcortical and upper brainstem which do not produce images.[4] A person with blindsight does not experience sensations, and yet, if you put her in a room filled with people and objects she can navigate through them as nimbly as you or I. In tests where blindsight subjects were shown cards in different locations and asked to point to them, the subjects objected that they could not see the cards referred to, yet could consistently point to them. If shown an object, then, on some level the blindsight person knows the object is there, but doesn't experience it. This phenomenon, which can occur with any of the senses, indicates a clear separation between mere sentience and sensation. Sensation becomes possible when an organism gains the ability to monitor (map) its sensorial stimuli.

The claim has often been made that a creature who experiences sensations must have at least a core self which is experiencing these. If sensations are appearing (so the argument goes) they must be appearing *to* someone or something— there must be a subject watching the picture show. This is an easy trap to fall into, but it must be avoided. It is often referred to as the homunculus fallacy or the Cartesian theater. A homunculus is a tiny person (the self) who sits in a theater and watches representations of the world as they are projected on a mind-screen (see Figure 2–5). This is problematic because it doesn't explain our visual sensations, for now we have to ask how the homunculus sees the representation, which means there must be another, even smaller, homunculus inside the homunculus, and this regress continues forever. The result is that nothing is explained using this concept.

We might agree that positing sensations as representations shown on a screen to a self is a bad idea and still demand a rudimentary form of self must exist as a

---

[4] The ancient pathway relays spatial information concerning objects—its function is to allow us to determine where an object is (so we can track it) rather than what an object is. The more recent pathway projects to V1 which again splits into different functional relays: the how and the what.

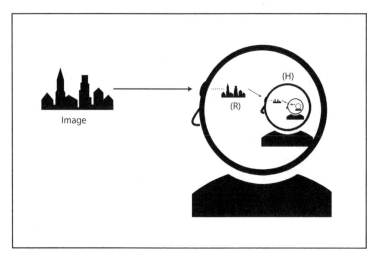

FIGURE 2–5

The homunculus problem arises when sensation is explained in terms of an image which is represented in the brain (R) as in a theatre, viewed by the self (H). This merely puts the explanation off to another level, for we must now explain how the self sees this image, which is explained in terms of another representation viewed by another self, and so on.

precondition to sensation. Mustn't there be a subject, someone or thing that experiences the sensations? But this, it seems, is just another form of the homunculus fallacy. It derives from another of our human penchants—for abstraction (we will discuss this penchant in more detail in later chapters). Granted, we humans have the ability to step back (up) and view our self as viewing sensations, but is this a necessity? That is, is it possible to have sensations without knowing we are having sensations? (Note this is different from the blindsight phenomenon. The blindsighted person has sentience without sensation. We are bumping up a level: can a person have sensations without being conscious of the sensations as theirs? My distinction between consciousness and self-consciousness hangs on this.)

The best way to imagine the sensations of a creature without a self is to analyze your own sensations on a basic level. Imagine you are experiencing ongoing pain from a toothache, a healing broken bone or a headache. I am asking you to reflect on your having a painful experience, but reflecting on a painful experience is different from actually undergoing the painful experience. When you are in the midst of pain, it is a part of you in a way that is inseparable. Again, we humans have the ability to step back and watch ourselves suffer. (Does this make the experience more painful?) We can view ourselves as having the pain as if it is something separate from us, but this is an abstraction. Once we realize this, we see that a creature lacking this abstract ability might still *feel* the sensation of pain, but won't have the capacity to feel it as *their* pain—they just feel. So also with visual sensations, auditory sensations, and so on. A purely sensate creature just feels. This is what the second meter on our consciousness detector measures.

What kind of creatures are we talking about? If we hooked our detector up to various creatures what readings might we get on the second meter? The answer is speculative, of course, but since we know we are working with a continuum based upon neurological complexity we should be able to make an educated guess. We know such a creature will have less neurological complexity than a human and more than an amoeba. It must have neurons. We also know there will be varying degrees of sensation, shading from pure sentience to vague sensations to more clearly delineated sensations, as the neuronal development makes these possible. If I had to guess, I would probably put C. *elegans*, a nematode worm, one of the simplest organisms to possess a nervous system, on the list of purely sensate creatures, that is, if I connected this worm to our detector the reading would look something like Figure 2–6.

This is just a guess, of course, but I'm willing to be generous in what creatures I allow sensation as a possibility. Again, the question arises as to how we might know such a thing. We can't, but we can infer from the neurological structure vaguely where an organism might fit on a continuum.

Consciousness Detector

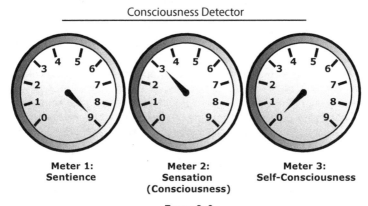

Meter 1:	Meter 2:	Meter 3:
Sentience	Sensation	Self-Consciousness
	(Consciousness)	

FIGURE 2–6

Consciousness detector, with readings consistent with being connected to the nematode worm C. elegans.

§6   LEVEL III: SELF-CONSCIOUS MIND

At the very lowest reading of the third meter, a proto-self begins to emerge. This occurs when a creature gains the ability to make its sensations explicit, that is, to experience its sensations. Level II organisms feel sensations, but are completely immersed in their flow. They may have elementary memory retention (learning ability), as does C. *elegans*, but do not have the capability of realizing that things are happening to *them* as opposed to just happening. Figure 2–7 shows the relation of the third meter to the other meters on our consciousness detector.

This ability to map not only internal and external inputs (sensation), but also to monitor these maps gives rise to the core self. The core self is a pulling together of various imaging processes, and with this capability eventually comes the realization that the organism is separate from other organisms and from the rest of the world.

Another way of putting this is to say that the organism gains a perspective. William James (1890) put it like this:

> One great splitting of the whole universe into two halves is made by each of us; and for each of us almost all of the interest attaches to one of the halves; but we all draw the line of division between them in a different place. When I say that we all call the two halves by the same names, and that those names are "*me*" and "*not-me*" respectively, it will at once be seen what I mean. The altogether unique kind of interest which each human mind feels in those parts of creation which it can call *me* or *mine* may be a moral riddle, but it is a fundamental psychological fact. No mind can take the same interest in his neighbor's me as in his own. The neighbor's me falls together with all the rest of things in one foreign mass against which his own me stands out in startling relief. (I:289)

You can observe this separation occurring by watching an infant grow. A healthy newborn human would probably register around 991, that is, would possess a core self, a vague awareness of being, but has not yet separated itself from the world as a separate entity (see Gopnik). This separation begins to occur at around eighteen months, and contributes to what is often known as the terrible two's. This is when the child begins to realize it is something special, and lets everyone know. You can almost think of this as a second birth—the birth of the self. A person can have no history prior to the developed self, for there is no thing (no self) to place in a historical context. A person once told me he clearly remembered his mother taking him outside at night and showing him the stars when he was but three months old. He claimed this initial experience of the vastness of the universe helped make him who he was. This is a nice story, but it's pure fabrication (though I have no doubt the teller was sincere). There are two reasons why it must be a fabrication: First, because there is no self at three months, which means memories cannot be recorded as belonging to anyone. An autobiography requires a subject. Not even vague experience-memories will be recorded until this subject has developed. Second, the concepts of a star, the vastness of the night sky, and so on, are all

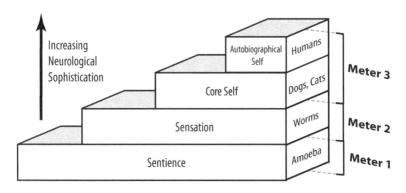

FIGURE 2–7
A diagram of our consciousness continuum indicating the meter readings on our consciousness detector. Neurology begins with sensation and becomes more complex as we move upwards on the diagram.

complex concepts beyond the ken of a three-month-old. I assume what happened was that his mother later related the story of how she had taken him outside at night as an infant and showed him the stars, and this was then fabricated into a memory, no doubt embellished over time until it became a certainty.

The developing self includes a growing affirmation that "I" am alive, and entails that sensations can be enjoyed as mine; there is a "way it is like to be me": objects are represented in a mind belonging to me. The highest level of development gives us the concept of a lived past and an anticipated future. We create a timeline of our past populated with memories (real and imagined) and of our projected future. The brain is continually computing as-if scenarios concerning our wants, hopes, goals and desires. It is only at this higher level of awareness that such computations are possible.

Emotions can be viewed as automatic responses to internal and external stimuli generated by the brain. In this sense, all conscious animals have emotions to some extent, but again, the complexity of the human brain indicates that we have more sophisticated responses than other animals. Just as we not only have sensations, but awareness of sensations, so also we have not merely emotions, but *feelings* of emotions. The responses from the nervous system begin a chemical chain reaction that is continually monitored and revised as new data is input. The feeling of emotions can itself generate feedback loops that change our emotional state. For example, the feeling of depression often colors our perception of the world in a negative light, which enhances the depression which further colors the world...

The as-if computations of the brain are simulations of real life events and thus evoke as-if emotional states as well. These are weaker versions of real emotional states that allow us to forecast the consequences of various action plans. These as-if computations have the benefit of saving us the considerable energy of going through the actual emotions. Emotions are exhausting because they involve so many actions and reactions. If you've ever watched a zombie movie and felt emotionally exhausted afterwards, you are aware of the cost of emotional responses. In movies like this, the body is tricked into an emotional response on a higher level than a mere as-if. When you are on the edge of your seat watching a thriller, your body is actually feeling fear, preparing to fight or flee, pumping adrenaline, preparing your muscles, focusing your attention.

Are humans the only denizens registering on meter three? Hardly. I tend to be very generous in positing core self-consciousness to other animals, but there is no doubt that humans are unique in possessing an autobiographical self. Your canine companion has many wonderful traits—probably has a core self-consciousness with rudimentary past recollections and future anticipations, including emotional responses—but he probably doesn't wonder what he'll be doing next year at this time. That humans are wonderfully special in their ability to do just this sort of thing is unquestionable.[5] Damasio:

---

[5] Almost every author on the subject of human neurology and/or consciousness notes the resistance they routinely receive when they claim humans are superior to other animals with respect to consciousness. This false modesty is puzzling. Is it a reaction to the out-dated view that humans are the final goal of evolution, occupying some privileged niche which allows them to control other species at will? Ramachandran claims it is the modern equivalent of the doctrine of original sin. Whatever the reason, it is misplaced. Humans have the most complex neurology on the planet and with this neurology comes abilities available to no other species. It does not follow from this that humans are the apex of evolution, and no neuroscientist (that

...the lower notches of the consciousness scale are by no means human alone. In all probability they are present in numerous nonhuman species that have brains complex enough to construct them. The fact that human consciousness, at its highest reaches, is hugely complicated, far-reaching, and therefore *distinctive* is so obvious that it does not require mention. (171)

You may be wondering how anyone could possibly know that dogs and cats, for example, don't possess autobiographical selves. For that matter, how do I know that you possess a consciousness like mine—that you aren't a zombie of sorts? This claim is obviously not mathematically provable, but the evidence is good. We know that conscious states depend upon the brain, and fMRI research indicates that those parts of the brain activated by higher reasoning abilities are non-existent in other animals, including the ape family. With respect to whether you are conscious like me, I draw an analogy between us. We have almost identical design including our neurological structure. Furthermore, you behave as I behave, that is, you behave as if you have an inner life like I do. Thus I conclude that you do have an inner life (are not a zombie) until evidence suggests otherwise. Believing that other humans have an inner life like me is a core value within my (and other humans') framework.

Does this mean that if I connected you to our consciousness detector you would always register a 999? No. We probably spend most of our waking lives in the 996-998 zone (and, particularly when sleeping or under anaesthesia, drop down into the 900 range). The important point is that we have the *capability* of moving to a 999.

§7 RETURN TO ZOMBIES

Now that we have explained the three meters on our consciousness detector and what they indicate, we can return to our original question: what constitutes a zombie? To determine this we have to stipulate that our meter measure not the current state of consciousness (which we have used it for up until now), but the highest conscious capacity of the individual in question. Otherwise, if we were continually connected to our detector it would no doubt show a constant fluctuation between, say, 993 and 999, while we are awake, and would probably remain mostly in the 995 range. This is because we seldom use our most explicit self-consciousness. In fact, we often perform less well when we do. Think of playing the piano, typing on your computer keyboard, or, as we have seen, driving your car. When you become explicitly conscious of your playing or typing you tend to make more mistakes than if you just go with the flow. But going with the flow is a lesser state of consciousness.[6]

I know of) claims this. Indeed, it could turn out that our complexity is disadvantageous to our ultimate survivability.

[6] We perform better in the lesser state, but only up to a point. Once you learn to type at a certain level of competence you can type best at that level without becoming explicitly conscious of your performance. But if you want to improve your level of competency, you will have to engage your explicit consciousness. Foer (2011) makes this point with respect to improving your memory.

Most of our actions, then, occur around the 995-997 range, but we would be diminished if we could not occasionally reach 999. Thus, a zombie might be defined as any human who lacks the ability to attain a 999 state at will.

Granted we would not wish to be such a creature, but they exist in many subtle forms due to various types of brain malfunction (usually due to strokes, which, as we have seen, can inflict damage to very specific areas of the brain). Humans existing in a deep coma, for example, could give us a 000 reading; lacking even sentience they are kept alive artificially. A perusal of the writings of neurologists such as Oliver Sacks gives interesting insight into the strangeness of neurological disorders. Such cases also tell us that our world is fabricated in very specific ways.

Would we be able to recognize a 998 zombie if we saw one? Probably not. There might be a momentary quirk or two, but odds are they would not be transparent to the general public. Most of our 999 behavior is opaque to others. Would the 998 zombie know what he was missing? Probably not. In the same way that a born-blind person does not know color perception and thus cannot truly understand its absence, a 998 zombie would not understand the lack of 999-explicitness. Part of the tragedy of Alzheimer's disease is the occasional return to explicitness, during which time the patient knows of their predicament. Without this awareness, the suffering would be limited to the friends and loved ones of the afflicted.

§8   BENEFITS & DETRIMENTS OF SELF-CONSCIOUSNESS

There must be benefits to both consciousness and our distinctively human self-consciousness. Without these benefits, all forms of consciousness would be invisible to natural selection and, because their complexity would prohibit genetic drift, would not have evolved (we will explain this in chapter 3). There are corresponding detriments to consciousness as well, though these will not have been sufficient to have been selected against, but may still be serious. In what follows I will briefly speculate on four benefits of self-consciousness along with their corresponding detriments.

MORE EFFECTIVE MONITORING

Probably the most important positive effect of self-consciousness is its ability to enhance our monitoring capabilities. Once we added self-consciousness to sensation we gained a more precise ability to monitor our internal milieu and our external environment. We can think of this as increased processing power which allows for better responses to threats.[7] By far the most valuable aspect of this heightened monitoring is the ability to anticipate our future in ways that allow us to take advantage of opportunities and avoid threats by preparing ourselves in advance.

We mentioned above that our brains continually map and re-map the future in as-if scenarios. As we take in new information from our sensors these maps

---

[7] Better responses to certain types of threats. The more ancient, more reflexive, brain structures are lightening fast compared to the more modern deliberative structures. We still have the ancient, but the newer structures add an additional level, giving us broader coverage.

are continually updated. Our brains monitor these maps accordingly (in a largely unconscious manner) and adjust our actions (which thereby changes our future). Consider the advantages of being able to do this. Our companion dog can anticipate the near-future. When you start putting on your boots he may get excited, may even bring you his leash, but other than these brief forays into the future he is immersed in the present moment. We, on the other hand, can look years or decades into the future: planning for next year's vacation, saving money for retirement, drafting a will to distribute our assets. Even considering the unreliable nature of our long term predictions, this still constitutes an advantage over living only in the present. Furthermore, this ability to anticipate the future enhances our curiosity. The better we get at anticipating the future the better the payoff for curiosity, and curiosity (though it occasionally kills cats) is, overall, a beneficial attribute.

The cat-killing aspect of curiosity is the first of at least two detrimental aspects of increased monitoring effectiveness. If we think of the brain as a blind control center, with nerve endings branching out like the picket lines of an advancing army (to reuse a metaphor), these nerve endings give us vital information about the world outside both the brain and the body. When we become conscious of the information input from these monitors we are aware, not only of their content, but of their lack of content. What lies beyond their scope? This nagging question leads us to develop our own external monitors that will extend our innate monitors. These extensions are referred to as technology. Put this way, the detriments of increased monitoring are the detriments of curiosity—of technology—not merely the unforeseen consequences that plague our shortsighted forays into technological development, but also the development of new technologies which may very well give us the capacity to destroy ourselves.

The second detrimental aspect of heightened consciousness of our sensations is the fact that, not only is our pleasure more pleasurable, but our painfulness is more painful. There are two levels here: first, having a core self that feels pain may be more painful that a nebulous pain feeling without a subject. That is, when pain is felt as my-pain rather than as pain-in-general, suffering is the result (if we want to make this the distinguishing characteristic between suffering and pain). C. elegans may feel pain, but it does not suffer. The second aspect contributing to suffering is our ability to anticipate pain, to calculate its end or lack of end. Just as anticipated pleasure is itself pleasurable, so also anticipated pain is itself painful, and may even increase the painfulness of the sensation when the anticipation is realized.

PRIVACY

The fact that we can even question whether or not humans or other animals have an inner life like our own points to the overwhelming isolation we experience as humans. On the one hand, what a wonderful thing this privacy is. Without it, if others could read our minds, we would be open books, our every thought a public record. Mental transparency would be disastrous to most human relationships, whether personal or political. But this boon also has a catch. This inwardness means we are alone in our search for meaning and truth; we are subject to all the vagaries of experience and logic which mislead us, and yet we must ultimately depend upon our own mental manipulations in order to obtain knowledge about the world and ourselves. We are imprisoned within our subjectivity. This subject will be explored in more detail in Part II of this text.

A less obvious (and more speculative) consequence of this privacy may not have fully manifested itself yet. Early humans may have lacked our autobiographical consciousness which may have contributed to more stable early societies. The reason for this is that the less individuality displayed, the more important the whole. Selfishness is lessened since the importance of the individual is subsumed under the importance of the group. The rise of individuality is thus correlated with an increase in personal selfishness which leads to a weakening of the group and a lessening of the importance of the whole. On the one hand this has given us democracy and individual human rights; on the other hand, continued polarization may result in a breakdown of social bonds, a situation in which no one is willing to sacrifice their own rights for the greater good.

PUBLICITY

The third consequence mediates the extremes of the second. Publicity, culture, is the result of our linguistic abilities, which are a result of our advanced neurology. Language makes culture possible. It allows us to share our inwardness with others and, in doing so, see that we are not alone. The more we come to know others via public expressions, the more we come to see that they are like us in important ways. In this sense, although we are alone in the world, we are partners with all other humans. We share many of the same core values just because we are human. Cultures vary, not because humans are radically different from each other, but because the environments people grow up in are radically different, and different environments demand different solutions for survival. We will discuss culture in more detail in Chapter 6.

Robert Wright (2001) and others have argued convincingly that it is our social nature, our ability to live together in large numbers, that has resulted in all the wonders we attribute to civilization. Humans had to overcome substantial obstacles in order to group together. It is still unclear, for instance, what pushed humans to abandon the hunter-gatherer lifestyle for the more sedentary life of farming, but once we did, farming allowed for larger population centers to develop than would otherwise have been possible. Wright's thesis is that the more humans cluster in one area, the more minds there are available to work out new innovations to improve lifestyles. This is necessary, for every advance that made larger civilizations more amenable also brought problems that needed to be solved. Animal husbandry may have allowed for larger population centers, but it also brought about the transfer of animal disease to humans. And these centers of innovation, as it turned out, were more often than not merely stages for despots to assert their power by means of endless wars and horrendous cruelty. Thus, for every advance made by a culture, there is a price to be paid—a promissory note toward future generations who, hopefully, will keep ahead of the game enough to solve their present problems while making their own for the future.

PLEASURE

We mentioned the excitement of a dog anticipating a walk, but we don't even have to go to anticipation to recognize the increased pleasure resulting from self-consciousness. Pleasurable sensations are felt as "belonging to us" on the lowest readings of the third meter on our consciousness detector. Horses cavort, dolphins wave-surf, birds cartwheel in the sky.

At the Gombe Stream Research Centre in Tanzania, a chimpanzee beside a stream was observed by scientists drawing her fingers repeatedly through the rippling water, transfixed, it seems, by the delicate play of light, sound, and touch on her body. (Humphrey 84)

There is always a danger of anthropomorphism when observing other species, but what are these displays if not creatures enjoying the fruits of pleasurable sensations? That chimpanzee beside the stream initiated other chimps into the pleasures she felt, and soon they were all sitting in the stream. We all feel such moments of *joie de vivre*: maybe while watching a glorious sunset, or drinking our morning tea, or feeling the warmth of the sun on your face as you relax on the beach, or the sound of a breeze though a pine forest, or curling up for a nap on the couch. "Life is good," is the thought that comes to mind during such contemplative moments. In order to experience this kind of pleasure there must be at least a core self, a consciousness of being alive. This, too, has survival value, at least at the higher reaches of consciousness, for awareness of the joy of life will increase the value you place upon your life, and increased life-value translates into a greater will to live.

Humans take joyfulness to new heights, for not only can we revel in experiences of the moment, we can plan them; we can arrange our lives around them in ways other animals cannot. (Though, as with many things, the spontaneous happenings may be the most joyful.) No one doubts that humans can find joy in living, and I think it is safe to agree that the ability to enjoy life increases the importance we place upon our lives. When life is good we look forward to living. But therein lies the rub, for the more pleasure we derive from the world the less we want to leave it behind, and yet leave it behind we must. Death looms for every human, and this constitutes a large anomaly within our framework.

We humans are the only creatures who explicitly see their own death as an inexorable and inescapable future reality. This realization colors our lives and valuations in ways we are not even aware. Just as heightened consciousness may increase our painful sensations, so also it may increase our dread of future non-existence.

§9   ON PHANTOM LIMBS & FALLING TREES

Where does the redness of red come from? The painfulness of pain? These properties do not exist in the object from which they seem to emanate. Likewise with respect to an object's smoothness or its smell. Nor does the pain we experience when we stub our toe exist in our toe. The fact that redness is the result of electrical pulses sent to the brain via the optic nerve indicates we can simulate these pulses and create redness without an object. The redness of red is a projection by the brain (or neurons, if a brain is not present).

Not only do we create the redness, but we, in turn, reify it, we stamp it on to the object in the external world. So also with pain and other sensations. That pain you feel in your toe exists in your brain, which then makes you think it is in your toe. This mapping is a useful function. Without it, every time we were hurt we would feel a sharp pain in our brain, but wouldn't know what was hurting. So it makes sense the brain would interpret the pain as occurring where the damage was done, but it doesn't alleviate the strangeness of it all. This function of the brain, to reify its synoptic firings to places external to itself, is an evolutionary followup to sentience. If you puncture the cell wall of an amoeba, the amoeba doesn't feel pain, but it responds immediately to the site of the attack. It makes sense that painfulness would also be located at the damage point. The painfulness of pain is a more precise, more insistent damage control response.[8]

There is no sound in the forest when a tree falls and there is no sentient creature there to hear it. So also, there is no color or smell in the room when no one is there to experience them. This means that those qualities do not exist in the objects themselves, but are the result of our brains' interpreting our sensory inputs. Objects do not possess or radiate color. They have a

> **REIFY:**
> To regard or treat an abstraction as if it had concrete or material existence.

molecular content which is such that, when light strikes the object and the reflected wavelengths happen to strike our sensory inputs, we see red, which we then mentally place back on the object, the source of our input, as an attribute. If there are no sentient creatures in the room, light is still reflected from the objects, but the electromagnetic radiation is wasted on the walls, like the flower in Gray's elegy: born to blush unseen, wasting its sweetness on the desert air. In a darkened room there is not even this.

We accept that we have this amazing ability to enchant the world. We can take an olfactory input and, like wizards, make it blossom into a sensation, projecting it back on to the world, painting the earth with our sensations, transforming it from a dull sublunar landscape into a canvas of colors, tastes, textures, smells and sounds. We can then follow our memory links, indexed to a particular sensation, and retrieve an image of ourselves as children smelling that very smell or feeling that very texture. But, just as amazing, we also do this with our own body, for all feeling exists primarily in the brain which then projects it to various parts of the body where the input occurred. Input from our skin surfaces is concisely mapped in the cortex (postcentral gyrus) in a representation known as the somatosensory homunculus, also known as a Penfield map (Figure 2–8). This gives rise to an odd phenomenon known as phantom limb syndrome, experienced by up to eighty percent of those who have lost a limb.

> Many patients with phantoms have a vivid sense of being able to move their missing limbs. They say things like "It's waving goodbye" or "It's reaching out to answer the phone." Of course, they know perfectly well that their hands aren't really doing these things—they aren't delusional, just armless—but subjectively they have a realistic sensation that they are moving the phantom. (Ramachandran 30)

When a limb, say an arm, is lost or removed the brain map for the arm remains. The job of the brain map is to represent the arm, and it continues to do so even if the arm is no longer there, sending its mapping up for higher processing where the

---

[8] The painfulness of pain is evidence that, in Sam Keen's words, "Mother Nature is a brutal bitch." (Becker 1997: xii) This painfulness evolved in the impersonal uncaring process of natural selection. Wouldn't it have been nice if something less hideous had evolved? A continuum of pain with an apex of what corresponds to a dull ache would have sufficed.

sensations are not only *felt*, but reified out into the world to where you think your arm should be.

Consider the following experiment conducted by Carrie Armel and V.S. Ramachandran (Armel 2003) in which a subject is sitting with his hands on a table in front of him. A partition is placed so that the subject is unable to see his right arm and hand, and a prosthetic arm and hand is placed where his arm would normally rest on the table (see Figure 2–9). His left hand is connected to a skin conductance response indicator (see box on page 29 for information on the SCR). When an experimenter then simultaneously stroked the subject's right hand and the hand of the prosthesis (in the same place), the subject reported the tactile sensations caused by the stroking were located on the rubber hand. More amazing still, when the experiment was repeated without the prosthesis, the subject experienced the tactile sensations as coming from the table in front of him. When band-aids were placed on both the right hand and on the table and then the band-aid on the table was suddenly ripped off, the skin conductance response indicated a change in emotions as there was an expectation of pain within the subject.

Nor is this the only amazing projection our brains are capable of. Electrical stimulation of the right amygdala can produce "vivid visual hallucinations, out-of-body sensations, déjà vu, and numerous types of illusions." (d'Aquili 1999: 44) Reflecting on these kinds of experiments should lead us to appreciate the power of the brain to influence and interpret our various sensory inputs.

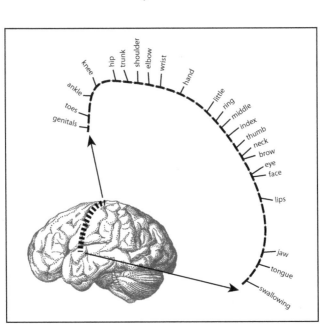

FIGURE 2–8

The cortical homunculus, or Penfield map, showing the areas of the cortex representing various skin surfaces.

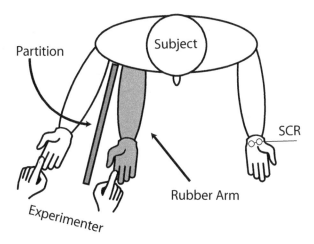

FIGURE 2–9
An illustration of the Amstel/Ramanchandran experiment in which the subject reified the sensations to a visible prosthesis rather than his real arm.

§10 CHAPTER SUMMARY

In this chapter we have differentiated some of the various ways in which organisms monitor and react to stimuli of various sorts. My point has been that these ways range from simple to complex and along this continuum we make arbitrary divisions, and as we progressively get more complex we begin to speak of consciousness and self-consciousness. It doesn't matter if you agree with where I draw the lines with respect to the levels of consciousness or if you disagree with what organisms I have speculated might belong within each level. I think it useful to speculate on the divisions even if we don't agree, especially since it clarifies how I will be using terms in following chapters. That said, there are two points that are not speculative; indeed, that should be seen to be beyond debate:

(1) Everything we humans experience is processed and interpreted by our brains, and because of this

(2) The world is not necessarily as it appears.

As organic creatures we must use our senses, internal and external, to glean information about ourselves and the world around us. That is, anything we know is input in some way into our system. These inputs are our senses (not just the familiar five—we also have internal sensors for pain, balance, and so on), and these are all connected to our nervous system,[9] the pathways of which culminate in the brain. By the time we become aware (conscious) of an input, that signal has already been processed and reprocessed. This processing opens a fundamental gap between the-world-as-it-appears-to-us and the-way-the-world-really-is. This gap is shown explicitly in our ability to reify sensations—to make them appear as if they exist in

---

[9] Processing occurs all the way up, not just in the brain proper. Feedback loops begin in the spinal cord and brain stem, which are not merely conduits to the brain. Consciousness of an action, though, cannot occur without brain processes.

MORE ON PHANTOM LIMBS

V.S. Ramachandran describes a patient, Victor, whose left arm had been amputated below the elbow. On a whim, he decided to test Victor's response to various stimuli and began touching his skin in various places with a dampened Q-tip. When he touched the left side of his face Victor reported feeling the sensation in his phantom hand. With repeated probing, Ramachandran discovered there was a map of the missing hand on Victor's face. The map corresponded precisely to the cortical homunculus (Figure 2–9).

> On one occasion I pressed a damp Q-tip against his cheek and sent a bead of water trickling down his face like a tear. He felt the water move down his cheek in the normal fashion, but claimed he could also feel the droplet trickling down the length of his phantom arm. Using his right index finger, he even traced the meandering path of the trickle through the empty air in front of his stump. Out of curiosity I asked him to elevate his stump and point the phantom upward toward the ceiling. To his astonishment he felt the next drop of water flowing up along the phantom, defying the law of gravity. (2011: 25)

Victor was excited by the finding, for it gave him a means of alleviating the aggravating itchiness of his phantom hand—he simply scratched the corresponding area of his face and found relief.

One explanation for this phenomenon is that the diminished use of the facial map in the absence of the corresponding body part(s) allows adjacent nerve fibers to invade the diminished territory of the limb (note that on the Penfield map that the facial area is situated adjacent to the hand). This theory is borne out by other cases: Italian researchers reported the amputation of a finger with a corresponding facial map, and a foot amputation that resulted in sensation from the penis being felt in the phantom foot.

Many cases of phantom limbs result in either pain or paralysis of the missing limb (often the pain is the result of the phantom limb being in an uncomfortable position which cannot be adjusted). Here again the brain does not realize the limb is missing and sends out motor commands to the limb which cannot be accomplished, resulting in the feeling of paralysis and discomfort. Ramachandran found that by placing a mirror so that the patient, looking down, saw a mirror image of his existing arm in the exact place where he felt his missing arm, the patient could free his phantom paralysis.

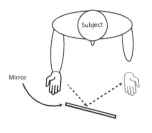

the world, like the pain within a phantom limb. In this sense we might say that all perception is hallucination.

These points alone are enough to engage us philosophically for the rest of this book. They should at least be sufficient to make you want to know more about the marvelous processor each of us possesses, if only to discern how it influences our perceptions, for these in turn influence our actions. This is the topic of the next chapter.

Notes / Questions

3. Operating Systems

• •

Operating systems are like underwear — no one really wants to see them.
— Bill Joy

SYNOPSIS

(1) Our human operating system consists of the non-reflective cognitive processes used to interpret the input from our senses. (2) The principle of non-contradiction, one of the fundamental rules of processing, is briefly examined. (3) Examples are given which indicate the way we see the world is determined by brain processes. Cognitive processing takes place prior to our conscious awareness of objects, and proceeds according to specific rules (algorithms) which dictate how we see the world. (4) Learning also occurs unconsciously. Different types of non-reflective knowledge are discussed briefly. (5) Our operating system is given to us genetically, but plays a part in learning as well. This gives rise to the age old nature-nurture debate. Current research indicates that the nature side is more heavily weighted than the nurture. (6) A brief introduction to natural selection will help explain why our operating system is not optimally designed. (7) Examples of the non-optimal design of our operating system and some of the practical consequences of this. (8) Time differentials in brain processes and what this means for us. (9) Chapter Summary.

CHAPTER OBJECTIVES

- to appreciate how much of our conscious experience is due to unconscious brain processes and why this is important.
- to gain an understanding of the process of natural selection: how it works and why this is important.
- to understand why we are not optimally suited for understanding the world around us

§1 FRAMEWORKS

hen personal computers first arrived in the 1980s many first-time users were terrified when confronted with a blank screen and a blinking cursor. The interface was called DOS or "disk operating system," and, though a layer removed from machine language, it was nonetheless intimidating, a diaphanous veil hiding the mysterious inner workings of the computer, especially when compared to the beautiful graphic user interfaces of today. Now we blithely push the buttons or touch the screens of our electronic devices without having a clue how they work, just as we drive our cars without knowing how the various mechanical and electronic systems hidden beneath the hood make it all possible. And why should we? There are experts who can fix our computers and cars when they break.

The complexity of the human body far overshadows that of cars and computers, so the same question arises: why bother to learn how the human body works when there are experts who can fix us when our systems fail? After all, we can only know so much. The reflective person, though, will at least want to know herself well enough to know the limits of her understanding, just as an athlete needs to know the limits of his endurance. Cars and computers are not the best analogy; they are useful tools, but your body, and especially your brain, is you. Its limits are your limits, and these limits might be crucial to achieving well-being.

Each of us has what I will refer to as a framework which enables us to interpret the world around us. Your framework is with you at all times. Once you become aware of it, you may be able to change small parts of it, but you cannot exist without it (just as a computer can do nothing without software). Raw data enters our framework via our senses, is processed by the system, and then output to consciousness (Figure 3–1). All we are ever conscious of is the processed data. The virtual cloud of consciousness we call our self is a result of these brain processes. We are not passive observers of the world, but active participants, continually processing and interpreting our surroundings. This raises several questions: What is the data like before it is processed? How do we know if the processed data (our view of the world) is similar to the original data (the way the world really is)? These are deep and abiding questions. When we take a picture with a digital camera, the software inside is already set to render the output (the photograph) to look like the world as

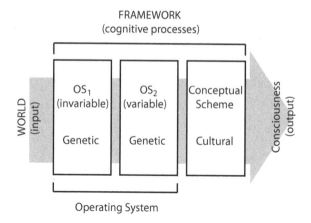

FRAMEWORK
(cognitive processes)

FIGURE 3–1

A representation of our human framework through which we interpret the world. The framework is composed of the operating system and the conceptual system.

we interpret it (see box on page 52). We have a standard to judge the output by, namely, what we see with our eyes. But the question we have raised is different, for there is no standard to judge our output—our output just is our standard. How, then, do we know if our conscious view of the world matches the world? It is one of our goals to answer this question as best we can.

I will divide frameworks into two systems, or levels. The first is what I will call our Operating System, which will be described in this chapter. I will further divide our operating system into two subsystems:

(1) OS_1: This most basic level of the operating system contains the genetic, invariable structures that allow us to live in and interact with the world. We have no control over this system. Unless damaged, our operating system is exactly like that found in every other human (and many non-human animals as well).

(2) OS_2: This level contains the genetic variables, genetic characteristics that vary from human to human. This might include intelligence, appearance, athletic abilities, and so on. We have limited control over our genetic variables: a) we may realize, or fail to realize, the potential given to us genetically; b) we may attempt to control the genes of our offspring (by, say, choosing our child from a genius sperm bank or looking for a spouse that has characteristics we want our children to have); c) we may influence the impact of some genes (whether they are turned off or on, for instance) by manipulating environmental factors.

The second major system I will call our Conceptual Scheme (the topic of chapter 5). We can reflect on our conceptual scheme in ways we are not capable of with our operating system. Conceptual schemes presuppose an operating system, and are highly customizable. Our overall framework presupposes a working relationship between our operating system and our conceptual scheme.

What exactly does an operating system do for us? Where did it come from? How does it affect us? These are all questions that must be addressed in a reflective investigation of ourselves. Let's begin with a look at several aspects of our operating system's core processing.

§2 THE PRINCIPLE OF NON-CONTRADICTION

The principle of non-contradiction, first formulated by Aristotle, is a fundamental rule of our operating system and, as such, is a major factor in determining how we see the world. There are several formulations:

(a) A thing cannot both be and not be at the same time in the same sense.

(b) A sentence cannot be both true and false at the same time in the same sense.

The principle of non-contradiction is part of our genetic makeup, and without it we could not survive. The very act of attempting to prove the principle presupposes it. (To prove the principle true, you must first assume it cannot also be false—which just is the principle you are trying to prove.)

Suppose you ask someone whether they believe in the existence of God, and they reply, "Of course I believe God exists." But as you continue to talk with them, it sounds as if they do not believe. Confused, you say, "I thought you believed in the existence of God," to which they reply, "I do believe God exists, but I also believe he doesn't exist." You might try to give the person the benefit of the doubt, assuming maybe they were using the word 'god' or 'exists' in two different ways. Short of that you would be completely stymied. This is the principle of non-contradiction at work. When the principle is broken, we don't know what to do, for our reasoning is based upon it. As such, it forms the very basis of what we mean when we say we are rational, or that the world is rational.

In *Through the Looking Glass*, the White Queen tells Alice that in her youth she "believed six impossible things before breakfast every morning." There are several problems with this statement. First, that we can intentionally believe anything on a whim, but more importantly, that we can believe impossible things at all—contradictory sentences. This is a function of the principle of non-contradiction. If you believe "It will rain sometime today," you cannot also, at the same time and in the exact same sense, believe "It will *not* rain sometime today."

We should clarify this as follows: We can believe contradictory things, but we cannot *knowingly* do so. For example, for many years people believed "The morning star is not the evening star." They could believe this because they did not know the morning star and the evening star were the same body, namely, the planet Venus. Once we know this, the statement becomes "Venus is not Venus," which no rational person can believe. (Go on; try it. Pick a sentence you know is true, then try with all your might to believe it false. Good luck.)

To say the principle of non-contradiction is a fundamental part of our operating system means reality might not conform to it. If the principle is part of our operating

CAMERAS AND EYES

When light enters a digital camera through the lens it is directed into an electronic sensor (CCD), which we can think of as containing a grid. Each cell in this grid is a picture element, or pixel. The sample of light that enters the grid is controlled by the aperture and shutter settings. When you take a picture, the electrical charge of each cell within the grid is measured and turned into a digital value. The more cells a camera has in its grid, the more detail it can capture. A twelve megapixel camera has an array with more than twelve million cells. (35mm film is estimated to be around twenty million pixels.)

Cameras can't see color; they only sense the intensity of the light. After the original measurement is made, this information is sent to a processor in the camera where a filter is used to break the light into three different wavelengths, corresponding to what we see as red, green and blue. Millions of colors can be represented by combining the varying intensities of these three. If we wanted the best possible image, we would send the light from the lens through three different filters, and then record these three numbers for each pixel location (most digital cameras use a more economical method based on an algorithm).

The human eye is a sensitive detector, able to detect a single photon (though a single photon doesn't exceed the minimum signal-to-noise ratio threshold of the noise filtering circuitry in the visual system). Thus, the images we see when our eyes are open are processed images, not raw. When we calibrate a camera to take "accurate" images, then, we are actually calibrating to an already-processed image. There is no way to calibrate our vision.

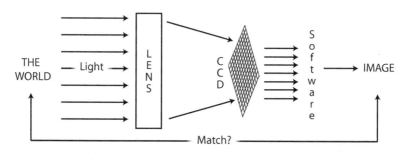

system, then it is a function of our brain processes, not necessarily a part of the external world. It seems, then, that we impose non-contradiction upon reality as a necessary precondition for understanding it. All data is filtered through our framework. It's a pretty good bet, though, that the world is rational in this way, that it conforms to the principle of non-contradiction. Our behavioral traits are honed by natural selection, which forces them to track the environment, at least to some extent (more on how this works in §6). This is not something we should worry about. Even if there are contradictions in the world around us, 1) we will never experience them as such as long as we can explain them away, and 2) they must not be especially lethal, since the non-contradiction gene has been passed along very successfully.

§3 PROCESSING IN THE VISUAL CORTEX

As I write this, I'm looking out a window at a large evergreen tree. Farther back is a forest of these trees, but I'm looking at a particular tree, closer to the window than the others. How do I distinguish this tree from the background of trees? It seems a simple enough question. The quick answer is: our brains absorb raw data from our eyes and process it using very specific algorithms, or rules, that determine where one object starts and another stops. Our brains identify boundaries in this fashion, and these boundaries determine what we call independent objects. Is that rectangle protruding at a right angle from the tree a part of this tree or part of another tree? There are more rules for determining this. What about distinguishing foreground and background? More rules.

We're already getting ahead of ourselves. Beneath all this computation is the presupposition that we have the ability to perceive various wavelengths of electromagnetic radiation, which is what allows a basic processor to see lines and gradations of color, which is the initial data needed for our boundary processing to begin. Once this has taken place another system is presupposed—memory. The processed world-picture must be continually relegated to memory, otherwise we wouldn't recognize the tree from moment to moment; and speaking of recognition—that's still another process, one that requires pulling an image from memory that matches in some way the one being processed. And we've still only scratched the surface. We are not yet aware we are seeing a tree. Everything so far has happened beneath the conscious level. Welcome to the operating system!

The visual system is one module in our operating system.[1] I want to consider a few simple examples of how one aspect of this module works. The function of our visual system is to construct our conscious world view. Consider the black dot in Figure 3–2, the period magnified. Why do we see dots on a page as periods, as two dimensional points? Why don't we think of a period as a very long three dimensional line seen from one end (the rotated view in Figure 3–2)? We can see it that way if we try. We can imagine every letter on this page extending infinitely deep into the page, but if this were so, then by shifting our head a bit we would begin to see this depth. But a period, all by itself, alone on a page—why do we see this as a point instead of a pole? This is what our operating system has to take into account. It interprets the period as a point because the odds are astronomically against our happening to view a line from the one perfect perspective from which it appears as a point instead of a line, and our operating system always goes with the odds. So when we perceive a dot by itself the rules based on probabilities eliminate the three dimensional option and interpret it as a point. Note the uncounted perspectives from which we view a line, and only one of those portray it as a point. We could, for instance, see a telephone pole lying on the ground as a circle, but what are the odds we would be in the one absolutely perfect perspective to see it as such?

---

[1] Cognitive functions are divided into modules, which are located in different parts of the brain. The modules themselves are further divided into modules nested within the larger module, which in turn have their own sub-modules. These vastly complex nested systems form the black box of neuroscience. Cognitive scientists know a great deal about inputs and outputs into these systems, but what happens within these nested systems is a mystery. To delve into these systems is to travel down the rabbit hole. The larger question is how all these modules come together to deliver a unified conscious awareness (the binding problem we have previously mentioned).

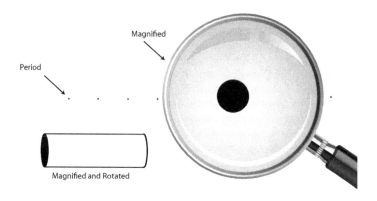

Figure 3–2

For all we know, the periods we see on a printed page could extend indefinitely down into the page, but the probability of this is so small the brain doesn't even consider it, automatically interpreting them as flat, two dimensional objects.

The odds are stacked against our just happening to see a line as a point; our brain recognizes this and doesn't even take those vastly improbable views into account. The brain thus forces us to see certain perspectives, but don't feel cheated. There are so many possibilities in perception that if some branches on the possibility tree were not pruned, we would never be able to see anything. This is what perceptual rules do for us, and the most basic of these are founded on the notion of simplicity.[2]

An example of how this processing can lead us astray is the Penrose (or impossible) triangle (Figure 3–3). You can build a three dimensional model of this triangle which, when looked at from the perfect perspective, looks exactly like this illustration (there is a sculpture of one in Perth, Australia). But what are the odds we would ever encounter such an object and be looking at it from that one specific perspective? Thus our brain is telling us it can't be three dimensional even though there are cues telling us it is. We can override this, but the default algorithm gives us the two dimensional interpretation.

This also happens when we consider background and foreground. In my example of looking out the window and seeing a tree, I have no problem distinguishing background and foreground, and this is usually true when we look at objects. But not always, and we can fool the visual system into not knowing which is which if we make both interpretations equally probable. In other words, the probabilities are usually high that background and foreground will differ markedly, making confusion improbable, but the more we lower these probabilities the more we are likely to be confused. Consider the familiar example in Figure 3–4, in which we see, alternatively, two people facing each other or a black vase. There is not enough information

---

[2] The principle of simplicity (Occam's razor): don't make something complex when something simple will work. Even if this leads to the occasional error, it's worth it. Imagine the energy it would take to calculate all the permutations of the world before deciding on one in particular as the best. Such processing would expend enormous amounts of time and energy, and thus would never be selected for in nature.

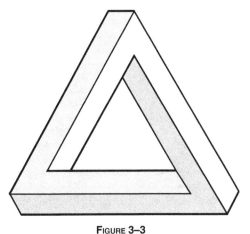

FIGURE 3–3

The impossible Penrose triangle. We can construct such a triangle, but it will have this look only from one, very precise, perspective.

FIGURE 3–4

A rendition of the familiar face-vase diagram which confuses foreground and background.

to tell definitively which is background and which is foreground, so our brain continually shifts back and forth between the two options.

Another example of built-in algorithmic processing is given by Ramachandran (2011). In Figure 3–5 notice that you can view the circles as either protruding out from the surface or sunk into the surface of the rectangle, but whichever way you view them, they are all the same. If you change your perspective from one to the other, they all change. Next, look at the top row of circles in Figure 3–6. Again, you can see these as either protruding or sunken, but whichever way you view them, the entire row is the same, and the bottom row will be the opposite. Now look at Figure 3–7. Some of the circles will appear sunken, others will appear to protrude, but you cannot change them at will. Focus on one circle and, while looking at it,

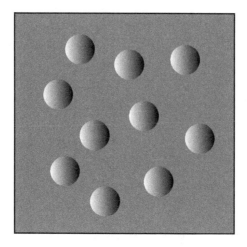

FIGURE 3–5
In this figure you can make the circles appear as either sunken or extruded, but whichever you choose to see, all of the circles will change accordingly.

rotate the book so that it is upside down. When you do this, the protruded circles will now appear sunken and the sunken circles will appear protruded. Now return to Figure 3–6, and adjust your perspective so that you see the top row of circles as extruded (the bottom row will appear sunken). Now tilt your head so that your right ear is resting on your shoulder while viewing the top row. The circles will now appear sunken on the top row and extruded on the bottom. This is all very interesting, but why does it happen?

The answer has to do, once again, with probabilities. Our brains assume any object we see will be top-lit (a pretty good assumption). Not only that, the light source is assumed to be located on the top of our head rather than external to us (which is why when we tilt our head and look at Figure 3–6, things change).

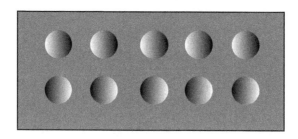

FIGURE 3–6
In this figure, if you see the top row as sunken, the bottom row will be extruded and vice versa.

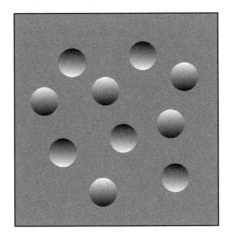

FIGURE 3–7
Some of the circles in this diagram are sunken, others extruded. If you focus on one and turn the book upside down you will see them all change to their opposite.

It's as if your brain assumes that the sun is stuck to the top of your head and remains stuck to it when you tilt your head 90 degrees! Why such a silly assumption? Because statistically speaking, your head is upright most of the time. Your ape ancestors rarely walked around looking at the world with their heads tilted. Your visual system therefore takes a shortcut; it makes the simplifying assumption that the sun is stuck to your head. The goal of vision is not to get things perfectly right all the time, but to do get it right often enough and quickly enough to survive as long as possible to leave behind as many babies as you can. As far as evolution is concerned, that's all that matters. Of course, this shortcut makes you vulnerable to certain incorrect judgments, as when you tilt your head, but this happens so rarely in real life that your brain can get away with being lazy like this. (Ramachandran 54)

Once you know that our operating system uses very specific rules for processing information about the world, it shouldn't surprise you that this sometimes leads to error and confusion. In fact, once you know the rules you can fool the system on purpose, as with the Penrose Triangle in Figure 3–3. Often when you find yourself in a confusing situation the problem is a lack of enough information to apply specific rules. This may be why we humans have such a hard time with extreme boundaries, both spatial and temporal (the end of the universe, the beginning of time). We process the world in a very practical way, most of which is unconscious, but our reflective abilities (our self-consciousness) allow us to think about aspects of the world never encountered in our earlier stages of development. Confusion arises when we try to extend our concepts beyond the practical sphere our brains evolved to deal with. The concept of boundary, for example, probably has its roots in our reach. We are inherently aware of what is within our reach, which constitutes a boundary of our practical abilities. As we became more reflective we extended this concept—the limits of our vision, hearing—even to inanimate objects such as property. An even higher abstraction extends boundaries to what we cannot see: space and time. Every thing has a boundary and the universe is a thing, so the universe must have a boundary; but what, then, lies outside the universe? When our brain attempts to apply the down-to-earth literal boundaries of our bodies to the highly abstract concepts of space and time, confusion results.

All of our basic processing takes place in the unconscious; it occurs before we are even aware of a pine tree or a triangle. But learning can also occur in the unconscious. In the next section we will discuss some of the ways in which this happens.

§4 NON-REFLECTIVE LEARNING

The world is always with us. In the good times we enjoy friends and family, we savor both scenery and excitement, but when our comfort dissipates, the world is what it always was—an environment packed with exigencies that will kill us without hesitation. We must learn how to survive in this fickle environment. All learning depends on storing information in memory. Instincts, fixed action behaviors, are not learned, but inherited. A bird, for instance, does not have to learn how to build a nest. A colt does not have to learn to walk, nor a baby to cry. These are all part of the individual organisms' operating systems, which have evolved for their benefit.[3] We often think of learning as a process that occurs in school when we learn the names of presidents and the state capitols. Reflective learning occurs when we consciously set out to learn facts about the world. Knowing yourself better, our goal in this text, also involves reflective learning, and this is the type we will be most concerned with. But we can also learn unawares, or non-reflectively. As Figure 3–8 shows, there are two broad categories of non-reflective learning. We will consider each in turn.

NON-ASSOCIATIVE LEARNING

Simple learning is said to occur when a given stimulus elicits a specific response. The organism in question associates a stimulus with a separate event, and changes its behavior accordingly. But it may be possible for an organism to learn without this kind of association taking place. Habituation and sensitization (mirror images of one another) are two types of non-associative learning.[4]

Habituation (desensitization). You move into a new apartment which is close to a busy highway. The traffic noise keeps you awake at night—for a while. In time, though, you become used to the noise and it no longer bothers you. Habituation

---

[3] As always, the more closely you look into a subject, the less you are able to make clear distinctions. This is true with every distinction we make in this chapter, including the distinctions between reflective and non-reflective knowledge, associative and non-associative knowledge, and so on. Take for instance the phenomenon of imprinting, first studied by Konrad Lorentz, when a hatchling attaches itself to the first thing it sees. The procedure of imprinting seems to be genetic, but isn't it also a form of learning?

[4] There is some question whether these are truly non-associative, but we will accept the distinction.

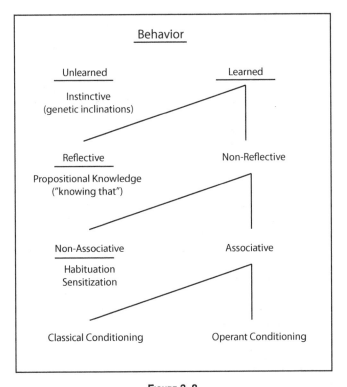

FIGURE 3–8
A schema of various types of behavior indicating how different types of learning might be classified.

has occurred. The probability of your responding to the traffic noise has declined. Habituation allows organisms to flourish in what might otherwise be inconceivably hostile environments.

Sensitization (dishabituation). As the mirror image of habituation, sensitization increases the probability of responding to a stimuli. The classical example has to do with a marine worm (*Nereis*) confined within a tube. When the worm was fed regularly it was found that the confinement increased the likelihood of responding to new stimuli of any kind (increased illumination or noise level) with food-seeking behavior. Thus, its food-seeking behavior had been sensitized (it would not ordinarily have been invoked by the new stimuli). Another example might be when you close your eyes to better hear the nuances in a musical piece, or a blind person's ability to distinguish braille symbols with their fingertips.

ASSOCIATIVE LEARNING

As we consider these types of non-reflective knowledge, keep in mind that calling these non-reflective does not mean they cannot be used reflectively. Rather, they are included here because they are methods by which an organism can learn without being aware it is learning. There are two widely recognized types of associative learning: classical conditioning and operant conditioning (Figure 3–9).

Classical conditioning was first studied by the Russian physiologist, Ivan Pavlov (1849-1936). While studying the digestive system of dogs he noticed his test subjects salivated profusely when given food (the salivation was, at first, an annoying by-product of his work on digestion), but after time they began salivating when they saw the trainer coming to feed them. The trainer is a relevant causal factor in the dog's getting food, but Pavlov showed that the stimulus need not be relevant—it could be completely arbitrary. He would ring a bell before the dogs were fed and, in time, the dogs would salivate merely upon the sound of the bell. An association was made between the bell and getting food.

Operant conditioning was first studied by Edward Thorndike (1874-1949), but made most famous by B.F. Skinner (1904-1990). Operant conditioning is similar to classical conditioning, but works on voluntary behavior as opposed to reflexive behavior. The salivation of Pavlov's dogs was a reflexive behavior which could be modified by forming associations between the unconditioned stimulus (the food) and a conditioned stimulus (the bell). In operant conditioning the dog's behavior isn't reflexive. Suppose you want to teach your dog to bark on your command. You say "speak" and if (and when) the dog barks you reward him. With repetition, this forms an association between the command "speak" and the voluntary behavior of barking. In essence, the dog is thinking "if I bark when she says 'speak,' I'm going to get a reward." Thus the dog must understand that the consequences of barking include a reward and that the command stimulating him to bark will gain him this. He thus learns to bark on command. In operant conditioning there is a consequence to the dog's response (the bark), while in classical conditioning there is no consequence to the dog's response (the salivation).

Our operating systems determine how we see the world. Non-reflective learning occurs by running our input from the world through modules in our brain which

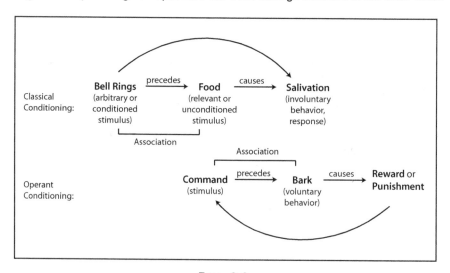

FIGURE 3–9
The difference between classical and operant conditioning. In classical conditioning the association of the subject between the conditioned and the unconditioned stimulus is (or can be) completely arbitrary. In operant conditioning there is a feedback loop between the final reward (or punishment) and the original stimulus.

interpret them in various ways without our even being aware of the processing. This learning is crucial for making us who we are in our early stages. But how much of who we are is genetic and how much is learned from our environment? We know our nature is due to a mixture of both, but is one dominant? The current answer is that genetics dominates environment, but this debate is a thorny one and needs some background of its own.

§5 Nature / Nurture

We know the brain processes information taken in by our senses. We also know the brain is built from our genetic blueprint in coordination with external (environmental) factors. We have already raised the question concerning how much of what we sense is determined by our operating system, and this leads to yet another question: How much of what we are and do is determined by our genetic complement? This is often referred to as the nature versus nurture question.

Plato believed we were born into this world with all knowledge already within us. Before birth we lived in a perfect world, but forgot everything when rudely thrown (born) into our present earthly existence. We spend our entire lives attempting to remember what we forgot—this remembering is what we call "learning." Plato gives a famous example in his dialog *The Meno* in which Socrates pulls a slave boy into the conversation and asks him pointed questions concerning geometric figures drawn in the sand. With a little prompting the boy has no problem producing correct answers. Socrates concludes that the only way an unlearned slave boy could know such things is if he already knew them and simply had to be prompted into remembering them. Plato, on one view, falls on the 100% genetic side of the debate, at least in the sense that we have the ideas in our heads, even if we don't remember them. Or you might say he falls in the middle, allowing that we must be nurtured into remembering.

A prominent modern position holds the exact opposite. The blank slate hypothesis is the claim that we are born into this world with minds that are completely blank. Everything we are and do is the result of learning, of experience imprinting upon our minds. John Locke (1632-1704) first formulated the idea of the blank slate as an argument against innate ideas (ideas we are born with). His rather crass position was that experience gives us simple ideas which we then combine into more complex concepts. We start, then, with minds that are blank tablets (*tabula rasa*) which are then imprinted by experience. The obvious objection to Locke's position is that there must be some kind of mental machinery in place that combines all those simple ideas into more complex ones, mental machinery which is not given to us by experience.

Locke wasn't interested in addressing this problem, for he had an ax to grind. He needed the blank slate hypothesis in order to undercut the divine right theory of government wherein rulers claimed to know (by self-evidence) that they were appointed to rule. The link is this: divine right positions hold that certain people (the aristocracy) are intrinsically better than others. These are the people ordained to rule everyone else. The blank slate hypothesis holds we are all born equal with respect to worth, intelligence, talent, and so on, bolstering the idea of egalitarianism.

So, if the blank slate hypothesis is true, the aristocracy was not born to rule, and had no divine right to such.

Attaching egalitarianism to the blank slate gave rise to the idea of the noble savage, popularized by Jean Jacques Rousseau (1712-1778), in which civilization corrupted the inherent nobility of humans. But how did we get from equal at birth to noble at birth? Equally noble? Why not equally ignoble? If we are truly blank slates at birth, then nothing follows with respect to our nobility. The important aspect seems to be the influence of civilization. Coupled with the inherent nobility of humans this would mean that all evil is learned evil; we are born good, but tainted by civilization. This idea has an even more important implication, for if all evil is learned, then it can be unlearned, an idea which leads to utopian idealism in which the state takes over the role of both teaching and unteaching in an attempt to return humans to their original condition. This idea was not lost on Plato, who, in *The Republic*, attempted to formulate just such a society.

> **EGALITARIANISM:**
>
> The doctrine of the equality of mankind and the desirability of political, economic and social equality.

This is the aspect of the blank slate concept that hits closest to home, for in the 20th century it was coupled with behaviorism in psychology—a marriage born in heaven. Behavior is learned, so if we begin with a blank slate we can teach a person to be whatever we want him to be. As John Watson once proclaimed:

> Give me a dozen healthy infants, well-formed, and my own specified world to bring them up in and I'll guarantee to take any one at random and train him to become any type of specialist I might select—doctor, lawyer, artist, merchant-chief, and yes, even beggar-man and thief, regardless of his talents, penchants, tendencies, abilities, vocations, and race of his ancestors. (Pinker 2003:19)

This idea gave rise to Skinner's radical behaviorism, and spread to anthropology via the influence of Franz Boas (1858-1942). Boas, whose famous students included Margaret Meade and Ashley Montagu, had the best of intentions. He propounded the blank slate in an effort to rid the world of prejudice and injustice, much as Locke had done four hundred years earlier. The idea was used as a stick with which to beat down those who offended its propounders.[5] Any reference to human nature or inherent intellectual or physical abilities roused the ire of the blank slaters, for they saw all such claims as forming the basis of future discrimination and its resulting oppression: not only will some races claim superiority, but if genetics rules, then trying to better humanity is a futile task.

While it is true that great evil can come from claims of genetic superiority, this is not evidence for the truth of the blank slate hypothesis. Bad things might happen because we are human, but this is part of our condition we have to deal with. Nor

---

[5] Pinker (2003) gives many examples of this. An interesting phenomenon began to arise as evidence against the blank slate mounted. Many intellectuals stuck to the hypothesis doggedly even in the face of contrary evidence. Their justification: we cannot afford to admit the blank slate idea to be false because of the (supposedly evil) consequences if it were. In other words, we should promote a falsehood because of the consequences of the truth. Lying, it seems, especially for the greater good, is an esteemed tradition, one not relegated only to politicians.

does it follow that trying to better humanity is futile. Genetics is important, but no one believes it is everything. Culture still plays a large part, including the part that teaches us to get along with other humans. Ironically, some of the greatest evils perpetrated upon humans have come from attempts to force individuals to conform to programs purposefully designed to better them, programs based firmly upon the notion of the blank slate. Marxism, as practiced in both Russia and China, is a good example.

In fact, we are not blank slates. Culture is not a set of arbitrary roles that happen to shape humans. It is the result of both genetics and human interaction. Cultures turn out to be similar because humans are similar; they are different because different environments dictate different human survival strategies. A culture that develops in the North African desert is going to be different from one that develops in a rain forest in South America. There is a set of characteristics all humans are born with—a human nature. The evidence for this is substantial. First, as we have already pointed out, we cannot learn without inborn genetic structures. Something must exist, an operating system, in order to process the data that comes in from the world. This operating system is built according to instructions in our genetic code, begins functioning before we are even born, and is essentially the same in all humans. If we think of the genes as a blueprint,[6] there are specific structures that will be constructed, though we may have to take environmental contingencies into account.[7]

If we wanted to find out how much of personality is due to genetics and how much to environment, we would want to take two individuals with exactly the same genetic code and raise them in separate environments. If there were no similarities between them, then we would know that environment was all important, but if there were significant similarities, this would constitute evidence for a human nature. Luckily, there is way to do this, for identical twins have exactly the same genetic code. The studies conducted on identical twins raised apart indicate genetic influence is substantial. Examples are telling.

Consider the identical twin sisters Daphne and Barbara. Raised outside London, they both left school at the age of fourteen, went to work in local government, met their future husbands at the age of sixteen at local town hall dances, suffered miscarriages at the same time, and then each gave birth to two boys and a girl. They feared many of the same things (blood and heights) and exhibited unusual habits (each drank her coffee cold; each developed the habit of pushing up her nose with the palm of the hand, a gesture they both called "squidging"). None of this may surprise you until you learn that separate families had adopted Daphne and Barbara as

---

[6] Marcus (2004) and others have argued against the blueprint analogy since there are not enough genes to specify exactly how all our cells develop. The alternate, and probably better, analogy is the recipe. All analogies will, of course, break down at some point.

[7] Psychopathy is a good example. Psychopaths are born with a damaged amygdala, which hinders their ability to empathize with other humans. They do not understand that others suffer as they do and so have no feelings or emotional attachments to other people. This is a genetic characteristic that is quite common in human society. There are many psychopaths among us. Most learn to deal with their lack in socially acceptable ways, but some, due to environmental circumstances (abusive parents are the usual suspect) may turn into serial killers.

infants; neither even knew of the other's existence until they were reunited at the age of forty. When they finally did meet, they were wearing almost identical clothing. (Haidt 32)

Examples like this are fun, but there is a serious point. Particular genes can now be tied to particular aspects of cognition, language and personality.[8] Identical twins are more similar than fraternal twins, and biological siblings are more similar than adoptive siblings, whether reared together or apart. This indicates that genes play an extremely important part in our development.

What does this mean for us? The human nature we are referring to constitutes not only our bodies but our brains, and this includes our operating systems. I am going to claim, in what follows, that our operating system is not particularly well-designed. There are two related parts to this claim. First, the mechanisms of the brain itself are not optimally designed for what they do, and second, we humans are not optimally adapted to our modern environment. Everything we say about the brain is also true of the body. We humans like to think of ourselves as optimally designed to live in our world and grasp its truths, but this is not so. Our systems work well enough and are enormously complex, but when you understand how they work you begin to see flaws (as we have already seen in our examples above concerning visual processing). Two questions arise: 1) How could flaws have developed in our operating system? and 2) What are the flaws? I will address these questions in order in the following sections.

§6 NATURAL SELECTION & OPTIMAL DEVELOPMENT

Understanding the origin and development of humanity by means of an evolutionary process is the key to understanding how flaws developed in both our bodies and our brains; and self-replication, the ability to create copies of one's self based on building instructions passed down generation by generation, is the key to evolution.[9] The best explanation for our present condition is that we have a past. We are the products of a long, complex historical development.

Let's start with a simple one-celled organism as an example. Call it O, and let's give it a tail (a flagellum) to help it move about in its watery environment. The basic instruction set for O will contain: (1) information on how to complete its own construction: how to move, take in nutrition and grow to maturity; (2) details on how to create another O, once mature; and (3) a mandate to create another O. In a simple organism (2) and (3) are combined in cell division and (1) might be minimally

---

[8] No one claims there is a gene for drinking cold coffee. What is being claimed is that the genes control the development into a particular personality type which might tend to have such a trait.

[9] Sex, by the way, is not necessary for replication; we humans adopted it, but whatever gets your instruction set into the next generation will do. Why sexual reproduction developed is problematic. Most theorists assume it came about to protect against predators glomming onto our genome and taking advantage of it. The mixing of genes in sexual reproduction is tantamount to continually changing the locks on a building in order to keep burglars out. The downside, from an evolutionary standpoint, is that only one-half of an organism's genes get passed down into the next generation. With asexual reproduction 100% get passed on.

important, but in sexual organisms we have to include not only the ability to mature and reproduce sexually, but the desire to reproduce. These are the basics. O must live long enough to enable it to make a copy of itself that contains these instructions, then it can die. If it fails to live long enough to make a copy, the instructions die when it dies. End of story.

So far we have O making an exact copy of itself, which copy then contains instructions to make an exact copy of itself, which it does, making an exact copy of itself, and so on. This is an ideal evolutionary organism which always faithfully passes its code on to its offspring without error, and which lives in an ideal (unchanging) environment with plenty of resources (food and shelter) and no predators. In this scenario, O_1 would be exactly like O_2, which would be exactly like O_n, even after thousands of generations. Figure 3–10 illustrates this, showing O with instruction set A. But conditions are always less than ideal, and complications arise. Both the instruction set and the environment are subject to change. A more realistic scenario, even though still ideal, would be one in which O makes more than one copy of itself. This would mean that by generation O_n there might be a vast number of O's, all of which would be exactly the same. This would be referred to as a population of O's. Let's use this concept to examine a less ideal world in which O_n turns out to be vastly different from O_1.

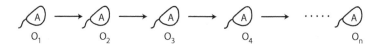

FIGURE 3–10

A situation in which there are no replication errors, environmental change or predators. If each organism (O) makes an error free copy of itself according to an instruction set (A), then the organism would never change throughout the generations.

MODIFYING THE INSTRUCTION SET

O's instruction set can be modified externally or internally. Externally, radiation damage from the sun might occur, modifying the code in various ways. Internally, an error might occur when the instruction set is being copied during replication. However the error occurs, there are three possible consequences of these errors (see Figure 3–11): (1) The modification may give rise to a phenotypic trait detrimental to the survival of O. For example, suppose the line of code that specifies how to build the flagellum is modified, resulting in a much shorter flagellum. Call this the X modification. Let's also suppose the flagellum is necessary in order to find food and avoid predators, which means a shorter flagellum translates into a smaller probability of finding food and a greater probability of being eaten, which means the X-modified O's may not grow to maturity and thus will not be able to replicate. Since they cannot replicate, this X-modified instruction set won't be passed on. All O's with this modification will die. (2) The modification may cause a phenotypic trait that is neutral with respect to survival. For example, maybe it causes a slight thickening in O's outer lining; not enough to hinder its growth and reproduction, but also not enough to protect it from predation. Call this the Y modification. This change has absolutely no effect on O's ability to grow and reproduce, so the Y-modified instruction set will be passed on to the next generation. Thus, within the future population of O's, some will possess this neutral trait and others won't. The trait will drift through the lineage, and may or may not become relevant in the future. (3) The modification may cause a phenotypic trait advantageous to O. For example, let's suppose the modification to O's instruction set results in a longer flagellum that enables the O's who have it to move around better in their environment. Call this the Z modification. Moving around better translates into being better able to find food and avoid predators, which means the Z-modified O's will have an advantage over other O's in the population. This means, over time, that the O's with this modification will eventually out-breed the original O's, completely replacing the original population. The long-tailed O's have become better adapted to their environment, better "designed." They have increased their evolutionary fitness. This process is known as natural selection. Notice how, as this process continues, the organism will become better adapted to its specific environment. In fact, over time, it will appear as if the organism was almost perfectly designed for its environment. That is, until the environment changes…

MODIFYING THE ENVIRONMENT

Natural selection also occurs due to environmental change. The selection method is still the same—random changes to the instruction set, but environmental change can introduce new pressures. Suppose, for example, the environment is slowly getting colder, and the present winter is the coldest yet—too cold for most O's to survive. If all O's died, this would be an extinction event. But in this case, remember the set of O's which had the, until now, neutral trait of a thicker external

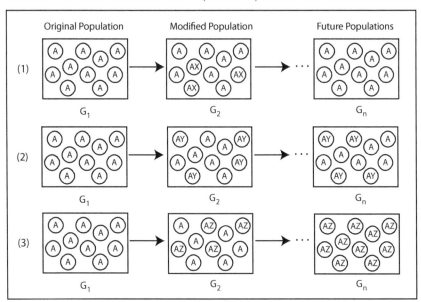

FIGURE 3–11
Errors in an instruction set can produce phenotypic traits in an organism that are (1) detrimental, (2) neutral, or (3) beneficial.

skin? This trait suddenly becomes important, for it allows those individual O's who possess it to survive. This line of code in the instruction set now becomes universal in the population. The O's that contain it are tracking the change in the environment. From a different perspective it might appear as if they had prepared themselves on purpose for the coming environmental change, but of course this is not so. Natural selection gives only the appearance of design.

Here's another way that environmental change can mold organisms. Suppose our population of O's gets caught up in flood waters that wash half the population away, taking them far downstream to an entirely new location. Call the O's in the original location O-1 and those in the new location O-2. The new location will have new and different challenges—new predators, different food sources, maybe different temperatures. If these challenges are too great, O-2 will simply die out. But let's suppose some had developed the ability to digest different food sources, to protect themselves against the new predators, and so on, and these flourished in their new location. The survivors have an instruction set better suited for their new environment so that their offspring will contain only these instructions (the rest have died). These O-2's will be different from O-1's, and over time, as they continue to reproduce and change their instruction sets independently of each other, tracking their own environments, the differences will become radical. Indeed, there may come a time when they are not even identifiable as the same organism ($O-1_n$ and $O-2_n$ are no longer both considered O's). If they are reintroduced to the same environment they will not breed with each other, and may even be hostile. This is called allopatric speciation.

EVOLUTION IS BLIND TO THE FUTURE

We're all familiar with artificial selection. We breed dogs, cats, horses and cows in this way. We want certain traits and we breed for these traits, mating animals with like traits and discarding the offspring which don't manifest the traits we're breeding for. Then we breed these again. In artificial selection the guiding factor is the trait the breeder is interested in honing. We look toward a future goal and breed accordingly, weeding out those which don't conform to the goal. But in natural selection there is no future goal, there is no breeder. No early organism could plan ahead, could say to itself, "I see I'm in a watery environment where speed matters, so let's build a longer tail into our offspring's genome." And yet natural selection results in an organism that seems designed to fit its environment.

Evolution is not guided. It occurs randomly, and because of this it does not bring about optimal design. It must work with what it has in hand, and this is what leads to non-optimal design. Consider the human eye, which is often used as an example of supreme wonder and design. We can admire it, but it is not optimally designed. As indicated in Figure 3–12, the wiring from brain to eye enters the rear of the eye in a mass known as the optic nerve. The eye sensors, rods and cones, are wired in such a way that the light coming through the lens must pass through the wiring before it reaches the sensors. Furthermore, this schema dictates there be no sensors at all where the optic bundle penetrates the rear of the retina. The result of this is the blind spot, a flaw which every human has and for which the brain must compensate. A better design, from an engineering standpoint, would be that of the cephalopod eye, which is wired from behind, eliminating the need for the optic nerve to pass through the retina and also clearing up the mass of nerves blocking the eye sensors. Figure

3–13 gives us a schematic view of what the human eye would look like if it were wired like a cephalopod eye.

The eye is not the only example of non-optimal design. In fact, the more we examine the human body from an engineering standpoint the more we notice the flaws. The spine is not optimal for supporting our upright frame, the male urinary tract travels in unnecessary spirals, and, as Robin Williams once remarked concerning the human reproductive organs, "there's an entertainment center built on top of a waste treatment facility!"

§7 GLITCHES IN THE OS

The blindness of evolution also results in an odd construction technique for the human brain, one in which the more modern human parts are built on top of, and depend upon, more ancient structures. These ancient systems, including the brain stem (reflexes) and the limbic system in the mid-brain (emotions), are lightning fast when compared to the newer system of deliberative thought located in the pre-frontal cortex. It's not hard to imagine why. If a saber-tooth tiger is preparing to pounce, the person programmed to analyze the angle, spin and speed of the feline descent in order to better compute the odds of its hitting its target will not live to pass on these genetic tendencies. Sometimes you just need to move. More deliberative systems would only have survival value, at least at first, for more mundane actions where time was not a critical factor. The way our brain is constructed, though, is such that inputs often have to travel through the ancient systems before being processed by the cortex. Gary Marcus (2008) cites an analogy comparing the brain to a Ukrainian power plant,

> where at least three layers of technology were in simultaneous use, stacked on top of one another. The recent computer technology operated not directly, but rather by controlling vacuum tubes (perhaps from the 1940s), which in turn controlled still older pneumatic mechanisms that relied on pressurized gases. If the power plant's engineers could afford the luxury of taking the whole system offline, they would no doubt prefer to start over, getting rid of the older systems altogether. But the continuous need for power precludes such an ambitious redesign. (12-13)

Not only does evolution proceed blindly, leading to non-optimal design, it also often progresses at a snail's pace. Its lethargy is a function of its blindness. If there were a designer, this wouldn't be a problem, but it's all trial and error with evolution, hit and miss. This evolutionary "straggle" is also a factor in extinction, which is usually the result of an organism not being able to adapt quickly enough to environmental change. Rapid change is a problem, and therein lies the rub, for human culture has changed with extreme rapidity in the last 30,000 years or so. This is less than an eye blink in evolutionary time (see box on page 71). In that period we humans went from living exclusively in small hunter-gatherer tribes to our present situation in which millions of us often crowd together within the confines of a relatively small area. The complexities of social interaction in such large societies are incalculable. Think of the differences just in economic complexity. A hunter-gatherer

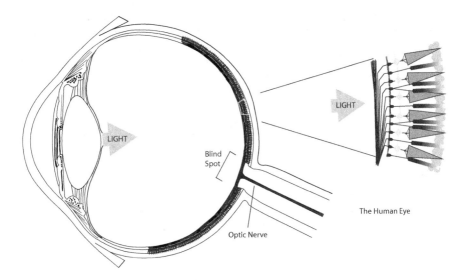

FIGURE 3–12

A diagram of the human eye showing the less than optimal wiring. (1) Light from the world has to pass through the wiring in order to reach the rod and cone cells, and (2) the wiring enters from the back of the eye, interfering with the receptors which creates a blind spot for which the brain must compensate.

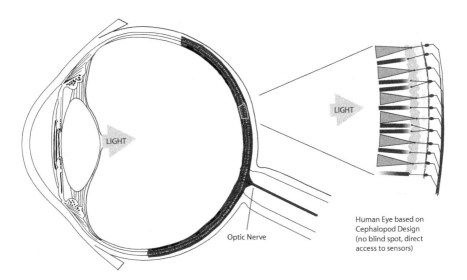

FIGURE 3–13

Compare the wiring diagram of the human eye with the cephalopod eye which is wired from behind. This means (1) there is no wiring to interfere with the light reaching the rods and cones, and (2) there is no blind spot.

tribe's economics depended on its hunting, gathering, and what it could get by barter from other tribes. Today's global economics includes multiple currencies, stock and bond exchanges, futures markets, instantaneous trading, and on and on. The human brain is a wondrous instrument, but it was formed, in part, to deal with the (comparatively simple) problems in a hunter-gatherer milieu. The importance of this point cannot be overstated: we often find that we have hunter-gatherer brains in a complex modern world.[10]

This means our brains are often out of synch with our times.[11] For example, in hunter-gatherer times there were three important but scarce resources that were necessary for human survival: fat, sugar, and salt. We developed a craving for these, in the same way we developed a craving for sex, insuring we would actively look for them and partake of them when found. Today, we still have those hunter-gatherer cravings, even though fat, sugar and salt are found on every corner: candy, hamburgers, french fries, colas, are all readily available, contributing to our current malaises of high blood pressure and obesity.

In §3 I gave an example of how our operating system works to generate our conscious perception of objects. Most people have no idea this kind of processing is going on behind the scenes. We are mainly concerned, in this chapter, with this unconscious (non-reflective) processing, but note the importance to consciousness. These non-reflective (or pre-reflective) processes determine how we see the world; they form our consciousness.

One example of a non-reflective process is our genetic propensity not only to look for causes to explain events that happen to us, but also to make causal connections between any two events that happen contiguously over time. If event A happens, followed by event B in close proximity, we attempt to connect the two, especially if we see this conjunction occur multiple times. The British philosopher, David Hume (1711-1776), put it this way:

> Our idea, therefore, of necessity and causation arises entirely from the uniformity observable in the operations of nature, where similar objects are constantly conjoined together, and the mind is determined by custom to infer the one from the appearance of the other. These two circumstances form the whole of that necessity, which we ascribe to matter. Beyond the constant conjunction of similar objects, and the consequent inference from one to the other, we have no notion of any necessity or connexion. (Section VIII)

---

[10] What caused this increase in change? Culture. Once cultural evolution began, with the advent of language, leading to the rise of consciousness, the focus of evolution switched from nature to culture. Deliberative thought allowed for increased technology, which is designed to increase our chances of survival. With culture, including increased technology and cooperation, humans can survive with genomes that would have been eliminated in a non-cultural milieu. We will talk about culture in Chapter 6.

[11] Not always, for evolution is not always lethargic. Consider just a few examples: our hunter-gatherer ancestors were all lactose intolerant (once breast feeding stopped), but since then our genes have mutated to allow 1/3 of all humans to consume dairy products without illness. This is directly related to the development of animal husbandry. Our hunter-gatherer ancestor could also not digest wheat products (containing gluten), but we moderns, again, have no such limitations, a fact related to the advent of farming. For more on the speed of evolution see Zuk, 2013

THE EYE-BLINK OF HUMAN HISTORY

Carl Sagan, in *Dragons of Eden*, summarized the history of the universe from its beginning to the present human civilization using the analogy of one year in a cosmic calendar. In this analogy, every billion years of the universe corresponds to about twenty-four days of the calendar (assuming the age of the universe to be approximately 15 billions years).

"It is disconcerting," says Sagan, "to find that in such a cosmic year the Earth does not condense out of interstellar matter until early September, dinosaurs emerge on Christmas Eve; flowers arise on December 28th; and men and women originate at 10:30 PM on New Year's Eve. All of recorded history occupies the last ten seconds of December 31; and the time from the waning of the Middle Ages to the present occupies little more than one second." (17)

Hume is describing the mechanism behind the forms of associative learning we discussed in §4. His point is that all we ever really see are events happening one after the other. The mind then connects these into a causal relationship. We never actually experience a causal relationship. If I throw a brick through a glass window, I experience the brick hitting the window and the window breaking, but I never experience causality. My mind interprets these two events as bound by a causal relationship. Causality is a mental projection.

The causal projection has survival value. If one of our ancestors saw a cave bear mutilate a human, a connection would be made between a cave bear and a mutilated corpse. Making this connection might then save his life in the future. This causal rule seems reasonable enough, but, like the rules for processing visual images, it is not infallible, and in fact has led us into a myriad of superstitions throughout the ages. This is the same rule, for instance, that led people to believe that black cats bring bad luck. Someone somewhere saw a black cat cross his trail and afterward slipped and broke his leg, and made the connection: the black cat caused me to break my leg. If you ever caught a cold and blamed it on someone ("she gave me her cold") or on going out in the rain the day before, you are guilty of the same type of error. These are all manifestations of our propensity to look for a cause, and find it in a proximate event. The causal law helped us survive, and its misuse did not lead to our not surviving, so it became a universal human trait.

This is just one example of how our unconscious processing works. There are many more of these biases, and becoming aware of them will help us not only understand how our brain works, but will also protect us from those who would take advantage of our ignorance. Now let's turn to a more radical example of how the brain creates our reality.

§8 LIBET'S TIME DIFFERENTIAL AND THE FASTBALL PROBLEM

If the star Betelgeuse, located on the shoulder of Orion, went supernova around the time the Spanish Armada sailed in its failed attempt to invade England, we still wouldn't know it. Betelgeuse is 450 light years away, that is, its light takes 450 years to reach Earth, which means we wouldn't see it go supernova for another twenty years or so. Light, unlike evolution, is not lethargic, but neither is it instantaneous, which means we are continually looking at the universe as it was in the past (the closest star, Alpha Centauri, is 4.24 light years distant).

We've seen that unconscious cognitive processing occurs and that it affects our behavior. This is unsettling, for it means we often act in ways contrary to our conscious desires. It also means we can be controlled once others discover how these processes work. But there are even more unsettling aspects of unconscious processing having to do with who we are and our freedom to act. The causes behind these drastic effects are traceable to mundane physical laws governing the speed of light. As we have seen, light is fast but finite, and we can detect this finitude even in the small span of the length of our bodies. When prodded on the foot by a probe like a pin, the electrical nerve impulse must travel the length of our body, which means we will feel a probe to the face faster than to the foot. We hurt before we even know we hurt. If you've ever cut yourself with a kitchen knife, you've probably experienced this. You look down and see the blood, and—wait for it—the pain arrives. We are behind the times. Literally. And it gets worse.

Professional baseball pitchers can throw a fastball at velocities ranging from 80 to 100 MPH, which means it will take the ball approximately less than 1/2 of one millisecond to reach home plate (there are 1000 milliseconds in a second). The problem is, it will take at least 200 ms for it to register in the batter's brain that the ball has left the pitcher's hand. The swing will take another 200 ms.

> To get an appreciation for the magnitude of the problem, consider that a fastball will travel about nine feet before your retina transmits and your brain processes the initial notification of the ball leaving the pitcher's hand. Full perception of the pitch takes considerably longer. The delay in processing means that when the ball appears to be at a certain position, it is no longer at that position. To see it "where it will be," the brain must integrate the speed of motion over time, estimate the degree of position shift, and combine this with the appearance of the object as seen at the present time... the "now" that the batter experiences when he initiates his swing is "virtual," generated by complicated subliminal computations. (Burton 70-71)

Our brains somehow manipulate all this data, making everything appear as if we can see the ball coming and (some even claim) hit a particular part of the ball. In fact, a batter has to initiate his swing before the ball leaves the pitcher's hand. "If the brain did not somehow compensate and project the image of the approaching baseball backward in time, you would see the ball approach the plate after you had already hit it." (73) This is our operating system at work, manipulating data into a stream that is both constant and understandable.

The same manipulation is taking place in our ordinary everyday communications. Extremely complex cognitive processing is taking place as we listen to someone talk. Not only do we have to hear and recognize the individual words and take into account the context, hand signals and other background information, we also have to constantly evaluate what is being said and how we will respond. All of this takes time. We are formulating responses to what is being said before we even become conscious of what was said.

If you are driving through town at 25 MPH and a child steps out into the road thirty feet in front of you, even if you are paying full attention (not talking or texting) and not impaired in any way, and even if the driving conditions are perfect, it will take approximately one-half of one second for the perception of the child to register in your brain. The brain sees the child, but you are not yet conscious of seeing the child. Your foot (unconsciously) moves to the brake, but this takes another second. At 25 MPH you're traveling at 36.7 feet per second. You've already hit the child and you aren't even fully conscious of the child yet. If you're texting, your foot hasn't even moved toward the brake pedal. Those who "remember" looking up from their phone and seeing the child before they hit it are seeing a series of events fabricated by their brain.

In a famous (and admittedly controversial) experiment Benjamin Libet measured the time differential between action and consciousness. He wired the brains of his subjects to detect the firing of neurons when decisions were made. He then told the subjects to move their hand whenever they chose. When they did so, the cortex lit up showing the conscious decision to move their hand, but approximately 250 ms before this conscious decision, the motor neurons had already fired to move the hand. In other words, the brain made an unconscious decision to move the hand which only then bubbled up to the conscious level. If this is true, then we are constantly out of synch with the world by about a quarter of a second. The brain, though, stitches everything together, just as it does with our blind spot, and makes it appear as if everything is happening simultaneously.

And what of our free will? The philosopher Benedict Spinoza (1632-1677) once gave an example of what it was like to say we humans act freely. He asks us to imagine a rock on the side of a mountain, subjected daily to wind and rain, which, over the years, gradually erode its base until one day it comes loose and falls. "I think I'll jump," says the rock as its base falls away. Are we no better than this rock? We will examine this question in Chapter 11.

This chapter has been concerned with unconscious brain processing. The function of our operating system is to give us the means by which to interact with the world in an intelligible way. We would like to think we have a direct link to the world and we're seeing everything just as it is and in real time. But even conservative interpretations of the cognitive processes we've reviewed here indicate this isn't even close to the way things happen. When you reflect on how we perceive the world you begin to realize the surreal quality of our conscious experience. We are living in a series of time delays, from stars to conversations, from seeing to choosing. We don't know whether the conscious images we have of the world around us, the output from our operating system, are anything like the raw data input into our senses.

So now we know the basics, at least that the brain interprets our experience and sends it on to what becomes our conscious awareness. It is to this conscious awareness that we must now turn, for this is the part of our world we are most familiar with. Before we talk in depth about our conceptual schemes, though, we must first understand the process by which we make sense of our world—theorizing.

4. Theorizing

· ·

In theory there is no difference between theory and practice. In practice there is.

— Yogi Berra

SYNOPSIS

We are unaware of and, for the most part, unable to change, what goes on in our operating system. Understanding the operating system is interesting, for it explains many of our actions that might otherwise seem odd. In this chapter we will be setting the groundwork for talk of how our reflective cognitive systems function. My overall thesis will be that the way we make sense of our world, whether our concerns are large or small, short term or long term, is always in terms of a theory. Because of the importance placed on theorizing, we will spend this entire chapter describing it. The discussion will be superficial, but will allow us to understand the basic process. (1) We begin with two theories concerning Columbus, and (2) use these to discuss the basic structure of theorizing. (3) A literary example to further illustrate how a theory functions. (4) Once we understand what a theory is, the question arises: what makes for a good, or adequate, theory? We will define 'adequacy' in terms of what works, and give five conditions for such. (5) Anomalies arise if the conditions for adequacy are not met. How these should be handled and how they are actually handled are two separate matters. (6) The Ptolemaic and Copernican theories of the universe are considered as examples of theorizing. (7) An historical view of theorizing and the aftermath of the acceptance of the Copernican world-view. (8) Chapter Summary.

CHAPTER OBJECTIVES

- understand how the process of theorizing works.
- give specific examples of how you use theorizing daily.
- examine how we handle anomalies and determine whether our methods are ad hoc.
- to begin to see how we choose between conflicting theories.
- to understand why some theories are better explanations than others.
- apply this understanding to other cultures, realizing others theorize as we do, but with different initial inputs.

§1 *THE PROBLEM OF COLUMBUS*

I n 1492 Columbus sailed the ocean blue. Every American school child knows this. The famous explorer's prestige may have been somewhat tarnished over the years—he has been portrayed as a gold-greedy religious zealot and a fumbling failure who mistreated the natives and died in poverty. The son of Genoese wool-weavers, Columbus passionately pitched four royal courts for venture capital to find the fastest route to the East Indies. He finally managed to persuade Ferdinand and Isabella, king and queen of a newly united Spain, to back his mission, which they did, reluctantly. He then purchased, provisioned and sailed away in three ships: the Pinta, the Nina, the Santa Maria, and bumbled upon a new world, landing on what is now San Salvador in the Bahama archipelago. For all his faults he is upheld as a passionate man whose persistence and dedication to cause allowed him to realize his dreams and follow his quest.

A nice story, but completely fabricated. In fact, we have all been deceived, with the help of Columbus himself. According to Manuel Rosa, instead of a wool-gatherer's son from Genoa, Columbus was a royal prince, the son of an exiled Polish King, who worked as a double-agent for King John II of Portugal (whom Isabella attempted to assassinate in 1483). Columbus infiltrated the Spanish court under an assumed identity on a covert mission to divert the Spanish away from the true spice-route to India. Instead of discovering a new world, Columbus was "allowed" by his employer, the king of Portugal, to make public the discovery of a world already known to the Portuguese.

Which of these stories is true? Each is a theory based upon a set of well-accepted facts, and yet the one tells a completely different tale. They cannot both be correct (the law of non-contradiction at work). How do we judge between them?

In this chapter I want to talk about this process—the process of theorizing. The case of Columbus is interesting as a case of historical revisionism, but the process involved, though mundane, is essential to how we humans get by in the world. We theorize. That's what we do. We do it hundreds or thousands of times every day. Furthermore, we maintain and manipulate thousands of theories in our minds continually throughout our lives, juggling the evidence, pro and con, making probability calculations and deciding what is and what is not believable based on these.

The thesis of this chapter is this: theorizing is an activity that allows us to get by in the world, to achieve our goals of comfort and well-being. We will speak abstractly of theorizing in this chapter, giving some rather esoteric scientific examples, but this is only to introduce you to the topic. In the next chapter I will bring theorizing down to the individual level.

§2 THE NUTS AND BOLTS OF THEORIZING.

It is a symptom of the modern age that we take theorizing so blithely. It was not always so. Theorizing was once thought to be an inelegant solution resorted to only when direct access to truth was not available. "*Hypotheses non fingo*," claimed Newton in disdain. "I do not hypothesize." Truth was available by direct perception; hypothesis was for those who could not claim such certainty. After reading the previous chapter you should be somewhat skeptical of the claim that we have direct access to the truth. If so, you have joined the ranks of modern thinkers, for whom theory is considered the *only* access to truth. You may yet think you have privileged access to some truths that do not require theory, but my goal in this chapter and the next is to show you this is not so. Let's begin with what a theory is not.

A theory is not merely a collection of data. A theory is interpretation of a collection of data, an extrapolation. Data refer to facts about the world. Used in a broad sense a fact is an event or object either external to us (cats, milk, a smirk, a machine gun) or internal to us (ideas, beliefs, a goal, an opinion), and a collection of facts is just a collection of facts, not a theory. Another way to put this is to say that a theory (of any complexity) will always be under-determined by the evidence to some degree. Under-determination means there is not enough evidence to warrant an absolutely certain guarantee. Under-determination leads to ambiguity, which guarantees the possibility of multiple interpretations. In our opening example, the same data-set yielded two different theories concerning Christopher Columbus.

To call something a theory does not mean it is unconfirmed, as in "That's *only* a theory." As used in contemporary science, 'theory' has nothing to do with confirmation. Rather, the most important characteristic of a theory is that it interprets, or makes sense of, a number of facts we refer to as evidence.

The two theories above, for example, make use of historical facts in order to portray Columbus and his adventures in a specific light. A vastly abbreviated listing of these facts might look something like this:

(1) Columbus was born of humble origins in Genoa.
(2) He had red hair.
(3) He married a high noble woman in 1479.
(4) He approached no less than four royal courts trying to get funding for his venture.
(5) He wrote out a will in which he declared himself a natural-born Italian.
(6) He set sail in 1492 in three ships: the Pinta, the Nina, the Santa Maria.
(7) He landed on what is known today as San Salvador, which he claimed for Spain.

(8) There was fierce competition in the 15th century between European nations (and especially between Spain and Portugal) to monopolize the lucrative spice trade with India.

(9) Dias, of Portugal, made progress toward discovering a promising route to India when he sailed to the southern tip of Africa in 1482.

(10) Columbus's calculations estimating the distance to India were widely thought to be ridiculous.

This is an arbitrary data-set. We could, of course, add a multitude of facts to this list, but we are only using this as an abbreviated example. With the exception of (1), both Columbus theories, the standard theory and the spy theory, accept this data-set. The theories themselves are interpretations of this set; both are under-determined, that is, both go beyond the data in an attempt to make sense of the set as a whole. This is what theories do. They allow us to make sense of a conglomeration of facts, and the cash value of making sense is to establish the truth. We can't yet delve into the intricacies of what this means, but a rudimentary notion, capturing our everyday usage is this: the purpose of a theory is to help us find out the way things really are (or were).

We want to know the-way-the-world-really-is. We would like to know if Columbus really was a double agent, whether there was a second shooter in the Kennedy assassination, where Jimmy Hoffa is buried, whether our best friend is lying to us. Knowing the truth has survival value. Those who, in our distant past, had a desire to seek out truth (those who were curious) tended to pass on more genes than those who didn't. Theories help us achieve this, which is why we engage in theorizing throughout our daily lives. A theory is "adequate" or a "good theory" according to how well we think it performs this task of determining the way the world is.

A theory takes a certain number of facts (a data-set) and interprets them in an attempt to make sense of them. The facts involved in such a theory must hang together in a certain way. They comprise a system, from which emerges an explanation of their complex relationships. Not only do the facts support the theory, but the theory then supports the facts, as illustrated in Figure 4–1.

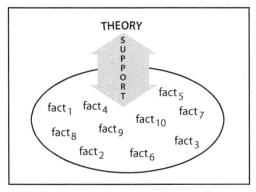

FIGURE 4–1

The complex relationship between a theory and the facts it explains. Facts serve as evidence for a theory, but a good theory will also serve to bolster belief in facts that are consistent with it.

✻

§3 A LITERARY EXAMPLE

A theory can be likened to the thesis statement of a literary work or story (a thesis statement is a theory that uses the facts of the story as evidence). Consider the following story:

Once upon a time there was a boy who tended sheep. He was told to be ever vigilant, as there were wolves about. For a while he was content, but in time grew bored, for sheep are not great companions and there were no wolfish threats. He decided one day to make his own excitement, and cried out, "Wolf! Wolf!" which brought the townspeople running to his aid. There was much hubbub and excitement, though when the townspeople discovered his prank he was severely chastised and warned not to repeat such behavior. Weeks passed and the boy's boredom grew, and, remembering the excitement of his previous proclamation, he performed a cost-benefit analysis and again cried out, "Wolf! Wolf!" Again the townspeople responded, running to his aid, and again he was severely chastised. Yet another week passed, and the boy was contemplating yet another performance when he spotted a wolf approaching the fold. He cried out, "Wolf! Wolf!" but no one came. They heard his cry, but, assumed he was up to his old tricks and went about their way. The boy, to his credit, tried to protect the sheep, and was eaten by the wolf for his trouble.

What is the thesis (or moral) of this story? Suppose we advance the following in answer to this question:

Thesis 1:   A boy continually cried wolf when there was no wolf, so no one believed him when a real wolf appeared.

This won't do at all, for it is not an interpretation, but a mere reiteration of the facts—a plot summary. An interpretation takes the facts and goes beyond them. Another try:

Thesis 2: Humans get bored when performing menial tasks.

It's true, humans do get bored when performing menial tasks, but how do we get here from the facts within the story? It does say he was bored, but his boredom is used to explain other, more important actions. Thesis 2 doesn't take either the ire of the townspeople or the appearance of the wolf at the end of the story into account at all. Nothing within the story explicitly contradicts Thesis 2, but the thesis doesn't handle enough of the data; it doesn't make sense of the story in its entirety. What about the following:

Thesis 3: Love wins in the end.

Thesis 2 looks good in light of Thesis 3, for the latter does nothing whatsoever to tie the facts of the story together. There is no evidence within the story that would lend support to this thesis. Finally, consider:

Thesis 4: If we continually lie, people will no longer believe us when we tell the truth.

Notice how Thesis 4 takes account of all the major facts in the story: the boy's boredom as an explanation for his lies, the wrath of the townspeople as an explanation of their no longer trusting him, and the ultimate consequences of his lying. I could easily cite lines from the story as evidence for this thesis, so we would say it is well-supported. In addition, there are no leftover facts that contradict it. We would be justified in saying, then, that Thesis 4 is an adequate theory with respect to the given data.

An objection might be raised against such examples, for literary examples use fictional "facts" as their basis. No matter, for the process is the same, and the fictional status of the facts is not relevant. Once written by an author, fictional facts exist in the world and demand an explanation as much as do phenomena not penned by persons.

✳

§4 ADEQUACY CONDITIONS

We need now to specify what sort of conditions a theory might have to meet that would allow us to claim it to be adequate. Here is a list of what might be considered the most important conditions (we could add more, but we are not attempting to be exhaustive):

    (a) Consistency: internal harmony, absence of internal contradictions.

    (b) Simplicity: structural economy, beauty, elegance.

    (c) Completeness: comprehensive explanatory power, no major facts left out (ideally, all relevant facts taken into account).

    (d) Interconnectivity: robust connections between facts within a theory.

    (e) Integration: orderliness, components mesh well with other theories and facts outside of them (conforms to our overall world-view).

Of these five, (a) may be the most important; indeed, it may be presupposed by all the others, and (b) may be the least important, but none are absolutely necessary in the sense they cannot be compromised to some degree. There is always give and take in the process of theorizing. We must always keep in mind the rank of the theory we are considering in the overall scope of our value system. This will differ from culture to culture, and within a culture from person to person, and for each person from year to year or even from day to day. In short, we all continually perform cost-benefit analyses on what is acceptable and what is not within our theories.

We can liken this process to other cost-benefit analyses in which we use parameters in our decision-making process. For example, suppose you want to buy a car. Your parameters (adequacy conditions) might include:

    (i) safety: functional design

    (ii) gas mileage: fuel efficiency

(iii)   cost: the sticker price of the car

(iv)   environmental efficiency: emissions data

(v)   non-functional design: sportiness, color, accessories

The ideal car would meet all of the above to your complete satisfaction, but what are the odds of this happening? Instead, you make trade-offs, and these will depend upon your value system at the time. If you are more concerned with environmental impact than price or pride, you will be willing to pay more and sacrifice sportiness. If money is the primary issue, you may deem (ii) and (iii) more important than all the rest.

In short, when it comes to judging our theories, we are and must be flexible. We must make judgments and adjustments, fine-tuning our hierarchies in order to meet the ever-shifting needs of our world.

> This plurality and interaction of desiderata [conditions] means that a narrow focus upon a single such cognitive ideal is not very helpful—they must stand in balance. To stress one to neglect of the rest is ultimately self-defeating: in each instance, these parameters are interlocked in a synthesis of coordinative tension. (Rescher 1979: 17)

We now turn to a brief examination of each of the adequacy requirements of a theory.

CONSISTENCY

Consider (2) in the Columbus data set. The color of Columbus' hair is important only in relation to other facts. Red hair is not characteristic of Italians, which means (2) clashes with (1), and this clash demands to be resolved. Similarly, (3) and (4) clash with (1). In Columbus' time, it was unheard of for a lowly peasant to marry into nobility or to move about freely in the court, having access to kings and their advisors. Of course, if we could justify accepting (3), this would make (4) more palatable, that is, if we allow that a lowly wool-gatherer did in fact manage to marry into nobility, maybe his wife's connections would make it possible to move about in royal circles. If we are aware of an inconsistency within a theory it must be resolved in some fashion, even if this means pushing its solution into the future or speaking about it as a mystery.

The importance of the consistency requirement harks back to our discussion of the principle of non-contradiction in chapter 3. If 'consistent' means non-contradictory, then the necessity of satisfying this condition is easily seen, for our aversion to contradiction is genetic. We will not allow explicit contradictions in our theories unless we have no other choice. Inconsistencies within a theory almost assuredly indicate the theory is not an accurate description of the world—is inadequate, in our parlance. This doesn't mean we won't give up the consistency condition if necessary, but giving it up is not to be taken lightly.

SIMPLICITY

We want our theories to be elegant in their simplicity. As we have noted before, simplicity is often defined in terms of a principle known as Occam's razor, which dictates we should not multiply entities beyond necessity. There are many different features that can be emphasized: lack of redundancy or extraneous and irrelevant information, connections, and so on. With this in mind, we can say the following:

> Given two theories which both meet all other adequacy conditions equally well, if one theory is simpler than the other, the simpler theory is the preferable theory.

For example, suppose you are to judge between two different computer programs, which do exactly the same thing (and do it equally well), except that one program contains 30 lines of code while the other contains 982. Which is the preferable program? Most programmers would agree that the simpler, more elegant, program is the better program, even though they both produce the exact same results. Why we would think the simpler program is the better program? The answer is usually given in terms of elegance, but perhaps the answer lies in the fact that sparseness is usually correlated to utility. The claim here is that we prefer simplicity because it has practical consequences. To use our coding example, simplicity may reflect a programmer's deep understanding and comprehension of the coding syntax. Or we might say we prefer the simpler code because it uses less computer memory and thus has practical value (which means our stipulation that both programs produced the same results was mistaken). One thing is clear: simplicity removes redundancy and strips a proof or program or theory down to its bare bones, allowing us to see the essentials (and maybe the beauty) of its form. But so what? Maybe we perceive this as beautiful because it mirrors the world in some way, that is, maybe our standard of beauty evolved based on what helps us survive (what works).[1] Simplicity, by definition, removes many possible causes of error, since there are fewer ways to fail (keep this in mind when we discuss completeness). This is why simplicity, while desirable, is not a necessary condition for a workable theory: a theory might be harmlessly complex (it might also be beautifully complex).

Simplicity interpreted in terms of beauty seems to be different, which is why it is tempting to separate beauty from simplicity as a separate condition. This seems to be the idea behind Keats's words in *Ode to a Grecian Urn*:

> Beauty is truth, truth beauty…

and also what physicist Paul Dirac may have meant when he said, "God used beautiful mathematics in creating the world." These seem to be making the explicit claim that we see something as beautiful because it mirrors the way things are. Thus, one problem with making beauty a condition for an adequate theory lies in assuming there is a single objective definition of beauty we could all agree upon. A second problem is the possibility of a theory or proof being beautiful but false, or needlessly beautiful.

COMPLETENESS

There are at least two sorts of completeness: comprehensive completeness, which involves the number of facts a theory contains, and explanatory completeness, which involves the number of facts a theory explains. The motive behind

---

[1] There have been numerous attempts to show how our aesthetic sense is an adaptation; beauty as utility is just one of them. Of course, our concept of beauty might not be an adaptation at all; it may simply be a by-product of the way our brains evolved.

completeness is that the more data a theory accumulates and consistently explains, the better chance the theory will be workable in other scenarios, that is, the better chance it will exhibit elegance, integration and interconnectivity. This seems reasonable, though there is always the possibility that completeness will become corpulence, for the extra data may ultimately be of little or no relevance.

Comprehensive completeness will lead us into a discussion of what is knowable and what is unknowable. I will make a few comments on this, but we must put off a detailed look at this topic until chapter 8. The main point here is that comprehensive completeness is always a matter of degree. No theory of any complexity will ever be complete in this sense. There will always be:

(1) More data to accumulate from various points of view. There is a limitless number of perspectives we will never be able to take into account.

(2) Historical data which it is now impossible to recover. We know about Columbus via historical inquiry. We use this data to put together a theory of his life and times, but think of all the facts that could confirm or disconfirm our theories. Suppose, for example, there was, at one time, a letter from Columbus to King John describing his efforts to mislead Ferdinand and Isabella, a letter destroyed by King John. This one piece of evidence would have confirmed the spy theory. Or imagine we could know what King John knew or what Columbus himself knew. These are all facts about the world forever lost to us, and their loss guarantees the comprehensive incompleteness of our theory.

(3) Current data which is beyond our means. This might mean beyond our current technology, or it might mean beyond our powers of comprehension. What if there are facts in the world that our brains are not capable of grasping?

We might think, then, there could be a reachable goal of comprehensive completeness if we but redefine completeness as the set of data it is possible for us to obtain. But even this won't work, for the more we work to achieve even this delimited completeness the less likely we are to reach it, for the move from incompleteness toward completeness runs through complexity. As our theories become more complex, as we accumulate more data, there is necessarily more to know—new questions are raised, finer distinctions made. Thus we can never approach the optimal possible completeness of a theory. We have to run as fast as we can just to stay where we are.

For this reason, simplicity and comprehensive completeness pull in opposite directions. If the completeness of a theory is proportional to the amount of data it incorporates, then the tendency will be toward complexity and away from simplicity. For example, the ancient Greeks spoke of four elements (earth, wind, fire and water). In the 19th century this number was raised to sixty, while today we claim in excess of one hundred elements. This kind of proliferation can be seen in all areas of science.

The conclusion, then, is that comprehensive completeness is impossible to achieve, and so becomes merely a guiding principle, a goal to strive for. Explanatory completeness, though, is different, for explanatory completeness is a reachable goal if we define what it means to explain a fact in terms of a system or theory. In this sense explanatory completeness might best be seen as a property that emerges as we achieve the other four adequacy conditions. To explain something just is to show its multiplicity of relationships to other relevant facts in a theory that is itself integrated with other theories we hold, all of which hold together in an elegant manner. This is the adequacy condition of completeness we should strive for (see Figure 4–2).

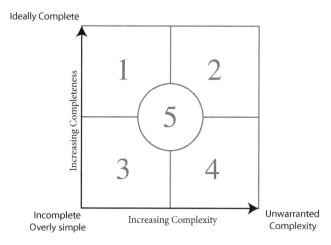

FIGURE 4–2

Graphing the relationship between Simplicity and Completeness: Area 1 might be the preferable state (approaching completeness with minimal complexity), but may be impossible. Area 2 (approaching completeness with increasing complexity) is a more realistic goal. Area 3 errs in most likely being oversimple or incomplete. Area 4 errs in being too complex with not enough data to warrant such. Area 5 is the "goldilocks" zone: a balance of simplicity and completeness.

INTERCONNECTIVITY

Interconnectivity is concerned with the connections within a theory. If we view our framework as one large theory incorporating many more specialized theories then these connecting points themselves might be theories. For now, though, consider the interconnectivity of smaller, individual theories such as our Columbus theory.

We can make an analogy here to a road map. Suppose you are traveling in an unfamiliar part of the country. You know vaguely where you want to go, but don't know how to get there. You have a map, but it is a strange map, for all it portrays is a list of the cities in the area (Figure 4–3, Map 1). Such a listing of cities tells you nothing of value; you may as well be looking at a phone directory. This is like getting a plot summary when you want a thesis. But what if, instead of a mere list, you also have a pictorial representation of the cities listed, showing their geographical relation to each other (as in Figure 4–3, Map 2)? This is better, but still not overly helpful. What you want is to be able to clearly see the relationships between the cities (Figure 4–3, Map 3). This is what an adequate theory should do—it should add to our understanding of the relationships between facts.

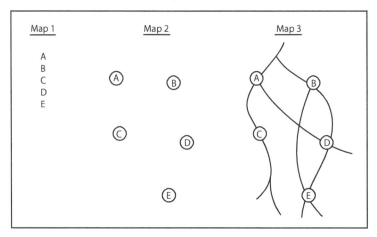

FIGURE 4–3

Cartographical interconnectivity. Map 1 shows no connections between cities, and is correspondingly useless. Map 2 shows limited spatial connections, but is still inadequate. Map 3 shows increased connectivity, making it even more useful.

Turning to our Columbus theories as a further example (Figure 4–4), the standard theory is founded upon (1), that Columbus was an Italian. This fails to relate facts (2), (3) and (4) as well as the spy theory. The spy theory also makes facts (8), (9) and (10) connect, while they remain extraneous for the standard theory. All in all, then, we would say that, given this arbitrary data-set, the spy theory is preferable to the standard theory with respect to the interconnectivity condition.

INTEGRATION

Returning to our Columbus data-set, notice how facts (8) and (9) differ from the others. They are not facts about Columbus and his life, but are features about the world in which he lived and moved. Any theory about the motives of Columbus must

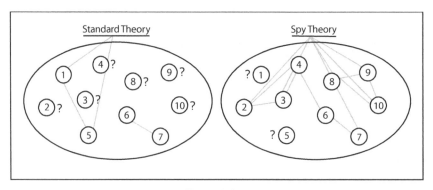

FIGURE 4–4

A comparison of the interconnectivity of facts in the data-set shared by the two Columbus theories. The spy theory is obviously more successful in meeting this condition.

also take these into account, for they influenced his actions. This is what I mean by integration. A theory about Columbus must fit in well with all our other theories.[2]

We have thousands of overlapping theories which impinge in different ways upon our Columbus theory (Figure 4–5 gives a simplified illustration of this). For example, we have a theory on what religious attitudes were like at the time. Our Columbus theory cannot stray too far from this without demanding adjustment of the religious theory (another value judgment: which theory gets adjusted?). We cannot portray Columbus as a Protestant since another well-verified theory says Protestantism did not yet exist. This would begin to interfere with our historical theories. Integration refers to the fit of a theory into all our theoretical frameworks as well, and as such is related to elegance. In this sense, our Columbus theory must integrate with our theories concerning causation, contradiction, the existence of an external world, and so on. Furthermore, all of these must be integrated with each other in as seamless a manner as possible.

This is true of our literary example as well. Our thesis concerning the cry-wolf story must take into account that wolves are dangerous (they eat sheep and the occasional boy), our theory of human motivation (boys get bored, adults get angry), sociological considerations (the "town" in townspeople and how they group together for protection), and so on. Without this integration, our cry-wolf thesis would cease to make sense.

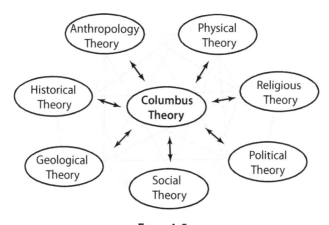

FIGURE 4–5

Integration: how well one theory "fits" into the schema of other theories you already hold to be well-accepted.

OVERALL COHERENCE

An adequate theory is one in which the five adequacy conditions listed above are met to our satisfaction. Figure 4–6 is an illustration of how we might measure these for two theories, one of which we deem adequate, the other inadequate. The reading of each individual meter isn't so important, as long as the total of the five is

---

[2] Integration could probably be reduced to consistency, for it broadens the consistency condition from consistency within the theory itself to consistency with facts and theories outside the theory. I separate the two because of this different aspect, but it all depends on what you mean by inside and outside a theory (a question which smacks of pebbles, rocks and boulders).

sufficient to meet our satisfaction. For example, maybe my cutoff is a total score of 300. If a theory has that score or higher I deem it adequate (pass); if lower I deem it inadequate (fail). The cutoff score will be different for different people. The lower the cutoff score the more gullible we deem someone to be. "They'll believe anything," we say. At some point gullibility infringes on survival value. Bad decisions can lead to disaster in many scenarios.

The "to our satisfaction" phrase is necessarily vague due to the variability within value systems from person to person. Not only do each of the conditions have their own internal tolerance, but each is also weighted against the others. For example, what I consider elegant you may consider inelegant—this is the internal tolerance; furthermore, I may rank elegance as the least important of the five conditions, while you may rank it the most important. If I rank elegance as the least important then I will be willing to accept more inelegance than you, according to how we judge elegance in the first place. (To show this on our diagram we would have to add multipliers for each condition.) This vagueness is not quite as bad as it seems, for everyone agrees the consistency condition is an extremely important condition and it is the least vague of the five. Furthermore, the failure of the other conditions can often (though not always) be seen in light of inconsistency: incompleteness leads to inconsistency because of gaps in our knowledge, simplicity is related to completeness, and both inelegance and lack of interconnectivity are often a direct result of inconsistencies.

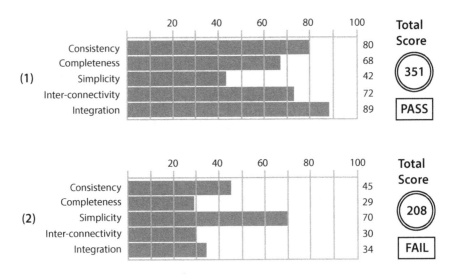

FIGURE 4–6

Hypothetical adequacy meters for two different theories. There is always give and take between the conditions, but we each have an unconscious (and imprecise) cutoff point at which we judge a theory adequate (pass) or inadequate (fail). In this example, I assume the cutoff is 300, which means theory (1) passes while theory (2) fails.

THE STRUCTURE OF SCIENTIFIC REVOLUTIONS

Thomas Kuhn, in his book *The Structure of Scientific Revolutions*, claimed that change is not gradual in science, but proceeds in revolutionary leaps. All scientific investigation has to be taken in a historical perspective, since the fundamental framework (Kuhn's word is 'paradigm') changes over time.

Science does not make smooth transitions in its accumulation of knowledge. Instead, once a theory is developed (a paradigm is formed), and accepted, science proceeds to work within the parameters of that theory. Kuhn refers to this process as normal science, which makes science essentially a problem-solving endeavor. Most scientists never question their paradigm; they are content to solve anomalies that arise within the given paradigm. Occasionally, though, a radical thinker appears (a Copernicus, Newton, or Einstein) who rethinks an entire paradigm. The result is what Kuhn calls a scientific revolution. It is during these revolutionary periods that science makes progress.

Kuhn claims that scientists using the old paradigm cannot even understand the new, radically different, paradigm. This is because, to some extent, our paradigms determine how we see the world. This inability to understand is called the incommensurability of paradigms. If two theories are commensurable, the holders of those theories can compare facts and determine who has the better theory. If two theories are incommensurable, this will not suffice, because the very basis of what constitutes a fact in each theory is different—those who hold different paradigms may not even see the same thing when they look out at the world.

Our theories seldom if ever survive intact in the wake of substantial extensions in our cognitive access to new sectors of nature (via new technology). The history of science is a sequence of episodes of leaping to the wrong conclusions because new observational findings indicate matters are not quite so simple as heretofore thought. Expanding our data via new technology "destabilizes the attained equilibrium between data and theory. This is the price we pay for operating a simplicity-geared cognitive methodology in an actually complex world." (Rescher 2006: 19)

Integration is the most modern of the adequacy conditions, appearing in its full glory only with the advent of the scientific method. Contained within integration is the idea of public verifiability, which includes the demand that experiments must be repeatable in order to be accepted as evidence. This puts stringent controls on what we allow as evidence and weeds out much useless information. In this sense, integration may also be the most important of the conditions, for we can imagine two theories being internally consistent, yet contradicting each other. Integration is the means of deciding between such. For example, you may live all alone in the woods, convinced that the government is out to enslave us. You see evidence of this every time a helicopter flies over, or you pick up unexplained static on your two-way radio. Your personal conspiracy theory is entirely consistent, but probably wouldn't stand up to public scrutiny. Thus, you may consider your theory adequate, but it is a stand-alone theory, and would not be successful explaining events in the world-at-large.

§5 ANOMALIES

An anomaly is a problem with a theory that occurs when one of the adequacy conditions is not met to our satisfaction. Because of the importance of the consistency condition we will focus mainly on this in our discussion of anomalies. Indeed, we might even define an anomaly as an inconsistency (of one kind or another) within a theory.

In the previous chapter we talked about our operating system and how a certain logical way of viewing the world is hard-wired within us. There we mentioned the law of non-contradiction as one of the fundamental laws of our operating system. Here we will see how this law is implemented, since we are calling an anomaly an inconsistency within a theory, by which we mean an infringement upon the law of non-contradiction. Since consistency is a fundamental adequacy condition for a theory, an anomaly within a theory guarantees we cannot completely trust that theory as a guide to the world around us. We should (and do) always attempt to eliminate anomalies within a theory.

We can imagine the following scenarios when dealing with inconsistencies:

(1) Those that are recognizable and can be eliminated.
(2) Those that are recognizable, but cannot be eliminated.
(3) Those that cannot be recognized (hidden).

(1) and (2) are the most straightforward scenarios. The proper method for resolving anomalies is to collect more data and reformulate the theory in light of the additional data, which will hopefully eliminate the inconsistency. In other words, anomalies are often due to shortsightedness, and as technology allows us to incorporate more data, we may come to see the anomaly in a new non-anomalous light. But sometimes, as in (2), we may not have the means to move to a higher level of knowledge, so we are stuck with the anomaly for the time being. In such cases, we know as long as the anomaly exists it is an indicator of the inadequacy of our theory. We continually refine our theories, adding data, reworking, hoping to eventually eliminate persistent anomalies.

There is no set number of anomalies which, when reached, guarantees that a theory must be given up. There are other factors to consider:

(a) The size and complexity of the theory: a large and very complex theory (quantum theory, general relativity) might have hundreds of anomalies, but as long as the theory is deemed workable it need not be given up.

(b) The availability of other theories: even if you know your theory is inadequate and should be replaced because of the anomalies within it, if you have no other theory to take its place (that is at least as adequate) you will not give it up.

Scenario (2) raises another concern, for there are also *improper* ways of handling anomalies. The most common improper method is called an *ad hoc* hypothesis. This is a quick fix for a theory that has no independent evidence to support it. Thus, an *ad hoc* hypothesis can be seen as a patch on a theory. The anomaly remains, but is covered over in such a way as to (temporarily) satisfy. What constitutes an *ad hoc* hypothesis is often a time-dependent value judgment. It's easy for us, in hindsight, to label an ancient fix *ad hoc, but* the question is, did those who formulated it base their fix on what was considered sound evidence at the time?

Why would anyone resort to an *ad hoc* hypothesis? One reason might be laziness. We might not want to do all the work involved in collecting more data and rethinking connections, so we hastily fix the problem and save ourselves a lot of work. More often, though, we are less reflective when we formulate such hypotheses. We tend to fall in love with our theories, that is, we often have a personal stake in a theory, whether because of the time spent constructing it or the benefits that accrue because we hold on to it, and because of this it often becomes very difficult to give up a theory. When this happens, the *ad hoc* option becomes very attractive.

Scenario (3) involves anomalies within a theory that we cannot see. The major cause of hidden anomalies lies in a lack of knowledge at the present moment—incompleteness. Hindsight makes it possible for us to say things like: "Now that I know fact p is true, I see that it conflicts with fact q." Before gaining the new

THE COSMOLOGY OF PHILOLAUS

Philolaus (c. 470-385 BCE) was a disciple of the philosopher-mathematician Pythagoras, and is famous for claiming the earth was not the center of the universe. Pythagoras, propounder of the theorem named after him, was also the founder of a mystical cult based on the idea that the world was composed of numbers. The Pythagoreans had many strange, mystical beliefs, but one of their main tenets was that numbers were fundamental in the construction of the universe. Each number was thought to have its own mystical significance, and the most important number was the number ten, represented by the *tetractys* (a), which was the number of completeness, or perfection. Thus, when Philolaus was constructing his cosmology, it was only natural to expect this to be the total number of objects in his universe. Here is where an anomaly arose, for when he totaled the number of known objects in the universe the number came to… nine. Not to be deterred, Philolaus invented a tenth planet he called "counter-earth," a planet that could not be observed because it revolved around the sun exactly opposite the earth (b), but which we know exists because, of course, there must be ten objects in the universe.

The fact that there were only nine bodies in the universe constituted an anomaly to Philolaus's overall theory, based on the Pythagorean notion of ten as the number of completeness. This anomaly is "solved" by adding a tenth planet, the counter-earth. With this addition, though, another anomaly appears: no one has ever seen this tenth planet, which leads to the further *ad hoc* placement of the planet in a position that explains why it has never been (and will never be) observed, namely, that it is in the same ecliptic as the earth, but on the exact opposite side of the sun. There is no independent reason for believing in a counter-earth other than to save the original theory.

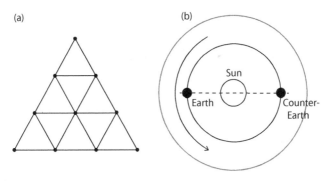

(a)　　　　　(b)

knowledge, fact p seemed perfectly secure within the theory. A second cause of hidden anomalies is a function of the complexity of a theory. An inconsistency may lie in the derivations from seemingly innocent, well accepted facts, but no one has yet seen these implications. Maybe the anomaly is buried so deeply within a complex set of derivations that it would take computing power not yet within our reach to discover it. The possibility of hidden anomalous derivations increases as the complexity of a theory increases.

As an example of an anomaly and how it might be handled, consider our two Columbus theories once again. We saw above that (2) in that data-set, Columbus' red hair, could be seen as problematic since Italians do not generally have red hair. Thus we might say that (2) constitutes an anomaly for the traditional theory, an anomaly solved by the spy theory, since red hair is a common trait among the Polish. But (2) is not a theory-breaker for the traditional theory. It is easily explained away, since red-haired Italians are not unheard of. Columbus could have had a Polish ancestor who settled in Italy, married and had red-haired children or grandchildren. So also with facts (3) and (4) for the traditional theory. Granted it was not normal that a commoner should marry a noble woman, but if we grant that it could happen, then, as we mentioned above, this could explain his access to the royal courts of Europe. In the same way (5) constitutes an anomaly for the spy theory, for that theory claims Columbus was not a natural-born Italian. But again, there are explanations available: first, the document might be a forgery, though this is *ad hoc* without additional information; or second, the document could have been part of Columbus-the-spy's ruse.

We see, then, that in a theory as complex as the Columbus theory, it is difficult to pin down an anomaly. The issue comes down to which theory makes the best sense of the data-set overall. Notice also that both Columbus theories are weak on completeness, for both are severely under-determined by the evidence (a perennial problem for historical theories). The more under-determined, the more ambiguous, which makes it more difficult to decide between competing theories.

§6 *The Cosmologies of Ptolemy & Copernicus*

We have seen the structure of theorizing in the above sections along with a few examples. In this section I want to give a large-scale example of theorizing using the competing cosmological theories of Ptolemy and Copernicus.

Ptolemy

Ptolemy (c. 90-168) was a Greco-Roman mathematician-astronomer-geographer who famously formulated a workable theory of the universe in which he proclaimed the earth was the center of the universe (Figure 4–7). All other heavenly bodies revolved in perfect circles around the earth. There are two reasons why Ptolemy ordered the universe in this way: first, and most obvious, this is the way things appear to us; second, and less obvious, is the philosophical baggage Ptolemy inherited from Aristotle. Greek thinkers believed circularity was a symbol of eternal, immutable perfection. The earth is obviously imperfect, but everything above it is perfect, a perfection manifested in perfectly circular orbits. Thus John Donne talks of us humans as "dull sublunary lovers." We are dull because we

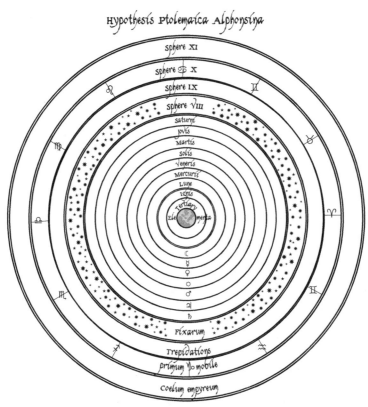

FIGURE 4–7

A view of the universe as proposed by Ptolemy. In this view, the earth is the center of the universe. The sun, like the planets, orbits the earth. Beyond the planets are the fixed stars (no star is farther away from the earth than any other star since all are in the same sphere), and beyond these are the heavenly realms responsible for all movement.

are sublunary, we live in a realm below the moon—the earth—which is imperfect, hence dull, or less perfect, compared to the sun, moon, planets and stars. This insistence on the perfect circularity of heavenly orbits led to an interesting anomaly: the retrograde motion of the planets.[3] If you observe a planet as it moves across the night sky, plotting its position on different nights, you might think you will plot a perfectly straight line as indicated in Figure 4–8 below, where each night the planet progresses further in its eastward movement. This is the movement we expect and is explained as the progression of the planet on its journey around the Earth. The

---

[3] Retrograde motion is actually the result of the relative motion of the planet approaching, and passing, Earth. It was not the only anomaly. Mountains on the moon constituted another. The moon, on this view, like the other spheres, had to be perfectly spherical—no flaws—but mountains and craters were flaws. Dante is said to have "explained" this by positing a crystal-line sphere that rose to a height above the highest mountain on the moon, so that if one could feel the surface of the moon it would be smooth like glass. This is most definitely an *ad hoc* hypothesis.

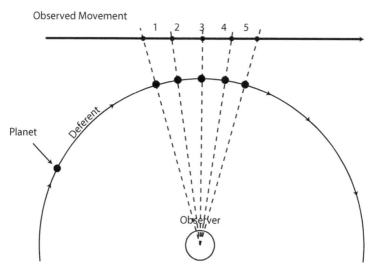

Observed Movement

Planet

Deferent

Observer

FIGURE 4–8

Expected movement of a planet through the night sky. If you are an observer on the earth looking up at a planet and plotting its position night by night as it traverses the night sky, you would expect it to progress as illustrated in this diagram.

problem is that there are times when what you actually see when you observe the planet's movement is indicated in Figure 4–9.

The planet moves in one direction for the first two observations (1 & 2), then reverses itself (retrogresses) for two observations (3 & 4), and then proceeds again in its original direction (5). This is odd enough when we observe it today, but it was devastating to a theory in which the planets were thought to move in absolutely perfect circles. Hence the anomaly: the theory states that all bodies moving around the earth must do so in perfectly circular orbits, and yet observation indicates the planets do not do so.

Ptolemaic astronomers solved the anomaly ingeniously with various devices such as epicycles and equants. If you think of the orbit of a planet as a cycle (a circular orbit), an epicycle is a cycle that lies upon that cycle. We would normally think of a planet as orbiting the earth on the deferent as in Figure 4–8, but this does not explain retrogression. What Ptolemy is asking us to believe is that a planet moves in circles (the epicycle) while orbiting the earth on the deferent. This is bizarre when

Observed Planetary
Movement

FIGURE 4–9

Retrograde motion of a planet. If you plot the course of a planet night by night, it appears to reverse itself at some point and then continue again in its original direction.

you think about it, and yet it solves the anomaly, for a planet on an epicyclic orbit will exhibit retrogressive behavior, that is, it will appear to move backward.[4]

Epicycles were an *ad hoc* hypothesis, a patch job on the Ptolemaic theory designed merely to handle the anomaly and thereby save the theory. Ptolemy's theory of the universe was the best cosmological theory for fourteen hundred years because it worked (was "adequate" in our parlance). It explained the movements of the heavenly bodies and successfully predicted events such as the appearance of constellations, planets, eclipses, and explained retrograde motions. As time passed, though, and technological advances made possible new observations with increasing accuracy, anomalies began to accumulate. Epicycles were never popular, even with ancient astronomers. No one liked the idea that the planets were doing these strange loops, even though they solved anomalies theoretically. This nagging inelegance may have paved the way for a more modern theory.

COPERNICUS

Nicolaus Copernicus (1473-1543) published his famous work, *On the Revolutions of the Heavenly Bodies*, just before his death in 1543. In this work he argued that the sun rather than the earth was the center of the universe (see Figure 4–10). We might like to think that, upon publication, there was a general rush to embrace the Copernican system, but in fact, for many decades, Ptolemy's theory worked better.

One of the largest anomalies for Copernicus' theory was our direct perception that the sun rises and sets, a view bolstered biblically by theologians who cited the instance in the book of Joshua where God stopped the sun from setting. Over time, though, it became clear that Copernicus' theory could explain everything that Ptolemy's could without resorting to the most egregious of the Ptolemaic *ad hoc* hypotheses, and thus the latter theory was eventually discarded. This advance was mostly due to improved technology which allowed for more accurate observations (the telescope).

The strength of Ptolemy's theory was that it was well-integrated with our common-sense view of the world, and also with Christian theology (which was itself interconnected). Theologians also argued that Ptolemy's view was correct because it gave the earth the prominent place demanded by the fact that it is the object of God's providence, the place where he sent his son. Thus the church refused to give up the theory in spite of the fact that Copernicus' theory was more complete. This gives us a good example of how our valuation of different adequacy conditions can influence our acceptance of a theory. I have illustrated this using adequacy meters in Figure 4–11.

It's fascinating that we can imagine two individuals, maybe Tycho Brahe and Ernst Kepler, one of whom believed Ptolemy, the other Copernicus, both watching a sunrise, but seeing two completely different events: one sees the sun rise, the other the earth turn. The ambiguity of the data, that it can be interpreted in such radically different ways, gives teeth to the claim that all theories are under-determined by their evidence.

---

[4] Consider watching a bicycle at night with a light attached to its spokes. You do not see the light move in a circle, but rather in loops. These loops are what give us the retrograde motion when applied to planets.

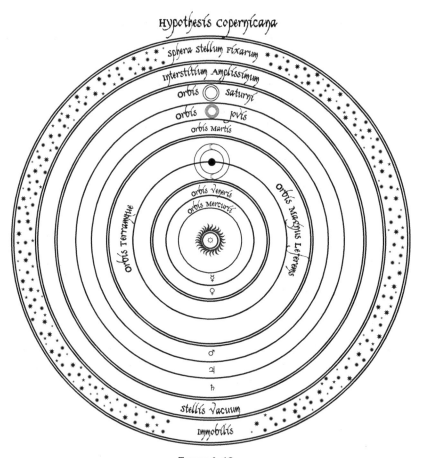

FIGURE 4–10

Copernicus' view of the universe in which the sun is at the center. The earth is now merely one of the planets circling the sun. The stars are still fixed, but now in the outermost sphere.

❃

§7 POSTSCRIPT: THEORY AND THE COPERNICAN WORLD-VIEW

Our example of the rise of the Copernican world-view is not accidental. Not only does it give a marvelous example of a conceptual shift, but shows the shift in the Western mind-set that occurred with the rise of theorizing. How perfect is this for a chapter on theorizing?

The wider philosophical perspective here has to do with the relationship of humans to the cosmos. As long as we lived in a compact universe, one in which the earth was the center around which all else travelled, with the stars pasted against a fixed sphere in the outermost reaches, and everything visible to the naked eye, we felt at home. It was a knowable and conceivably finite universe. No star was any farther away than any other star and we humans were at the center of everything.

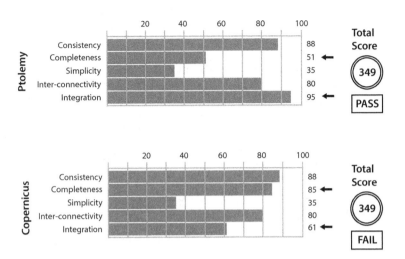

FIGURE 4–11
Tycho Brahe rejected the then new Copernican universe for the tried and true Ptolemaic universe. His judgment on the two theories can be illustrated using our adequacy meters. Note the only difference in the meters lies in the readings for completeness and integration, and the total score is the same for both, yet one (Copernicus) fails, while the other passes. Brahe's valuation of integration over completeness leads to a multiplier effect for the integration number (not shown) which is what would raise the total score of the Ptolemaic universe.

The ancient Greeks were never really fooled by all this. The myth of Prometheus is telling: we humans were mistakes, creatures who could not even survive on their own. We do not fit in the world and must be rescued by Prometheus, whose giving of fire to humans is seen as the gift of technology which allowed us to survive the indifference (or malevolence) of the gods. Thus was tragedy inseparable from the Greek world-view. Stoicism and Epicureanism were both attempts to rescue humans from this illegitimacy, and their views on the gods are telling. Epicurus allowed the gods their separate place on Olympos, claiming we should not expect them to interfere in our lives. We should use them only as examples of how a truly carefree life should be lived. The Stoics, on the other hand, claimed the gods look out for us, are providential. Both of these are philosophies of consolation. They are not interested in discovering truths about the universe, but in making people content. Thus, providence was embraced by the Stoics as a means of making humans feel as if they are a part of the universe.

Early Christianity had a similar dichotomy. In its early stages Christianity was dominated in the South (North Africa) by Gnosticism, which claimed there were two principles, a good and an evil, doing battle with each other. The evil principle created an illusory universe in which humans live, and the good principle (the Christian god) is trying to rescue us from this illusion. The evil principle has thrown a veil of ignorance over us. We think this is the real world when it is but a figment. The world as we perceive it is an illusion from which we are rescued only with the help of god. The repression and eventual destruction of the Gnostic church by the Roman church (with the help of the rise of Islam) represented a triumph for providence. With the fall of Gnosticism, providence was restored and with it at least some of the at-homeness of humans and their universe.[5]

Christianity embraced the Ptolemaic world-view, which made Christians comfortable in knowing the world. God was the guarantor of this knowledge. Direct perception of the universe (the sun circles the earth) is confirmed by the goodness of god himself, for a good god would not let our senses deceive us. We can know the truth by opening our eyes. Everything is connected to us at the center. Astrology confirms this direct connection of the stars and planets with our universe and was accordingly well-accepted by the medieval church (many popes would make no move without first consulting their astrologers).

> **POSTULATE OF VISIBILITY:**
> Everything is visible to the human eye. Our eyes can see just as far as they need to see to take in all natural objects.

The Church's position was that since god guarantees our direct access to truth, we have no need for theory. Thus, theory is set against truth, demoted to a lower status. The truth was visible, directly accessible; those who theorized were letting their curiosity get the better of them. Curiosity was epitomized as the pull of philosophy, which led to heresy and thus had to be curtailed (a view which ultimately justified the Inquisition). Thus Christians were comfortable in their discomfort: yes, they were hell-destined from birth, but the truth about their salvation, like that about the world in general, was readily available. Their very discontent led to their cure, and all was right and comfortable within their world. As Eliot puts it in the poem "East Coker":

Our only health is the disease
If we obey the dying nurse
Whose constant care is not to please
But to remind of our, and Adam's curse,
And that, to be restored, our sickness must grow worse.

With the advent of the Copernican world-view, everything changed. Humans were no longer at the center of the universe. Eventually the view of the infinite universe became the accepted view, and in direct proportion humans became less comfortable with their disenchantment. Direct perception, which tells us the sun

---

[5] Except that the problem of evil, solved by Gnosticism, which did not allow evil to taint god, now loomed large; this was solved in a different way by Augustine, who placed the blame squarely on humans instead of an evil god. This move alienated humans in a different way; not from the world per se, which also became tainted, but from god. Note the way this is put: this is a solution to a major anomaly in the Christian doctrine, of which the most promising solution is Gnosticism. Christianity feels it must maintain god as creator of the universe (possibly for omnipotence reasons, see chapter 12), but then must deal with an imperfect world. Having to save humanity from his own creation begins to smack of an *ad hoc* hypothesis. This entire issue depends on a tension in the very foundation of Christianity, namely, that humans are ordered to continually defy their humanity. They must work against their most basic desires. There is a telling difference here between the use of providence by the Stoics and the Christians. The Stoics appealed to providence (as against the Epicureans) in order to make humans more at home in the world, while the Christians appealed to providence (as against the Gnostics), which led to our being less at home in the world.

Medieval Intrigue

Copernicus, on his deathbed in 1543, turned the task of printing his work over to his student, Rheticus, a mathematician sent by Philipp Melanchthon (an ally of Martin Luther) to study with Copernicus. Rheticus supervised the printing process, but had to leave Nuremberg, and so turned the task over to Andreas Osiander, a priest and theologian. Osiander did two things: 1) he added an unauthorized and unsigned preface, and 2) he changed the title of the work. The first edition of the printed work contained both of these additions. Osiander has been much maligned for his interference, but it's clear he made the changes not out of antipathy toward Copernicus or his views, but rather to help insure their propagation.

THE PREFACE. In medieval times, theory (hypothesis) was equated with partial access and reduced certainty. The church allowed wide latitude on this subject. Giordano Bruno was burned at the stake in 1600 for maintaining the universe was infinite, but he could have saved himself merely by maintaining his position was a hypothesis rather than the truth. He refused to do so. This was a fate Osiander may have been trying to save Copernicus from, though, since Copernicus was on his deathbed, it is more likely he was trying to gain a wider audience for the work. The preface was entitled, "To the reader on the hypotheses in this work," and proceeded to enjoin that it be taken in this light, as a hypothesis to consider in order to make calculations easier than Ptolemy's system. Those close to Copernicus were furious with Osiander, knowing Copernicus himself would never have diluted his strong truth claim.

THE TITLE CHANGE. Copernicus wanted his work entitled *De revolutionibus orbium mundi* (On the Revolutions of the Bodies in the Universe). Osiander intentionally changed this to *De revolutionibus orbium coelestium* (On the Revolutions of the Heavenly Bodies). Why the subtle change from "bodies in the universe" to "heavenly bodies"? "Heavenly bodies" was a technical phrase referring to a class of objects known to astronomers with only partial access and reduced certainty (to claim more was to impinge upon the majesty of God, though notice the tension here with the postulate of visibility). To put the earth in the same class with the heavenly bodies was thus to claim the same reduced knowledge with respect to the earth. This was radical, for the earth was held to be subject to direct knowledge. Thus by making this change Osiander hoped the title alone would not stop scholars from reading the treatise.

circles the earth, could no longer be trusted (nor could god be trusted not to allow us to be deceived). Thus theory, which presupposes indirect perception, displaced truth. Indirect perception was now found to be more trustworthy than direct perception, and indirect perception is the realm of theory, that is, theorizing rose to prominence with the renunciation of direct perception. Direct perception now carried with it the very aura of inaccessibility and unknowability which the church had once relegated to theory.

Humans have, throughout ancient and medieval times, attempted to protect themselves from an uncaring universe, but the rise of theorizing, epitomized by the Copernican shift, made this more difficult than ever before. Truth via direct perception was given freely by god because it helped humans live in the world; it had utility, it led to well-being (salvation). Theory (using indirect perception) might have had superficial utility, but ultimately led only to unhappiness. Humans already knew the one true way; everything else was subsidiary and ultimately useless. This is why curiosity was suppressed in medieval times. Erasmus' interpretation of the story of Cain and Abel is telling: god was pleased with Abel's sacrifice because animal husbandry requires very little technology, relying entirely on the providence of god; he was displeased with Cain's sacrifice because agricultural management requires too much technology, which indicates a lack of faith in god's ability to provide. The medieval view of technology was thus always conflicted: technology is a result of curiosity which is a result of dissatisfaction with one's lifestyle. Technology is designed to make us more comfortable, but we are supposed to be uncomfortable, for this is our natural state. Technology presumed human unhappiness with this state, a desire for something better, which was a slap in god's face.

This theological viewpoint (that what is true is useful) is interesting and will be revisited, for this can also be an evolutionary viewpoint. It is only much later, though, that the reverse is contemplated: that what is useful is true. We have not touched on this position yet, but it will become important when we emphasize the regulative nature of theorizing.

§8 CHAPTER SUMMARY

In this chapter we have examined the structure of theorizing, defining a theory as an interpretation of data designed to help us get by in the world. To this extent, an adequate theory is one that works in various ways. (For now we are assuming that a theory works because it mirrors the way things really are in the world.) The most important condition for guaranteeing this adequacy is consistency, but we also considered four other related conditions: simplicity, completeness, interconnectivity and integration. There are no set rules on how much of each we need; judging adequacy is based on our value systems. We do know, however, that if these conditions fail, there is a problem with our theory, even if we don't allow the theory to crash because of it. This is what we refer to as an anomaly, and there are good and bad ways of handling anomalies. We can always collect more data and reformulate our theory, but if we judge our theory too important to give up we might patch it instead of throwing it out. This patch is called an *ad hoc* hypothesis. When to judge a fix as *ad hoc* is often as vague as deciding among adequacy conditions.

I have devoted an entire chapter to theorizing because I have claimed, at the beginning of this chapter, that we humans use theorizing all the time in our everyday lives. I haven't argued for this claim yet; that will be the topic of the next chapter. There, I will bring theorizing down to the personal level which will allow me to continue our discussion of the operating system from chapter 3. We all have our own personal theories that we carry with us throughout life, theories through which we interpret everything we see, hear and do, everything we believe or refuse to believe. This reflective part of the operating system is the part we can tinker with, and is what I will refer to as our conceptual scheme.

NOTES / QUESTIONS

5. Conceptual Schemes

. . . .

We are like sailors who on the open sea must reconstruct their ship but are never able to start afresh from the bottom. Where a beam is taken away a new one must at once be placed, and for this the rest of the ship is used as support. In this way, by using the old beams and driftwood the ship can be shaped entirely anew, but only by gradual reconstruction.

- Otto von Neurath

SYNOPSIS

We have seen, in chapter 3, that each of us has a framework which allows us to function in the world. There we examined the operating system, the non-reflective part of our framework. In chapter 4 I made the claim that we get by in the world by means of theorizing, and we looked at the process of theorizing with that end in mind. We are now in a position not only to back up this claim concerning theorizing, but also to expand the notion to include what I call our conceptual scheme, which functions as a kind of master theory. (1) From the esoteric scientific example of Copernicus in the last chapter we move to consider every day examples of theorizing. (2) What a conceptual scheme is: the concept of a personal theory. (3) The similarities of our conceptual schemes to theorizing. (4) Core values and conceptual schemes. (5) Cognitive dissonance: anomalies within conceptual schemes. (6) A look at various attempts to map our conceptual schemes. (7) Why craft a conceptual scheme? (8) Chapter Summary.

CHAPTER OBJECTIVES

- realize the ubiquity of theorizing throughout our lives.
- apply the concept of theorizing to our personal lives in terms of our conceptual schemes.
- understand how our conceptual schemes function, how they can be changed and manipulated by ourselves and by others.
- understand the various ways in which we attempt to overcome cognitive dissonance.
- identify our own core values and reflect upon their strengths and weaknesses.
- appreciate the connections between the various beliefs that make up our conceptual schemes.
- craft our conceptual schemes, and in doing so take a more active role in how we live our lives.

§1 MUNDANE THEORIZING

John Doe was worried, couldn't sleep, could barely function. His wife was having an affair. He was sure of it. He had been in a part of town he was not usually in at a time he was not usually out and about, had stopped in for a quick cup of coffee at an out-of-the-way coffee shop, ordered and paid for a cup to go, and was turning to leave when, through the brilliant haze of morning sunshine, in the far back corner, almost hidden from public view, he caught sight of Jane, his wife. He automatically raised an arm to catch her attention when it registered that she was sitting very close to a man he did not know; indeed, their arms were wrapped together and they were laughing intimately. The man turned his head as John watched and, as if in slow motion, kissed Jane on the cheek—not a peck of friendship, but a gentle, intimate, lingering, loving kiss. Her eyes closed in response, her hand seeking out his, fingers entwining. John abruptly turned and walked, like an automaton, to his car, where he sat at the wheel, unable to comprehend what he had seen. They loved each other, he and his wife, were happy together, had two kids, never fought. There must be an explanation. Maybe he had been mistaken. The sun had been in his eyes. He fought back a wave of nausea. No, he had not been mistaken, and now, as he thought about it, there had been more than a few incidences of strange behavior lately. Just a few days ago he had gotten a call from the school saying Jane was not there to pick up the children, asking what should be done. He was on his way to pick them up himself when she called and said she had been delayed in traffic, but was at the school now. Other evidence came to mind: her odd glances, reserved behavior, stilted laughs. It was true; she was having an affair. Their marriage was over.

In the last chapter, on theorizing, most of our examples were relegated to scientific or historical instances where we were trying to make sense of a collection of facts. The above example concerning John and Jane is different. It does involve making sense of facts, but is a much more personal instance, dealing with events that impinge upon our everyday lives and our mental health.

I have made the claim that theorizing is not relegated to esoteric, academic formulations, but is something that we engage in constantly, and this is an example of what I mean. John has a theory about his marriage—all is right within his world: his wife loves him, his kids are happy, his job is going well, his future bright, until, by chance, he comes upon a piece of evidence, his wife in the coffee shop with another man, that constitutes an anomaly to this world-view. Note the consistency condition is in place—it cannot both be true that his relationship with his wife is what he thinks it is AND that she is being kissed by another man in a coffee shop. Anomalies demand explanation and his first response is to gather more evidence; he thinks back over the last few days, retrieving memories that might help him understand his situation, and there he finds more anomalous evidence that seems to support a revamping of his theory from that of a happy marriage to that of a marriage in trouble. The difference between this kind of example and those in the last chapter is that this theory is *his* theory, it is personal in a way that cosmological theories and historical theories are not (though they could be). Let's continue the story of John and Jane:

> The next day, John confronted Jane with what he had seen in the coffee shop. Embarrassed, she explained she was planning a surprise birthday party for him and the man he saw her with in the coffee shop was a party planner. When he asked about the kiss and the hand-holding she was shocked: he must have been mistaken, she would never allow such a thing to happen. As John considered the sincerity of her response he realized she was right, he could have made a mistake; and the more he considered it, the more he realized he was probably overreacting. He remembered the sun was in his eyes; he probably imagined the whole thing... and so he convinced himself his wife was in fact faithful and all was well with his world once again.

John was sure he would have to relinquish his happy-marriage-theory, but his wife provided him with the surprise-birthday-party-solution, which nicely handled all the anomalous information except for the alleged kiss. But he recalculated the probabilities that he might be mistaken, and lowered the odds that he really saw what he thought he saw. He then did a cost-benefit analysis and concluded he didn't really see them kiss; maybe the man was bending over and in the bright glare he mistook what had happened. This smacks of an *ad hoc* hypothesis. The question is: What is his justification for believing he was mistaken in what he saw? He did, after all, clearly recognize her in the back corner of the coffee shop. What pushes him to believe he was mistaken is the value he places on the happy-marriage-theory (hence the cost-benefit analysis). He desperately wants to believe in it, so he disregards the contrary evidence, explaining it away, and patches up his endangered theory.

Using this example as a model should help you understand the ubiquity of theorizing. If your car doesn't start you gather evidence and formulate a theory: "My starter is broken" or "My battery is dead." If you know nothing about cars, you take your car to a mechanic and he does the same: he collects data, but since he knows more about how cars work, he formulates a better theory, then proceeds to work on the car based on this. If he "fixes" the car and it still won't start, the non-start constitutes an anomaly (a disconfirmation) and he will have to reformulate and try again. Doctors do the same: you tell a doctor your symptoms (data collection) and she makes a diagnosis (formulates a theory) based on this and prescribes medicine for your condition. If you die the next day, this constitutes an anomaly and she will reformulate if another patient comes to her with the same symptoms in the future.

We have theories about god, the weather, politicians, Aunt Mary, our pets, our finances. Every belief we have is a theory of sorts; some are miniature, others more comprehensive. Once you understand how theorizing works you can see that we engage in the activity continually. We are particularly aware of this when we experience events we don't immediately understand, that are not effortlessly incorporated into our theories. Whether we observe an example of physical suffering such as the aftermath of an earthquake, read about what many claim was a miraculous event, or hear a bump in the night, we immediately formulate a theory in order to try to understand it, or rearrange a current theory in order to try to make the new data fit. We are theorizing animals, *homo theoreticus*; we are constantly taking in data from our senses, incorporating it into our multitudinous theories, doing cost-benefit analyses against the adequacy conditions, running what-if scenarios, calculating probabilities based on our value system, formulating *ad hoc* hypotheses, reformulating, recalculating.

※

§2 Conceptual Schemes

In chapter 3 we saw that our framework processes the sensory input we receive from both our own bodies and from the external world and directs output when necessary (Figure 5–1). All this occurs before we become conscious of the input, which means we have no direct access to the world. All conscious data is processed data. If we have no direct access to the world, then we must weigh the (indirect) evidence we have and formulate theories about the world. This is why we spent an entire chapter on the process of theorizing, for theories are our only access to the world. We are now in a position to consider the conscious processing system that performs our cognitive theorizing—what I will refer to as our conceptual scheme. Of course, not everything within the workings of the conceptual scheme is available

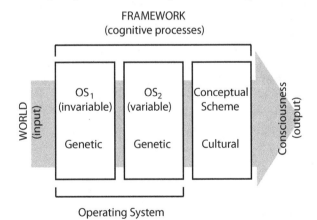

FRAMEWORK
(cognitive processes)

FIGURE 5–1

A representation of our framework, which I have divided into the Operating System (unconscious processing) and the Conceptual Scheme (conscious processing). We can reflect upon our conceptual schemes and thus mold them in ways not possible with the operating system.

to reflection, so the reflective/non-reflective distinction may be confusing, but I will continue to use it because consciousness, and in particular self-consciousness, is what characterizes the conceptual scheme, for it is from this that the self emerges. The self is at least capable of reflecting on its conceptual scheme (of which it is a part) even if it never does so. As we have seen, I don't doubt that dogs and cats and cows, birds and reptiles, dolphins and whales, all have some sort of conceptual scheme—I think all brained organisms do—but we will focus here on the human conceptual scheme and then, if you like, you can draw analogies to other organisms based on their neurological similarity to humans.

I have now expanded the concept of theorizing to include every belief we have, making the process of theorizing a fundamental part of cognition. There is no theoretical point of view which stands in contrast to a practical point of view. We are all theoreticians, and theorizing is an imminently practical exercise.

A conceptual scheme is a web of beliefs (hopes, wants, goals, desires) which together constitute our individual world-view. Since beliefs themselves are theories, we can say that a conceptual scheme is a web of theories, it is the master theory through which we see the world, and we are the master theoreticians. It is a collection, a weaving together, of everything we believe. As such, it is through our conceptual schemes that we define ourselves, and through which we derive meaning from the world. The overall goal of a conceptual scheme is what we called, in chapter 1, well-being.

Our conceptual schemes are formed non-reflectively, for the most part, by our parents, peers, teachers and from general lived experience based on standard brain processes. This is a continual formative process, but we humans have the ability to interfere in this process. We can take an active role in the on-going construction of our conceptual schemes, questioning them, reformulating them and thereby remaking not only our world-view, but our very selves. This is the benefit of self-consciousness. Many people never avail themselves of this opportunity, which seems to me a great loss. Why should our genetics (our operating system) and other people's beliefs, which they impose upon us, completely determine our way of viewing the world? We can't change many of our genetic propensities, but by becoming aware of them we can avoid their pitfalls, and we can definitely change our non-genetic beliefs. We can take control and remake our conceptual schemes and by doing so change our lives for the better. Our brains are not optimized for truth. We are naturally deceived in many ways and if we want to avoid these pitfalls, if the truth is of interest to us, then we will want to reflect upon and possibly rearrange our conceptual schemes.

§3   CONCEPTUAL SCHEMES AS THEORIES.

FUNCTIONAL SIMILARITIES

A conceptual scheme is an interrelated web of hopes, wants, goals, and desires, through which we interpret the world. In other words: each individual has at her disposal an aggregate of ideas by means of which she defines herself, and through which she interprets the world. A conceptual scheme, then, is a personal theory, a theory unique to each and every individual. It is a conglomeration of a multitude of theories, all of which we balance against each other continually, much as the facts within a theory are continually balanced.

I call conceptual schemes theories because they look like theories, act like theories and have the same purpose as theories.

(1) Their function is to allow us to "make sense" of the world around us.

(2) The consistency condition, as well as the other adequacy conditions outlined in chapter 4, is also a condition for an adequate conceptual scheme.

(3) Anomalies arise within a conceptual scheme and are seen as problems that need to be resolved.

(4) There are good and bad ways of handling anomalies within our conceptual scheme.

As another general example, consider the movie *The Truman Show*, in which an orphaned baby (Truman) becomes the protagonist of a wildly popular reality television show—unbeknownst to Truman, who has no idea that his entire world is constructed for public viewing. His parents, friends and associates are all actors hired to play their parts. A huge dome-shaped set has been constructed to mimic the world, complete with sun, stars, and rainstorms. There are cameras everywhere, and every part of Truman's life is orchestrated. This is a modern equivalent of Plato's allegory of the cave, but instead of being chained to a wall inside a cave, Truman lives in a fabricated world, on an island where nothing is as it seems. The producers implant a fear of drowning to allay his curiosity, thus keeping him securely within the confines of the set. He is a slave, born into bondage... Truman's conceptual scheme, then, formulated completely by others, is one in which he is an ordinary person living an ordinary life. But his world-view is obviously out of synch with reality (as all Truman Show viewers are aware).

The movie opens *in medias re*, with Truman as an adult having trouble maintaining his conceptual scheme. In an early scene he is driving to work when one of the set lights (the North Star) falls from the top of the dome and crashes into the street in front of Truman's car. He gets out and examines the light, which is labeled "Sirius." This is an anomaly demanding explanation, for which he has none. The set technicians provide one for him, though, for when he gets back in his car a radio blurb explains that an aircraft flying over has lost some parts. On another day there is a radio glitch while he is driving to work and suddenly he can hear all the background technical communications concerning the show. He tries to adjust his radio, but he hears strange voices instead of music: "He's approaching Lancaster street." Truman looks out, and sure enough, he is approaching Lancaster street. The glitch is remedied and, once again, an explanation is provided, but anomalies like these continue to accumulate and slowly Truman's entire world view is endangered.

ADEQUACY CONDITIONS: CONSISTENCY

The law of non-contradiction, as we would expect, is in full effect with respect to our conceptual schemes. This is the least reflective of the adequacy conditions, being part of our operating system. We don't learn to abide by it, we just do. Even small children rebel at explicit contradiction. Consider the child who, during the Christmas season, notices Santa Clauses on every street corner. The child turns

---

FROM THE ORIGINAL MOVIE SCRIPT: THE MATRIX

MORPHEUS: We are trained in this world to accept only what is rational and logical. Have you ever wondered why?

Neo shakes his head.

MORPHEUS: As children, we do not separate the possible from the impossible which is why the younger a mind is the easier it is to free while a mind like yours can be very difficult.

NEO: Free from what?

MORPHEUS: From the Matrix… Do you want to know what it is, Neo?

[Neo swallows and nods his head.]

It's that feeling you have had all your life. That feeling that something was wrong with the world. You don't know what it is but it's there, like a splinter in your mind, driving you mad, driving you to me. But what is it?…

The Matrix is everywhere, it's all around us, here even in this room. You can see it out your window, or on your television. You feel it when you go to work, or go to church or pay your taxes. It is the world that has been pulled over your eyes to blind you from the truth.

NEO: What truth?

MORPHEUS: That you are a slave, Neo. That you, like everyone else, were born into bondage… kept inside a prison that you cannot smell, taste, or touch. A prison for your mind.

---

to the parent and asks, "Which one is the *real* Santa?" This question presupposes the law of non-contradiction; the child recognizes that all these red-dressed jolly figures cannot, at the same time and in the same sense, be Santa Claus, and the existence of more than one constitutes an anomaly. The parent easily handles the anomaly with a lie: "The real Santa lives at the North Pole. These are all Santa's helpers." And the child, in all innocence, trusting the veracity of the parent, is satisfied. There is so much evidence within the child's life for the existence of Santa Claus: general talk, a web of deception, the gayly wrapped presents that magically appear under the tree on Christmas Eve, the cookies and milk set out that night that are consumed by morning. But as the child becomes more sophisticated, contradictions begin to emerge. Rumors begin to circulate in children-circles that Santa Claus doesn't exist, but what do those kids know? I remember growing up in Florida and being worried that we didn't have a chimney. I asked my parents, "How does Santa deliver our presents when we don't have a chimney?" "Not to worry," was their response, "Santa has a passkey. He can come right in the front door." Eventually we see through these deceptions, which are usually justified after the fact in the name of the greater good. Thus is Santa Claus diminished within our conceptual schemes.

OTHER ADEQUACY CONDITIONS

Of the remaining four conditions, all of which, remember, are related in some way to the consistency condition, simplicity may be the most reflective. We unthinkingly use consistency when constructing or maintaining a theory, but we explicitly strive to make our theories elegant in their simplicity and directness, whether from aesthetic or consistency considerations (or both). Integration refers to how well our own personal beliefs mesh with the beliefs of other people. Interconnectivity plays a special role within conceptual schemes, for the number of connections involved between the parts of our conceptual scheme determine the importance of those parts, which then relates to the amount of dissonance we feel when those are threatened. We will discuss this in the next section. Finally, completeness, in its relevant sense as explanatory completeness, is driven by our curiosity concerning the world and its workings.

§4 CORE VALUES & CONCEPTUAL SCHEMES

A conceptual scheme, like any theory, provides a way for an individual to make sense of the world. But our conceptual scheme is not just any theory; it is our own theory, defining not only our self, what we are, but our relationship to others, and because of this, making sense takes on a more important role. For humans, our bodily states and our relationship to the world is reflected in emotional states, the most important of which are related to pleasure and pain. As we have seen, our self-consciousness intensifies these, giving humans not merely the ability to feel pain, but to suffer. So also with pleasure. We might say that well-being is to pleasure what suffering is to pain—a heightened, more all-encompassing state of mind.

Pleasurable feelings are the result of chemicals released in the brain as a reward. That warm fuzzy feeling John gets when he is satisfied with his wife's explanation and they embrace is a shot of oxytocin, a neuromodulator which allows for, among other things, the bonding of mother and child. That feeling of exhilaration experienced by an athlete when he completes an arduous task is dopamine. These are rewards for achieving cognitive homeostasis, which is amenable to our survival.

When things are not right with the world, when they seem out-of-place, we begin to feel edgy, anxious. Imagine a Neolithic hunter prowling the forest, senses alert. There is danger about. He sees movement where there shouldn't be movement. He notices the absence of noise in the forest. These are anomalies. His brain responds before he is even conscious of these experiences, using chemicals to prepare him to fight, fly or freeze. His awareness manifests itself as a feeling of discomfort; something is not right. This discomfort, then, has survival value, and it has translated into modern life in many ways. Some of these may be trivial, but not always, for our lives are still full of dangers, real or perceived. I once got off at the wrong subway station while visiting New York City and decided to walk to my destination. I was immediately uncomfortable: buildings were in disrepair, there were what appeared to be disreputable people loitering in groups on street corners, graffiti and garbage were abundant. I began compiling theoretical scenarios on the result of my actions (as-if scenarios, probability calculations and cost-benefit analyses), none of which turned out well, so I returned to the station and got on the next train.

I will refer to the feeling of unease that I experienced as cognitive dissonance, a term from social psychology made famous by Leon Festinger (1956). It refers to the uncomfortable feeling we get when anomalies arise within our conceptual scheme, that is, when we are confronted with contradictory ideas. Before we can understand cognitive dissonance, though, we must first look at our belief valuations.

Imagine your conceptual scheme as a vast interconnected network of beliefs. When a new datum attempts to connect itself to this web it is subject, first, to the consistency requirement. Your subconscious processing pulls all the relevant beliefs on hand and compares them to the new datum and checks for consistency. If it meets the condition on a first pass it is allowed in and interconnections are made to other relevant beliefs. This may change in time. For example, as we explore the implications of our beliefs we may come to see there are contradictions involved that we did not see at first. If a datum fails the consistency requirement, interconnections become impossible without further processing. There are three possibilities here. Either:

1. the datum must be rejected (a refusal to believe), or
2. the datum must be reinterpreted in light of the present belief structure, or
3. the belief structure must be reinterpreted in light of the datum.

Which option is taken will depend upon the valuations we put upon both the datum being considered and our current beliefs.

A core value within a conceptual scheme is any belief that is highly interconnected with other beliefs within the conceptual scheme. If we consider beliefs (goals, hopes, wants, desires) as strands within our interconnected web (as indicated in Figure 5–2a), then the more connections a belief has to other strands, the more important it will be. Thus, a crucial factor in being a core value is the extent of seismic disturbance of the cognitive terrain should this value be lost. An example should illustrate this.

Suppose I have the belief, "My family is going on a picnic tomorrow," and it rains on that day so that we cannot go on the picnic. Rain, in this case, is a datum that constitutes an anomaly to my picnic-belief. It is impossible to deny that it is raining, so options (1) and (2) are not available. The fact of the rain is too strong. In order to deny it I would have to rearrange all my beliefs concerning the way the world works, and I am not willing to do this for a picnic, so I give up the picnic-belief. The picnic-belief is not a core value (nor is it directly connected to a core value, as illustrated in Figure 5–2b), and I suffer little or no cognitive dissonance when I contemplate giving it up. We could add value to it in various ways; for example, we could make it so that the purpose of the picnic was to allow us to meet with someone who was very important to us and whom we might not get to see again for a long time. By adding to the story in this way we connect it to other parts of our conceptual scheme (including, maybe, a core value), and by adding connections we increase value. When I am forced to give up a belief I tear it away from all other connections, thus inflicting damage on those connections. This is the seismic disturbance referred to above.

§5 RELIEVING COGNITIVE DISSONANCE

Suppose I, as most of us do, expect to live a long and satisfying life, and am then diagnosed with terminal cancer. Accepting this dying-of-cancer belief (giving up my long-and-happy-life expectation) will cause massive damage to my conceptual scheme. Many strands will be torn asunder, for the belief that I will live a long

(a)

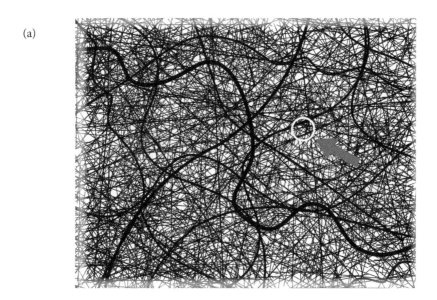

(b)

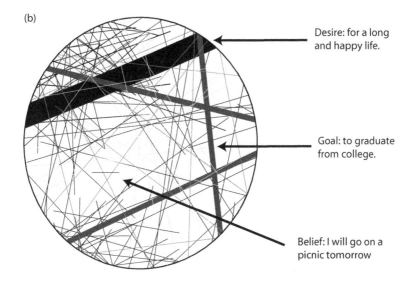

Desire: for a long and happy life.

Goal: to graduate from college.

Belief: I will go on a picnic tomorrow

FIGURE 5–2
A schematic view of a conceptual scheme as a web of beliefs. The thickness of a belief is a function of its interconnections: the more connections the thicker. Thickness, in turn, is an indicator of value. (a) is an overall perspective of a portion of a conceptual scheme; (b) is a closer view showing the strands of varying importance.

FIGURE 5–3
Dilbert encounters cognitive dissonance.

and satisfying life is a core value, is highly interconnected with other parts of my conceptual scheme. In this case, (1) is a tempting option. I might simply deny that I have cancer ("The doctors must be wrong."), or deny that it is terminal ("I can beat this!"). This response, known as Denial, is a common defense mechanism when a core value is threatened. We simply refuse to believe the datum in the form in which it first appears, which gives us time to slowly let the truth sink in without severely damaging our psyche.

To see how denial works, consider a large dam holding back a substantial volume of water. If, after weeks of heavy rain, the dam begins to fail, there are two available options: I can open the sluice gates and let the water out slowly, or do nothing and watch the dam disintegrate. If I take the first option there may be damage done downstream, but not nearly so much as when the dam fails catastrophically. Denial is equivalent to my opening the sluice gates. Refusing to believe the full-strength datum gives me time to begin to reorganize my conceptual scheme, preparing for the worst case. Denial involves deceiving myself, believing a lie, but it's only a white lie, for ideally we use it temporarily, and for the greater good. We usually reserve the term 'self-deception' for when it becomes more than a temporary fix, but while denial is a less extreme form of self-deception—more healthy—it is self-deception nonetheless. Self-deception allows us to hold contradictory beliefs, which, as we have seen, we cannot do explicitly. We cannot hold two beliefs that we know are contradictory, but if we can somehow become unaware that they are contradictory, then we can believe them. This is what our brain allows with self-deception. We fail to see the contradiction between two obviously contradictory beliefs. Self-deceptions are to conceptual schemes what *ad hoc* hypotheses are to theories.[1]

We humans are masters of self-deception. We know what we want to believe, what we must believe, and we proceed to believe it, often in the face of facts to the contrary. Our success in this endeavor is directly proportional to the value we put on the beliefs in question. For example, consider a woman who has a son who is her only remaining relation. She raises the son fully expecting he will be there to care for her in her old age. She depends on him and constructs her future based on his presence. But her son goes off to war and is killed. What is she to do? She refuses to believe he is dead. She keeps his room as it was before he left, speaks of him in the present tense, and expects him home at any time. Every day that passes

---

[1] For deception to occur, a deceiver has to know something the deceivee does not. The oddness of self-deception lies in the fact that we are both deceiver and deceivee at the same time.

without his arrival constitutes an anomaly to her world-view and yet she cannot accept his death.

Our concept of self is one of our most important beliefs and is thus often subject to self-deception. There is a phenomenon which I refer to as the American Idol effect, after the television show *American Idol*. On that show people who truly believe they can sing well come up against reality in the form of a panel of judges. The judges' decision that they cannot sing is an anomaly to the performers' belief that they can, and if that belief is an important part of how they view themselves, then they cannot give it up easily, for to do so is to force a reformulation of that self-image. The American Idol effect goes beyond mere singing, though; it applies to any

THE GREAT DISAPPOINTMENT

In the 19th century, William Miller (1782-1849), a Baptist preacher, theorized (predicted) that Christ would return to earth somewhere between March 21, 1843 and March 21, 1844. Many of his followers took the March 21, 1844 date as definitive and began spreading the prophecy. Many sold or gave away all their earthly possessions as the day approached. Needless to say, the day came and went (becoming known afterward as The Great Disappointment), constituting a major anomaly to the Millerite program. Many gave up their beliefs, but a large number insisted the date was correct, but that Miller had misinterpreted it as an earthly event—the second coming. These followers claimed that an invisible, heavenly event had occurred instead (Does Philolaus' counter-earth come to mind?) Out of this group a new church was formed: the Seventh Day Adventists. Leon Festinger wrote a book, *When Prohecies Fail*, in which he examined in detail such odd responses. It was there that he introduced the notion of cognitive dissonance.

The Great Disappointment is interesting not just for its *ad hoc* responses, but also as a study in evidence. Miller did not arrive at the March 21 date randomly. He based the date on a carefully plotted timeline founded on a passage in the Book of Daniel (8:14) which said: "Unto two thousand and three hundred days; then shall the sanctuary be cleansed." Note the presuppositions behind his calculations:

(1) He assumed the cleansing of the sanctuary was equivalent to the return of Christ (which is based on the further assumption that the Old Testament prophets were speaking of Jesus, who is assumed to be the Jewish messiah).

(2) He assumed that the days referred to in the passage should be interpreted as years in actual time.

(3) He assumed (as did Bishop Ussher, who famously established the creation date of the earth at 4004 BC) that earthly millenniums must correspond to the seven days of creation. On the seventh day, God rested, thus the 7th millennium was Christ's rule on earth, which means the time period from creation until Christ's return must be 6,000 years. All this, based on a metaphor.

There is no clear evidence for any of these assumptions, and yet together they were used as grist for Miller's calculations of the second coming.

This phenomenon is not limited to the past. Harold Camping prophesied more recently that the world would end on May 21, 2011 (Camping). Many people believed his prophecy; some even sold their homes and gave away their savings in order to preach the end of the world. We're still here.

case in which the persona someone projects is radically different from reality. This could be a person's voice, their physical appearance (weight, beauty, dress), their athletic prowess, their social skills. I'm not making a judgment on those involved (I may be doing the same thing). The point is that the deception in these cases is deemed necessary by the person, for it helps them get by in the world. It contributes to their well-being, and I personally wouldn't want to be the one responsible for destroying their attempt. I would hope, instead, that at some point they would gain the strength to examine their conceptual scheme and rearrange it on their own. Why? Not because they should necessarily conform to someone else's viewpoint, but because a conceptual scheme radically out of synch with reality often inhibits a person's ability to interact with the world in various ways.

Losing or damaging a core value always (by definition) results in radical reorganization within a conceptual scheme, and radical reorganization within a conceptual scheme is always cognitively stressful.

§6   ON MAPPING CONCEPTUAL SCHEMES

The notion of conceptual schemes that determine (to some extent) how we view the world is not a new idea. The German philosopher Immanuel Kant is generally given credit for the modern idea that input from the outside world passes through filters or categories of the mind, thus denying direct access to the external world. This raises the question not only of what the world is like when we are not experiencing it (what Kant called the thing-in-itself), but what the categories are like that process the information. This latter question has been answered in various ways. Phrenology was an early science, now deemed a pseudo-science, that believed the brain was composed of modules which represented various mental faculties. The skull was thought to conform to these areas so that one could map the mental faculties by means of an exploration of the cranium. Modern neuroscience also uses the concept of modules, locating brain functions within specific areas of the brain, but not in as crude a fashion as phrenology once did. Furthermore, no one today claims you can locate specific beliefs in specific parts of the brain. The best explanation of memories, which is what our beliefs boil down to, is that they are stored throughout the brain rather than in one specific locale.

It is not the task of neuroscientists to explore the conceptual scheme. They are more concerned with what we have called the operating system, which includes the basic brain functions. Exploring the conceptual scheme has traditionally been relegated to psychology. Freud talked of the unconscious, by which he meant the underlying brain processes that we would incorporate, for the most part, into our notion of the framework. He thought the workings of the brain were suppressed, or repressed, by various personal and social valuations of which we are unaware. One way of expressing this is in terms of the id, the ego, and the super-ego, which were designated by Freud as constructs to help us understand the workings of the mind. The id usually represents what we have called the operating system, and is based on the pleasure principle, while the ego attempts to make the instinctual desires of the id conform to reality. To accomplish this it uses strategies such as repression, denial, and sublimation to cover the goings-on beneath the surface. In order to explore the area of the psyche lying beneath the protective coverings of the ego, we must find a way to neutralize the processing system. One way to do this is by free association. The idea here is for one person (the analyst) to say a word after which you (the subject) immediately say whatever comes to mind without thinking about it. If you are with someone you trust (your analyst), so that you are not reserved in the least, then you should be able to bypass the protective processing and find out the core thoughts of your conceptual scheme. This is also one of the motivating factors behind the Rorschach, or inkblot, tests, in which the subject is shown a series of ambiguous drawings or inkblots (as in Figure 5–4) and asked to interpret them. Since there is no fact of the matter, no correct answer, the subjects' interpretations allow the therapist to map their conceptual scheme and gain insight into their mental processes.

Behaviorists, particularly radical or analytical behaviorists, have nothing but disdain for such practices. They claim there are no mental processes, no beliefs, feelings, mental states, indeed, no mind. All that actually exist are dispositions to behave in certain ways. This is an extreme reductionist doctrine insofar as it denies mental states altogether, reducing them to external behavior. When you say, for example, that you believe in god, this means only that you are disposed to behave in certain ways at certain times in certain situations. To say that I am afraid of cats means nothing more than that I am disposed to exhibit anxious behavior when in the presence of felines.

Behaviorism, as a preeminent psychological doctrine, declined with the corresponding rise of neuroscience and cognitive psychology, with their emphasis upon genetics, for it had linked itself too closely to the blank slate and environmental influence. Though its radical doctrines have fallen by the wayside, behaviorism itself remains a valuable explanatory position. The point to be salvaged for our purposes is that behavior is indeed the best indicator, in most cases, of our mental states. We can only deduce that other people have an inner life (subjectivity), as we know

FIGURE 5–4
A reproduction of the first of Rorschach's inkblot cards.

THE INVERTED COLOR SPECTRUM AND BEHAVIORISM

It is possible that the way I view colors (my color spectrum) is entirely different from the way you view colors. Our color spectrums could, theoretically, be inverted with respect to one another. This is interesting because if this were true, there is no way we would ever be able to tell.

When I am driving and pull up to a stop light, I see what I call red. You, on the other hand, see a different color, say, what I would call blue, but you call it red, as I do. Thus, we would both agree that the light is red and would stop accordingly. This is true across the board.

The spectrum problem becomes an argument against radical behaviorism (the claim that there are no mental states, only behaviors), because it is obvious that the inverted spectrum is a possibility, and yet behaviorism cannot account for it. If all mental states reduce to behavior, it makes no sense to say that we might be experiencing different colors even though our behaviors are always the same; and yet clearly it does make sense. Thus radical behaviorism cannot handle one of our intuitions concerning experience.

we do from personal experience, by noticing that they behave like we do in similar situations.

Another part of the behaviorist tradition makes the claim that our conceptual scheme parses the world according to the concepts we use in our language, which means our language influences the way we see the world. The most famous advocate of this was Benjamin Whorf, who, along with his mentor Edward Sapir, subscribed to what has now come to be known as the Sapir-Whorf hypothesis. The radical claim made by this hypothesis can be seen if we change the phrase "language influences the way we see the world" to "language completely determines the way we see the world." While the former is obviously true, the latter has been shown to be false.[2] Thus, while the Sapir-Whorf hypothesis has been discredited as it was originally formulated, no one can deny that there is some truth to it. As Hofstadter (2001) has remarked:

… we are prepared to see, and we see easily, things for which our language and culture hand us ready-made labels. When those labels are lacking, even though the phenomena may be all around us, we may quite easily fail to see them at all. The perceptual attractors that we each possess (some coming from without, some coming from within, some on the scale of mere words, some on a much grander scale) are the filters through which we scan and sort reality, and thereby they determine what we perceive on high and low levels. (524)

Consider, for instance, the diagram shown in Figure 5–5. If you have no idea what this diagram represents, then you should enjoy the experience. For you, the diagram is like a Rorschach inkblot, an uninterpreted set of marks on the page. It is still processed data, for your operating system has already worked its magic, allowing you to see lines on a two dimensional surface, but your conceptual scheme does not know what to make of it. This may be how an infant sees the world, as an

---

[2] See, for example, Pinker (2003: Chapter 12).

uninterpreted mass of lines and colors; as William James once put it: as "one great blooming, buzzing confusion." We can imagine a flesh-colored blob approaching the infant and giving it sustenance, all the while repeating the term 'Mommy,' so that an association is formed between the flesh-colored blob and the term. The child has thus divided the world, separating Mommy from the rest. If we think of words as corresponding to concepts, then the process of learning just is the process of dividing the world into more and more specific concepts.

The diagram in Figure 5–5 is uninterpreted because you have no concept (no category) to fit it into, but once I tell you that it is a diagram of a bear climbing a tree (seen from the opposite side), a category is formed, and from now on you will immediately interpret it that way. You will never again experience that particular grouping of lines as uninterpreted data. Thus did Wordsworth lament the passing of the childlike view of the world in "Intimations of Immortality":

Turn wheresoe'er I may,
by night or day,
The things which I have seen I now can see no more.

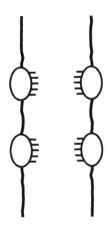

FIGURE 5–5

If you are unaware of what this diagram represents, then it appears to you as a Rorschach inkblot appears: as totally uninterpreted data.

§7   WHY CRAFT OUR CONCEPTUAL SCHEME?

As reflective individuals we can gain control over our conceptual schemes to a certain degree. Since our conceptual schemes at least partially determine how we see the world, it would seem we should take some interest not only in crafting them, but in crafting them carefully. To craft a conceptual scheme is to construct one's self concept, for our conceptual scheme includes our own self-image. This doesn't mean that a crafted (philosophically formulated) conceptual scheme is necessary in order to get by in the world. Most people probably never take the time to do much crafting, but it makes sense that a crafted conceptual scheme would be more useful than one that is formed willy-nilly by external factors. Our life-quest, as first mentioned in chapter 1, involves our search for meaning and value, and is thus part and parcel with this crafting. This is why our life-quest is a combination of both discovery and invention.

We humans are narrative creatures. From a very early age we tell stories in order to explain disparate facts. Indeed, a theory is a kind of weaving together of facts, which is why some people are so good at theorizing—at telling stories. Narratives make facts easier to remember, which means they help us make sense of the world. The storyteller at the heart of our conceptual scheme, our self, is itself a story we have constructed. It emerges from the theoretical constructions of the conceptual scheme, and is the result of multifarious brain processes, a story we weave together.

To craft a conceptual scheme is to articulate your beliefs, hopes, wants and desires. The word 'articulate' here means, for our purposes, to specify, to express distinctly, to put into words. We often think we know something, but when asked to speak about it we fumble around for words. Thinking about what you believe and why you believe it clarifies these in your mind and thus strengthens the structures that make you who you are. To the extent that you have never reflected upon your beliefs, your identity as the person you think you are is less stable. Reflection inhibits self-deception. We will talk more about the self in chapter 13, but it is clear that the conceptual scheme is crucial in its development. Indeed, as I have already said, the self emerges from the hopes, wants, goals, and desires that comprise it.

The good news is, that if you have read these chapters carefully, you are already beginning to craft your conceptual scheme, for you now know more about how you, as a person-in-the-world, function.

§8 CHAPTER SUMMARY

In this chapter we have brought the concept of theorizing home, taking it out of the hands of scientists, historians, and theologians, and showing how everyone uses it all the time throughout their lives. This led us to a discussion of our own personal theories, what I have called our conceptual schemes, through which we see the world. Conceptual schemes are complex interconnected belief-systems; they are that part of our cognitive framework which we can reflect upon and change.

As a theory, our conceptual schemes function like all other theories. They allow us to interpret the world, they adhere to adequacy requirements, particularly the consistency requirement, and when anomalies arise that threaten them, these are handled in similar ways to other types of theories.

Not only do I have a conceptual scheme, but so do you, and so do other people. The conceptual schemes of others are a major influence on our own (as ours is on theirs). It is to this broader aspect of integration that we must now turn.

NOTES / QUESTIONS

6. Extending Our Conceptual Schemes

Hell is other people.

- Sartre, No Exit

SYNOPSIS

(1) We begin with a brief look at the concept of feral children. This is of interest because it raises the question of the possibility of a private language. Private languages, or their impossibility, underline the importance of language to sociability. (2) The concept of an idea is explained, and how ideas become objectified or made public. (3) A brief digression on the importance of analogy to cognition. (4) Yet another digression, this time on the concept of reverse engineering. This will help us further explain the concept of the selfish gene, which in turn leads to a discussion of the meme. (5) We continue the notion of objectified ideas by introducing the concept of the meme, which is the vehicle of cultural evolution. (6) The effect of consciousness on biological evolution is explored. (7) A brief look at social groups, their formation and complexity. (8) The concept of reciprocal altruism, which has allowed human relationships to prosper. (9) The dialectical movement involved in sociality, in which we are introduced to some of the complications to which social complexity gives rise. (10) Chapter Summary.

CHAPTER OBJECTIVES

- become aware of some of the subtleties of social behavior
- understand more clearly what it means to say that we are "social animals"

---

§1 FERAL CHILDREN AND PRIVATE LANGUAGES

Before dawn on January 9, 1800, a remarkable creature came out of the woods near the village of Saint-Sernin in southern France. No one expected him. No one recognized him. He was human in bodily form and walked erect. Everything else about him suggested an animal. He was naked except for the tatters of a shirt and showed no modesty, no awareness of himself as a human person related in any way to the people who had captured him. He could not speak and made only weird, meaningless cries. (Shattuck 5)

So begins Richard Shattuck's account of the "wild boy of Aveyron" entitled *The Forbidden Experiment*. Accounts of feral children have fascinated humans since the earliest recorded history. The Babylonian epic *Gilgamesh* tells of Enkidu, the feral man, who had never seen a human before he was introduced to (and seduced by) a temple prostitute. Romulus and Remus, the mythical founders of Rome, were said to have been suckled and raised by a she wolf, and we have already mentioned Rousseau's theoretical account of the noble savage. Shattuck's account is troubling from the start because of the reference to the tattered shirt, for doesn't this smack of cultural taint? Indeed, it was later determined that the wild boy was in fact an intelligent deaf-mute who had been abandoned by his family, all of which dispels the enchantment of a noble savage entering civilization.

Feral children are to sociologists what identical twins are to geneticists—pure specimens that set the limit for determining the influences of the domain in question.[1] Identical twins, with their identical genomes, allow scientists to determine the influence of culture (environment) on the individual. Feral children do the same sort of thing, allowing scientists (in theory) to determine the influence of specifically human cultural practices on the individual. The problem with the latter is that we cannot run experiments on children by depriving them of contact with other

---

[1] Hermits are also of interest as idealized thought experiments, a true hermit being a person who has no living relations and has separated himself entirely from civilization, which he will never rejoin.

humans. (This is the reference to the forbidden experiment in the title of Shattuck's book.) The inherent problem in the concept of studying feral children is that we cannot know they are truly feral unless we set up the experiment and precisely specify the initial conditions (which is forbidden). Otherwise we are always unsure of the effects on the child. Ideally, we would have identical twins, one of which became feral as an infant, as did Mowglie and Tarzan, while the other grew up within civilized society.

Imagine a true feral child, one who has never had contact with another human. If such a child could develop their own private language it would be a language with no objective basis (no anchor outside the mind of the individual) by which to fix its rules and so could be changed continually at the whim (and memory) of the user. But rules that are allowed to change at any time in any way do not really constitute rules, and language depends on rules for its existence. Thus, a truly private language may very well be impossible. This is the conclusion of Ludwig Wittgenstein in his work, *Philosophical Investigations*. For him, a private language is one which can, in principle, be understood by only one person, its inventor. There are various interpretations of Wittgenstein's private language argument, whether, for instance, he is making a statement about the importance of the effervescence of memory, but these need not concern us here. We are concerned primarily with the social nature of language, for language is what makes culture possible. Feral children are of interest in this context for they have no culture by definition, since culture necessarily involves at least two humans.

§2 *IDEAS, BELIEFS, AND OBJECTIFICATION.*

For our usage, an idea is any object apprehended or conceived of by the mind. An idea thus need not correspond to an actual physical object. I can have an idea of a unicorn as well as an idea of an automobile. I can also have an idea of an idea. Our discussion in chapter 5 concerning conceptual schemes was an elaboration of the connections we make between ideas. We generally think of these ideas as residing internally (within our mind), what we will refer to as subjective ideas. But our subjective ideas can become external, or objective, by means of social interaction via language. In particular, language allows us to share ideas publicly. This process with respect to ideas is called objectification.

Abstract general terms, crucial to linguistic development, are objectified ideas which occur when we recognize specific objects or actions as being the same in some respect (having characteristics in common). This recognition is a form of associative learning, and as such is a fundamental feature of our cognitive processing. For example, the word 'cow' can refer to any or all cows; it is not, and cannot be, cow-specific. Once we agree to use the word 'cow' to designate objects with commonly-held characteristics, the word 'cow' becomes objective in the sense that it is now itself an object that can be referred to by many different people (those who share the language).

Languages may depend on rules, but these rules need not be written down (as indicated by primary oral cultures). Instead, linguistic rules are based on agreed-upon behavior. If I say, "Bring me the milk," and you bring me a brick, all other things being equal, your behavior indicates we have failed to agree upon an anchor for the term 'milk.'

I'm always in awe when it is announced that daylight savings time will begin in the spring and everyone in the country moves their clocks forward by one hour on a certain date. You can rebel against this conformity, but you will lose. But why should I be in such awe of daylight savings time conformity when the same principle is at work every time I drive a car and every time I speak a word and someone understands what I mean? I could rebel against this public conformity, too, but I would lose. I could, that is, decide to drive on the left instead of the right or use the word 'hot' for 'cold' and vice versa, but the resulting confusions would quickly become disastrous.

Language gives rise to a plethora of objective behaviors. With the advent of city-dwelling (made possible by agricultural developments) and the resulting population pressures, humans had to formulate rules to live by. But the existence of rules dictates the formation of other institutions, for punishments must be meted out if the rules are broken, and this necessitates law-making and law-enforcing institutions, that is, government. And what if someone is arrested and wants to argue his case? Now we will need lawyers and courts and judges. Once these are established and everyone acknowledges their existence and function, they become objective in the same way words are within a language. These public institutions further give rise to public roles. People are identified as participating within these institutions, and are thus identified as, say, lawyers, judges, criminals, doctors. All this behavior is predicated by and dependent upon an ephemeral cloud of objectified ideas that depend for their existence simply upon the agreement of groups of people.[2]

We can liken this ephemerality to the value of our money (Figure 6–1). The ancient idea of the monetary system was that coin would be issued based on something of value stored safely away. In medieval times, goldsmiths (forerunners of bankers) would hold a person's gold and issue paper based on the value of the gold. The person holding the paper could then turn the paper in to the goldsmith and get the gold, or he could trade the paper to someone else for other commodities. This was the origin of the concept of paper money. When governments began printing paper money the concept demanded they could only print money for which they had gold in reserve to back it up (like goldsmiths). This was known as the gold standard. But eventually, the complexity of economies led the U.S. to abandon the gold standard. The result is fiat money, or money with no gold to back it up. Upon what, then, is the value of our money based? Public perception. As long as enough people believe in our currency it retains its value. If doubt arises, devaluation follows. This relationship is dialectical:[3] the value of the dollar depends on public perception, and public perception depends upon the value of the dollar. If the public

---

[2] I think the attraction to dystopian scenarios (dystopia is the opposite of utopia), for example, after a nuclear holocaust or viral epidemic, is the same attraction we find toward feral children. A dystopia is an ideal thought experiment, a starting over, though not completely—there is the baggage of the previous culture to deal with, as if in a reincarnation with a past. Both of these indulge our desire to abstract certain aspects of our lives to see what the result would be like.

[3] A relationship between any two things is termed dialectical when one influences and thus changes the other, and that change in turn influences and changes the one, which change in turn influences and changes the other, and so on.

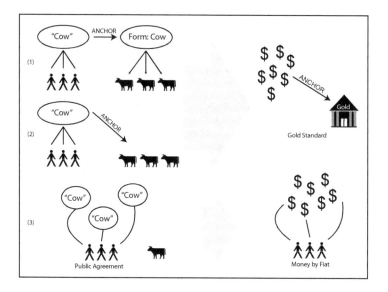

FIGURE 6–1

The concept of anchoring. In the top diagram our language anchors are compared to a currency anchor (the gold standard). (1) is the Platonic notion that anchors our concept of an object in another world (the world of the forms (see box on page 129). (2) is the modern view that our words are anchored in objects in the world (the museum view). Finally, (3) is the idea considered here that there is no external anchor to our words. There is only agreed-upon behavior. This is compared to the economic example of leaving the gold standard.

trust were to fail, the value of the dollar would spiral, which would generate more distrust, and so on.

This same kind of dialectical relation exists between our individual selves and objective ideas, especially those concerning the formulation of our self-image. For example, I might define myself in terms of a public idea such as artistic or quirky or judge or thief, or some combination of these. If so, my idea of myself is formed around the characteristics of my perception of the public idea and the informal societal rules which define it. My interaction with these ideas can change these ideas, which in turn can change my self-concept, which can lead to further changes in the ideas…

§3 ASIDE: ANALOGY AND COGNITION

There is an important relationship between abstract general ideas and the concept of analogy as the core of human cognition. Forming abstract general concepts via associations of ideas and then making further associations between these complex concepts may very well form the basis of our cognitive processes.

[E]very concept we have is essentially nothing but a tightly packaged bundle of analogies, and... all we do when we think is to move fluidly from concept to concept—in other words, to leap from one analogy-bundle to another—and... such concept-to-concept leaps are themselves made via analogical connection... (Hofstadter 499)

We originally form our concepts by experiencing the world. We usually label these with words from our language. Thus a child sees an animal and stores this sensation in its memory under a label provided by culture: 'dog.' Later, another animal is observed which is similar though different, but is also labeled 'dog.' Thus does the child begin to populate its concept of dog. A child who has only experienced one or two dogs and then experiences a cat for the first time, may respond with "Doggy!" This conceptual error is corrected by the parents and eventually the child is able to distinguish between dogs and cats with ease, making its own delineations concerning the world. When a barking animal appears the child now knows it to be a dog rather than a cat or a cow.

All this indicates that we share an objectified idea of dog, which is extremely useful for communication purposes, for it gives us an objective standard by which to anchor our concepts. This might give us the illusion that we are somehow sharing the exact same concept, that there really is a concept "out there" existing extramentally. This is what Plato thought (see box below). Indeed, this may have been the source of his positing a world of forms in which such ideas existed, but there is no need to create such fictions. There is only agreed-upon behavior. To say there is an objectified idea of a dog is just to say that we both exhibit dog-recognition-behavior (but see box on page 131).

Meanwhile, our individual concepts are extremely diverse, for not only do we have the concept of dog, but we then compare aspects of this concept with other concepts and create myriads of combinations. This analogical ability, the ability to recognize abstruse similarities between parts of things, allows us to compose even more complex concepts based on those being compared. Consider, for example, a dog's hind leg. I remember the first time I heard a particular hole at a golf course being described as one that takes a "dogleg to the left." We immediately know what this means, that is, we see the analogy between the layout of a golf course

---

PLATO'S WORLD OF THE FORMS

Plato (428-348 BC) believed that human knowledge consisted in our being able to grasp concepts that exist in another world (the world of the forms). These forms were eternal and unchanging, unaffected by anything we do in this world. For example, when we look at two circles drawn on a piece of paper, how do we know they are both circles? We know this, says Plato, because we recognize the "one thing" they share, namely, the abstract, eternal form of circularity. We do this by means of a mental act which gives us access to the extramental form-world.

This sounds strange to us today. We prefer to say that 'circle' is an abstract general term we use to refer to specific kinds of figures, and that this term is based upon agreed-upon behavior. Plato, though, was dealing with issues no one else had dealt with during his time, and so succumbed to the human penchant for reification (projecting mental states into reality). The beauty of the Platonic approach, of course, is that it gives the words in our language an absolute anchor, not subject to human whim.

green and a dog's hind leg. Seeing this opens other possibilities. A quick internet search shows that the word 'dogleg' also applies to a stair configuration in which there is a landing midway which turns and continues upward, a shift pattern on a floor-mounted manual transmission in a car, a guided powered turn with respect to a rocket's upward trajectory, and the jagged pixelated graphics on a computer screen.[4] All of these are doglegs.

Once we understand the complexity of our concepts, how they are shaped by experience and analogy, we begin to understand their fuzziness. The beauty of their fuzziness is their flexibility in allowing us to make (often obscure) tangential connections. The downside lies in the fact that we humans like to make black and white distinctions where there are none (pebble-rock fallacy).

The ultimate goal of communication is to replicate the ideas existing within my head in your head (see Figure 6–2). This would be impossible with a private language, but if we can first objectify our ideas, anchor them publicly to agreed-upon behavior, we can then have some certainty that your ideas are matching my ideas. The reception will always be under-determined by the signal (since the reception is a theory and all theories are under-determined by evidence), but this semantic ambiguity gives rise to all the joys and traumas of interpretation.

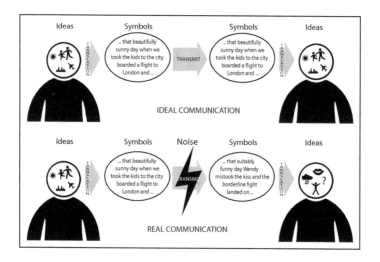

FIGURE 6–2
The goal of communication is to reproduce the ideas in my head in your head. Ideally this would take place with perfect replication. This goal was the impetus behind the Platonic forms. If there is an absolute, unchanging reference for our words, these could be reproduced with absolute fidelity from speaker to speaker. The real world is much less precise.

---

[4] This latter is interesting because pixelated graphics do not particularly look like dogs' legs, but they do look like the stairway configuration mentioned above, so it may be that the term evolved from the stairway configuration usage and refers only obliquely to the dogleg concept. That is, it piggy-backs (?!) upon the dog-leg usage.

EMBODIED PERCEPTION

Embodied perception is the idea that our concept formation is not completely arbitrary, but rather depends to a great extent upon the makeup of our bodies and our brains and our experience of the world delimited by these. I think this must be correct. Our concept of boundaries, for example, is established by the limits of our reach. We then extend this by means of metaphor. George Lakoff (1999, 2003) gives numerous examples of how our fundamental concepts (space, time, self) are based on metaphors with foundations in our bodily experience. The infant, for example experiences other humans, particularly parents, looming over her continually—humans upon whom the child depends completely. In other words, physical size becomes associated with physical strength. The child then comes to associate the looming with power (on top or over = powerful), and this is transferred metaphorically into "above" as powerful, dominant, regal; and "below" as weak, subservient, lowly. This concept, then, spreads (again, via metaphor) throughout our language.

I have control *over* her. I am on *top* of the situation. He's in a *superior* position. He's at the *height* of his power. He's in the *high* command. He's in the *upper* echelon. His power *rose*. He ranks *above* me in strength. He is *under* my control. He *fell* from power. His power is on the *decline*. He is my social *inferior*. He is *low* man on the totem pole (1999: 15)

This idea, that there is an experiential, bodily, basis behind our metaphors, and that metaphors (which are analogies formed by means of association) are the basis of our cognition, is radical. Embracing it will change your interpretation of the basic philosophical concepts we use to think about our world.

§4 REVERSE ENGINEERING

So far I have considered language and its place in expanding our individual conceptual schemes into the public domain. Language allows us to objectify our ideas, which we symbolize in words. Before I move on to consider the effects of these objectifications, though, I must first discuss how we come to understand and explain the actions of others. The problem is that we are blind to each others intentions, which is a function of the privacy of our mental states. All we have to go on is behavior.

You say you love me, but I saw you kissing another man in a cafe. Thus your behavior belies your words.

How do we understand the workings of a process to which we are blind? We assume purposive behavior and then try to fit the subjective intentions into a theoretical framework that explains the actions.

I assume you would only kiss another man that way if you were attracted to him, but this means you don't love me like you say you do.

This is how I attempt to gain insight into your mind, and this same type of reasoning allows us to look at other, similarly purposive activities. Thus the issues here are important because understanding them will clarify the way we use the concepts of design, purpose and function in a way that will lend itself to understanding not only human intentions but social rules and physical systems as well.

When a radically new technology is developed, it is immediately scrutinized by potential competitors (predators?). If they can obtain a copy they will be able to disassemble it, determine how it works and produce their own (possibly cheaper) version. This process is known as reverse engineering, and is particularly interesting in cases concerning sophisticated technological weaponry. When we take a widget apart in order to determine how it works we presuppose that everything within it has a specific relationship to the function of the widget. For example, if I am interested in how a toaster works, when I scrutinize the parts of the toaster I will always keep in mind that the function of the toaster is to toast. Knowing this is the end result sheds light on (gives meaning to) the parts of the toaster. I might ask: "Why would a designer include this particular wire?" and the answer might be: "Because it connects the heating element to the timing mechanism that allows the user to control the degree to which the bread is toasted."

Most designers do not include irrelevant parts which would affect production costs, weight, size, and so on. If irrelevant parts are included, it is usually either by mistake or in order to intentionally deceive those attempting the reverse engineering. This might be true, for example, of a sophisticated bomb made by terrorists, which might include superfluous wiring and other items in order to mislead the bomb squad personnel who are attempting to disarm it. Still, in such cases, even the superfluous parts have a purpose, and the bomb squad personnel, knowing this, have to keep the possibility in mind. It is rare to find an example where there is simply no reason why a part is included in a finished product. Daniel Dennett (1995) gives a humorous example of a case in which two inventors had designed an electronic component for a military application:

> Their prototype had two circuit boards, and the top one kept sagging, so, casting about for a quick fix, they spotted a brass doorknob in the lab which had just the right thickness. They took it off its door and jammed it into place between the two circuit boards on the prototype. Sometime later, one of these engineers was called in to look at a problem the military was having with the actual manufactured systems, and found to his amazement that between the circuit board in each unit was a very precisely milled brass duplicate of the original doorknob. (199)

This is an example of what has been referred to as a frozen accident, a characteristic the original purpose of which has disappeared though the characteristic itself continues to be passed on to future generations. The QWERTY keyboard attached to most computers is another example. The specific arrangement of the keys on most keyboards is not the optimal arrangement for speed. This arrangement (called QWERTY because of the first five letters on the keyboard) was designed for mechanical typewriters to ensure the least amount of interference with the keys as they physically struck the inked ribbon. This is an irrelevant concern with computers, but the arrangement was frozen in the design for various practical considerations. Notice the difficulty this arrangement might cause a future reverse engineer who doesn't know the history of keyboard development.[5]

The important point here is that we assume every characteristic within an object with a specific function has a reason for being (*raisonné d'être*), a purpose, whether it was an historical accident or a misdirection of some sort. When we look at a biological organism we assume the same—there is a reason for every characteristic. Postulating these reasons as explanations, though, can often lead to trouble. There are some seemingly obvious examples: the pleasure involved in sex probably evolved in order to entice us into having sex, which obviously benefits the transmission of one's DNA. But we noted, in chapter 3, the concept of genetic drift, in which random mutations are neither beneficial or detrimental to the organism at the time of mutation and thus tend to drift through the lineage. This may be the origin of the color of our eyes, for instance, which doesn't seem to be crucial to our survival. Genetic drift, then, muddies our ability to understand traits as purposive.

To take our original example, suppose a one-celled organism suffered a mutation that thickened the cell wall ever so slightly—not enough to protect it from predators, but also not enough to hinder it in any way. In a future scenario, if the environment changed, this slight thickening might make the difference between life and death. Those organisms who did not possess the trait would die, leaving only those who possessed it, and these would pass that trait on to their offspring. Observing the organism in its present environment we might be tempted to explain the development of the thickened cell wall as a protection against the environment, but this would be incorrect. Its present function is that it protects the organism, but this does not fully explain how the organism came to possess it (though it might explain how it came to dominate the population).

We could also imagine a scenario in which a trait was passed on for a very specific reason, but then turned out to be useful for other reasons as well. Stephen J. Gould named such examples exaptations (as opposed to adaptations). For example, we might ask why birds evolved wings. An incorrect answer to this is that birds evolved wings in order to fly; incorrect, for it presupposes evolutionary foresight (that flying was the goal and wings developed with that in mind) and we have already seen that evolution is blind to the future. The better way to answer this is to say that birds developed wings and it later turned out they could use them to fly. Scientists speculate that the membranous connections between the phalanges of ancient wading birds may have allowed them to better spot their prey beneath the surface of the water (by using them to shade the light). If this was in fact an adaptation, it was only later that this trait was further exapted into gliding and later into flying. On a more mundane level, if you are using your exercise machine as a convenient spot on which to hang your discarded clothing after work, then you have already experienced exaptation first hand.

Thus, we must be very careful when we try to specify the origin of any specific trait.[6] In general, though, it makes sense to consider the traits of an organism in

---

[5] This is the basis of my earlier claim that knowing the history of a developing system is essential to understanding that system.

[6] Stephen J. Gould often chastised evolutionary biologists for inventing numerous tales to reverse engineer traits found in organisms. He called these "just so stories" after Kipling's collection of "explanations" for various animal characteristics (such as the leopard's spots and the elephant's trunk).

REVERSE ENGINEERING THE CLITORIS

"In the clitoris alone we see a sexual organ so pure of purpose that it needn't moonlight as a secretory or excretory device." (Angier 58) Angier wonders, then, "why is it that women are the ones with the organ dedicated exclusively to pleasure, when men are the ones who are supposed to be dedicated exclusively to sexual pleasure. Men are portrayed as wanting to go at it all the time, women as preferring a good cuddle; yet a man feels preposterously peacockish if he climaxes three or four times in a night, compared to the fifty or hundred orgasms that a sexually athletic woman can have in an hour or two. Maybe you thought it was some sort of cosmic joke... As it happens, evolutionary thinkers are engaged in a vigorous debate over the point, or pointlessness, of the clitoris and its bosom buddy, the female orgasm. They are asking whether the capacity for orgasm does a woman any good and thus can be counted an adaptation that has been selected over the wash of time, or whether it is, to borrow a phrase from Stephen Jay Gould, a glorious accident." (65) The female orgasm, it seems, is unnecessary from a biological point of view; that is, it has no fitness function, no evolutionary benefit. We can understand the evolution of the male orgasm, which spews sperm by the millions into the female. This is the evolutionary shotgun approach: produce enough of something and at least some are bound to reach the goal. But females can conceive without explosions—no orgasm is needed. With this in mind, here are three major evolutionary explanations for the existence of the clitoris and its corresponding female orgasm:

1. *The clitoris is a vestigial penis.* The fertilized egg is bisexual; it contains everything needed to make either a male or a female human, depending on which genetic switches are turned on (or not turned on). Clitoris and penis both develop from the same genital ridge within the fetus. If the decision is male, a penis is produced; if female, the clitoris is merely leftover material, "like male nipples" The clitoris is thus an unnecessary remnant just happened to give women pleasure..

2. *The clitoris is a vestigial clitoris.* On this view the clitoris was, in the ancient past, an adaptation, but is now no longer necessary in the way that it was before. Like our craving for salt, which once served to stimulate us to imbibe the precious and rare mineral whenever it was discovered, but which now serves merely to increase our blood pressure, since salt is ubiquitous in modern society, so also the clitoris was at one time necessary to help ensure a woman became pregnant. On this view, ancient females were not monogamous, but had sex with multiple males, multiple times, in multiple places. The clitoris, with its orgasmic potential, rewarded this behavior (still evident in female Bonobos), which, it seems, would help guarantee pregnancy.

3. *The clitoris is, and always was, an adaptation.* On this view the clitoris exists, not in order to spur the female into sex, but rather to urge her to take control of her sexuality. In Angier's words, "The clitoris not only applauds when a woman flaunts her mastery; it will give a standing ovation." (70) The clitoris will not normally respond to wham-bam-thank-you-ma'am sex, and provides a substantial reward for the woman's success in slowing her partners' poundings. This may give her incentive to stay with a partner who gives her this pleasure—and may also take better care of the offspring.

There is also evidence that the female orgasm is beneficial to pregnancy, which means it would be to the man's benefit to allow the female to achieve orgasm. On this theory (propounded by Baker and Bellis, in their book *Sperm Wars*), "the timing of a woman's orgasm relative to a man's ejaculation influences whether or not his semen has a shot at fertilizing her eggs. If a woman climaxes shortly after her partner ejaculates, her cervix, the gateway to the uterus, will do a spectacular thing. As it pulses rhythmically, the cervix reaches down like a fish's mouth and sucks in the semen deposited at its doorstep." (Angier 73)

These clitoral explanations may be no different, but the speculation is interesting nonetheless.

light of their purpose with respect to survival. That is, natural selection gives the appearance of design which is what allows us to speak of the traits as having a purpose. This also happens in cultural selection, to which we must now turn. (We have seen an example of this already in the example above where 'dogleg' applied to a pixelated graphic.)

§5 MEMES

A meme is an objectified idea. Once objectified ideas take on lives of their own they are beyond the control of the individual or individuals who originally conceived of them. Richard Dawkins first formulated the concept of a meme in his 1962 book, *The Selfish Gene*, in which he focused on the gene as the vehicle of evolution. The sole purpose of a gene is to replicate itself. Our bodies, indeed, our selves, are machines, built by our genes to facilitate getting copies of themselves into the next generation. Understanding this concept can change the way you look at developmental histories.[7]

Your DNA is a group of genes that have joined forces over the years since life first developed, becoming more and more complex as time passed. Two genes will combine forces only if their association is mutually beneficial. Our 25,000 (plus or minus) genes have clumped together to form both our bodies and our minds, but the purpose of these macro-bodies, these external shells, is merely to allow the individual genes to push themselves into the next generation.

We can speak loosely and say that genes "want" to replicate; that is their sole "desire" or "purpose." Again, genes, as sections of DNA strands, do not have any wants or desires, but it is enlightening, at times, to speak as if they do. We speak this way because, as we saw above, we can reverse engineer genes as we might a mechanical invention, and ask their purpose. Genes are referred to as "selfish" because their purpose is their own replication. Genes are interested in you as a whole only insofar as you can pass them along to the next generation. Once you have fulfilled this function you are no longer valuable, which is why we grow old and die. Memes are to social evolution what genes are to biological evolution, that is, genes are the vehicles of biological evolution while memes are the vehicles of cultural evolution.

Humans are, by nature, imitators. Indeed, some have claimed that this ability, *mimesis*, is what makes us uniquely human.

> When you imitate someone else, something is passed on. This 'something' can then be passed on again, and again, and so take on a life of its own. We might call this thing an idea, an instruction, a behavior, a piece of information... It is the 'meme'. (Blackmore 4)

---

[7] Dawkins' claim concerning the gene as the vehicle of evolution is controversial. Acceptance of it denies the plausibility of group selection, and indeed, it looks like group selection can only apply in very specific scenarios, though the concept is slowly making a limited comeback on the evolutionary scene (see, e.g., Wilson 2012).

Imitation is at the heart of cognition, for it is the basis of our ability to draw analogies. When we see a behavior, say maybe a dance move, we store a copy in memory, and based on this make an analogy from the memory of that behavior to what we can do. Imitation and analogy both seem to depend on the recognition of things as being the same in some way. This recognition is what makes a behavior replicable. DNA makes a physical copy of itself, which is passed into the next generation. Our brains make copies of ideas which have been objectified (made public).

The spread of certain memes is often described as viral or epidemic. Dawkins tells the following story:

> When I was about nine, my father taught me to fold a square of paper to make an origami Chinese junk... I went back to school and infected my friends with the skill, and it then spread around the school with the speed of the measles and pretty much the same epidemiological time-course... my father himself originally picked up the Chinese Junk meme during an almost identical epidemic at the same school 25 years earlier. The earlier virus was launched by the school matron. Long after the old matron's departure, I had reintroduced her meme to a new cohort of small boys. (in Blackmore ix)

Think for a moment of an idea as something that, like a gene, "desires" to pass itself on, to make copies of itself. When such an idea becomes public it has this chance. I remember going to Disney World as a child where there was a rather silly ride called "It's a Small World," in which you sat in a boat and floated through a maze of dolls and decorations. It was all very boring and I wouldn't even remember it if it hadn't been for the song that was played over and over in the background: "It's a small world after all; it's a small world after all..." Anyone I ever talked to that heard that song still remembered it (and most hated it as well). The song was a meme, and a very successful one. Whatever it was about that song (the rhythm, the words, the repetition), it stuck, and so made copies of itself in our brains. There were other songs in other rides at Disney World that I don't remember at all. Less successful memes.

Just as the phenotype of a gene can be extended past the organism itself (the beaver's dam), so also the phenotype of a meme (an idea) can be extended. Consider, for example, the book-meme, a highly successful meme which has replicated itself endlessly since someone first thought of making one. If we consider the book-meme as a replicator that desires to make copies of itself, we might see libraries and bookstores, reading groups, book reviews and even writers as simply a book's way of insuring its own survival. These would all be considered part of the extended phenotype of a book.[8] Just as our bodies, brains and consciousness are all extensions used by our genes to help ensure their replication, so also libraries and bookstores are extensions of the book-meme to ensure its replication.

Once you appreciate this idea it gives you an entirely new view of culture, for culture is simply an expression of our humanity, which is an expression of our genes. That is, culture is to humans what the milky froth is to a cappuccino—a byproduct.

---

[8] Or maybe a book is a complex group of memes like our DNA is a complex group of genes. It utilizes the memes of printing, paper, binding, and so on, and all these use the book to pass themselves on, which in turn uses libraries and bookstores.

On a more personal level, memes continually vie for your attention, filling your head with "noise" that can only be shut down with some effort. A meme wants to be reproduced, and going public is the only way this will happen on a vast scale, so it is to the meme's advantage to pop into your head and pester you until you spread it. You see now how successful that it's-a-small-world mene really is—it succeeded in making itself prominent enough in my mind so that I included it in this chapter, which you are now reading, which means it has spread into your head. If you've never heard the song before, whatever you do, don't look it up and listen to it. Stop the madness!

Memes are as blind to the future as any evolutionary process, and so may eventually lead to consequences not in their (or our) best interest. Memes can hurt and kill individual humans, but memes don't care—all they want to do is reproduce. Racism, for instance, is a meme, as are nationalism and religion. Certain religions in particular are highly successful memes. Imagine the advantages of a meme that has, built into it, the following instructions: (1) never question or discard the meme, even in the face of contradiction, (2) spread the meme to as many people as possible, (3) threaten with eternal damnation those who do not possess the meme.

We often think of genes and memes as having to benefit us individually, but this is not so. We are the expression of a large number of genes which only want to push themselves into the next generation. Consider the pig, which by complete accident happened to have the genetic trait flesh-that-is-tasty-to-humans. You might think the pig, if it could think this way, would consider this a terrible gene, leading to the ill-treatment and destruction of many individual pigs. And yet, from the pig-gene's perspective, the trait of tasting-good-to-humans is the best thing that ever happened to pigs, for, liking the taste, we do our best to multiply pig genes as much as possible—and we're good at it. The "new white meat" ad campaign was just a pig-gene's way of getting itself reproduced.

Sober and Wilson (1999) tell the story of an ant, a snail and a trematode parasite. The ant performs an extremely odd behavior. It climbs to the highest grass stalk it can find and sits there, transfixed, awaiting its demise. The fate it awaits is the fate it is asking for by sitting astride the highest stalk, for there it is most likely to be consumed by grazing cattle or sheep. Why this suicidal behavior? Enter the trematode parasite *Dicrocoelium dendriticum*, which spends the adult stage of its life cycle in the liver of cows and sheep.

> The eggs [of the trematode] exit with the feces of the mammalian host and are eaten by land snails, which serve as hosts for an asexual stage of the parasite life cycle. Two generations are spent within the snail before the parasite forms yet another stage, the cercaria, which exits the snail enveloped in a mucus mass that is ingested by ants. About fifty cercariae enter the ant along with its meal. Once inside, the parasites bore through the stomach wall and one of them migrates to the brain of the ant (the subesophagal ganglion), where it forms a thin-walled cyst known as the brain worm. The other cercariae form thick-walled cysts. The brain worm changes the behavior of the ant, causing it to spend large amounts of time on the tips of grass blades. (18)

Once ingested by grazing cattle or sheep, the thick-walled cysts migrate to the mammalian liver where they live out their adult life cycle until being shat out once again and eaten by snails. Daniel Dennett has compared this behavior to that of religious terrorists who will strap bombs to themselves and fly airplanes into large buildings. Memes have infected their brains, and their own destruction ensures the survival of the meme. This should give us pause to appreciate the power of memes.

§6 CULTURAL VS BIOLOGICAL EVOLUTION

Evolution never stops. As long as there are mutations occurring our genome is changing, even if the mutations just drift through time. Evolution never stops, but the advent of human consciousness has slowed its already lethargic pace, has made it less likely that some genes will be bred out of the gene pool.[9] There was a time in human history when being born even partially blind was a death sentence, as it still is to animals in the wild. Consider a lion cub who is born blind or lame or sickly (we will say due to a genetic mutation within the sex cells of its mother). Since it will not be able to feed itself or protect itself from predators it will die young and that particular mutation will die with it. Every cub the mother has that possesses that mutation will die before it reproduces, so the gene will not be passed on.

So also with humans. It's considered bad form in modern society to kill a child born blind, but it was not always so. In a primary oral society[10] the blind may have become "remembers" and so would have had a useful function, but before that to be born blind meant being a burden that society would not be willing to bear. Today, though, blindness is no longer a burden, and for those with poor eyesight, eyeglasses are an easy fix, so that as we age we need not die from lack of sight. So also with disease.

At some point in our history humans or proto-humans developed the ability to think about the future in a reflective manner. Squirrels gather nuts in anticipation of winter, but this is not a reflective behavior. As long as behavior is purely instinctual organisms are completely determined by a combination of evolutionary and environmental factors. They are born, grow, search for food, mature, reproduce and die, a cycle interspersed with floods, earthquakes, famines, sickness, and accidents. This process is as determined as that of the life cycle of a star or the formation of a galaxy or solar system. In order to control this process one must become conscious of the process or of some small part of it. This is what reflective learning allows.

Imagine the early human or proto-human who maybe saw a mammoth fall from a cliff and realized (by analogy) that he might be able to make that happen on purpose. There is a significant difference between a cheetah chasing and killing a gazelle and a band of humans driving a mammoth herd over a cliff, and within this difference lies the key to the importance of culture. Reflection allows us to change the process of evolution for our benefit. It allows us to build tools to extend

---

[9] Consciousness slows biological evolution, at least at first. The ability to manipulate genetics, though, may accelerate biological evolution.

[10] A primary oral society is one untainted by exposure to writing or print. There are no such societies left today. Without writing, all histories have to be committed to memory and transmitted by word of mouth. Thus, certain individuals within society would be designated as rememberers in order to provide this function. These were the poets (such as Homer), for poetic structures provided mnemonic devices making it easier to remember large amounts of data. There was a time when all cultures were primary oral cultures.

the power of our eyes, hands, and feet; it allows us to use these tools to protect ourselves from the ravages of fate, to rise above nature in all its tooth and claw red-ness. In doing so we are changing our futures, controlling them in a way that the blindness of evolution would never allow. We have bypassed some of our biological processes with cultural processes by becoming progressively more reflective.

§7 SOCIAL GROUPS

A social group, in its broadest definition, is composed of individuals who share a belief or set of beliefs. On this definition there is a social group whose members all have blue as their favorite color and have nothing else in common. Such a broad definition is of little interest since it doesn't help us explain behavior. On the other hand, we could get very precise and define a group in terms of its structure, leader-ship, rules, sanctions, and so on, but here we have erred in the opposite direction. For our purposes we simply need to appreciate the complexity of group behavior and so will work with our own, very lax, definition. For our purpose:

> (SG) A social group is formed when individuals interact on the basis of common core values with which they identify.

Thus, a social group can be seen as a collection of conceptual schemes which have specific ideas or sets of ideas in common. For example, suppose a person is an avid bicyclist and so shares many core bicyclist-values with other avid bicyclists. On the broadest definition of a social group this person would belong to the bicyclist group even if he was a hermit bicyclist and never interacted with anyone. On our preferred definition (SG), though, he does not belong to the social group bicyclists because he is asocial. There are pros and cons for both views, but the above defini-tion is preferred because it insists on sociality. Hermits are not members of social groups no matter what their interests (and there is no social group composed of all hermits).

SG is thus strong enough to exclude hermits, but lax enough to allow for vary-ing interpretations with respect to certain aspects of sociality. For example, can a person be a member of a social group without explicitly identifying with that group or even denying membership in the group? Heroin addicts who admit they are addicts form a social group, but what about the heroin addict who is in denial about his addiction? Or, consider a person who denies membership in a group out of igno-rance. A person may, for example, be a registered Democrat, may refer to himself as a Democrat and think of himself as a Democrat, yet not only agree with all the commonly held planks in the Republican party, but also vote Republican in every election. Does this person belong to the Republican social group even though he denies membership in that group? I take it nothing important hangs on the answer to these questions. I would consider neither the heroin addict who is in denial nor the closet Republican as members of the respective social groups, but you might disagree depending on your interpretation of what it means to interact.

Regardless of how you interpret SG, you are not usually considered a mem-ber of a social group by those who are bona fide members of a group unless you consciously identify with the core values of the group. Individuals not holding the core values, even though asserting membership in a group, might be denigrated by those who do hold the core values. In my youth I experienced this quite often. As an adrenaline junkie, I got involved in many different activities: skydiving, scuba diving, hang gliding, rock climbing, but did not want to make these my vocation. I just wanted the experiences. I would join a group of, say, skydivers, who would take me in and teach me their sport. Most of the skydivers I knew spent every waking moment skydiving, and if you didn't, you weren't really a skydiver. When I first began I fit this profile and was accepted without question into the group, but as my enthusiasm waned I would only participate every other weekend or so, and they became distant. I participated in their sport, but I was seen as an outsider, a weekend warrior, because I did not hold their core values. Again, notice the laxness of our definition, for who determines the core values of a group? If a group has become institutionalized there may be guidelines for becoming a member (the American Medical Association or the American Bar Association), but in many social groups membership is determined in an *ad hoc* fashion.

Social groups can be nested within other social groups indefinitely, that is, there is no limit to the levels of nesting that can occur. For example, a person might belong to all of the following social groups: Americans, cigarette smokers, Baptists, and males. Of these, both the Americans, cigarette smokers and Baptists are partially nested within the male group.

A social group functions like a social (or objective) conceptual scheme, it is a web of external beliefs, hopes, goals, some of which are more important than others. The beliefs within a social group also have to make sense, which means consistency is required within the group, and there is a corresponding notion of cognitive dissonance within the group when things do not make sense or when someone or something threatens the core values of a group. Since a social group is nothing more than a collection of commonly linked conceptual schemes, individual cognitive dissonance connected with core values of a social group will either emanate to the group as a whole or will result in the individual leaving the group. A social group is said to be suffering from stress or dissonance only insofar as its individual members are, that is, a social group has no ontological status beyond that of its collective members.

Social groups cluster around objectified core values. These core values are memes. Any desire, hope, goal or belief that you have that you share with another person somewhere is a meme vying to pass itself on. If you transfer your excitement about the wonders of skydiving to a friend, this is a meme successfully passing itself on. The American Parachutist Association, an organized group which provides benefits to its members in the form of insurance and information, is like a bookstore, just another ploy used by a meme to pass itself on. So also with the American Medical Association, the function of which has less to do with healing the sick than ensuring the financial success of its members, keeping the defined group exclusive by means of a rigorous selection process.

§8   RECIPROCAL ALTRUISM

We have seen that genes are selfish. Their only desire is to replicate. How then, is it possible that altruistic (unselfish) behavior has evolved? Imagine a society of altruistic organisms, each helping the other when needed. In evolutionary terms this means expending energy helping others reproduce when it could be spent helping yourself reproduce. Within this utopia suppose a mutation occurs which makes one of the offspring selfish instead of altruistic. This selfish organism has a much better chance of reproducing (and thus passing on its selfishness) than the altruistic organisms since it is devoting all of its time and energy to itself rather than to others. Thus the selfish gene will flourish and eventually breed the altruists out of the gene pool. Guaranteed. Whence, then, altruism?

The answer lies in something called reciprocal altruism in which organisms exhibit unselfish behavior, but only on the condition that it is reciprocated. One example of this occurs among vampire bats. These bats must feed every sixty hours or they will die, but hunts are not always successful, so at the end of every hunt those who were successful share with those who were not. But the bats will not share with those who have not themselves shared in the past. Cheaters (or free-riders) cannot be allowed within such a society for the reason inferred above — cheaters always prosper at the expense of the altruistic. This is a nice quandary: you enhance your fitness (your ability to pass on your genes) by sharing reciprocally, but this behavior opens the door for cheaters who are detrimental to your fitness. Thus, along with reciprocal altruism some sort of cheater detection method must develop. With bats, for instance, this means they must be able to keep track of the individual bats within their social group, note which ones cheat, and then refuse to share blood with them.

There are some interesting consequences of this behavior. In early human hunter-gatherer societies handling cheaters was not a problem, for these societies were composed of close-knit kin-groups who were intimately acquainted with each other. Cheaters were easy to spot and easy to punish. But as population increased so also did anonymity, which is ideal for an aspiring cheat. This may have prompted the development of the moral emotions such as guilt, honor, trust, and so on. It also emphasized the importance of reputation.

Reputation is a fascinating concept, having its roots in remote societies whose lives are intertwined with easily stolen assets, such as sheep or cattle. Scottish herdsmen developed a reputation for horrendous violence against those who dared steal from them, all of which ensured that, knowing this reputation, one would think twice before doing so. Reputations are social entities, spread by word of mouth; they depend on what people say and they are crucial in remote societies for discouraging cheats. Anti-cheat devices thus gave rise to notions of honor and friendship in which individuals are trusted not to cheat. To break these bonds was anathema. All of this in order to discourage cheating.[11]

Self-deception, that *ad hoc* handling of cognitive dissonance within our conceptual schemes, may also have its root in reciprocity responses. Cheaters must be convincing. Humans have developed intricate and subtle methods that allow us

---

[11] Nisbet and Cohen (*Culture of Honor*) describe this development. Gladwell (*Outliers*) popularized it (in chapter 6) showing the descent of the fierce Scots and their role in populating the southern states in America, leading to a culture of honor in the South that was much different from that of the North.

THE TRAGEDY OF THE COMMONS

The problem of cheaters arises in a concept developed by Garrett Hardin based on the old Colonial use of the commons area, acreage set aside for the use of all townspeople on which they could graze their cattle. The problem is that it is always in a person's best interest to graze as many cattle as possible on the commons (since it is free), but in doing so the commons is destroyed (over-grazed). The civic-minded person (the altruist) who limits the number of cattle he grazes on the commons will be the loser, and the commons will always end up destroyed.

The problem of the commons shows up today in many different areas. One is pollution of our natural resources. Lakes, rivers and oceans, as well as the air we breath, are commons (at least in theory). Corporations are notorious for using these commons as dumping grounds for toxic waste. Any corporation who takes the high road and refuses to pollute loses money (and the other companies will continue to pollute). On a more personal level, would you pay more money for a car or a house that is more eco-friendly? Would you do this even when you realize that other people won't? It seems as though the tragedy of the commons is a form of collective short-sightedness, or maybe the cultural equivalent of self-deception.

---

to surmise that a person is lying to us. The consummate cheater must circumvent these and learn to fool the system, and what better way to be convincing than to convince yourself. If you believe your own lies, then you are much more convincing when trying to foist those lies upon others.

The most important aspect of reciprocal altruism is that it may contain the germ of morality, for within reciprocal altruism lies the notion of empathy, which seems to be necessary for morality (see Baron-Cohen). Morality is primarily a social concept; it developed as a means of allowing individuals with different beliefs, hopes and desires to live together. In order for this to happen, at some basic level you must make the analogy that you are like me in certain ways—we are both human. This analogy must be expanded beyond mere externals. We must come to see that not only are we alike on the outside, but that we have the same ultimate concerns: our basic needs must be met, we don't like to suffer pain, we want to be loved and accepted, we want to achieve well-being. Once this analogy is made we might accept those other than kin into our trusting circle. The more we know about the way we humans function, the closer we can draw these analogies. We will examine the moral aspect of reciprocal altruism in more detail in chapter 14.

§9 DIALECTICAL RELATIONSHIPS

The relationship between individual humans and between individual humans and the social groups they construct is dialectical. Each is constantly changing according to input from the other and vice versa. Society thus forms a complex adaptive system, a dynamic system which cannot be understood simply in terms of its individual components. Sociology is the discipline that studies such systems, but complexity warrants, and has founded, a discipline of its own.

PRISONERS' DILEMMA

The prisoners' dilemma is a game theoretic device that illustrates some of the problems inherent in human relations. The game is usually set up using prisoners as an example, but I want to change the scenario slightly.

Imagine a college professor who assigns each student within a class a different research project, on which the entire course grade will depend. The way he will grade the project is a bit odd. First he randomly groups all students into pairs (you do not know who you are paired with). He then grades the projects based on the matrix below. All students are fully aware of this matrix. Here is how to read the matrix: If both students within a pair do the work and turn in their projects they will both get a B in the class (box on the lower right). If neither of them turns in their project they will both get a D in the class (box on the upper left). If only one of them turns in their project then the one who turned it in will fail the class (F), while the one who turned in nothing will get an A.

		Other Student	Other Student
Don't do the work	You	D,D	A,F
Do the work	You	F,A	B,B

What would you do? This game is called a dilemma because most people playing the game first decide that cooperating would be the best strategy. But once you realize that cooperating is the best (most rational) strategy, you realize your paired partner will come to the same decision, and if so then you should not turn in your project and get and A for doing nothing. But then, isn't your partner thinking the same thing?

There is no right way to play the game, but examining it is enlightening. This game was part of the strategic preparation for nuclear warfare and first strike strategies in the 1960's and 70's. You would hope, in such cases, that both sides would decide not to launch, but if you know the other side won't launch the temptation might be to launch.

This complex relationship has ramifications on how I think about myself, for I am constantly analyzing and adjusting my self-image in light of other people and what they think of me. This is the dialectic: I try to see myself as you see me and, if you are important enough to me, I will adjust my self-image to conform more closely to what I ascertain you want me to be like. This change causes a corresponding change in the way you see me, a change I will also have to adjust to. But this isn't all, for you are doing the same thing with respect to your self-image and my perception of you, and all of this is happening simultaneously.

Our ability to display multiple façades has led to the idea of social masks. We continually wear masks based on personas we create for each occasion based on the individuals or groups within which we move. I put on my skydiver-mask when I go skydiving, my good-son mask when I visit my parents, my professor mask when I teach. But we are not so simple as to require only one mask at a time. Our masks are nested as deep as our social groups.

Most people inherently divide their behavior into public and private. The private mask is for the people we trust and we tend to think of this as taking off our masks, but there's no reason to think this is our true self. It is just a persona we are comfortable with in the presence of friends or family. This public-private distinction gives rise to interesting anomalies. In the presence of trusted friends, for example, we can desist with public niceties that control and shape our behavior: we need not dress the same, we can swear, tell crude jokes, expel noxious gasses, and drop all pretences of political correctness. When you are in such a private arena you can "be yourself." But are you really being yourself? Such thoughts lead to the question: what am I like without a mask? Erving Goffman (1959) claims there is no true self behind our masks. We just are a compilation of our masks. Here psychology, biology and sociology merge.

If you laugh at a racist joke when you are with your friends, are you a racist? If you allow your friends to make sexist comments without correcting them are you a sexist? I think we would be too hasty, too simplistic, to make a black and white judgment in such cases without understanding more about the person. Social relations are complex because humans are complex. We make valuations and cost-benefit analyses based on those valuations continually. Do I value this person as a friend? Why? How important is it that I keep this person as a friend?

We reverse engineer the selves of other people by observing the groups they adhere to. But other people know we will be reverse engineering their behavior in this way and so might act with this in mind (just as the terrorist includes fake wires and switches in his bombs). And of course we know that they know that we know… Politicians are particularly good examples since their livelihood depends upon their public persona. A politician might go to church, for example, in order to foster his conservative religious followers, but they might be suspicious that this is just an act, based on some of his legislation (which constitutes anomalous behavior). A politician who upholds conservative religious values and then is caught propositioning another person of the same sex in an airport restroom is publicly ridiculed and reviled as two-faced or hypocritical. We want those making our public policy to be true to their publicly proclaimed beliefs since they are setting public policy.

Everybody lies. That is, if lying consists in hiding parts of our self from some people at some time, then everybody lies. Thank goodness. I remember having a good friend once confess a horrible secret to me. He did so because he thought everything should be open between us and that our friendship would be better for it. But I never viewed him the same afterward and our friendship never recovered. As we have seen (in chapter 2), part of the beauty of subjectivity is that we live within layers that even we do not understand. This is why extreme conditions often show us things about ourselves that we did not know before. But does this mean that we all have a hidden self that constitutes what we really are? I think not. The search for the true self is equivalent to the search for the real world, and is every bit as futile. (We will examine the concept of self in more detail in chapter 13.)

THE HANDICAP PRINCIPLE AND RELIABLE COMMUNICATION

We've all heard stories of extreme altruism manifested in particular species, from the wounded-wing behavior of a mother bird protecting its young to sentinels who signal the presence of predators at their own peril. Zahavi and Zahavi (1997) proposed a different theory to account for this behavior that belies its altruism.

Consider the gazelle. When a predator approaches, certain gazelles begin to bounce on all four legs, a practice called stotting. The traditional explanation of stotting is that the gazelles are acting altruistically—they are warning their fellow gazelles of the presence of danger, but in doing so they are wasting precious energy that could be used to escape. Zohavi claims this behavior is not altruistic. Instead, the stotting is a communication, not between gazelles, but between the stotting gazelles and the predator. The message is this: "Don't even think about chasing me. I've got so much energy and strength that I can bounce around like this and still outrun you. You need to chase those other gazelles if you want to eat."

Instead of altruistic behavior, then, this is purely selfish behavior. It is also a fascinating example of one variation on how reliable communication techniques might evolve. Couldn't a less fit gazelle pull the stotting technique and fool the predator? If a gazelle has the stotting gene but not the fitness to pull off an escape, then it will be more likely to be eaten by the predator since it has expended its energy and will not be able to outrun the other gazelles (remember: you don't have to be the fastest gazelle, you just can't be the slowest). This cheater gazelle, then, will not pass on its genes. Thus only the fit gazelles will stot, and the predator "knows" this.

Another aspect of the handicap principle is manifested in male peacocks. Here the message is to the female, for fitness impresses females, who are looking for a fit mate—one who has good genes. The huge tail of the male peacock is a handicap and thus the male is touting the fact that he can carry this plumage and still escape predators (he is, after all, alive and strutting).

Thorstein Veblen (1899) captured this aspect in human behavior with his concept of conspicuous consumption. Conspicuous consumption is public behavior designed to deliver a message of power: "Don't mess with me. I can spend more money on one car than you can make in ten years."

Conspicuous consumption, though, is not limited to the wealthy. It is a relative concept and can be practiced by any particular income group to impress other members within that group. For instance, a person within the middle class may want others to perceive her as being part of the upper middle class. The way to do this would be to spend extravagantly and conspicuously on frivolous items. This lifestyle must be sustained over time or else it could be funded on loans or temporary riches. If sustained, however, it is an honest signalling technique.

§10 CHAPTER SUMMARY

We have seen how social groups function around the core values of humans and that these core values can be seen as memes trying to replicate. However we choose to define social groups or view their core values, the importance of the social nature of humans cannot be overestimated:

> The very way we walk, move, gesture, speak is shaped from the earliest moments by our awareness that we appear before others, that we stand in public space, and that this space is potentially one of respect or contempt, of pride or shame. (Taylor 15)

In sociality lies all the wonder and the horror of being human. On the one hand it fosters emotions which are the very foundation of morality—an emphasis on empathy and reciprocity. What is the golden rule but a codification of this principle? On the other hand, it fosters anxiety, guilt, shame, revenge, and deception, highlighting the deceptive and violent nature of humanity.

> Humans are well equipped for the demands of reciprocal altruism. They remember each other as individuals (perhaps with the help of dedicated regions of the brain), and have an eagle eye and a flypaper memory for cheaters. They feel moralistic emotions—liking, sympathy, gratitude, guilt, shame, and anger—that are uncanny implementations of the strategies for reciprocal altruism in computer simulations and mathematical models. Experiments have confirmed the prediction that people are most inclined to help a stranger when they can do so at low cost, when the stranger is in need, and when the stranger is in a position to reciprocate. They like people who grant them favors, grant favors to those they like, feel guilty when they have withheld a possible favor, and punish those who withhold favors from them. (Pinker 2003:255)

Notice how we keep coming back to questions of how we know. I have emphasized this by speaking of blindness in many respects, from the blindness of physical and biological processes with respect to the future, to the blindness we suffer with respect to knowing the intentions of others. This is a fundamental fact about humanity and we have evolved elaborate mechanisms to try and overcome it, but at the end of the day... we are what we are.

NOTES / QUESTIONS

Part 2: Explications

7. Truth

It's a basic truth of the human condition that everybody lies. The only variable is about what. The weird thing about telling someone they're dying is it tends to focus their priorities. You find out what matters to them. What they're willing to die for. What they're willing to lie for.

- House M.D., Three Stories, 2004

SYNOPSIS

Thinking about the concept of truth will raise some interesting questions concerning the external world and what we can know about it. (1) The age old philosophical question "What is truth?" is examined, revealing the answer to be trivial. This will allow us to define truth according to what we will call the correct description theory, in which sentences are true when they correctly describe the world. (2) All historical attempts to precisely define knowledge have failed, but this shouldn't bother us. By now we are used to embracing somewhat slippery solutions. (3) The fuss about truth is not for nothing. If true sentences are those that correctly describe the world, then possessing true sentences should improve our ability to get by in the world. (4) A distinction is drawn between objective and subjective sentences. Objective sentences are anchored in the external world in a way subjective sentences are not. (5) Reference frames are based on the same notion of an anchor (or lack of such). The absolute reference frame is the highest possible reference frame, a god's-eye-view of the world. We humans are stuck in relative reference frames. (6) Enlightenment occurs when we rise to a higher reference frame, where 'higher' is defined in terms of adequacy conditions. (7) An historical note on reference frames in which it is noted that the general movement has been from absolute to relative. The cash value of this in terms of meaning. (8) Chapter Summary.

CHAPTER OBJECTIVES

- understand the function of truth and related concepts
- understand the difference between absolute and relative reference frames
- appreciate the historical movement away from absolute reference frames
- expand upon the concept of anchoring as discussed in previous chapters

§1 WHAT IS TRUTH?

hat is truth? The question conjures mental images of a sage sitting atop a mountain or wise men in scholarly attire. It is often thought to be at the heart of the philosophical enterprise. And yet, the question is misleading, for its answer, though important for delineating our world view in many different ways, is trivial in its everyday formulation. To see why, let's begin with a commonsense definition, one that captures this everyday usage:

A sentence is true when it correctly describes the world.

We will call this the correct description theory, since a sentence is said to be true if and only if it correctly describes the way the world really is.[1] Suppose, for example, a person says: "I saw your wife kissing a man in a cafe yesterday." If this is a true statement, then the man's wife really was kissing another man in a cafe yesterday. If it is a false statement, then she was not. It does not matter whether the person reporting the incident is sincere or insincere. He may have really thought it was the person's wife, but was mistaken, in which case he is not reporting a truth—his statement does not correctly describe the way things really were (see Figure 7–1).

Using the correct description theory of truth we can always determine what makes a sentence true, that is, we can always know what would have to happen in the world to make a sentence true: a sentence is true if it correctly describes the world, false if it does not. This is why I claim the answer to the question "What is truth?" is trivial, for the answer is always the same. Consider another sentence: "It is raining outside." What would make this statement true? Answer: If the sentence correctly describes the world—if it really is raining outside. What would make the sentence "God exists." true? If the sentence correctly describes the world—if God really exists. See? Trivial.

---

[1] The technical name is "the correspondence theory of truth." I think this theory really does capture our ordinary intuitions about truth, but I also think it is flawed. I will not correct it, though, until chapter 10.

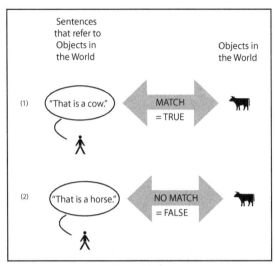

FIGURE 7–1
The correct description theory of truth in which a sentence is true if and only if it correctly describes the world. In (1) there is a match between the sentence and the world, which means the sentence is true. In (2) there is no match, which makes the sentence false.

The most important question is not about what truth is, but rather about how we know whether or not our sentences or beliefs are true. The short answer to this latter question is that we construct a theory. If we judge the theory adequate then we are justified in saying a sentence or belief is true, that it correctly describes the world. This knowledge claim will always be subject to correction, but this goes without saying.

§2 TRUTH AND KNOWLEDGE

There are objects in the world and there are things humans say (or believe) about objects in the world. What we say or believe about objects in the world is formulated in sentences, and these sentences are the kinds of things that are true or false, not the objects. It makes no sense to say of a chair: "That is a very true chair" (we are obviously not talking of the true used by carpenters).

We have earlier distinguished two types of knowledge: reflective knowledge ("knowing that" something is true, often referred to as propositional knowledge) and non-reflective knowledge ("knowing how" to do something). Non-reflective knowledge is often a necessary precondition for reflective knowledge. For example, knowing how to read is a necessary precondition for many other types of learning. In what follows we will focus almost exclusively on reflective knowledge.

Philosophers, for the most part, have given up attempting to provide a tight definition of reflective knowledge. The best we can do is to say that knowledge is justified true belief, plus something else. Truth is undeniably a necessary condition for knowledge. It would be odd for someone to claim to know a falsehood, for example, to say, "She knows the sun orbits the earth." Instead, we would say "She thinks the sun orbits the earth, but she is wrong." Knowledge claims seem to carry truth claims within them as an essential feature.

Justification also seems to be an inherent feature of any knowledge claim, for we can come to have a true belief for insufficient reasons, and this insufficiency seems to negate the knowledge claim. For example, suppose you overhear a conversation between two people in a crowd. One says, "The Lions lost their game today," but, due to the background noise, you hear: "The Lions won their game today." Because of this you come to believe the Lions won their game, and in fact they did win the game. Thus, your belief is true, but do you really *know* they won the game? The fact that you came to hold your belief based on faulty evidence seems to negate the knowledge claim.

This is why the condition of justification is added to true belief, for we can now explain your lack of knowledge in the above situation by saying that you were not justified in believing the Lions won. But a similar problem arises with justification. Suppose you always look at the old grandfather clock in the hallway to see what time it is before you leave for work. The clock has always been right in the past, so when you now look at it you come to believe what it indicates, namely, that it is 8 AM. You are justified in believing this (since the clock has always been right in the past), and let's suppose it is true—it really is 8 AM. What you don't know is that the clock stopped yesterday at 8 PM (and a stopped clock is right twice a day). So here you have a justified true belief that it is 8 AM, but do you really know?

§3   T<small>HE</small> I<small>MPORTANCE OF</small> T<small>RUTH</small>

What's the big deal about truth? The big deal is this: if our sentences are true, if they correctly describe the way the world is, then it makes sense they will enable us to get by better than if we were working with false sentences (those that do not correctly describe the world). Imagine two groups of people trying to solve a puzzle or a maze and each group is given a set of instructions which should help them. The instructions given to one group contain all true sentences relevant to their situation while those given to the second group have a mixture of true and false sentences. Which group is more likely to succeed in their task?

The niggling need to know is embedded deep within our genes, and for good reason. Knowledge is essential for successful replication in an always changing world, for our lot cannot depend upon sharp teeth, keen senses, wings or blazing speed. Some ancient Greeks blamed this on Prometheus, who was put in charge of handing out traits to the creatures of the earth. He supposedly gave all the good traits away before humans arrived, though this seems a bit too ironic a tale for a god named Foresight. Prometheus' gift to humans, stolen from the gods and symbolized by fire, was knowledge, technology—the ability to view the future and prepare for it. Our inherent curiosity was at first directed solely toward survival, but once that was assured the impulse to know did not simply disappear. If survival is no longer our sole concern upon what should we then turn our curious eye? We turn it toward whatever we will, whatever strikes our fancy, and this aimless curiosity has resulted in explorations of our globe and beyond, from the outreaches of the stars to the innermost recesses of the atom.

During the middle ages Christian theologians disparaged curiosity, blaming all human ills upon Eve's inability to just say no to ripened fruit proffered by sly serpents. Odysseus, too, was a prime target, for his curiosity was legendary. Dante, in his *Inferno*, provides a fine ending for him, claiming that his restless mind led him to take one more sea voyage in his old age, in which he sailed beyond the pillars of Hercules[2] only to be destroyed by a whirlpool in the vast uncharted sea. Odysseus relates his tale to Dante:

> Neither my fondness for my son nor pity
> for my old father nor the love I owed
> Penelope, which would have gladdened her,
> was able to defeat in me the longing—
> I had to gain experience of the world
> and of the vices and the worth of men. (94-99)

Odysseus' speech to his would-be followers when he is trying to raise a crew is telling:

> ...you must not deny
> experience of that which lies beyond
> the sun, and of the world that is unpeopled.
> Consider well the seed that gave you birth:
> you were not made to live your lives as brutes,
> but to be followers of worth and knowledge. (115-120)

Odysseus is confined to the eighth level of hell (out of nine levels) for his troubles. But why? Why condemn curiosity? Because curiosity is the enemy of the status quo. It is dangerous to any dictatorial, top-down power structure that attempts to control humans, whether "for their own good" or for the good of the dictator himself. Great evils have been perpetrated upon humanity in the name of the greater good.

§4 OBJECTIVE & SUBJECTIVE SENTENCES

Most of us agree there is a world outside of us that many of our sentences describe, whether they are about the weather, the solar system, the color of a person's hair, an idea or an institution, or an event in history. We will call sentences that describe features of the external world objective sentences. Examples of objective sentences might be as follows:

(1) The earth is the third planet from the sun.
(2) It is snowing outside.
(3) Caesar crossed the Rubicon.

Since the truth of an objective sentence is dependent upon some fact in the world, it makes no sense to say it is "true for me, though not for you." It is either

---

[2] The pillars of Hercules, or Gibraltar, were a symbol of the boundary of human knowledge. To sail past them was to venture into the unknown.

true or it is false—period. In Figure 7–2, the sentence "That is a tree" cannot be true for one person and false for another. If it is true, then it is true for all. I have heard people say, for example, "I know you don't believe that god exists, but it's true for me that he exists." In this case, "true for me" simply means "I *believe* it to be true." It does not mean that the truth of the sentence depends on the person believing it. The sentence "God exists" is an objective sentence and thus is true if and only if there is a god.

We will call a sentence subjective if its truth is grounded in our own value judgments. For example:

(1) I like ice cream.
(2) Eisenhower will go down in history as the best president ever.
(3) That inkblot looks like an elephant.

It makes perfect sense to say, of a subjective sentence, that it is "true for me, but not for you," for the truth of such is grounded within each person's own beliefs.

Subjective sentences are an odd set that revolve around our preferences. They are true because of what we prefer or think at the time, and this can change. Because of this subjectivity we are said to have privileged access to subjective sentences. When I say, truly, (a) "I like ice cream", then this statement corrrectly describes a belief that I have. But once stated, my preference becomes public property—it has been objectified. Thus you can now say, referring to me: (b) "He likes ice cream." (a) is a subjective sentence—its truth is grounded upon my preference for ice cream. It

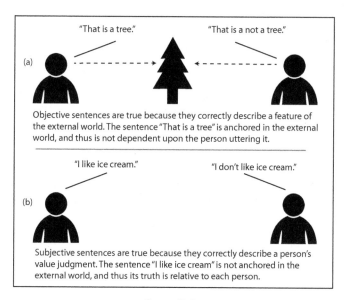

FIGURE 7–2

(a) illustrates objective sentences in which the truth of a sentence depends upon (is anchored to) an external object. If two people disagree about the truth of an objective sentence they cannot both be right. (b) illustrates subjective sentences in which the truth of the sentence depends upon each individual. If two people disagree about the truth of a subjective sentence they can both be right.

is "true for me" no matter how much you argue. If it's true that I like ice cream, then there is nothing you can say that will convince me that I don't.[3]

(b), on the other hand, is objective—it is grounded upon historical fact, namely, what I said about liking ice cream. The person, other than me, uttering (b) can be mistaken concerning my preferences in a way that I cannot be. If this distinction is still unclear, imagine taking a bite of ice cream. I ask you how you like it and you reply, truly, "I really like it," to which I respond, "No you don't." This is absurd. One person cannot dispute another's preferences. This is what I mean when I say that you have privileged access to your own preferences.

We have divided sentences into two categories, objective and subjective. Granted, there are clear examples of both, but there are also examples where it may be debatable which category they belong to. These fall into two groups, both having to do with valuation:

1. Aesthetic Truths: sentences about what is beautiful.
2. Moral Truths: sentences about what is good and bad, right and wrong.

Plato believed that aesthetic sentences were objective (he didn't think that beauty is in the eye of the beholder). The reason a sculpture was beautiful was because it partook in an objective form of beauty. Thus, if a sculpture did so partake, making it beautiful, and you thought it was not beautiful, you would be wrong. We might agree that what is considered art is objective even if we aren't Platonists, for we might agree that a certain group of people, maybe art curators, sets the standard for art. On this view, if the curators say it's art, then it's art. "The Mona Lisa is art" would thus be an objective statement since its truth is not grounded on our own individual preferences, but rather on an objectified set of preferences.

This same looseness applies to moral sentences. An ethical objectivist is one who thinks the truth of moral sentences is grounded in a reality external to humans, in a god maybe, or etched in the fabric of the universe. An ethical subjectivist, on the other hand, is one who claims that the truth of moral statements depends on each individual, rather than on anything external to us. In other words, moral sentences, like "Murder is wrong" are like "I like ice cream" sentences—matters of taste. As with aesthetic sentences, though, you don't have to go to the opposite extreme in order to deny this. You might claim that moral rules are objective in the curator-sense, that is, a group of individuals band together and formulate rules to live by, just as we might agree art curators determine what constitutes art. These are deep questions, touching as they do on the foundations of our value systems. We will discuss this in more detail in chapter 14.

There has been a movement from ancient times to modern times in which we today are less inclined to anchor our moral and aesthetic sentences outside of ourselves, and are more inclined to anchor them within. This movement seems to point toward an increasing subjectivity (see §7 below).

---

[3] Almost. It is possible for someone, in certain instances, to know me better than I know myself. For example, maybe I've forgotten my preferences: I'm about to order something on a menu and my wife says, "You don't like that." I disagree, but upon receiving the dish and tasting it I realize she was right. This only happens when I am relying on memory. If I am tasting it at the moment and say that I like it, then I cannot be wrong.

§5 Reference Frames

In *The Republic* (Book VII) Plato gives us a famous allegory of a cave in which we are asked to imagine a row of prisoners facing a wall on which they see the shadows of objects. The prisoners have been chained to the wall their entire lives, so they have never experienced anything else and thus take these shadows to be their entire reality. In fact, these shadows are caused by a great fire behind the prisoners. There are people on the wall between the prisoners and the fire who parade about holding up stick figures of various objects (see Figure 7–3) and it is the shadows of these stick figures, cast by the fire, that the prisoners see and which they take to be real.

We can imagine the prisoners conversing about what they see, having named the shadows just as we name objects in our world. What interests us is what happens when one of the prisoners is unchained and led back behind the wall and the parapet to observe the true cause of what he has seen on the wall before him all his life.

> And now look again, and see what will naturally follow if the prisoners are released and disabused of their error. At first, when any of them is liberated and compelled suddenly to stand up and turn his neck round and walk and look towards the light, he will suffer sharp pains; the glare will distress him, and he will be unable to see the realities of which in his former state he had seen the shadows; and then conceive someone saying to him, that what he saw before was an illusion, but that now, when he is approaching nearer to being and his eye is turned towards more real existence, he has a clearer vision, what will be his reply? And you may further imagine that his instructor is pointing to the objects as they pass and requiring him to name them, will he not be perplexed? Will he not fancy that the shadows which he formerly saw are truer than the objects which are now shown to him? (515c-e)

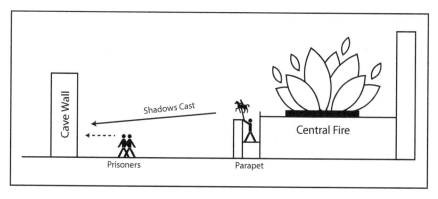

Figure 7–3

In Plato's cave allegory, prisoners are chained so that they can only see the cave wall before them, on which are shadows of stick figures held by individuals on the parapet above them. Having been in this position all their lives, the prisoners think the shadows are real.

As the prisoner's eyes become accustomed to the glare of the fire (which for Plato is a picture of the learning process), he realizes what he had taken to be true is not true at all—the shadows on the wall are merely the effect of a completely different reality.

We will use the phrase "reference frame" as synonymous with a point of view from which an individual or a group of individuals interprets the world. In this sense, there are various levels of reference frames. In general, the higher reference frames incorporate more data (all data below them) and are equated with a more comprehensive view of the world, one in which the facts are interconnected in a way that was lacking in the lower levels. In other words, we can define 'higher' here as a better fit with our adequacy conditions. Thus, Plato's prisoner moves to a higher reference frame when he sees his previous world-view as inadequate.

Reference frames, then, are really no different from what we have called individual frameworks. A reference frame is simply a person's perspective on reality. I distinguish reference frames from frameworks only in order to talk about the difference between individual, or relative reference frames, and an absolute reference frame, a theoretical construct which is the highest possible reference frame, one that ideally meets all the adequacy conditions: it is (1) internally harmonious, containing no contradictions, (2) beautifully elegant in its structure (any addition would be superfluous, any detraction a diminishment), (3) maximally comprehensive (incorporating all known facts), and (4) maximally interconnected (the condition of integration does not apply since there is nothing outside an absolute reference frame to integrate). As a theoretical construct we can call such a reference frame a god's-eye-view of the universe. This can be a useful theoretical tool even if you do not believe in a god, that is, talk of an absolute reference frame does not presuppose the existence of a sentient creator.

Isaac Newton (1643-1727) was a proponent of an absolute reference frame in his adherence to the concepts of absolute space and time. He believed both were created by god, who could always be used as an absolute fixed reference (at least in theory). Space was created as a container for everything, from stars to planets and people. As a container, we can imagine it originally empty and then populated by god with the rest of creation. God could look down from his position above the container and see everything within. This is the god's-eye-view of all of space from outside of space. According to this, you may find yourself physically lost at times—you may not know where you are—but god knows, for there is always a fixed reference point to judge your position. So also, if space is absolute and thus external to us (since it would exist even if we didn't), sentences about space are objective sentences.

Time was similarly absolute for Newton, for time, like space, was created by god.[4] This meant there was always a standard by which it could be said that one thing in the universe happened before or after or at the same time as something else. You may not be sure which event occurred first in a certain situation, but god is not fooled. He has the clock by which all other clocks are set.

---

[4] St. Augustine propounded this view in the fifth century. He realized that this raised the question: "What was God doing before he created time?" Augustine said he would not answer this question, as some were wont to do, with the response: "Creating hells for those who ask such questions."

The alternative to absolute space and time, relative space and time, was first proposed by Immanuel Kant in his *Critique of Pure Reason*. There he claimed space and time were mental constructs. According to Einstein, who made Kant's position scientifically respectable, if there were no objects there would be no space. Space just is what separates two objects. This means there is no one correct place where something exists, since places are relative to observers.

Imagine, for instance, a stoplight at a busy intersection (see Figure 7–4). You are in your car (B) and pull up to the light as it turns red. There are cars in front, behind and on all sides of you, all waiting for the light to turn green. Suddenly you realize your car is slowly moving backward (like it does sometimes if you are stopped on a hill). You slam your foot hard on the brake pedal and only then realize you were not moving. You had seen the car on your left (A) creeping slowly forward in your peripheral vision, but you had nothing to help you establish who was moving and, thinking it was you, slammed on your brakes. This confusion is the result of your being immersed in relative reference frames. To establish who is moving in such a situation we must find a third, external, reference frame from which to judge.

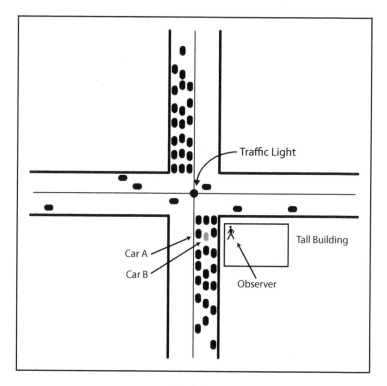

FIGURE 7–4

A distinction between absolute and relative viewpoints. Relative viewpoints are immersed in the world with other viewpoints, as are the drivers of cars A and B. There may be times when B, for example, is fooled with respect to his motion. The absolute viewpoint is the highest possible viewpoint, illustrated here by the observer looking down on the intersection from a tall building. This observer is not fooled with respect to the motion of the cars below, for he is not immersed in the situation.

Such a reference frame, incorporating both of the others would be considered a higher reference frame.

Suppose that instead of being in a car at the intersection you are on the roof of a tall building overlooking the intersection. You, the observer, are looking down at the same scenario. You see car A creeping slowly forward, but you are not even tempted to think that car B is moving. There is no confusion as to who is moving because you are in a higher reference frame which allows you a more comprehensive picture of the situation.[5]

Einstein also proposed the relativity of time. Consider the following thought experiment:

> Suppose everything stops. Everything. People stop, trains and cars stop, atoms and electrons stop. Everything stops... and then everything starts moving again. Does it make any sense to ask: "How long did everything stop?"

If time is absolute, god would be above the scene with his clock, timing the stoppage; but if time is relative, where there is no god's-eye-view, then time just is the movement of things, so that, if everything stopped, so would time, and the question "How long did everything stop moving?" would be rendered meaningless.

Note the connection between reference frames and objective and subjective sentences. If there is an absolute reference frame, then we can be wrong (absolutely), not only in our judgments about space and time, but about what is good and bad, valuable or not valuable. This is because the standard that judges us is outside of us or any other set of human constructs. On the other hand, if there is no absolute reference frame, then judgments within a reference frame are correct or incorrect in reference either to their own internal system or to another reference frame which is also relative. There is no absolute fact of the matter.

§6 ENLIGHTENMENT

Within a set of reference frames, moving from a lower reference frame to what one perceives as a higher reference frame is often described as enlightenment or a conversion experience, since, from the higher perspective, one's previous perspective seems limited and parochial, or at most incomplete.

The prisoner in Plato's cave allegory is enlightened when he walks behind the parapet, for he sees the true cause of the shadows on the wall he once thought real. His new reference frame is more complete than his previous one, offering explanations for previously unexplained objects, and in the process falsifying many

---

[5] Galileo formulated the principle of relativity, one formulation of which says: "You must look outside to see if you are moving." Einstein used this principle as one of the two fundamental principles in his special theory of relativity, namely, "All laws of science remain the same in all reference frames moving uniformly with respect to one another." (The other fundamental principle was the constant speed of light.) The special theory is called "special" because it only works in very specific reference frames, namely, those moving uniformly with respect to one another. The general theory, formulated ten years later, removed this condition, making it more complete.

of the prisoner's prior beliefs. So also Truman in *The Truman Show* is enlightened when he steps outside the dome-shaped set into the real world, as is Neo in *The Matrix* when he wakes up in the real world outside of the matrix. All of these are world-changing experiences, which is why enlightenment is often equated with religious experience. But enlightenment need not be quite so radical. On a mundane level, enlightenment is occurring whenever we change our theories, no matter how small the improvement, and since every belief we have is a theory, every change in our belief structure can be seen as a mini-enlightenment. Even anomalies can be enlightening, for indicating a theory is false may be enlightening even if we don't see how to fix it. Remember the man who saw his wife with another man in the coffee shop? That might be considered a moment of enlightenment, since he came to view his wife in a completely novel way, one that eclipsed his previous view of her as faithful and loving.

Improving on any of the adequacy conditions of a theory can be enlightening. We might discover consistency between aspects we previously thought inconsistent, or we might experience the beauty of a consistent set of sentences, the simple elegance in the way that sentences hang together. We might subsume a number of sentences under one sentence, or open an entirely new branch of knowledge to scrutiny. We might come to see connections between diverse theories we had never thought of as related before or we might come to appreciate the interconnections within a specific theory. All of these are enlightenment experiences.

Granted that even the smallest addition to our store of knowledge is enlightening, we usually reserve the term for significant changes in our theories. If so, we might define 'enlightenment' using the notion of core values. In this sense your level of enlightenment is determined by the seismic effect of the knowledge upon your conceptual scheme. When I learn a new fact about nature (a Volvox is the only biological creature on the planet that has a wheel), I might find this interesting, but not particularly relevant to my life in general, but when I learn a new fact that is highly relevant (I have terminal cancer), it cannot help but change my core values, which means its effect will ripple throughout my conceptual scheme.

Not all enlightenment brings joy and happiness. Since we have tied the term to a modification of core values, cognitive dissonance is never far away. An enlightenment experience can either bring about or relieve cognitive dissonance. To continue the coffee shop example, the first enlightenment (when the man saw his wife with another man) brought on cognitive dissonance, but later the wife's explanation of her interaction with the man, which was accepted, was also an enlightenment experience, for it re-explained the facts from yet another point of view, leaving the previous core values intact.

The feeling of enlightenment is primarily associated with relief from cognitive dissonance, and is probably identical with the feeling of certainty. These feelings are dopamine rushes given by the brain as a reward for reducing dissonance. They are often confused with confirmation of our beliefs. The wonderful feeling of peace we feel when we've solved one of life's conundrums is a feeling of being right. We will devote an entire chapter to certainty (chapter 9), but for now keep in mind that the feelings connected to enlightenment are never a guarantee of truthfulness, for we can have all these wonderful feelings and still be wrong. Enlightenment, like romantic love, is often passionate, but short-lived.

The god's-eye-view (the absolute reference frame) is an abstraction. It is an attractive nuisance which, when properly used, can shed light on our cognitive

RELATIVITY & REFERENCE FRAMES

Imagine you are in a spaceship traveling at the speed of light (approximately 186,000 miles per second) and you decide to run an experiment in which you will measure the time it takes to throw a ball a specified distance. Observer A, who is on the spaceship with you, measures the time and distance and records that the ball took exactly 1 second to travel 50 feet. A second observer, B, on the ground, performs the same measurement as you zip by overhead (he obviously has amazing measuring abilities). This second (outside) observer records the same time, but the distance has increased dramatically. So the same time elapsed, but the ball was seen to have traveled 50 feet by one observer and 186,000 miles plus 50 feet by another. What's going on here? Same ball, same experiment and yet two different measurements.

The explanation lies in the fact that the measurements are conducted in different reference frames. Observer B, since he is outside the spaceship (in a higher reference frame), is also measuring the distance the spaceship travels as the ball moves forward. Observer A is inside, moving with the spaceship.

Which is the correct reference frame? The question, according to Einstein, is meaningless. There is no correct reference frame. It might be tempting to say that since Observer B's reference frame is a higher reference frame his is the correct one. But to judge one reference frame correct there must be a third reference frame to which we have access, which acts as a standard, and there is no such reference frame in the universe.

According to Einstein, nothing can travel faster than the speed of light. This gives us a problem, for Observer B records the ball moving at the speed of light plus the speed at which you threw the ball. Though the extra is miniscule, it still exceeds the speed of light, which is prohibited according to the theory of relativity. What to do? Usually when we have a speed calculation (mph = distance x time) and the distance increases, we increase the time accordingly. Thus 100 mph = 100 miles in 1 hour. If we increase the distance to 200 miles we must increase the speed to balance the equation (200 mph = 200 miles in 1 hour). But what if, as per Einstein, increasing the left side of the equation is not allowed? Then we must increase the time. (100 mph = 200 miles in 2 hours). Thus does Einstein's theory of relativity dictate that time slows as speed increases, for increasing the time variable is equivalent to slowing time (from the perspective of the outside observer). This is fine until we realize that the inside observer made no such adjustment, so the elapsed times will be different for Observer A and Observer B. Thus, time is reference frame dependent.

This time-relativity leads to some interesting conundrums, one of which is known as the Twin Paradox. Imagine twins are born. One grows up to be a banker, the other an astronaut. The astronaut boards a spaceship and travels through space at speeds approximating the speed of light and then returns to earth. According to the astronaut twin, the time spent traveling in space amounted to about a week, but when he greets his twin brother, his twin is an old man who claims his brother was gone for decades. This paradox occurs because time ran slower for the astronaut twin because he traveled at speeds approximating the speed of light (not only does time slow, but measuring device slow as well, so the traveller doesn't notice).

This aspect of the theory of relativity was tested in 1974 with atomic clocks. The theory predicts that even at speeds less than the speed of light there will be a time differential. The difference will be miniscule, but atomic clocks are so accurate they can detect the small differences involved. Thus an atomic clock was placed in a jet plane which was flown around the world. On the ground was another atomic clock, synchronized with the one on the plane at the start of the journey. Scientists calculated how much slower the clock on the plane should run based on its speed and distance. When the plane landed the difference in time between the clocks was precisely as predicted.

This concept of time (which is inextricably bound to space, or distance traveled) means that the concept of absolute simultaneity is illusory. Events can only be said to be simultaneous if viewed within the same reference frame.

meanderings, but when misused can lead us down blind alleys where we are apt to be mentally mugged. We have mentioned the human penchant to abstract many times: it is what leads us to reify our sensations like redness on to the world, and what led Plato to invent an entire world of forms. The god's-eye-view is particularly attractive because it is attached to truth and enlightenment and all the dopamine drips that go along with these. This attractiveness lies in the lure of anchors. We do not like our beliefs, hopes, wants and goals to be merely our own, we want to know they have meaning. Remember we described meaning as arising from connections, which also relates meaning to core values, since these are a function of the number of connections they have. And therein lies the lure of the god's-eye-view, for it promises to connect you to everything.

This helps us understand the connection between religious forms of enlightenment and absolute reference frames both in the Eastern and the Western traditions. Most religious enlightened states occur when one rises above the morass of human cares (the relative reference frames) and comes to understand the inter-relatedness of all reality. This may involve becoming one with all things or an experience of complete understanding. This nirvana or bliss-state occurs when one gains the highest reference frame and sees all things from a god's perspective. This may be expressed as a comprehension of god's mind or his purpose or plan for humans, which gives meaning to all things. The concepts of All or Oneness are ubiquitous in experiences of religious enlightenment. All facts about the world, previously disparate and disjointed are now seen as intimately interrelated. There is one plan and we are all a part of it.

Remaining within a relative reference frame is like piloting a ship amongst dangerous rocks and reefs. You have an anchor, but it is never dropped, and you are responsible for threading your way between the dangerous outcroppings. There is another solution, though; you can drop anchor and fasten yourself to the unmoving sea bottom and permanently eliminate the threat of destruction. As an analogy, this is of limited value, but hopefully it gets across the function and the lure of the god's-eye-view. There may very well be places which serve as anchors along your life's passage, but beware the easy solution, the siren song of the absolute reference frame.

The external world functions as a secure anchor for our truth claims. It gives solace to some to know that there is an external world to which our sentences can be compared, even if we may have a difficult time knowing whether or not there is a match. So far in our discussion of truth we have assumed that we have access to this external world (via theory), but I have used this only as a starting point. In chapter 10 I will argue that the correct description theory of truth is insufficient for properly handling our concept of truth.

⋯⋰⋯

§7   HISTORICAL ASIDE ON REFERENCE FRAMES

As a general historical progression from ancient to modern, humans have tended to move steadily away from belief in absolute reference frames, embracing belief in relative reference frames. When a person or group of people hold a reference frame to be absolute they are never lost. They are secure in knowing the rules of the game. The problem is only whether or not they are following the rules. Condemnation is the consequence that one suffers by not following the absolute guidelines. This was always true in the ancient past, from the Homeric epoch with the warrior ethos to Plato and Aristotle in classical Greece, and remains true today for any reference frame claiming absolute status: Christianity, Judaism, Islam.[6]

Consolation seems to be a necessary condition for a religion. Absolute religions give consolation by making people feel at home in the world. If the rules of a religion are too harsh, it will not survive. When religions do include harsh rules, they always provide a means for circumventing these (for the not-quite-so-truly-dedicated members). As an example of this, consider the heretical sect of the Cathari in the middle ages, which solved the harshness of a total ban on sex by means of a division between the *Perfecti* and the *Credentes*. The *Credentes* were allowed to have sex, which kept them out of heaven, but they would always have another chance in the next life via the doctrine of reincarnation. This second-chance-allowance may be the function of all concepts such as reincarnation, levels of holiness, purgatorial transits, and karma within various religions.

The trend in modern societies is toward relative and away from absolute reference frames. This gives rise to what is often referred to as the modern existential predicament, the feeling of anxiety, of not being at home in the world. Another way to put this is to distinguish between Meaning (uppercase) and meaning (lowercase), where Meaning (uppercase) connotes overall universal significance (bestowed upon us by an absolute reference frame), while meaning (lowercase) is meaning that is relative to an individual's life, but no more. Put this way, the modern existential predicament is explained as a loss of or move away from Meaning. Max Weber (2001) described this as the disenchantment of the modern world.

Within an objectively given conceptual scheme you can face condemnation, but never Meaninglessness. If, on the other hand, you are at least partly responsible for crafting the core values within your own conceptual scheme (which is what occurs in a relative reference frame), you might very well have to confront Meaninglessness.

An example of the shift from absolute to relative reference frames can be found in the movement away from the teleological view, espoused by philosophers, naturalists and theologians from Aristotle to Darwin. This viewpoint held that everything in nature is created for a specific purpose (*telos*, in Greek, means purpose). Theologians in the 18th and 19th centuries took this to ludicrous extremes, claiming, for example, cork trees exist on earth in order that we might have a means to stop our wine bottles, and that coal is found in the bowels of the earth in order that we might have fuel to burn. It was always acceptable, even for the scientist, to ask of any phenomenon: "Why is it here?" or "What is its purpose in the grand scheme of things?"

This viewpoint began to decline with the advent of Darwinism. Particularly within science, such why questions were no longer asked, for according to the theory of evolution by natural selection there is no overriding purpose for anything (note the term 'overriding' and its relation to a higher reference frame). There are only

---

[6] Absolute reference frames are like axiomatic systems (which we will discuss in the next chapter). Their foundations (the rules of the game) have to be justified somehow. This is always difficult, for it must boil down to self-evidence. What makes this particularly ironic is that the degree of condemnation inflicted upon those who don't think your rules are self-evident is often inversely related to the strength of your first principles.

adaptations caused by random mutations which make an organism more or less fit to its environment.

There was a certain symmetry in the old view, lacking in the modern view, for on that older view not only was an organism adapted to its environment, but the environment was adapted to the organism. This was true because god made it that way. Stephen J. Gould (1988) quotes the 19th century zoologist Edward Blyth as pointing out the difference between the old and the new viewpoints. Blyth speaks of a bird called a ptarmigan:

> It is the grand and beautiful, the sublime and comprehensive, system which pervades the universe... and which is so well exemplified in the adaptation of the ptarmigan to the mountain top, and the mountain top to the habits of the ptarmigan.

Blyth's quote presumes both are perfectly adapted to one another, but as Gould points out:

> Darwin's system permits us to speak of the ptarmigan adapting to the mountain top, for natural selection produces such apparent "order" in a world devoid of intrinsic purpose. But we can no longer speak of the mountain top adapting to the ptarmigan, and in this loss lies both the grandeur and the despair of "this view of life"—Darwin's own designation for his reconstructed world. (60)

This view of life is the life of relative reference frames without recourse to the god's-eye-view.

§8 CHAPTER SUMMARY

We began this chapter with true sentences firmly anchored to the external world. The question "What is truth?" was thus easily answered: sentences are true if and only if they correctly describe the way the world really is. This answer conforms to the way we ordinarily use the term, but, as we will see, it is an abstraction that is not without problems, for it creates an unbridgeable gap between us and the world which our sentences are supposed to describe. How can we know whether or not the proper match takes place? We theorize. Thus theories, as we have described them, are used to bridge the gap between ourselves and the world as best as possible.

The correct description theory of truth is comforting for it dictates that there is a connection between our beliefs and the world even if the link is tenuous. Someone must know, if only god himself, and if not him, then at least there is a theoretical god's-eye-view that would solve our arguments if we could ever attain it. In the end, using the external world to define the truth of our sentences is like insisting on the existence of Santa Claus once we have grown up and realized that he doesn't provide presents at Christmas. He no longer serves a useful function.

I will suggest, in chapter 10, that we drop the façade and redefine truth simply as coherence. If our sentences or theories fulfill the adequacy conditions we have set for them, then we are justified in saying they are true. Period. Fulfilling the adequacy

A NOTE ON THE RISE OF CONSCIOUSNESS

Ancient people had no concept that the beauty of an object or the goodness or badness of an action could be dependent upon personal preferences. This is a thoroughly modern idea which depends upon a reflective consciousness not possessed in earlier times. In other words, reflective consciousness, as we know it, is a fairly recent development in human history. This thesis is put forward in order to explain the movement in human history toward subjectivity, that is, the interior (cognitive) movement which corresponds to the rise in the importance of the individual in human history.

According to this thesis there was a time when humans were not as reflectively self-aware as we are today. In other words, humans did not see themselves as individuals, did not distinguish themselves from the group in the way that we do.

Some of the historical changes in attitude that serve as evidence for the rise in the importance of the individual are as follows:

- Freedom versus slavery. In ancient times the institution of slavery was an accepted idea, even to the slaves themselves. This begins to change, in the West, in the 17th and 18th centuries.

- Self-expression in the arts. In ancient times self-expression was never a function of art; in modern times this has become the major function of art.

- Relativism in morality. In ancient times, moral rules were seen as absolute, that is, as having their origin outside of humans. In modern times, relativism dominates.

- Tolerance for cruelty to others. In ancient times individual pain and suffering was tolerated to an extent we no longer understand. Families in medieval times would routinely attend hangings and other brutal punishments (boiling in oil, dismemberment).

- Increasing insistence on democratic political institutions instead of autocratic, dictatorial systems.

We would expect that, with the rise of importance of the individual, these practices would no longer be tolerated. The question arises as to why this shift in consciousness occurred. There have been many theories, but my favorite explains the shift occurring in correlation with the shift from oral culture to, first, written culture, then print culture. Writing and print force us to separate our selves from the world in a way oral culture does not. This, in turn, leads to greater levels of abstraction.

conditions means our sentences and the theories they are a part of will help us get around better in the world, enabling us to do what we deem most important in our lives, but they are purely methodological—they indicate nothing about the external world. Public agreement becomes the touchstone of our beliefs rather than the external world itself.

We know that truth is important. The cash value of saying that our sentences are true, or that we value knowledge, is that these help us survive and thrive in the world. We will now turn, in the following chapters, to examine the scope and limits of our ability, as humans, to procure truth, and how we can best be said to know when we have it.

Notes / Questions

8. Our Knowledge

· ·

Nothing more strikingly betokens the imperfection and limitedness of our knowledge than the ironic circumstance of the uneliminable incompleteness of our knowledge regarding our knowledge itself, which arises because we do not and cannot know the details of our ignorance.

—Nicholas Rescher (2010: 97)

SYNOPSIS

In the last chapter we considered truth—touched the surface really, but enough to give you an inkling of what the term involves. We will now begin to apply this to see what it means to say we know something. (1) The world is a vast source of prospective truths which can never be completely encapsulated by our finite investigations; we will never exhaust the potential truths that we can explore. (2) What we mean by perception. At base, this is the only true source of our knowledge. (3) A look at how induction works, with special consideration given to the scientific method as the most successful form of induction. The downside of induction is that it only results in probabilities. Deduction promises to solve this problem. (4) A look at how deduction works. Deduction gives us necessity in our reasonings, but this is not all it appears to be. The conclusion is that deductive methods are ultimately based upon inductive methods. (5) An historical note on the movement from a deductive methodology (Plato) to an inductive one (Aristotle) and the corresponding changes to Western thinking. (6) On the wonders of inductive reasoning. Inductive methodologies can be ingenious, allowing us to discover truths we would not have thought possible to discover. (7) The importance of memory for our truth claims. Knowledge is nothing more than what we can remember about the facts we perceive. If all our knowledge ultimately depends upon memory, then the largest obstacle to knowing might be ourselves. (8) Chapter Summary.

CHAPTER OBJECTIVES

- appreciate the vastness of potential knowledge and fleeting nature of our present knowledge.
- provide a foundation for understanding why our knowledge will always lack absolute certitude
- understand how important memory is in our every day life (and how we attempt to protect ourselves from its fallibility)
- become aware of barriers (to knowledge) that exist between us and the world

§1 *ON THE SCOPE OF OUR KNOWLEDGE*

The amount of data we humans are collecting is increasing at an astonishing rate. All of the data from all of the missions collected by NASA from 1958 to 2000 can be stored on a one terabyte drive (a terabyte is 1,000 gigabytes), while the recent Lunar Reconnaissance Orbiter alone returned over 192 terabytes of data. The Sloan Digital Sky Survey (SDSS I, not to mention SDSS II & III) has made photometric observations of over 500 million objects (over 35% of the sky). These are just two of a multitude of data collection projects that are returning massive amounts of information to earth for analysis. In fact, the data already surpasses our ability to mine it thoroughly. Amateurs have been enlisted to spot the obvious (galaxy types, supernovas, planets), but most of the information will never be thoroughly sifted.

Information itself is not knowledge. Knowledge seems to be something more; an organized set of information rather than a jumble of facts. This need not be spelled out in great detail, but is a point to keep in mind, especially in light of our emphasis on the importance of connectivity. What is important to us is connecting pieces of information (by analogy, inference, and so on); indeed, this may constitute what we mean by cognition itself.

A fact is an actual aspect of the world's state of affairs, a feature of reality. Truths, as we have seen, are linguistically stated facts. Traditionally, every fact corresponds to a potential truth awaiting linguistic embodiment. The ideal of science has always been to continually advance our technological proficiency until we have taken account of all facts. Figure 8–1 gives a schematic illustration of this, in which we can imagine all three circles as time-dependent and thus as capable of growth. It may seem odd that the outer circle increases (our god's-eye-view of the universe), but new facts are continually created as the universe changes, and this is true even if the total amount of matter and energy is continuous, for the rearrangement of these is constant. So also, as a time relevant concept, the potentially knowable continually increases. In Aristotle's day it was not possible to view individual atoms, germs, cells, or see the stars and galaxies beyond the bounds of human perception. Thus, we might say that these were not then the potential objects of knowledge (in the same sense) that they are now. This growth in knowledge potential corresponds

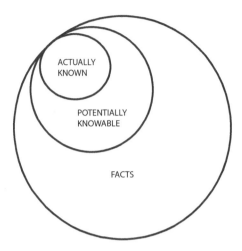

FIGURE 8–1

A schematic illustration of what we know. All three circles are time-dependent and continually increasing. The outer circle increases due to the constant changing features of the world, the middle circle increases with technological advances, and the small circle increases as we utilize this technology to collect data.

with the growth of our actual knowledge, for it is technology that extends our potential, and, unless we never use the technology in question, our knowledge will increase accordingly.

The pleasing thought that all three circles will at some undefined point in the future merge into one is but a pipe dream. For facts, it seems, are inexhaustible. The complex diversity of the world around us guarantees there will always be more that can be said concerning any particular aspect of the world than is actually said. Figure 8–2 depicts the situation with a more accurate representation. In this figure we have to imagine all three circles expanding, but with the two outer circles expanding at a greater rate than what is actually known.

Every fact has features that are beyond the scope of our comprehension. Fiction differs from fact in that facts have what Rescher (2006) has called "unlimited depth." Fiction has limited depth because the framework upon which any fictional story rests is fabricated by us, which means the work will lack the multitude of connections existing within reality. If you ever find yourself in a virtual world, push its boundaries and you will eventually encounter its emptiness.[1]

There is a vast, indefinitely large, number of facts in the world, a number far beyond our ability, as humans, to comprehend. This is true for the following reasons:

(1) We may simply not be intelligent enough to grasp some of the complexities involved. When you consider there are approximately 7×10^{22} stars in the universe which are arranged in over 100 billion galaxies, which themselves are arranged in clusters and superclusters, giving a rough

---

[1] This has been a theme of several movies, one of which is, again, *The Truman Show,* where there are multiple devices in place to try to keep Truman from pushing past the boundaries which would then show his world to be fictional. This raises interesting questions with respect to our own odd perception of boundaries (we touched on boundary processing in chapter 3).

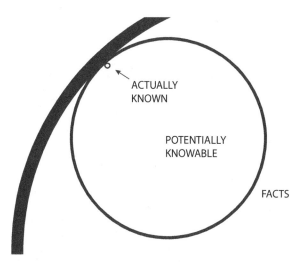

ACTUALLY
KNOWN

POTENTIALLY
KNOWABLE

FACTS

FIGURE 8–2

A more to scale model of Figure 8–1, showing how little we know compared to what we can potentially know, and how much we do not know (most of which we will never know).

estimate of 10^{90} atoms in the universe, all of which are arranged in various relationships to each other, forming an incomprehensible matrix the details of which are awaiting linguistic manifestation. Furthermore, each of those atoms is composed of multiple atomic and subatomic particles, all of which have the same complex relationships as their larger sisters. Stephen Hawking (2010) and others (for example, Green 2011) speak of the multiverse, in which there are as many as 10^{500} universes like ours, all with different sets of natural laws. When you understand this vastness you begin to understand one of the limitations on our knowledge.[2]

(2) Since events happen within the scope of an ever-moving time frame, from the standpoint of our present we are continually losing the ability to recover facts that will never again be divulged due to the opacity of the past. We don't have to contemplate the state of the universe to bring this home; simply contemplate the death of any one person and realize all the aspects of that person that will never be known. Or consider a past event such as the civil war in American history, and all the unknowable facts

---

[2] We don't have to go cosmological in order to understand this vastness. Consider the game of chess. It has been estimated that from the initial position there are 10^{120} possible variations which would have to be calculated by any machine trying to solve a chess game by brute force calculation. If we assume the machine can calculate at the rate of one variation every microsecond (there are 1,000 microseconds in a second), then it would take it 10^{90} years to complete the calculation. Our human operating systems face this problem continually when pruning our decision trees (though obviously on a much less vast scale). We make myriads of instantaneous decisions concerning what is relevant and what isn't on a preconscious level when discerning objects, their depth, their background, and so on.

THE DAY THE UNIVERSE EXPANDED

On December 28, 1995 the known universe expanded. On that date scientists pointed the Hubble telescope at a black speck in the sky near the constellation we call the Big Dipper. The point in the sky was about the size of a grain of sand held at arms length (approximately 1/28,000,000 of the total sky), and contained almost no known astronomical objects. The scientists created a layered exposure over ten days, not knowing whether they were wasting precious Hubble-time until the final image was processed. In that image (known as the Hubble Deep-Field) they were amazed to find more than three thousand galaxies never before seen by humans.

In 2004 the experiment was repeated with an improved camera in a different part of the sky (in the constellation Fornax) and the result (known as the Hubble Ultra-Deep-Field) showed more than 10,000 new galaxies. An average-size galaxy contains anywhere from 100 billion to 1 trillion stars, (the Milky Way has around 100 billion). So if we assume 500 billion stars per galaxy, this gives us 5 trillion new objects in the Ultra-Deep-Field photograph alone (not to mention planets orbiting the stars). It is estimated that there are over 100 billion galaxies in the universe.

contained within its scope. Here are a few examples of the innumerable facts we will never know about the civil war:

(a) The youngest Confederate soldier to die of a gunshot wound at the battle of Gettysburg.
(b) The velocity of the 723rd cannonball fired by the Union in the battle of Fredricksburg.
(c) The name of the person who fired that cannonball.
(d) The number of people who died of natural causes on Robert E. Lee's birthday in 1864.

All such facts are forever lost to us due simply to the nature of reality.

(3) There are other, in principle, limits to our knowledge. Heisenberg's uncertainty principle, for example, tells us we can know either the position or the momentum of an electron, but never both. This limitation is due to neither a technological nor an intellectual deficiency, but to the very nature of the world. Related to this, at least in its symmetry, is Gödel's Theorem, which proves the set of whole numbers could be shown to be complete, but only at the cost of its becoming inconsistent; and if we make it consistent, then it will always be incomplete.

These limitations show why it is always a mistake to proclaim we will one day achieve the god's-eye-view in which all knowledge is encompassed. On the other hand, it is also a mistake to claim we will never know some particular aspect of the universe, for we humans are ingenious investigators of our domain. The physicist Michio Kaku (2009) makes this clear:

Let me remind you of a speech given by Nobel laureate Albert A. Michelson in 1894 at the dedication of the Ryerson Physical Lab at the University of Chicago, in which he declared that it was impossible to discover any new physics: "The more important fundamental laws and facts of physical science have all been discovered, and these are now so firmly established that the possibility of their ever being supplanted in consequence of new discoveries is exceedingly remote..." ... His remarks were uttered on the eve of some of the greatest upheavals in scientific history, the quantum revolution of 1900, and the relativity revolution of 1905. The point is that things that are impossible today violate the known laws of physics, but the laws of physics, as we know them, can change. (285)

Kaku also tells of the famous French positivist philosopher Auguste Compte, who claimed, in 1825, that it would always be impossible for science to determine what stars were made of—they're just too far away. And yet a few years later the science of spectroscopy allowed scientists to analyze light from the stars and thus determine their chemical makeup. Even today such claims are made with seeming authority, as, for example, by the astronomer John Barrow: "All the great questions about the nature of the Universe—from its beginning to its end—turn out to be unanswerable." (287) The statement makes sense—the space-time boundaries of the universe seem incredibly distant, but what new discoveries, I wonder, are in the works that will one day make him eat those words?

§2 PERCEPTION

We usually use the term 'perception' to refer to our consciousness of objects via the five senses, but this is arbitrary, for there are other types of perceptions we could include in this term. Internal perceptions, for example, are those sent to your brain from various organs and parts of your body. These are processed in the brain by the insula, which relays its signals to the emotional center of the brain (primarily the amygdala), where they are interpreted as emotional states (your external sensory inputs are also sent to the emotional center). You know, for example, where your hands and feet are without looking, for there are continuous sensory inputs from the ligaments in your joints which are relayed to the insula via the spinal cord. Pain sensation is another example. Below this conscious level, though, are the sensory inputs from your vital organs, bones and muscles, all of which are constantly

> **EXTEROCEPTION**
> Perception of the external world via the five senses: sight, sound, smell, hearing, and touch.
>
> **INTEROCEPTION**
> Perception of pain and the movement of interal organs.
>
> **PROPRIOCEPTION**
> Perception of the body's movement and the location of the various parts of the body in relation to each other

monitored. Is this sense experience? Surely it is, for it is the result of input sensors being processed by the brain, which is exactly what happens with respect to taste, smell, touch, hearing and sight.

We will focus our attention on our conscious perceptions. My brain is monitoring my heart rate and lung capacity, indeed my entire metabolism, as I write this, but since I am not conscious of this we will not call this perception. We usually equate perceptions with objects in the world, but of course this need not be the case, and even if there is an object we aren't necessarily sure we are seeing it as it really is. Figure 8–3 illustrates these possibilities. The top ellipse contains within it all external objects, including boys, bats and bobsleds, but also atoms, neutrinos and stars— any object existing in the world (including the perceiver's body). The bottom ellipse contains all of our perceptions, including those of sunsets, the smell of sweat, and the feel of silk on your fingers, but also pink elephants, phantom limbs, and dreams. With this in mind, let's consider each of the numbered sections of Figure 8–3:

Section (1) indicates facts we either have not or cannot perceive at this time, even with technological extensions. This includes the sorts of historical facts we mentioned above. In the 1800s, germs were beyond the scope of our perception. Before December 28, 1995 there were thousands of galaxies (and all the stars contained within) that were beyond our perception (see box on page 176). As our technology improves we become aware of more and more entities, whether we look inward toward the subatomic or outward toward the galactic. There doesn't seem to be an end in sight.

Section (2) indicates perceptions with no corresponding objects. At this very moment I am conjuring a mental picture of a unicorn. Now I've turned it into a flying unicorn, and now it's pink. There is obviously no object that corresponds to this perception. If we create these perceptions intentionally we say we are using our imagination; if they appear unintentionally, like phantom-limb pain, they are hallucinations (though we might induce hallucinations intentionally). There may be times when we cannot tell the difference. Descartes, for instance, tells us that we cannot distinguish between waking states and dreaming states. So also, you may be nothing more than a brain in a vat in a scientist's laboratory, and all of your perceived reality may be caused by electrical stimulations. This is another scenario brought out by the movie, *The Matrix*. We will have more to say about this in the next chapter.

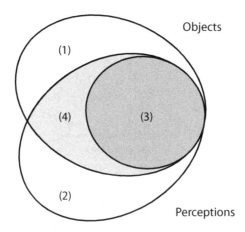

FIGURE 8–3
The relationship between perception (bottom ellipse) and objects in the world (top ellipse). (1) is unperceived objects, (2) is perceptions with no object, (3) is incorrectly perceived objects, and (4) is correctly perceived objects.

Sections (3) and (4) in Figure 8–3 both contain perceptions with a corresponding object. Section (3) is composed of those in which the object is not correctly represented, for whatever reason.[3] We call these illusions or misrepresentations (see Figure 8–4). When you look at a straw in a glass of water the straw appears bent; when you look at a long straight stretch of railroad tracks, the tracks appear to converge in the distance. Our senses fool us continually and we learn to adjust accordingly.

Section (4) is the realm of perception in the way we ordinarily use the term; a perception of objects that are not misrepresented. I look out the window and see trees and cars and people, and there really are trees and cars and people outside.

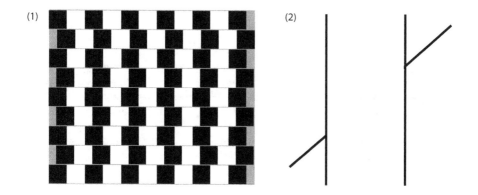

(1) (2)

FIGURE 8–4

Examples of standard optical illusions: (1) The cafe-wall illusion. The horizontal lines appear skewed, but they are straight. (2) The Poggendorf illusion. The oblique line segment appears to be offset, but isn't.

Of course, nothing is as simple as it seems. Difficulties arise when we insist on matching objects in the world to our perceptions, difficulties raised, for example by the position we have referred to earlier as embodied perception. The classical (and still predominant) view of the brain is that it is a data processor that just happens to be connected to a particular body, but which could be connected it to a different body, or to a machine, and would parse the data in essentially the same way (I consider this an example of the abstraction fallacy). Embodied perception denies this, claiming that the processor is inextricable from the processed. We will discuss this mismatch between subject and object further in chapter 10, but one example from Ramachandran (2011) will give you an idea:

> ... if you bite into a pencil (as if it were a bridle bit) to stretch your mouth into a wide, fake smile, you will have difficulty detecting another person's

---

[3] This is relative, of course, for the degree of representational correspondence may always be askew. In other words, is there ever a correct representation of an object? and if so, what would this be like? To imply there is one correct representation returns us to the question of what the world is like before it is processed by our operating system. A misrepresentation may be a perception that merely differs in some way from what the majority of perceivers would agree to.

smile (but not a frown). This is because biting the pencil activates many of the same muscles as a smile, and this floods your brain's mirror-neuron system, creating a confusion between action and perception. (Certain mirror neurons fire when you make a facial expression and when you observe the same expression on another person's face.) The experiment shows that actions and perception are much more closely intertwined in the brain than is usually assumed. (143)

If this is so, then there is a tighter relationship between our self-conscious perceptions and our bodies then the standard view implies. How tight remains to be seen.

§3 SOURCES OF KNOWLEDGE: INDUCTION

I mentioned two questions concerning truth in the previous chapter. The first, "What is truth?" was seen to be trivial, at least in the sense that its answer is always the same: a sentence (any sentence) is true if it correctly describes the world. The second, "How do you know when you have truth?" I brushed over with the answer: "We theorize." We must now elaborate on this.

My position is that there is but one way to truth: by means of theory. But, traditionally, theory has utilized two methodologies:

(1) Induction. Associated concepts: experience, theorizing, scientific method, contingency, probability

(2) Deduction. Associated concepts: intuition, rationalism, mathematics, necessity, absolute certainty

Induction, the most successful form of which is called the scientific method, begins with our experiencing the world. On its most basic level this is what we have called (in chapter 2) sentience, but we are more interested here in the reflective experience we called sensation. We collect sense data and attempt to integrate it into our existing framework. If there is no easy fit we formulate new hypotheses. These hypotheses can then be tested, for they allow us to make predictions about the future (see Figure 8–5). We go through this process many times every day of our lives. For example, I once had someone tell me that as she left for work one morning (she lived alone in her own home), there in the hallway by the front door was an empty beer bottle and an old blanket. She clearly remembered locking up the night before. Note how she proceeded according to the inductive method:

The experienced fact of the beer bottle and blanket gave rise to an anomaly: where did they come from? She immediately formulated a theory (someone somehow got inside the house) which generated predictions (there should be signs of forced entry, the person is still in the house). She then tested her theory: she looked for corroborating data, but none could be found (no signs of forced entry, no one in the house). Theory failed. Reformulate. The person could have left and locked the door behind them. Anomaly: but how

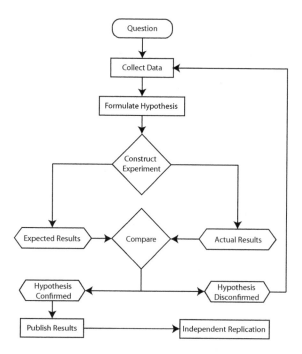

FIGURE 8–5

A flow chart of some of the processes involved in the scientific method. Once a question has been formulated, relevant data is collected in order to answer the question and a hypothesis is proposed that answers the question. This hypothesis generates future predictions which can be tested by means of an experiment. If the experiment confirms the hypothesis, the results will be published so that other, independent experiments can confirm the test results. If the experiment disconfirms the hypothesis, there is a return to the earlier stage of data gathering.

did they get in? Hypothesis: memory failed; she must not have locked the door after all. No way to verify that one.[4]

That's induction in a nutshell, though nutshells are fragile things, for our brief foray has been a vast oversimplification. Testing a hypothesis by means of its future predictions is a method fraught with danger, for, as we have seen, our brains are not optimally designed for truth-finding. For example, we cannot simply base our views on predictions fulfilled because predictions can be accidentally fulfilled. Remember our black cat belief back in chapter 3. If I believe that black cats cause bad luck (my hypothesis), I might test this the next time I see a black cat: I await the bad luck, and sure enough, later that day my car has a flat tire. I then conclude that my

---

[4] There are other unanswered questions: why did they break in? Nothing was stolen; no food was eaten. Did they just need a place to sleep? None of these questions were ever answered, but they obviously still bothered her when she told me the story. We do not like untidy strands in our conceptual schemes. This is the pull of curiosity.

black-cat-hypothesis has been confirmed. But it should be clear there is no confirmation, only an accidental connection. I may have gotten the flat even without the black cat's intervention. Because of these sorts of biases scientists must proceed with extreme caution when formulating experiments and drawing conclusions from them. Truth claims demand multiple experiments with independently repeatable results, blinds, double-blinds, triple-blinds—all of which are put in place to avoid our human tendency to jump to conclusions.

My thesis is that humans have theorized for thousands of years (though they would not admit to it until recent times), but not until the scientific method was developed did this theorizing become a plausible method of insuring that our reasonings lead to truth rather than falsehood. The scientific method is a set of algorithms through which we run our experiences, which enable us to generate true sentences more than false sentences—an extremely successful set of algorithms, I might add. The reason the scientific method is so highly touted today is that it, by far, exceeds any other available set of algorithms that attempt to do the same thing. Compared head-to-head with any other method used for obtaining knowledge—faith, prayer, intuition, communion with the spirits, dice rolling, guessing, coin-flipping, bottle-spinning, astrology, various peel and pip divinations, oracular pronouncements, I Ching, dowsing, tarot, numerology, palmistry, oneiromancy, crystal gazing, entrail and tealeaf deciphering, crystal ball-gazing, and so on—none is as consistently successful as the scientific method. Not even close.

Imagine a conversation between two stone-age men concerning whether or not to enter a cave.

A: Do you think there's a bear in that cave?
B: Nah, there's no bear.
A: How do you know?
B: God spoke to me last night. He told me there is no bear in that cave!

If A goes in the cave and there is no bear, our human logical shortcomings see this as confirmation that god talks to B, but consistent repetition of this procedure could end in A's getting eaten 50% of the time (or more). Sporadic results are the hallmark of non-scientific truth methods, and none is more successful than another when it comes to making future predictions.

What is the difference in the highly successful scientific method of theorizing and the less successful pre-scientific methods? In a word: publicity. The scientific method demands that experimental results be replicated by different people in different settings, and this safeguards us from the multiple human biases that play havoc with our otherwise subjective speculations. Without publicity, you may stumble upon the truth from time to time, but you will not find it consistently.

There is a downside. Induction via the scientific method can yield wonderful new truths about the world, but it can never claim absolute necessity—it is always and only known with some degree of probability. We will refer to this lack of necessity as contingency. For example, from sense experience you can never deduce a universal proposition such as "All swans are white," for no matter how much data you gather (no matter how many white swans you observe), you can never be absolutely sure that a disconfirming piece of evidence (a black swan) will not appear in the future (and all it takes is one to ruin a universal statement). Hence, the probabilistic nature of inductive (empirical) knowledge. Consider the following example of inductive reasoning:

(1) All the weather reports today indicate rain.
(2) Today is overcast and the clouds look threatening.
(3) The radar shows thunderstorm activity approaching the area.

(4) It will rain sometime today.

The premises (1)-(3) function as evidence for the conclusion (4). Even if we assume the truth of all the premises, though, we can only claim (4) with some degree of probability. We know that no matter how it looks or what the experts and their instruments are saying, they are often wrong. Even if we say that it is highly probable it will rain today it could still not rain. So also if we said it was highly improbable that it will not rain, it still could. Our inability to generate truth with 100% accuracy by means of induction is a function of our knowledge limitations (which itself is a function of the complexity of the world we live in).

Nassim Taleb (2007) tries to help us understand that improbable events occur all the time and will always take us by surprise. He gives an example of a turkey who, using the inductive method, observes day after day after day that the farmer arrives in the morning and feeds him. This justifies his concluding that tomorrow the farmer will also arrive and feed him, for he always has in the past; but, of course, one day the farmer arrives and, instead of feeding him, chops off his head and serves him as the main course for Thanksgiving dinner. From our higher reference frame we understand that the turkey's reasoning is fallacious, but we are, of course immersed in our own reference frames.

The contingent nature of conclusions drawn by means of the scientific method is indicated by the fact that these conclusions only follow with a certain amount of probability. Theorizing will always and only give us probable results—never absolutely certain results—and it is because of this lack of certainty that deduction is appealing.

§4 SOURCES OF KNOWLEDGE: DEDUCTION

The beauty of the deductive method is that it gives necessity to our derivations in a way that induction cannot, and with necessity comes certainty, which we humans adore. Consider the following valid argument form:

(1) Building A is taller than building B.
(2) Building B is taller than building C.

(3) Building A is taller than building C.

In logic, a valid argument is defined as follows: if the premises of the argument are true, then the conclusion of the argument must also be true. (1) and (2) are the premises of the above argument. Note that if you assume they are true, then there is no possible way the conclusion (3) can be false. That is, the conclusion follows *with absolute necessity* from its premises!

Let's get more specific by plugging in values for our variables in the above argument. Here's one possibility (as illustrated in Figure 8–6):

(1) The Petronas Towers are taller than the Eiffel Tower.
(2) The Eiffel Tower is taller than the Taj Mahal.
_____
(3) The Petronas Towers are taller than the Taj Mahal.

Call this argument A1. Since A1 exhibits the same form as the valid argument form above, it must also be valid (validity applies to the form of an argument, which means any substitution instance will also be valid). We have no problem seeing this, as exhibited in Figure 8–6, Argument (1). But now look at another example, A2:

(4) The Eiffel Tower is taller than the Taj Mahal.
(5) The Taj Mahal is taller than the Petronas Towers.
_____
(6) The Eiffel Tower is taller than the Petronas Towers.

A2 also exhibits the same valid form and thus it, too, must be valid, even though it has a false premise (5) and a false conclusion (6). This is because the definition of validity is formulated as a hypothetical: "*If* the premises are true, then the conclusion must be true." This still holds, for the premises are *not* both true, so the conclusion can be false. But if (4) and (5) were true, then of course (6) would be necessarily true as well. This is all that is required for validity.

The important point of this discussion is to recognize our seeming ability to obtain necessity via deduction, a feat impossible with induction. Valid argument forms are to deduction what the scientific method is to induction, with one huge exception: the former generates necessarily true propositions while the latter generates only contingently true propositions. With deduction, given the truth of the

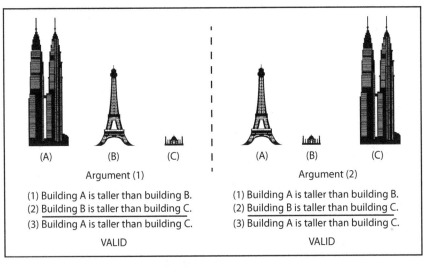

FIGURE 8–6

Validity. The validity of an argument form does not depend upon the truth of its premises or conclusion. Validity says only that if the premises are true then the conclusion must be true as well.

IMPROBABLE EVENTS

What are the odds that I could find a person who could win ten coin-flip games in a row? The odds of finding someone who has correctly guessed heads or tails ten times in a row seems small, but it is easily achieved. In fact, I could produce a person who has won even more, but let's stick with ten. Here's the procedure: I simply set up a single-elimination tournament with the following structure:

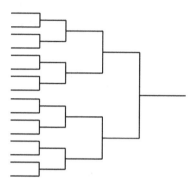

and, voila, the winner will be a person who has won ten straight coin-flip games. The above bracket shows four sets of coin flips, but by increasing the number of people we could increase the coin flips, and there will always be a winner. For our ten-straight winner we would need to start with 1,028 people (2^9). To find a person who has won 100 straight games we would start with 2^{99} (since there are less than 2^{33} people living on earth, this would be physically impossible; the total number of people who have *ever* lived on earth, including those alive now is less than 2^{37}).

Here's one more improbability that works on the same principle: think of all your direct ancestors, stretching back over thousands of years. What are the odds that not one of them died before having a child? And yet here you are!

---

premises we can be absolutely certain that the conclusion is true. This feature of valid arguments also applies to larger deductive systems known as formal or axiomatic systems. The deductive method always begins with a set of sentences (either premises or axioms) from which deductions are made. Premises and axioms have the same function: they are accepted starting points for deduction, but what does it mean to be accepted?

We know we can generate true conclusions by using valid argument forms. In other words validity is a truth preserving algorithm—plug in true premises and out comes a true conclusion. But this means we must first be assured that the premises we plug in are true. There are only two ways to do this: we must use either deduction or induction. But of course, if we use deductive arguments to prove the premises true then the same problem arises with respect to these arguments—their premises must also be proved by means of valid deductive arguments, and the premises of those arguments must be proved by means of valid deductive arguments, and so on. This generates a potentially infinite regress of arguments, which means we cannot depend on deduction to justify our premises.

If, on the other hand, we use induction we lose the necessity that is the justification for using deduction in the first place. That is, if we formulate inductive arguments for the premises of our deductive argument, then the premises of our deductive argument will only be true with a degree of probability and this probability will be transferred to the conclusion. The conclusion will never be more certain than the premises on which it is based.

One solution to this problem is to rely on self-evidence as a justification. An example of this can be found in the American Declaration of Independence, where Jefferson proudly proclaims, "We hold these truths to be self-evident, that all men are created equal, that they are endowed by their Creator with certain unalienable Rights, that among these are Life, Liberty and the pursuit of Happiness." I doubt these were self-evident to King George, and therein lies the problem of self-evidence. What is self-evident to you may not be self-evident to me and vice versa. Furthermore, our intuitions of self-evidence do not necessarily conform to the way the world is. Consider, for example, one of Euclid's postulates (his term for axioms), the fifth or parallel lines postulate:

> Given any line and any point not on that line, one and only one line can be drawn through that point that is parallel to the first line.

When you understand the terms as used by Euclid, this sentence really does seem necessarily true. Once you have drawn a line (B) through point (P) that is parallel to the first line (A), how could you possibly draw a second line through the same point (on the same plane) that is also parallel with the first line? (Figure 8–7) Thus did Euclid proclaim the self-evidence of his starting points. But the fifth postulate was questionable almost from the start (even Euclid was uncomfortable with it), and in fact has turned out not to be a correct description of the universe according to Einstein's theory of relativity, in which he adopted a non-Euclidean geometry, that is, a geometry without the fifth postulate. Over and over again modern science, from cosmology to neuroscience, has demonstrated that our common sense (upon which we base our claims of self-evidence and obviousness) cannot be trusted.

But, you might object, we surely do use universal propositions in our arguments. How is this possible? Consider the following argument:

(1) All mammals are warm-blooded creatures.
(2) All bats are mammals.
_____
(3) All bats are warm-blooded creatures.

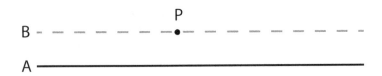

FIGURE 8–7
An illustration of Euclid's 5th postulate, where A is the first line and P is a point not on that line. The postulate claims that one and only one line (B) can be drawn through P that is parallel to A.

This is a valid argument and its premises are true, so the conclusion is also true. But how do we know the premises are true? Knowledge gained from sense experience will never yield propositions that are necessarily true or universal, but we can construct categories by fiat (by definition and agreed upon behavior) and claim our universal propositions are necessarily true. We are justified in treating them as universal, for no sense experience can refute them. We have designed them this way. For example, given the present meaning of the terms, the sentence "All bats are mammals" is necessarily true, since, if you know the meaning of the terms involved, you need not check all bats in the world to see if they are mammals. By definition, if you come across something that isn't a mammal, it won't be a bat. These meanings may change, but within our definitional system right now, they hold fast. Note how this differs from "All swans are white." The color white is not a part of the concept of a swan in the way that being a mammal is part of the concept of a bat. I could build whiteness into the concept of a swan, but then I would have to call black swans something else, maybe "blans." Thus, our concepts are malleable. To say that "All bats are mammals" is a faux necessity of sorts; a necessity we have agreed upon.[5]

What actually happens when we formulate universal sentences is this: we go out into the world and collect data, noticing the similarities and differences of things. We note, for instance, that there are a lot of animals that share certain characteristics and we call these, say, "mammals" to distinguish them from other animals that do not share these characteristics. We can then go out into the world and look for more instances that fit into these categories. Thus, the categories are based on experience (induction), and we turn them into universals by defining them as such. Once we have defined a category we can then use deduction to draw conclusions that hold with absolute necessity (Figure 8–8). But notice again that this is always provisional upon the acceptance of our starting point, which is established with induction. Thus, the conclusion of this argument:

(1) All bats are mammals.
(2) This creature in my hand is a bat.
_____
(3) This creature in my hand is a mammal.

follows with absolute necessity if we grant that we accept the universal proposition (1) as a definition (a human construct), and that we have correctly identified the creature in hand. Necessity is always provisional. It is not to be found in nature.

To summarize, there are two overriding points of interest in the last two sections: First, although traditionally there were said to be two methods for obtaining truth, induction and deduction, we have seen that the deduction ultimately reduces to, or depends upon, induction. Second, we must reiterate that the most successful methodology for utilizing induction is the scientific method, which is a modern rendition of the process we have called theorizing.

---

[5] It used to be held that characteristics such as "being a mammal" were essential properties of bats (and humans). The search for essential properties was a search for what makes something what it is. For example, humans were rational animals. Other properties, like the whiteness of feathers or the color of our hair were said to be accidental properties. We, today, realize that all properties are accidental, having evolved randomly over time. Essences are relegated to definitions.

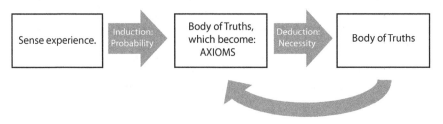

FIGURE 8–8

The ultimate source of all our reflective knowledge is experience by means of induction. We then take this inductive knowledge, stipulate it as true and from these "axioms" deduce other truths based on the relationships of the categories we have created. These deductions can then be used to deduce even more truths.

§5 HISTORICAL ASIDE: METHODOLOGICAL MODIFICATIONS

Plato's system of knowledge was based solely on deduction. He believed, as we have seen, that knowledge is obtained when the human mind grasps truths in a separate world, the world of forms. This other world was the source of all our knowledge, which means we do not need sense experience, for it will only lead us astray. In theory, a philosopher could sit in a closet, never experiencing the world, accessing instead the world of the forms, and know all there is to know about everything. Plato's most famous student, Aristotle, rebelled against this otherworldly nature of knowledge, and embedded the forms (which he agreed must be grasped in order to obtain knowledge) firmly within this world. For Plato, if you are to recognize a cow as a cow you must mentally grasp the form "cow" in the world of forms; while for Aristotle you can only grasp the form by looking at the cow itself, for the form is inseparable from the object in which it inheres. Thus, we have two radically different methodologies developing simultaneously: Plato's deductive method and Aristotle's inductive method.

An historical accident led to a loss of the works of Aristotle in Western Europe, while Plato's remained available. This may have had something to do with the fact that Plato wrote for popular consumption—his philosophy was encapsulated in literary dialogues—while Aristotle left behind only lecture notes. These lecture notes were transferred to the famous library of Alexandria in Egypt, which was part of the empire of Alexander the Great (who was a student of Aristotle's). With the disintegration of Alexander's empire, communication between the West and the East broke down, and so the West lost access to Aristotle's work. (This schism between East and West, briefly patched by the Romans, was further cemented by the rise of Islam in the seventh century.) Plato's works, however, remained, and when the early Christian church fathers were attempting to systematize their theology they used Plato's framework as their basis.

Plato's philosophy fit well with the Christian view. In his world of forms was the form of the good, the highest and most abstract form; a form which contained all other forms. Furthermore, the forms themselves were perfect, eternal and unchanging. The church fathers thus adapted the form of the good into the Christian god and used Plato's arguments for the forms as arguments for the existence of god. The problem arose as to how we humans could access god. In short, we can't, for we are imperfect, but god can access us, and thus he gave humans special revelation (the Bible) which served as the source of all knowledge. To put this in the terminology of this chapter: Christianity developed an axiomatic system in which the fundamental truths were found in the Bible. These axioms were unquestionably necessary truths and were knowable with absolute certainty—after all, they were from god.

Note the ramifications of this: the Bible, which is given by god, tells us all we need to know about how to live in this world. Thus, there is no incentive for humans to go out into the world to find knowledge. Sense experience is not a source of knowledge. The result has been labeled the dark ages. The darkness of the dark ages lies in its stagnation. Scholasticism was the reigning methodology for learning and consisted in arranging and rearranging Biblical truths in endlessly different formulations (all consistent with the basic ideas of early theorizing). These systems were grounded in the ratiocinations of humans using only the Bible as a touchstone for their consistency.

Enter Islam, which rapidly spread via warfare through North Africa, decimating the Christian churches there and cementing Rome as the center of Christianity instead of Carthage. The Islamic armies crossed the straits of Gibraltar, captured Spain, crossed the Pyrenees and were only just stopped from taking France by Charles Martel (grandfather of Charlemagne) at the battle of Tours in 722. Slowly the French pushed Islam back into Spain, where they clung tenaciously for another 500 years (giving rise to wonderful literary figures such as Rolland and El Cid). The Islamic toehold in Spain meant extensive interaction (for the first time) between the two cultures. Islamic theologians always had access to Aristotelian texts and used them in the same way Western theologians had used Plato, and now, for the first time, these texts became accessible to the West, where they began to be incorporated into Christian theology.

Thomas Aquinas (1225-1274) was the first Christian theologian to systematically use Aristotle in a reinterpretation of Christian theology. Just as Aristotle had emphasized finding truth in nature, Aquinas introduced a new type of revelation, natural revelation, which was seen to complement special revelation. With the advent of natural revelation, god could be found in nature as well as in the Bible, and this gave humans incentive to go out into the world and use their senses to discover new facts and features, all of which were seen to glorify god. The powers that be rebelled, but Pandora's box was open. The fruits of induction were too tasty to resist, and it was a short step from using induction to glorify god to using it simply to assuage that irresistible urge to know more. This urge eventually resulted in the development of the scientific method, which eventually turned its back on the church, following its own path of discovery.

This is the power of a shift in methodology. The Platonic view stifled the West for centuries (it was no coincidence that the great strides made in science and mathematics were initially Arabic). This change in methodologies, from deduction to induction, was what eventually gave rise to science and technology and all the consequences, both good and bad, these have since engendered.

§6 THE WONDER OF INDUCTION

Zadig was an ancient Babylonian philosopher who was once able to give an extremely accurate description of a princess's lost dog, even though he had never seen the dog. Here is what he deciphered from dog tracks in the sand:

> Long faint streaks upon the little elevations of sand between the foot-marks convinced me that it was a she dog with pendent dugs, show-ing that she must have had puppies not many days since. Other scrap-ings of the sand, which always lay close to the marks of the forepaws, indicated that she had very long ears; and, as the imprint of one foot was always fainter than those of the other three, I judged that the lady dog of our august Queen was, if I may venture to say so, a little lame. (Gere 8)

Zadig was too good at his trade. He was said to have been executed for making it possible to potentially meddle with ancient sacred truths, that is, his calculations were indistinguishable from magic. This same method was also used by Sherlock Holmes. Consider the classic example from Conan Doyle's "Sign of the Four," where Watson tests Holmes' abilities by giving him a watch he has recently acquired from his brother.

> I handed him over the watch with some slight feeling of amusement in my heart, for the test was, as I thought, an impossible one, and I intended it as a lesson against the somewhat dogmatic tone which he occasionally assumed.

> Holmes, looks the watch over carefully, lamenting that it had been recently cleaned, which no doubt destroyed valuable evidence. But still, he says, "I should judge that the watch belonged to your elder brother, who inherited it from your father... The W. suggests your own name. The date of the watch is nearly fifty years back and the initials are as old as the watch; so it was made for the last generation. Jewelry usually descends to the eldest son, and he is most likely to have the same name as the father. Your father has, if I remember right, been dead many years. It has, therefore, been in the hands of your eldest brother."

Watson admits that this is correct, and Holmes continues:

> "He was a man of untidy habits—very untidy and careless. He was left with good prospects, but he threw away his chances, lived for some time in pov-erty with occasional short intervals of prosperity, and finally, taking to drink, he died. That is all I can gather."

Watson is angry, thinking Holmes has been prying into his private life, but Holmes assures him that he deduced everything with a certain amount of probability.[6]

---

[6] Note that he "deduced everything with a certain amount of probability," which means he really didn't deduce it at all in the sense in which we have been using the term 'deduce.' Holmes is using the term in the more general sense of reasoning—using our reason to come to conclusions, which includes both induction and deduction. Holmes's deductions are, in fact, astonishingly tenuous.

"What seems strange to you is only so because you do not follow my train of thought or observe the small facts upon which large inferences may depend. For example, I began by stating that your brother was careless. When you observe the lower part of the watch-case you notice that it is not only dented in two places, but it is cut and marked all over from the habit of keeping other hard objects, such as coins or keys, in the same pocket. Surely it is no great feat to assume that a man who treats a fifty-guinea watch so cavalierly must be a careless man. Neither is it a very far-fetched inference that a man who inherits one article of such value is pretty well provided for in other respects... It is very customary for pawnbrokers in England, when they take a watch, to scratch the number of the ticket with a pin-point upon the inside of the case. It is more handy than a label, as there is no risk of the number being lost or transposed. There are no less than four such numbers visible to my lens on the inside of this case. Inference—that your brother was often at low water. Secondary inference—that he had occasional bursts of prosperity, or he could not have redeemed the pledge. Finally, I ask you to look at the inner plate, which contains the keyhole. Look at the thousands of scratches all round the hole—marks where the key has slipped. What sober man's key could have scored those grooves? But you will never see a drunkard's watch without them. He winds it at night, and he leaves these traces of his unsteady hand. Where is the mystery in all this?

Zadig's audience is amazed (if not delighted) by the magic of his reasoning (as was Watson of Holmes' reasoning). Arthur C. Clark once claimed that any sufficiently advanced technology is indistinguishable from magic, and the reasoning powers involved are often driven by methodologies unknown to the majority of us mortals. Thomas Huxley once referred to this type of reasoning as "retrospective prophecy," and it has the same magical effect as Holmes' upon those who do not follow the train of thought or observe the small facts upon which large inferences are made. (I wonder if some enlightenment experiences are not sometimes colored by the surprise of not fully understanding the origins of our epiphanies, so that they become divine inspirations.)

Human ingenuity allows us to discover truths that seem unobtainable, and not just in myth and fiction. Jared Diamond, for example, relates the puzzle of the Anasazi, who lived in the Chaco Canyon area of Northwestern New Mexico for more than five hundred years, from about A.D. 600 to around 1150, and then disappeared. Those who came after them, reoccupying their impressive pueblo dwellings, gave them their name, which simply means "ancient ones." It was long thought impossible to determine when and for how long these people lived in their dwellings and why they ultimately left, but there are several particularly telling techniques that shed light on these questions.

First, consider the tree ring dating method, known as dendrochronology. Every school child knows a tree's rings indicate how old it is. This only becomes useful to archaeologists, though, if certain conditions prevail. For instance, in tropical rain forests tree growth is almost always constant, which makes it difficult to date very far into the past. Add to this that trees tend to rot rather quickly in the tropics. But in the arid Southwest, not only is the environment conducive to tree preservation, but the variance in rainfall from year to year means the trees grow with rings that vary from year to year: wider during a wet season, narrower during a dry season. These rings not only show the type of weather during the tree's growth, but also make for distinctive ring patterns when taken as a group, which allows for dating trees back thousands of years ago.

Thus, using recent trees whose dates are well known (since we know precisely when they were cut), we find a distinctive ring pattern in the early growth years of an older tree—one that is, say, 200 years old. We then look for this same pattern in (preferably) the later growth period of a still older tree (of which we don't know the cut date). When a match is found this older tree pushes back our chronology and we then look for a pattern in this tree's early years and compare it to growth patters in even older trees, slowly pushing back our knowledge of the precise dates and weather patterns of the area. This is truly reminiscent of retrospective prophecy.

For a second retrospective methodology, consider packrat middens. Diamond (2005) gives us the background:

In 1849, hungry gold miners crossing the Nevada desert noticed some glistening balls of a candy-like substance on a cliff, licked or ate the balls, and discovered them to be sweet tasting, but then they developed nausea. Eventually it was realized that the balls were hardened deposits made by small rodents, called packrats, that protect themselves by building nests of sticks, plant fragments, and mammal dung gathered in the vicinity, plus food remains, discarded bones, and their own feces. Not being toilet trained, the rats urinate in their nests, and sugar and other substances crystallize from their urine as it dries out, cementing the midden to a brick-like consistency. In effect, the hungry gold miners were eating dried rat urine laced with rat feces and rat garbage. (145)

The beauty of the packrat midden is twofold. Packrats never stray far from their nests in order to minimize both energy expenditure and the risk of predation by other more aggressive species. Also, as their name implies, they collect an assortment of vegetation within their nests, not to mention their feces (which allows us to determine their diet) and anything else they find of interest. In protective areas such as caves and overhangs packrat middens can last up to 40,000 years.

By identifying the remains of the dozens of urine-encrusted plant species in a midden, paleobotanists can reconstruct a snapshot of the vegetation growing near the midden at the time that the rats were accumulating it, while zoologists can reconstruct something of the fauna from the insect and vertebrate remains. In effect, a packrat midden is a paleontologist's dream: a time capsule preserving a sample of the local vegetation, gathered within a few dozen yards of the spot within a period of a few decades, at a date fixed by radiocarbon-dating the midden.(146)

One of the fascinating pieces of information that emerges from this is that the now treeless desert in the Chaco Canyon was at one time a verdant pine forest. It can also be seen when this forest disappeared. Other methods of analysis (strontium isotope ratios) indicate exactly where the Anasazi went to get logs for their roofs once they had deforested their own area.

These examples illustrate not only how we can obtain knowledge in surprising ways using various methods, but also how the different disciplines and methodologies compliment each other with their interconnections (integration).

§7 MEMORY AS A SOURCE OF KNOWLEDGE

The source of truth lies in the inductive method. But whatever its original source, what is ultimately important is our ability to recall what we need when we need it, and this depends either on our memory or on memory substitutes that utilize either analog or digital technologies (audio and video recordings, writing).

We will accept that we can gain knowledge both from sense experience and from defined categories, but the knowledge we use in everyday life depends on our memory. For example, when you go into a meeting, or even into dinner with your family, you rely on your memory to recognize people and carry on conversations with them. Even in a single conversation you must remember the point of the conversation and what has been said in order to carry on. The primary source of your knowledge of the conversation is auditory (external), but once the data are learned your source becomes your memory (internal). In other words, knowledge we consistently use in our everyday life is filtered through our memory. Consider the following:

(1) There are sentences I do not have to commit to memory, for example, "There are three balls before me at this moment." I can confirm the truth of this sentence continually as I stare at the balls before me, so I don't need to remember it. But the knowledge we use consistently in our daily life is not like this.

(2) We look outside before we go to work and see it is raining, and thus formulate the true sentence "Today is a rainy day." We still know this to be true even after we turn away and prepare for our day; we remember it is raining and dress accordingly. As we leave we will confirm the truth of the sentence continually: we feel the rain on our skin, see and hear it hitting the windshield. In this way sense experience acts as a touchstone to confirm the knowledge stored in our memory. This is true when you check your address book for a telephone number or consult a photograph of your childhood.

(3) I learned the Pythagorean Theorem in high school geometry class, where it was proved to my satisfaction. Thus, I know the Pythagorean theorem is true. When I speak of this theorem now, I base my knowledge claim on my memory of once having understood the proof for it, or on my memory that some authority figure proved it at some time in the past. I do not have to re-prove it every time in order to be sure, though I could do so, if need be, as a touchstone in order to verify my memory. The same thing happens when I say I know that "Albany is the capital of New York."

We can see, then, that memory is a crucial component in the practical application of our knowledge. The source of our knowledge of any given sentence may have been sense experience at one time, for example, "I learned it in class," but moments after it has been committed to memory (learned), the source of that knowledge is no longer sense experience, but memory itself.

So how reliable is our memory? Whenever this question is asked, I am reminded of the Challenger Study. The modern public touchstone for memory is September

11, 2001, when terrorists destroyed the World Trade Center and damaged the Pentagon. Everyone who was old enough at the time remembers where they were and what they were doing when they first heard the news. In the 1960s and 1970s the public memory touchstone was the Kennedy assassination; in the 1980s it was the explosion of the space shuttle Challenger. At the time of the Challenger explosion, a psychologist, Ulric Neisser, was studying the human ability to recall dramatic events (called flashbulb memories).[7] The day after the Challenger disaster he asked his class to write down where they were, what they were doing, and how they heard about the event. When he interviewed these students two and a half years later, twenty-five percent of them gave accounts that were radically different from those they had written down, and less than ten percent had all the facts correct. These were facts they assumed they knew, based on their memory of events. And this was only two and a half years after the event! (see Neisser & Harsch)

Memory, it turns out, is not passive. All representations are dependent upon individual frameworks, which means there is no single objective representation of an event in the present, only a representation woven together from within an individual's framework. Only things (objects) endure, and they but for a short while— they abide and then disappear; they dissipate into the past, which is nothingness. Their being holds them in the present. The past does not exist as a multifaceted storyboard or timeline which we can somehow access in order to pluck historical nuggets of knowledge. There are only remnants we humans use to try to put together a present narrative about what once was. Remnants of the near past are memories, but these fade and eventually disappear altogether when their holder dies. Other remnants are more substantial: words written, recordings, photographs, carvings, buildings.

A specific memory is not stored in one place in the brain. My memory, say, of having a conversation with you, cannot merely be recalled from one memory address, like pulling a photograph from a folder. Human memory, unlike computer memory, is not address-dependent, but rather context-dependent. Because of this the memory of our conversation will be stored in pieces, part of which will be in the visual center because I remember seeing you, part will be in the brain module that handles spatial recognition, part will reside in the auditory complex because we talked, and part in the emotional complex because I felt specific emotions based on the valuation that I put on the topics of our conversation. When we remember, all these strands are pulled together and reconstructed. What this means, for any memory, is that the memory is constructed by the different modules within our framework, some of which are filtered through our conceptual scheme and might very well depend on our wants, hopes, beliefs, goals and desires. We are biased constructionists. It may benefit your comfort level *not* to remember certain aspects of events within your past.

It is, of course, well known that memory cannot be trusted; everyone knows how unreliable eyewitness accounts are. But we don't really take this mistrust to heart, maybe because it constitutes an anomaly to our view of ourselves as having absolutely certain knowledge about events that happened in our past. Think for a minute how radical the fact of our unreliable memory is, that is, think about all the things

---

[7] Flashbulb memories are interesting because they disprove the standard view (going all the way back to Plato) that memories tend to fade unless constantly repeated. They prove that, when necessary, the brain can move information instantaneously into long term memory.

within your world view that depend upon memories you are certain are correct. These include memories of events within your past, which themselves constitute your very notion of selfhood, or who you see yourself as. Who you are, who you consider yourself to be, could very well be based upon faulty, possibly even fraudulently reconstructed, memories.

I had a conversation with my mother not long ago during which I mentioned how nice I thought it was that her mother (my grandmother) had mentioned me, of all people, as she was dying. My mother looked puzzled and said, "She did?" I was appalled. "You're the one who told me she did," I responded, but my mother had no memory of this occurrence. From that moment I could no longer be sure my grandmother mentioned me as she lay dying, which I regret, for it was a fond memory. Did I fabricate the memory of my mother relating the story to me? Or has she forgotten what really happened? Was it a reified dream? A dream I enjoyed and which slowly burrowed its way into my memory as a real event? Such is the tenuous nature of our memories.

One way to protect ourselves from memory loss is to make memories public. Memories shared or written down can serve as touchstones for our lives. If, for instance, I knew someone else was with my mother when my grandmother died, I could ask them for independent verification her dying words. Memories made public are objectified remnants of our subjective recollections. Of course, by manipulating the objective touchstones our memory itself can be manipulated. (A digitally manipulated photograph left in a drawer can recreate a person's memories.) In the movie *Bladerunner*, a cyborg, Rachel, is given implanted memories (accompanied by photographs with handwritten notes on the back from her "mother") which make her believe she is human. Dekker destroys this ruse by telling her some of her most private memories ("Remember the spider…"). She is horrified, as we would be, to discover someone else knows what only she could know. Her entire life narrative, her self, was a lie. In another movie, *Memento,* a man, Leonard, has lost his ability to make new memories and is being manipulated by others who take advantage of his condition. If he doesn't write something down immediately he won't remember it, but how does he know to trust what is written? We are all Rachels and Leonards to some extent. Our memories may not be implanted in toto as Rachel's are, but they are often implanted, manipulated, by us in order to make our selves into who we want to be. Our memories don't fade as fast as Leonard's, but they all fade, and those memories not objectified in some way will be lost, as Roy in *Bladerunner* says, "like tears in the rain."

§8 CHAPTER SUMMARY

In this chapter we have seen that the potential for knowledge accumulation is vast—indefinite if not infinite. But at the same time that vastness means there will forever be knowledge beyond our grasp. This inability is a function of the human condition, and as such is neither a new concern nor a major one, though it may bother some that there are inherent limits to our knowledge. More importantly, we now have two new complications which will haunt us from this point onward. The first stems from the fact that the source of our knowledge is ultimately sense experience which will never result in necessary truths, only those that are true with some degree of probability. Again, this may bother those who feel more comfortable when they can make indubitable claims about the world, but we may simply have to face the facts. In the modern world there is no basis for absolute truth claims.

The second complication is memory. Sense experience may be the source of our reflective knowledge, but memory is also crucial. The fallibility of memory introduces yet another barrier between us and the world, and barriers lead to uncertainty. Not only do we process all information that comes in through our senses before it is recorded in memory, but the recording itself is interpretive rather than representative, and then we have to worry about our recall. Does our recollection of an event match the event as it was recorded? Does it match the event as it really happened? Our solution to the vagaries of memory is to make touchstones to them by means of publicity. Recorded memories (journals, movies, recordings) are objective extensions of our own memory. It is no coincidence that the same publicity that gave us the scientific method and thus made theorizing a respectable method for obtaining truth is also the solution that guarantees our memories and frees us from our prison of subjectivity. We will return to this solution in chapter 10, and apply it in a different way.

In the next chapter we will examine the concept of certainty. We all feel certain that some of our beliefs are true (this is the root of the claim to self-evidence), but what does this mean? Can our certainty serve as a justification for our beliefs?

NOTES / QUESTIONS

9. Certainty

. . . .

*"Why do you doubt your senses?" [asks Marley's Ghost]
"Because," said Scrooge, "a little thing affects them. A slight
disorder of the stomach makes them cheats. You may be an
undigested bit of beef, a blot of mustard, a crumb of cheese, a
fragment of an underdone potato. There's more of gravy than of
grave about you, whatever you are!"*

- Charles Dickens, A Christmas Carol

SYNOPSIS

(1) Certainty is a psychological state engendered by a reflection upon our evidence for our beliefs. (2) Technically, there are no degrees of certainty, only degrees of uncertainty. Certainty, as a psychological state, is unattached to reality, and thus cannot be taken as a guarantee of truth. (3) Certainty is transferred by means of derivation, as in a formal (axiomatic) system. (4) Sooner or later all our justifications for our beliefs will resort to self-evidence, that is, to beliefs we "just know" to be truth. At base, all certainty is certainty in our own ability to determine truth from falsehood. (5) Certainty is systemic, that is, it is a function of our entire conceptual scheme. (6) Certainty demands action and affects the way we handle anomalies within our conceptual scheme. It makes us intolerant of alternatives and thus limits our belief-choices. (7) Religious conceptions of faith and trust can be interpreted in terms of our analysis of certainty. Seen in this light these terms are ubiquitous to our reasoning about the world. (8) We should view absolute certainty with a jaundiced eye, for it clouds our vision and inhibits our ability to understand our own actions. (9) A historical perspective on the search for foundations. (10) Chapter Summary.

CHAPTER OBJECTIVES
- understand what certainty is, how it is engendered, and its effect upon our beliefs
- undermine your faith in certainty as a guarantee of truth
- further develop the concept of anchors in our belief system

§1 CERTAINTY & UNCERTAINTY

ertainty and uncertainty are states of mind engendered by our judging whether the evidence for the belief is sufficient to meet our own subjective standards (the standards within our own framework).[1] In other words, in order to become certain of a belief we must be satisfied that the evidence for it is *substantial*. For example, if I am listening to a news report and hear experts predicting an economic decline in the coming months, I may remain indifferent. We are bombarded with so much information every day we cannot process everything. But if the information is of interest, I must determine whether or not it is reliable, and to do so I must take note of the evidence I have for it. This might be as simple as realizing the source as a trusted source, or it might entail research.

When I say we must be satisfied the evidence for a belief is substantial, the term 'substantial' is relative to a standard subjectively determined by each individual. If I am a member of a conservative or liberal political organization and my favorite talk show host, whom I trust, claims the current administration is the cause of all our country's woes, I may unthinkingly believe everything this person says. If someone questions this belief, though, I may reflect on why I believe it, and the result will be a degree of either certainty or uncertainty. Suppose the evidence for my belief in this case lies in the authority of the source, which I judge to be substantial. I do not question this authority; I am satisfied with the shallowness of my reflection.

If we are not satisfied the evidence for a belief is substantial (or if we become aware of evidence against the belief), we become uncertain; and the level of our uncertainty will be directly proportional to our evidential dissatisfaction. We may, of course, still hold on to a belief even if we are less than certain of it. The point at which our uncertainty demands non-belief remains unspecified.

---

[1] To say that certainty is engendered in this way is not to claim we are always conscious of the process. Certainty may very well bubble up from our unconscious processing of events.

§2 DEGREES OF CERTAINTY

I will argue that there are no degrees of certainty (though we will continue to speak as if there are). We are either certain or we are uncertain. There are, however, degrees of uncertainty.[2] We often speak as though there are degrees of certainty. We say, for example, "I'm fairly certain" or "I'm absolutely certain." This seems to imply a scale of certainty that shades into uncertainty, but a little reflection indicates this is not the most accurate description.

Suppose $s(C_n)$, where s is a sentence and n is a measurement of the level of certainty for a person at a specific time. (You would read this formula as "I am certain to an nth degree that s is true." If, on a scale of one to ten where ten is absolute certainty, you placed your certainty level for a sentence at the highest level, you would say "I am certain to the 10th degree that s is true." This would be represented as $s(C_{10})$. For example, if s = "I now live in the state of Michigan," then $s(C_{10})$; and if r = "I was living in Michigan in 1989," then $r(C_5)$, because I am not sure off hand where I was living in 1989. Thus we would say "I am more certain of s than I am of r."

This example implies degrees of certainty. The state $s(C_{10})$ is what we would refer to as being absolutely certain of s. But even the smallest lessening of this, say $s(C_9)$, introduces uncertainty. Thus, we are either absolutely certain of s or we are uncertain of s to some extent. This seems to indicate that it is uncertainty that is subject to degree, not certainty, despite our ordinary usage. Figure 9–1 indicates our usage of the term 'certainty,' with degrees applying only to uncertainty.

Accordingly, to say "I am certain that s" is to say "I am absolutely certain that s." So also, it makes no sense to say "I'm certain that s, but not absolutely certain," for to say you are not absolutely certain implies there is something prohibiting you from being absolutely certain, that is, something is causing you to hold back from complete immersion in the state of certainty. This is uncertainty. Figure 9–2 is yet another way to look at this.

It should be obvious that I cannot be certain of things I am uncertain of. Consider:

(1) "I am fairly certain my pit bull is safe around babies, but not absolutely certain."

Here the "fairly" indicates a lack of certainty. In other words, you are uncertain you should allow your pit bull around babies. But it makes no sense to say

(2) "I am both absolutely certain and fairly certain my pit bull is safe around babies."

Based on this analysis we may be tempted to equate the uncertainty/certainty distinction with the belief/knowledge distinction. This is because we often use the term 'know' as synonymous with 'certain,' as in, "I know that 2+2=4." While it's true there are degrees of belief, but no degrees of knowledge, and that knowledge occupies the topmost position on the belief scale, there are fundamental differences in knowledge and certainty. First, knowledge is itself a belief state. Certainty is not a state of uncertainty. Second, what causes the change from mere belief to knowledge is the truth connection. This does not apply to certainty. Truth is a necessary

---

[2] Nothing important hangs on this claim. If you prefer instead to say there really are degrees of certainty nothing will change, but it seems that, upon a close analysis, the way we usually talk about certainy belies our actual mental states.

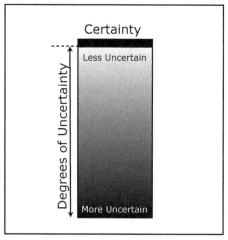

FIGURE 9–1

Uncertainty is the state subject to degrees rather than certainty. Certainty emerges as our uncertainty dissipates.

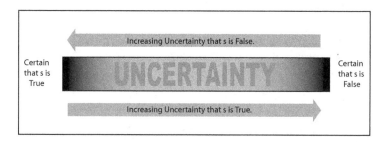

FIGURE 9–2

If you are certain that a sentence is true, then you are also certain that its negation is false. As you become more uncertain of its truth you thereby become less uncertain of its falsehood.

condition of knowledge, but not of certainty. You can be absolutely certain of the truth of a belief or sentence and be wrong, but you cannot know a sentence is true when it is, in fact, false. You might *think* you know it, but you are wrong. For example, a thousand years ago, many people believed, and were absolutely certain that, the sun moved around the earth. Based on the level of scientific inquiry at the time we might even say they were justified in believing this to be true. But it wasn't true. They thought it was, but they were wrong. In retrospect we see that they could not have known it, because it was false. This does not change the fact that they were certain, though.

We will continue to talk about sentences as having degrees of certainty (since this is common usage), but keep in mind that the degrees are actually degrees of uncertainty which lessens as certainty is approached. Thus, when we say, as above, "I am fairly certain my pit bull is safe around babies" we are actually uncertain, but

LEGAL EVIDENTIARY STANDARDS

The burden of proof, in the American legal system, shifts, depending upon the type of trial. For criminal trials it rests upon the prosecution, which is why the defense only offers evidence that counters the claims of the prosecutor. (For the insanity defense the burden shifts to the defendant.) What follows are four standards of evidence used by judges and/or juries to determine cases:

(1) Some Credible Evidence or Probable Cause (used for obtaining search warrants, wire taps, or in child services proceedings): a bare minimum of materially credible evidence is provided. (Valmonte v Commissioner NYS D.S.S. Mar 1994 2nd Circuit)

(2) Preponderance of Evidence (all civil cases unless otherwise provided by law): a superiority in weight, force, importance, and so on. A party must show their case is "more likely than not" the correct version. 51% is all that is needed. (Miller v Minister of Pensions)

(3) Clear and Convincing (intra-adjudicative, that is, used to settle administrative details in court hearings, both civil and criminal): more than a preponderance, but less than conclusive. Substantially more likely than not.

(4) Beyond a Reasonable Doubt (only applies in criminal proceedings): The judge or jury must be entirely convinced (morally certain) of the guilt of the defendant (98-99% certain)—they can have no doubt of the defendant's guilt.

Proof beyond a reasonable doubt is proof to a moral certainty, as distinguished from an absolute certainty (Victor v Nebraska, Supreme Court ruling). The following diagram illustrates how these four different standards compare:

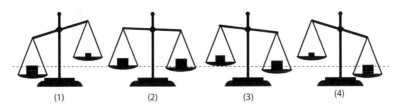

(1)   (2)   (3)   (4)

There is simply no way to anchor certainty in any objective way so that every person on a jury, or every judge that reviews a case, will be using the same standard. While we can probably judge the difference between, say, 55% and 99%, how would we judge the difference between 95% and 99%?

we speak as if we are certain, though to a lesser degree than absolute certainty. Better, would be to say, "I am almost certain my pit bull is safe around babies."

Unlike knowledge, certainty is a completely internal state; it does not depend upon having met adequacy conditions, and no external fact about the world could ever make you claim, "I thought I was absolutely certain, but I was wrong." This is illustrated in Figure 9–3, in which the larger circle contains everything I believe to be true, and the smaller circle everything I am absolutely certain is true. This indicates that many of the sentences I believe to be true are in fact false, and these include many of the sentences I believe to be absolutely certain. Certainty is never a guarantee of truth. Since it is possible to be absolutely certain and still be wrong, we should never use our certainty as either an indicator or guarantor of truth—and yet we continually do so.

All it takes to show that certainty does not guarantee truth is one case in which a person was absolutely certain of something and then turned out to be wrong. For instance, I once had an argument with my wife about the location of our car keys. She claimed I had them, while I was certain I had given them to her. I was so certain I even had a mental movie to prove it—I could clearly remember her asking for the keys and my handing them to her. Finally, to prove my point, I thrust my hand into my pocket to show her there were no keys there... and there they were. I was flabbergasted. I was absolutely certain, but wrong. If you even admit that this is a possible scenario, then you must also admit: certainty is never a guarantee of truth.

§3   TRANSFERRING CERTAINTY

The certainty of one sentence can be transferred to another via derivation (implication). If I am certain of the sentence

(1) Each of the ten metal bars on the table weighs one pound.

then I can deduce rigorously that

(2) The cumulative weight of the metal bars on the table is 10 pounds.

Thus, I can be as certain of (2) as I am of (1). (I say "can be" rather than "am" for reasons that will be clarified below.)

The certainty of a derivation will never exceed that from which it is derived (and may be less than that from which it is derived). For example, if, having weighed each metal bar, my degree of certainty for (1) is eight (n=8), then my degree of certainty for (2), which I know only as a derivation from (1), cannot exceed eight.

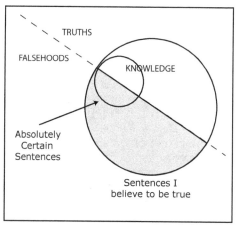

FIGURE 9–3

In this diagram the large circle encompasses everything we believe to be true, the smaller circle everything we are absolutely certain is true (obviously we are only absolutely certain of a small subset of our beliefs). We are probably wrong about many of the things we believe to be true and this includes many of the things we are absolutely certain are true, which means that certainty does not guarantee the truth of our beliefs in any way.

"Securely derived" is itself cashed in terms of certainty, which means the degree of certainty in a conclusion may be less than that of the premises. For example, perhaps due to the complexity of the concepts, I may be less certain of what I derive from my premises even though perfectly certain of the premises. We might say, in this case that the derivation is downgraded, having been filtered through the uncertainty of the implication process.

If multiple premises are involved in a deduction, then the degree of certainty in the conclusion will never be greater than the least certain premise. Thus if we have the following argument, where (1) and (2) are premises and (3) is the conclusion,

(1) $s(C_4)$
(2) $r(C_{10})$
$\overline{}$
(3) $t(C_n)$

then, in the conclusion, necessarily, $n \leq 4$. Here, (1) is the least certain premise, having a degree of certainty that equals four. This guarantees that the degree of certainty in the conclusion, (3), will never exceed four, despite the fact that one of the premises, (2), is absolutely certain. This is true within all axiomatic systems as well: the derivations comprising the system are never stronger than the weakest axiom. Consider a more concrete example:

(4) Acme always makes good products.
(5) This product is made by Acme.
$\overline{}$
(6) This will be a good product.

The second premise (5) is more likely to be certain than the first (4), especially if we're holding the product in hand and see the Acme stamp on it (though if the product is in high demand it may be a knockoff). As for the first premise, what are the odds that any company will *always* make a good product? This being so, if (4) and (5) are our only evidence for the conclusion, our certainty concerning (6) can never exceed the certainty we have in (4).

Similarly, if we are certain of a sentence, s, then we are as certain of s as we are for any grounds we could give for s. This is the reverse process of implication. In implication we hold specific premises and then deduce conclusions. The premises, in such cases, constitute our grounds for believing the conclusion. But we often hold a sentence to be true in an unreflective manner, and only when questioned search for grounds. When we do this, the reasons (grounds) we uncover must be as certain as the sentence we are attempting to ground. Once we discover a ground for our sentence, we want to be able to turn around and deduce it from that ground. For example, suppose I am having a debate with someone about whether it is morally wrong to steal money from a person who will never miss what I steal. Suppose my belief (formulated in a sentence, s) is that it is morally wrong to do this. When I am asked why it would be wrong I might reply, "Because it is always wrong to steal." This is the ground for my sentence (belief), "It would be wrong to take money from someone even if they would never miss it."

Even small children, when asked why they believe something, will attempt to find a ground for their belief and this ground will be equal to or greater than the belief itself with respect to certainty. For example, when asked "Why do you believe in Santa Claus?" the child might answer, "Because I've seen him!" and, if serious, he will be as certain of this as he is that Santa Claus exists.

We might note here how arguments function exactly like axiomatic systems. An argument is an axiomatic system writ small. In an axiomatic system you start with axioms about which you are certain and then proceed to deduce truths from these. This is why what you prove in an axiomatic system can never be more secure than your weakest axiom. This is exactly what you do in an argument. You formulate premises and then deduce a conclusion and the conclusion can never be more certain than its weakest premise. This means you must prove your premises to everyone's satisfaction, but in order to do this you must formulate arguments for them. This leads to the infinite regress we mentioned in the previous chapter. This is why the appeal to intuition or self-evidence has become so important. It is thought that this appeal in some way anchors our beliefs upon absolute certainty. Let's turn now to examine why self-evidence won't fulfill our hopes for an anchor.

§4 SELF-EVIDENCE

We have seen that our evidence for our beliefs, though ultimately resting on experience, will usually depend on our ability to recall information from memory. Much of this evidence depends upon some kind of authority, whether from a person, a text, or some other source. But the question always arises with respect to such evidence: why should I believe this? For example, suppose I believe "Neptune is the farthest planet from the sun" because I looked it up in a reputable encyclopedia and am, at this very moment looking at an illustration of the solar system that indicates it is true. Memory issues aside, why should I trust the source? Maybe the source is a well known and trusted encyclopedia, but according to whom? This means we have to trust whoever claimed it was well known and trusted. Or maybe we trust it because it has always been correct in the past, but this fact (like Acme always making good products) is always subject to change, and how do we know it hasn't? We believe that Neptune is the farthest planet from the sun ultimately because we are satisfied that the evidence is sufficient to warrant our belief, and we ourselves are the final judge in determining such things. How do we know we are a good judge? We just know. End of story. This is known as self-evidence.

This is a stunning conclusion. All our beliefs are ultimately founded on the belief that we are capable of distinguishing between truth and falsehood.[3] For example, most of us believe there are objects in the world such as cows and trees, and that we have some kind of access to these via our senses, that is, we are not living in an illusory world like that in the movie The Matrix. But how do we know this? We just know. When we consider such scenarios a feeling of certainty descends on us like a comfortable blanket. We just couldn't be wrong about this; we are not living in an illusory world. What we have, then, is faith in our ability to judge truth from falsehood. All our chains of justification are like this, eventually all of them rely solely

---

[3] Even the belief that we are capable of distinguishing between truth and falsehood is founded upon this belief, which is problematic, but no more problematic than all our other beliefs being founded upon it.

upon self-evidence. When continually pushed to justify our beliefs we all, at some point, will resort to the "I just know" defense. It is inconceivable to us that we could be wrong concerning our most cherished beliefs.

 A sentence (belief) is inconceivable to us if we cannot incorporate it into our conceptual scheme (and the more inconceivable something is, the harder time we will have incorporating it). What is inconceivable is not that a sentence could be wrong, but that *we* could be. In other words, what is impossible for us to grasp is not the falseness of the sentence (we really could be living in a matrix), but rather that our conceptual schemes could be so entirely mistaken. Thus, what we are certain of is the truth of our entire world view. For example, when questioned, "How do you know that god exists?" the answer might be, "I just know." In this case, for this person, it is not inconceivable that god not exist (such things are easily imagined, though the avid believer may deny it); the fact is the person doesn't want the sentence to be false, for cognitive dissonance looms. For the devout believer, the sentence "God exists" is on par with the sentence "There is an external world," which cannot be given up without seismic disruption on a massive scale. For the casual believer, on the other hand, the sentence "God exists" might be more like the sentence "I have classes to attend at school tomorrow." If a winter storm threatens the truth of this latter sentence, their conceptual scheme can be rearranged with very little damage. So also, a casual believer might easily shrug off belief in god when faced with a minor anomaly.

We all have a set of unquestionable beliefs which form the basis of our everyday view concerning the world. For example, "There is an external world" is a sentence most people believe to be true without question, and this truth allows us to believe other mundane propositions about the world without question, for example, that this chair exists beyond my perception of it (which is deduced from the previous sentence with equal certitude). If our conceptual scheme is working really well for us, then this will be our final line of defense when we are asked why we believe certain things. "I just know," is a claim based on the coherence of our conceptual scheme. (We will discuss the notion of coherence in the next chapter.)

It's easy to see why some might want a more objective basis for their beliefs, might need an anchor or touchstone to reality the same way we use a photograph to anchor our memories to the world. Because of this, some people claim that their intuitions are actually tied to the world in some special way, but there is no reason to believe they are. The person who makes such a claim is actually believing in their own ability to know when something is or isn't tied to the world; but how do they know they have this ability? They just know!

⁂

§5 ENGENDERING CERTAINTY

We have seen that in order to become certain of a belief we must deem the evidence for it to be substantial. Anything less will render us uncertain. Suppose, for example, I am participating in a game show. If I answer the question correctly I will win $5,000; if incorrect I receive nothing. The question is: "What planet is farthest from the sun?" Suppose the answer that immediately comes to mind is "Neptune is the planet farthest from the sun." The meta-cognitive process, based on this scenario might be as follows:

> This answer comes to mind based on my background knowledge of the solar system, but since I am interested in collecting the prize money, I reflect further on my background knowledge to see if it is justified.

Contingent facts such as these must have a basis in memory, so my reflection will take the form of examining my memories concerning the order of the planets. I might remember a specific picture of the planets showing Neptune as the farthest from the sun. This memory is so clear it engenders certainty.

If I become certain because of a memory, then this (my memory) is the ground of my belief, and we all know we can be mistaken about our memories, so, in this case I have decided my memory is not mistaken (even though there is no way I could possibly know this). Thus, my certainty is grounded upon the fact that I am certain of my own ability to recall a correct memory concerning the position of Neptune among the planets. Or perhaps I have the option to phone a friend who happens to be an expert on astronomy. She assures me that yes, Neptune is the farthest planet from the sun. My certainty is now grounded on the authority of my friend. But how do I know she is trustworthy? My certainty is ultimately grounded, not on her authority, but on my own ability to determine whether or not she is trustworthy as an authority. All certainty is ultimately based on a belief in our own ability to determine truth from falsehood.

We have a host of beliefs, the truth of which we take for granted, and from which we continually deduce propositions about the world which we use every day, but we do not speak of or reflect on the certainty of these until the truth of one is questioned and we reflect upon this aspect of it. For example, I believe there is an external world, and because of this I also believe this chair, in which I am sitting, exists independently of my thinking about it. I take this proposition for granted when I sit down, but I am not reflectively certain of it until I question the truth of it. Most people go through their entire life sitting in chairs without ever considering whether or not chairs exist.

Our reasoning follows the path of least resistance. Unless you have given me good grounds for doubting the existence of the chair, I won't even do the mental work necessary to check it. Instead, I fall back on the overall security of my conceptual scheme, which serves as a guarantor for the existence of the chair. When we do reflect, we say we are certain of such propositions based on the certainty that our conceptual scheme is working well.[4]

The cognitive state of uncertainty is also engendered by reflecting upon the evidence we have for any given belief or sentence. Becoming less certain of a belief or sentence is, at the same time, to become more certain of the truth of its negation. Consider the following two sentences:

(1) "The battle of Waterloo was fought in 1800"

(2) "The battle of Waterloo was *not* fought in 1800"

---

[4] There are times when we don't trust our conceptual schemes, for example, when we are under the influence of alcohol or drugs, or if we are aware of our bouts with insanity.

If I am certain sentence (1) is true, then I am also certain sentence (2) is false. As I begin to doubt the truth of sentence (1), to the same extent I will also begin to believe sentence (2) is true (see Figure 9–2).

As the graph in Figure 9–4 indicates, there may come a time, in the progression of your belief-state, when you become completely ambivalent with respect to belief in a sentence. You may be uncertain of the truth of a sentence either because of a lack of evidence for it or because of evidence against it, but how long you continue to believe a sentence when you are uncertain of its truth will depend, not upon the evidence, but upon the importance of the sentence within the scope of your conceptual scheme.

Uncertainty (like certainty) is always a function of evidence or the lack of evidence. Most people assume their beliefs are based on hard facts until forced to justify them all the way back to the I-just-know foundation, at which time the subjective roots of justification are made manifest. But our use of this internal justification is not arbitrary; it depends on the relation of the belief in question to our belief system as a whole. If a belief constitutes a core value within your conceptual scheme and you find you have no external evidence for that belief, then, rather than give it up, you may resort to your internal evidence ("I just know"). In this way we can be absolutely certain of propositions which we are aware have no external evidence to support them.

Certainty, then, is a psychological state (a feeling) engendered within the context of our conceptual scheme, and as such is unattached to the external world. This is why it is dangerous to base our belief states solely upon our feelings of certainty: "a slight disorder of the stomach makes them cheats."

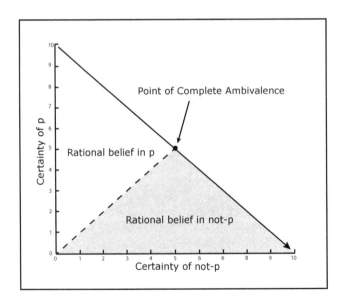

FIGURE 9–4
There comes a point (as we become more uncertain of a sentence) that we are no longer able to believe it. When our certainty in the truth of a sentence decreases, our certainty in the truth of its negation increases.

§6 CHARACTERISTICS & CONSEQUENCES OF CERTAINTY

There are specific characteristics and consequences that arise from the mindset of certitude that are of interest to us. We cannot touch on all of these, but will focus on those that have relevance to our overall discussion. I will limit the characteristics of certainty to two, and discuss the consequences surrounding each of these. The following topics are relevant:

(1) The effect of certainty on our actions.

(2) The effect of certainty on the way we handle anomalies.

CERTAINTY DEMANDS ACTION.

If a person claims to be absolutely certain of something, has the motivation and the ability to act accordingly, and yet refuses to do so, we can rightly question either their claim of absolute certainty or their rationality. For example, suppose you have a friend who is stockbroker, who tells you he knows of a stock that will triple invested earnings within a week if acted on immediately. When asked how sure he is of this information, he replies, "I'm absolutely certain." You happen to know he has available cash and a desire for wealth and has been looking for good investment opportunities himself, so you ask if he is going to invest in the stock. He replies that he isn't. In this scenario you would rightly question his certainty that the stock will perform as he says it will. He must be less certain than he maintains, otherwise what would stop him from investing?[5] Indeed, we can go so far as to say, if someone is absolutely certain of the truth of a proposition and yet fails to act as if it is true when able to do so, then that person is acting irrationally.[6]

There is a corollary here concerning intolerance. If you are absolutely certain about one of your beliefs, then when other people have opposing beliefs, insofar as those people are sufficiently like you, you may not understand why they don't believe what you believe. You may thus become intolerant of their behavior, and your intolerance may have the best of intentions. Consider a religious position that contains, as one of its tenets, the claim that if you do not believe in a specific way you will go to hell forever when you die. If you believe this with absolute certainty, then you will be intolerant of those who deny it, for in doing so they are not only threatening their own futures, but those of others.[7] Surely, the only way a person will be convinced to strap a bomb to his body and detonate it in a crowd is if he is certain that either he will make a difference by doing so, or will be rewarded in an

---

[5] Certainty and the perception of risk are inversely related. Believing a claim to be true might be risky if we are uncertain of it, but as we become certain of it our perception of the risk lessens. Betting the ranch on a poker hand might seem risky, but not if you are certain the hand has been fixed in advance in your favor.

[6] This point also applies to inaction. That is, certainty concerning a claim can also lead you not to act. In this sense, we would say that if a person is certain it would be irrational to act. For example, if you are certain you saw someone put poison in your food then, *ceterus paribus*, it would be irrational for you to eat the food (assuming you don't want to die, and so on).

[7] This was, as a matter of fact, the justification for the Inquisition in the middle ages.

afterlife (or both). The oddest part of this behavior is that it is consistent with truly caring for the future of others.

CERTAINTY AFFECTS HOW WE HANDLE ANOMALIES.

If a person claims to be absolutely certain of something, any anomalies that arise against this will be dismissed as mere appearances (as opposed to facts), or their solutions will be pushed into the indefinite future. This is not bad *per se*, but has potentially insidious consequences. This is a natural result of being absolutely certain of a belief, for if a belief you hold *must* be true (as you are assured it is in your state of certitude) then any fact that contradicts it *must* be false, and if it cannot be shown to be false in the present because we lack the resources or abilities to fully comprehend and explain it, then in the future we will be vindicated in having relegated it to a mere appearance.

For example, suppose you live in an apartment in which you continually hear and see strange phenomena: bumps in the night, lights and music. Based on these phenomena your friends suggest the apartment is haunted, but you remain a firm realist; you are certain there is no supernatural world. Notice first, to harken back to our previous point, to the extent you are certain there are no ghosts, you will exhibit no fear in going about your apartment, that is, your actions will correspond with your belief-state concerning the supernatural. What of those anomalies? When you hear bumps in the night, you will explain these noises in natural, as opposed to super-natural, terms. You may even decide to investigate the anomalous phenomena with sensors, cameras, sound equipment, and you will make the claim, whether implicit or explicit, that your position will be vindicated at some point in the future. "You'll see!" is the mantra of the person certain of his beliefs.

A theory of any complexity will always have anomalies. But if the theory overall (excluding these anomalies) meets our adequacy conditions, and thus works very well, then we won't discard it. Instead, we will attempt to explain the anomalies. One of the most successful ways of doing this is the future-pleading ploy: we push the anomalies into the future with the claim that as our knowledge increases, one day we will see the anomalous facts are not anomalous at all. We will one day be enlightened, see the larger picture, and thus see how the facts all fit together despite present appearances. This is standard theoretical operating procedure. It saves our theories and helps us avoid needless cognitive dissonance. The problem is, sometimes cognitive dissonance points to a valid problem within our theory and the future-pleading ploy becomes an *ad hoc* solution to pressing problems. In other words, the future-pleading ploy can easily become a means of self-deception.

FURTHER CONSEQUENCES.

We might say that certainty is a fine mesh that filters out contrary evidence. We tend to accept evidence that confirms our certitude and dismiss evidence that disconfirms it. This is a mental heuristic known as the confirmation bias (see box on page 213).

In the same way that certainty rules out contrary evidence, it also rules out choices that are intertwined with such evidence. This is true for several reasons. First, in the most straightforward sense, being certain that something is true means that you no longer have the choice to believe it to be false. This is because we can-not believe something we know to be false. Second, though, your certainty might lead you to make life-choices that rule out further life-choices. For instance, to the extent that you are certain that the earth is the center of the universe, you have eliminated a career as an astronomer in mainstream academia from your future.

Certainty, then, is connected to core valuations. In fact, we can probably say that if we placed all our beliefs on a continuum of importance, from little or no importance to those of core value importance, we would also, at the same time, be plotting the strength of their certitude (or incertitude). This makes sense. To question anything of which we are absolutely certain is, by definition, to cause seismic disturbance within our conceptual scheme, which is how we defined a core value. Furthermore, what caused this seismic disturbance was the interconnections to other beliefs, so those things about which we are most certain are those that have multiple connections with other parts of our conceptual schemes.

In a sense, then, certainty is the opposite of cognitive dissonance. Certainty is a comfortable feeling. If we are certain, we need not worry about being proved wrong. We are safe within the confines of our beliefs. Anomalies introduce uncertainty, which is what makes us feel cognitive dissonance, which is an uncomfortable feeling. Small wonder we adore certitude. But this adoration is dangerous, for, as we have seen, certainty does not guarantee truth, and easily leads the unwary astray.

CONFIRMATION BIAS

What cognitive psychologists refer to as the "confirmation bias" is the tendency we humans have, once we have embraced a theory (position, belief), to see confirming data rather than disconfirming data with respect to that theory. A simple example is given by psychologist Peter Wason, who conducted an experiment in which he presented his subjects with a series of three numbers and then asked them for a rule that would explain the series. Before formulating their rule, the subjects were encouraged to submit further examples of the sequence to the administrator, who would inform them whether their examples were in fact instances of the correct rule. Consider the following series:

2, 4, 6

The test subjects would invariably submit examples such as: 8, 10, 12 as possible examples of the series. They would receive a positive answer, that yes, this was also an example of the series rule, and would then formulate their suggestion, which was usually: "a series of three ascending even numbers which increases by two." What most subjects did *not* do was submit examples that might *disconfirm* the stated series, such as 3, 5, 7. Because of this, most test subjects never considered the possibility that the rule was simply: "any three numbers placed in ascending order." For instance, 1, 9, 10 or 123, 140, 198.

Wason's explanation of the results was that we formulate an initial hypothesis upon seeing the data and then filter all subsequent data through that hypothesis. Hence the bias. Believing we have already hit upon the series we think only of other series that would confirm what we think is true.

§7 FAITH AND TRUST

We are now in a position to understand what is sometimes taken to be baffling talk with respect to faith, usually in religious traditions, and particularly within traditional Christian thought. The talk is baffling because it often sets up a dichotomy between faith and reason, holding the two, at least at times, to be inconsistent. On the extreme view, reason is derided, as in Tertullian's (possibly misinterpreted) phrase, "I believe because it is absurd," or Martin Luther, who personified reason as a whore, and commanded us to throw dung in her face.

I think this dichotomy is a mistake. Consider one of the paradigm cases of faith within Christianity: the story of Abraham. Abraham and his wife Sarah were very old when they conceived a son, Isaac. This son was important, for god had promised Abraham that his offspring would be as numerous as the sands of the sea, and would become the basis of a new nation of people. One day god spoke to Abraham:

"Take your son, your only son, whom you love—Isaac—and go to the region of Moriah. Sacrifice him there as a burnt offering on a mountain I will show you." (Genesis 22:2 NIV)

Abraham obediently packed up his mule and, along with Isaac, headed out. When the time came, he prepared Isaac for the sacrifice, raised the knife, and was about to kill his son when an angel appeared and gave him a message from god:

"Do not lay a hand on the boy," he said. "Do not do anything to him. Now I know that you fear God, because you have not withheld from me your son, your only son." (Genesis 22:12 NIV)

Abraham had faith that, even if he sacrificed his only son, the son of his old age, god would still keep his promise and make his offspring as numerous as the sands of the sea. Or, to put Abraham in a more flattering light, he had faith that god would provide an alternative sacrifice before he killed his son. In this sense, Abraham's faith is equivalent to trust. He trusted in god to fulfill his promise (or to save his son). This also seems to be what Paul had in mind in the New Testament when he said, "faith is confidence in what we hope for and assurance about what we do not see." (Hebrews 11:1 NIV) He references Abraham in this respect:

By faith Abraham, when God tested him, offered Isaac as a sacrifice. He who had embraced the promises was about to sacrifice his one and only son, even though God had said to him, "It is through Isaac that your offspring will be reckoned." Abraham reasoned that God could even raise the dead, and so in a manner of speaking he did receive Isaac back from death. (Hebrews 11:17-19 NIV)

This is explained in the sense that Abraham was absolutely certain that god would fulfill his promise (Paul goes with a flattering interpretation), even in the face of evidence to the contrary. As Paul points out, Abraham never lived to see this promise fulfilled, but he lived as if it would be. Given Abraham's certitude in god's promise, it would have been irrational for him to have acted otherwise. Furthermore, this certitude led him to reinterpret evidence in light of his belief: the facts dictated that by killing Isaac he would have no offspring, but certitude changed what appeared to be a fact into a mere appearance. That is, it only appeared he would be left without offspring; the truth was: god would provide. The belief that an anomalous fact was not a fact at all but an appearance, would be justified in the future. These are all characteristics of certainty.

We can apply these same characteristics to a modern theory. We will use Einstein's theory of relativity, though any complex theory would do. The theory of relativity was Einstein's attempt to explain certain problems within the standard view of his time (Newton's). Einstein's was a mathematically beautiful theory and won wide acceptance from those who understood it, and from many more who trusted their advice. But the theory led to conclusions contradicting the way people viewed the world. To cite just a few:

(1) Einstein claimed that space and time were connected; an alteration in one would lead to an alteration in the other. In particular, traveling at a high rate of speed leads to a contraction of both time and space.

(2) Light is a particle, with a defined finite speed limit.

(3) Gravity can be seen as nothing more than a distortion in the fabric of space (or, better, space-time) caused by the mass of objects. This means the appearance of the position of celestial bodies could be distorted by massive objects, since light (as a particle) is affected by gravitational fields.

(4) Other odd phenomenon deduced from the theory, such as black holes, which no one knew how to verify.

With all these anomalous implications why wasn't the theory rejected immediately? First, because it worked. It explained phenomena that had been persistently anomalous within Newton's theory (such as the movement of Mercury's perihelion). Those who understood this, and saw the beauty of Einstein's derivations, trusted (had faith) that, when put to the test, it would pass. In other words, at the time of its formulation scientists were unable to fully confirm the theory and its derivations, so its contradictions (anomalies) had to remain until a future day when they could be shown to be merely apparent contradictions (the future-pleading ploy). Thus the basis of the acceptance of relativity theory was faith in its future ability to explain what had never been properly explained. This faith was shown to be justified as confirmations of the theory accumulated throughout the twentieth century.[8]

Thus, faith is not belief in the face of evidence to the contrary, or belief without evidence, or even, as Mark Twain once put it, "belief in something you know isn't true." No one believes anything without having what they take to be sufficient evidence to justify their belief. We have already pointed out that this view of faith, as a methodology for sorting true facts from false ones, is no more successful than rolling dice or flipping a coin. When people believe in the face of evidence to the contrary, this often simply means their core values are in danger and they are putting off rearrangement by pleading the future.

---

[8] To cite a few examples: time dilation was confirmed with the advent of atomic clocks and high speed jet planes, light affected by gravitational fields was confirmed by Eddington during an eclipse of the sun, black holes have been observed (or at least their effects have been) due to their gravitation effects on other celestial bodies.

§8 CERTAINTY AND THE EXAMINED LIFE

Our conceptual schemes function as coordinated systems. We have beliefs about the world that form the basis for all our deductions about the world. The belief in the external world, for example, or the belief that we exist and have a body, a self, separate from other bodies and selves. We draw implications from these axioms continually, and to the extent that the derivations are obvious, these are as certain as the axioms themselves. The result is that we hold our entire framework to be certain, and this certainty makes us comfortable, makes us feel at home in the world, and so contributes to our well-being.

Certainty, then, is unavoidable. It is as much a part of our mental lives as our emotions and it is part and parcel with our reasoning. There is no doubting its evolutionary efficacy. There is survival value in certainty, for it focuses us on realities we can deal with and thus prunes many possible branches from our decision trees by making us intolerant to alternatives. It rewards us with dopamine which imbues us with a sense of well-being and safety. The very characteristics that make it valuable, though, also make it dangerous for those attempting to live an examined life.

Despite the comfort it offers, we should resist the siren song of certainty. At times it is harmless. Remember our deductive argument from the previous chapter:

(1)   Building A is taller than building B.
(2)   Building B is taller than building C.

(3)   Building A is taller than building C.

In this argument, once you understand the concepts involved, you see that the conclusion, (3), follows with absolute necessity from the premises. When we think about this argument we are absolutely certain that if three buildings have the relationship specified in (1) and (2), then (3) must also be true. This certainty is harmless. Where certainty becomes dangerous is when it arises concerning facts about the world that influence the lives of others. For example,

(4)   God has commanded that all non-believers be converted.
(5)   We must do as god commands.

(6)   We must attempt to convert all non-believers.

Premises (4) and (5) are often assumed to be necessarily true because of some special connection between god and humans. Furthermore, they connect to the core valuations of some, which means they will have an affect on the lives of those who believe them, spurring them to action. Whenever we are tempted to bask in the absolute certainty of one of our beliefs we should remember: we could still be wrong. This instilling of doubt, which evaporates absolute certainty, will allow us to be more tolerant of other points of view.

Reciprocal altruism gives us the ability to overcome our absolute certainty and maintain relations with others despite our different world-views. A truly reciprocal relationship implies that one person empathizes with another. That is, I come to realize that humans are all similar in important ways, but at the same time, we all have different world views, and though I think mine is correct I realize that you

DESCARTES' AXIOMATIC SYSTEM

The French philosopher Rene Descartes (1596-1650), who was also the discoverer of analytic geometry, was enthralled by Euclid's method of deduction. In his *System of Geometry*, Euclid deduced the truths of geometry from five simple axioms (or postulates), and Descartes decided he would apply the same method to his philosophical search for truth. The burning question was: what propositions should he use as his starting point (axioms)? He knew they had to be absolutely certain (which he took to be a guarantee of truth), for the deductions within an axiomatic system are only as strong as the weakest axiom.

We can liken the axioms within an axiomatic system to the foundation of a building: no matter how well constructed the superstructure, it will never be stronger than the weakest part of the foundation. Thus Descartes decided to guarantee the soundness of his axioms by imposing several filters through which any proposition would have to pass in order to be considered as an axiom. These filters were:

1. The dream hypothesis: How do you know you are not dreaming at this very moment?

2. The evil genius hypothesis: How do you know you are not being deceived by an evil genius at this very moment?

With these two hypotheses in place, are there any indubitable propositions? Most propositions won't pass even the first test, much less the second. The first hypothesis turns on the fact that there is no criterion that would allow us to distinguish between sleep states and awake states. You could be dreaming right now, even as you are reading about dreaming. Furthermore, there's no test that could ever prove you aren't dreaming since you might be dreaming the test and its results. The second hypothesis asks us to imagine an all-powerful being who gets his jollies by consistently deceiving us. You might think, for example, that $2 + 2 = 4$, but this might be false and the evil genius is deceiving you into thinking it is obviously true.

It looks like Descartes set an impossible test for himself, but he finds one (and only one) proposition that makes it through both filters unscathed, namely, "I exist." This is characterized in the famous phrase, "*Cogito, ergo sum*" ("I think, therefore I am"). "I exist" makes it through filter one since you must exist in order to dream; and it makes it through filter two since you must exist in order to be deceived. The problem is that this is the only proposition that passes through both filters, and it's impossible to deduce anything of substance from it. All you can be certain of is that you are a thinking thing, and you can only be certain of this when you are actually thinking about it, for otherwise you are relying on memory, which is subject to the two doubt hypotheses. You cannot conclude from the fact that you exist that you have a body, for the doubt hypotheses are still in place. So Descartes is left with but one axiom and nothing to deduce from it. This calls for a desperate move on his part: he proves the existence of a good god via a version of the ontological argument, and then, since a good god would not deceive us, uses this to destroy the doubt hypotheses.

This move is illicit, of course, for it begs the question. Descartes can't prove the existence of god without getting rid of the doubt hypotheses, but he must prove god's existence in order to get rid of them. Hence the desperate move. If Descartes' attempt to ground philosophy on certitude was unsuccessful, why is he known as the father of modern philosophy? The answer lies in the fact that he attempted to found a system of knowledge on himself rather than on god. Descartes was the first philosopher to contemplate throwing off an objective anchor, even if he ultimately failed to do so.

think yours is correct to the same degree. This thought in itself is often enough to lower our certainty level sufficiently to take in others as brothers and sisters (fellow humans) while still maintaining a level of comfort with our own world view. (We will develop this further in chapter 14.)

繠

§9 HISTORICAL PERSPECTIVE

We humans have, for thousands of years, sought answers to questions important to us; questions such as: Why are we here? What happens after death? What is the meaning of life? How should I live? These questions are extensions of questions we would normally ask in every day life. If I wake up in a strange place I want to know how I got there; when I go on a journey I want to know what happens when I get to my destination. Questions about why we exist and what happens to us after death, then, are the same questions, but applied to our entire life rather than specific episodes within it. Having answers to these questions gives us comfort, allays our fears, dissolves our dissonance. The problem is that the answers, when applied to life-as-a-whole, are not as easy to come by. If only we could have a god's-eye-view and thereby understand the whole of our history or see into the future and determine whether there is life after death. Going outside of ourselves and our existential situation in this manner has always been seen as the only way to find answers to the otherwise impossible-to-answer questions we have posed. We have referred to this method in terms of anchors: we humans attempt to anchor our lives and our beliefs in something outside of ourselves in order to achieve the comfort we so desperately desire.

Traditionally, the gods provided us with this safe harbor. Even if we didn't know their intentions, as the Stoics claimed, it was helpful to know they had a plan for us. Plato invented his own safe harbor—his world of forms was an extramental place that was the basis of all our knowledge about the world. The forms within that world were eternal and unchanging, and thus could be trusted as anchor points. Christian and Muslim theologians later bestowed these attributes upon their god, who revealed truth to humans via divine revelation. We have seen how this Platonic viewpoint limited the incentive to investigate the world and how the introduction of Aristotelian texts to the West fostered new ways of thinking that led eventually to the scientific method. But with science came a host of new anomalies. Christianity, as the religion of the West, tried to protect those who would listen from the encroaching vastness of the universe; it tried to convince us that we, on the earth, were at the center, not only of the universe, but of god's care and concern, but the more we knew about our world the less convincing this became, and if god can no longer anchor us in this vastness, where then can we turn?

Unwilling to give up anchors altogether, humans sought sanctuary in more secular foundations. Science attempted to discover the world in-and-of-itself, mathematicians developed set theory and axiomatic systems grounded in mathematico-Platonic worlds, while philosophers and political thinkers turned to self-evidence and intuition. In fact, all of these are different names for the same thing; all are attempts to anchor systems to some external, unmoving foundation, and all ultimately rely on some version of self-evidence. This methodology is illustrated in Figure 9–5.

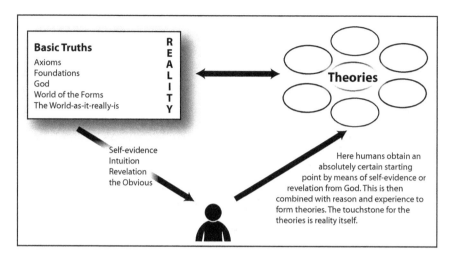

FIGURE 9–5

The anchoring of our knowledge system within external, objective systems. These systems are accessed, not by means of experience, but rather by non-experiential means such as intuition, revelation, and so on, which is why they can be held to be necessarily true with absolute certainty. This privileged access to eternal truths then serves as a guarantee for the deductions and theories based upon them.

I have been suggesting (and in the next chapter will address the topic directly) that this search is not only futile, but self-defeating. My suggestion is to stop trying to reach a forever unreachable world and realize instead that the ground for our axioms, instead of being the external world or the fabric of the universe or a world of forms, is found in the overall adequacy of our own human frameworks. This forms what might be called a non-vicious circular justification rather than a top-down authoritative one (Figure 9–6). We accept our axioms, our starting points, not because they are attached to the world in some peculiar way or because we have some privileged access to them, but because the deductions we make from them cohere well with everything else we believe and thus allow us to get by in the world and do what we want to do. The touchstone of our theories, both personal and scientific, is how well they integrate with other well-integrated, publicly held theories.

§10   CHAPTER SUMMARY

If you have read this chapter carefully you will be aware that it raises large issues with respect to our ability to know with certainty the way the world really is outside of us. This is simply a working out of what we have been saying since chapter 1. There, and in the following chapters, we made the point that all our conscious experience is processed, and this processing introduces a gap between us and the world, giving rise to the question: what is the world really like? The correct description theory of truth cements this view by defining truth in terms of this separation—we must somehow bridge this gap in order to obtain truth. What we have now seen is that all of our knowledge is ultimately based upon our own faith in our ability to

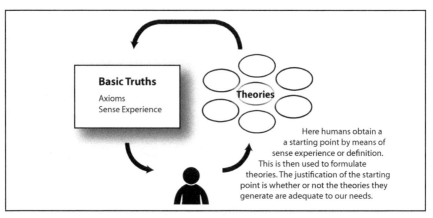

FIGURE 9–6
Anchoring without external, objective objects. Instead, we use our experience of the world (which will never give us necessary truths) and use this to formulate theories, which in turn justify our starting points.

distinguish what is true from what is false, which means the gap has become an unbridgeable chasm.

Certainty misleads us, for it gives us the feeling we have crossed this chasm, and cannot possibly be wrong about our beliefs. But do not be deceived; certainty is merely a psychological state and does not guarantee the truth of anything. Unreflective people often base extremely important decisions solely upon their feelings of certainty, as if this feeling could somehow imbue their position with truth. It does not.

We can make this point another way using the symmetry between certainty and cognitive dissonance. We can feel needless cognitive dissonance if what we see as an anomaly to our beliefs is in fact not an anomaly at all. Remember John, who saw his wife in the coffee shop with another man? What if she really was there to plan a party for him? Then the cognitive dissonance John felt was needless, for dissonance is but a feeling that bubbles up from a particular interpretation of data, and we humans often misinterpret data. Thus, cognitive dissonance itself is not a guarantee of any fact about reality. So also with certainty. Certainty is a feeling that bubbles up from a particular interpretation of data, an interpretation which may be incorrect.

When we judge evidence for any belief we use our own internal value scale, a scale that is notoriously unreliable, for it can be influenced by many other sources. We can remedy this subjectivity by going public, by testing our beliefs in certain ways. This is the idea behind the success of the scientific method. If a scientist is going to put forth a belief (a theory), then it must be testable and that test must yield results that are repeatable by others who run the same test. In other words, it must not be what we will refer to in the next chapter as a standalone theory. It must show interconnectivity with your own beliefs and must be fully integrated with other public theories that are considered similarly well verified. These are our touchstones. These tests may not securely anchor our beliefs to an unmovable external foundation, but they do anchor them to a public set of beliefs which, as it turns out, is all the foundation we need.

NOTES / QUESTIONS

10. Coherence

We must all hang together or assuredly we shall all hang separately.

—Ben Franklin

SYNOPSIS

The point of this chapter is to attempt to replace the correct description theory of truth with a coherence theory. (1) I will begin by way of an example showing how Kant attempted to breach the unbridgeable gap created by the correct description theory of truth. (2) This should give us a means of understanding how a coherence theory works, which is explicated here. (3) The question then arises: if we have done away with the external world as an anchor for the truth of our sentences, what is the function of the external world? (4) Some objections to the coherence theory are discussed. These usually involve a misunderstanding as to how the theory works, but discussing them will clarify the theory and how it differs from the correct description theory. (5) The anchor for the truth of our sentences, according to the coherence theory, lies in the public acceptance of a theory and its coherence with other publicly accepted theories. The fact is, those theories which manifest this trait are those that work the best. Those that don't, what I call standalone theories, do not function nearly as well. (6) Chapter Summary.

CHAPTER OBJECTIVES

- formulate a better basis for our truth claims—one that doesn't involve us in skepticism
- extend the concept of anchors and agreed-upon behavior to the concept of truth
- understand how we actually justify our beliefs

§1 *INTRODUCTION VIA KANT*

I mmanuel Kant was a 18th century German philosopher who has had a massive influence on how we think about both ourselves and the world. Everything we have said about how the world is filtered by brain processes is built upon what Kant said over 200 years ago. Of course, he didn't have detailed information about the brain, but he knew we probably weren't seeing the world as it really is. Thus, he made a distinction between our own perception of the world (the world-as-perceived) and the real world (the world-as-it-really-is). According to Kant we humans are stuck in the world-as-perceived, but our reason is constantly trying to expand into the world-as-it-really-is. We try to explain the former by forming mental constructs in the latter. The world-as-it-really-is is unknowable; we cannot transcend the world-as-perceived. This was the conclusion we arrived at in the last chapter, and is the essence of what I mean when I say that we are imprisoned within our subjectivity.

SKEPTICISM
A philosophical position that claims we cannot know anything.

If we are limited to the world-as-perceived, then there are at least two problems with the correct description theory of truth: first, it assumes that we, in the world-as-perceived, manufacture sentences about the world-as-it-really-is, and these sentences are true if and only if they correctly describe that world. But we can never know whether or not they correctly describe it. This is the inherent skepticism of the correct description theory. We can never say that our sentences are true because there is an unbridgeable gap between them and the world they refer to. We are bottled up within our subjectivity.

A second problem with the correct description theory of truth is that it makes perfect sense to ask whether the correct description theory is itself a correct description. By its own definition, a sentence is true if and only if that sentence correctly describes the way things really are, so what then of the sentence, "The correct description theory of truth is true"? If you are using the correct description theory as your definition of truth (and we have seen it to be the commonsense definition of truth) then of course you think it is true, but this begs the question at issue. How do we know the correct description theory is true? It is true if it correctly describes the world, but we cannot assume what we are trying to prove. Thus the correct description theory of truth once again relies on our own assumptions about reality and what seems to be obvious.

There is a way out of this conundrum, though it will be disappointing to those who desire a firm anchor to an objective world of absolute, necessary truths. I will explain the alternative to the correct description theory of truth by way of a discussion of Kant's handling of the distinction between the two worlds (the world-as-perceived versus the world-as-it-really-is), using his moral theory as an example. We can then apply this to our discussion of truth in general and perhaps see how we can overcome the inherent skepticism of the correct description theory. I am not interested in Kant's view per se and thus will not try to give a completely accurate portrayal of it. I am more interested in illustrating certain aspects of the problems involved and how they can be solved.

THE PROBLEM

In moral theory, the question is: how do we know what is the right thing to do? The answer seems to lie in the world-as-it-really-is, but Kant claimed there was no way for us, here in the world-as-perceived, to know the world-as-it-really-is. So how do we know what to do when faced with a moral dilemma? Another way to put this is: how do we know that our moral rules match the moral rules in the world-as-it-really is (see Figure 10–1). This is the same question concerning knowledge in general, but here is applied specifically to morality. Let's use the god's-eye-view terminology: how do we know that the moral rules that we humans formulate are god's rules? If our rules correctly describe the rules in god's book, then we have a match—we have acted morally; if not, we have acted immorally.

For example, suppose I borrow money from you and promise to pay it back at a future date. When that date comes, I have a choice: to pay you back or not to pay you back. What would be the moral thing to do? No matter which choice I make, I will be acting as if I have formulated a subjective rule. If I decide to pay you back, my subjective rule is: I should always keep my promises. If I decide not to pay you back,

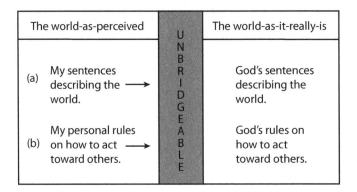

FIGURE 10–1

The problem with the correct description theory of truth is that it posits an unbridgeable chasm between our subjective world (the world-as-perceived) and the objective world (the world-as-it-really-is). This is true not only for sentences about the world (a), but also for moral rules (b). We must cross this gap if we are to match our sentences (or moral rules) to god's.

my subjective rule is: I need not always keep my promises. What I want to know is, which of these rules matches the objective rule in god's book of moral rules? If my rule (the rule that appears right to me) matches the rule in god's book (the right rule), then I have acted rightly; if it doesn't I have acted wrongly. This view captures the common sense view of a set of moral rules that does not depend upon us. That is, if you think the rightness or wrongness of your actions depends on something other than your own opinion, then this may be how you evaluate the morality of your actions. The problem, as always, is: how do I know if my rules match god's rules?

KANT'S SOLUTION

Kant believed he had a clue that would allow him to bridge the unbridgeable gap between our rules and god's book of rules—a clue that would allow us to peruse god's book, and so know how to act when confronted with moral decisions. This clue, which would allow us to know the world-as-it-really-is was based on his belief that a moral rule, in order to be a moral rule, must be universal in scope. In other words, a moral law cannot apply to one set of people and not to another set. It must apply to all or none. If it is a moral rule that we should not murder, then this rule applies, not just to white males, but also to black males, females, and so on. It must apply universally. Let's grant this point. From this, Kant deduced that any rule in god's book of moral rules must be universal in scope. With this in mind, when we formulate our own moral rules of action, if we can universalize them so that they can apply to everyone, then they, too, must be god's rules as well.

Let's recap: the only way to know we are acting morally is if our own moral rules (the rules we decide to act on) match the rules in god's book, but god's rules are hidden from us. We know, though, that each of those hidden rules must be universal in scope—they must apply to everyone—so in order to match our own rules to god's rules we test them to see whether or not they can be universalized. If they cannot be universalized, they aren't moral. This gives us a method to check our rules against god's. Kant called this test the Categorical Imperative (C):

> (C) Only act on a moral rule of your own if you can universalize it without contradiction.

If followed, (C) should allow us to compile a list of moral rules which matches the list of moral rules in god's book.[1] First, a word of explanation concerning (C). The "without contradiction" part may be a bit confusing. Kant did not mean for us to look at the consequences of our actions when determining morality. In our example above, suppose I decide not to pay back the money I owe you. This means I must ask: "Can I universalize what I'm about to do?" that is, "Can there be a moral rule that lets everyone break a promise whenever they like?" This is how we universalize one of our rules. You might think we cannot universalize this rule because it would lead to horrible consequences where no one could ever trust anyone, but for Kant consequences never determine the rightness or wrongness of an action. "Without contradiction" refers instead to a logical contradiction. The proper way to universalize would be to see that instituting such a rule (where everyone can break promises

---

[1] (C), of course, is also a rule. If you are wondering how we know this rule is correct, hold that thought. The answer is that it is a constitutive rule which derives its proof from its own derivations, but this will make more sense later.

whenever they like) would contradict, and thus destroy, the very concept of a promise. You cannot promise to do something if everyone knows you have no obligation to do it—this is contradictory. This is the sort of contradiction Kant has in mind. There are many difficulties with Kant's notion of (C) and its application, but none of these need concern us here. As long as you understand the basic principle that by universalizing our own rules using (C) we can generate a list of rules that match the rules in god's book. In other words, (C) gives us a way to know that our own personally formulated moral rules match god's absolute moral rules (see Figure 10–2).

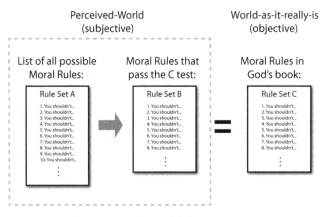

Figure 10–2

The moral rules that pass the C-test (Rule Set B) are the same one's that would appear in god's book of moral rules (Rule Set C). Thus we (in the subjective world) have a way of re-creating god's book (in the objective world). God's book thus becomes redundant. We no longer need it. Furthermore, every human who uses the C-test will end up with the exact same rule set (B).

An interesting consequence of this view is that, if we assume all humans are rational in the same way, then by using (C) we will all come up with the exact same set of rules. Kant believed that all humans were rational in the same sense, and thus the rules he formulated would be formulated by all. Let's grant this point for purposes of understanding the argument. If we all reason about the world in the same way and we all equally apply (C) to our personal moral rules, we will in fact derive the same set of rules. You won't think promise-breaking is moral, while I think it immoral. We will always agree on this and all other moral rules. Kant calls this the result of a rational community of believers. The important thing to note is that the list of moral rules I generate using (C) will not only agree with every other person's list of rules, but will also match god's list of rules.

EXPANDING THE CONCEPT

Now let's add a new piece of information to this story: there is no objective list of rules; no god's book of rules in the world-as-it-really-is. What changes with this additional knowledge? Not the list of rules we derived using (C). We are now all using (C) just as before, and everyone is generating the exact same list of moral rules. All we have lost is the objective anchor of our rules in the world-as-it-really-is, but of course we could never know those for sure anyway, so there really is no loss. We have substituted the objectivity of the transcendent out-there with the objectivity of agreed-upon behavior (publicity). If you use (C) you are actually creating your own list of moral rules. We all are, and yet we come up with the same set because of the way we process information. If you and I come up with different rules, then one of us has calculated wrong.

With this in mind, we can imagine two groups of people, both of which use (C), but use it for different reasons:

(a) Those who use (C) to match their own rules to the book of god's rules.

(b) Those who use (C) to create their own morality (there is no book of god's rules).

Note, first, that the list of rules generated by those in (a) is the same as the list generated by those in (b) because both groups are using (C). Now, keep in mind that the book of god's rules does not exist. This means the people in (a) are mistaken; they think they are using (C) to match their rules to god's, but in actuality they are doing exactly what those in (b) are doing, namely, creating their own moral rules (since the book of god's rules does not exist). And yet, according to Kant, there is a difference between the two. Those people in group (a) are enslaved, while those in group (b) are free. This is part of the originality of what Kant gives us. He redefines freedom as a function of awareness (reflection). Only those in (b) are free even though the results are the same as those in (a). We will have more to say about this notion of freedom in chapter 11, but for now, what is of interest is the contrasting viewpoints, (a) and (b).

§2 A COHERENCE THEORY OF TRUTH

Let's now look at a bare bones summary of our explanation of Kant's moral system and apply this to truth in general. Here are the steps:

(1) We began with an external standard which was impossible for us to know.

(2) This led to the formulation of (C), which ostensively allowed us to access the standard.

(3) Since our own rules now matched the external standard, the external standard became redundant, unnecessary, so it was discarded.

(4) We are left with no need for an external standard.

Let's now apply these points to our theory of truth:

(1) We began with what we called the correct description theory of truth. This theory assumes there is a world outside of us, an external standard, which our sentences must match in order to be said to be true. This conforms well with our everyday usage, but as we have seen, commonsense intuitions are not always optimal. As we have pointed out, the correct description theory of truth has inherent problems, the most important of which is that it posits a gap between the knower

KANT'S METHOD: THE REST OF THE STORY

The methodology we have described, used by Kant to access and then discard god's book of rules in the world-as-it-really-is, was later utilized by GWF Hegel (1770-1831), who turned it into a major movement of thought in history. Typical of Hegel, he analyzed this movement as having three stages, which can be seen as the evolutionary movement of truth and how it develops through history (Hegel referred to this as the dialectic). The stages are as follows:

- the positing of a hypothesis or position in order to solve a problem
- internal contradictions develop within this hypothesis
- the hypothesis, in its original form, disappears, giving rise to a higher position

We can see several of the themes we have discussed in this text in these stages, for this can also be seen as a snapshot of theorizing: a theory is formed, anomalies arise and may eventually dictate a theory be revised. The third stage is a move to a higher reference frame, a completely new way of seeing the world that falsifies the previous view. For instance, for Kant, the idea that there is an objective set of moral rules (god's book of rules) is first posited, but raises the question of how to gain access to such. The categorical imperative (C) is formulated to reach this, but once it allows us to reach god's book we see god's book doesn't really exist. But note that we had to think it existed, otherwise we would never have had the incentive to formulate (C) in order to reach it. Thus falsehood is necessary in order to attain truth.

A perfect example of the Hegelian dialectical movement is seen in Baum's classic, *The Wizard of Oz* (I have a hunch that Baum was a Hegelian). In that story, Dorothy, the Lion, the Tin Man and the Scarecrow each have something they want to achieve. Dorothy wants to go home, the Lion wants courage, the Tin Man wants a heart and the Scarecrow wants a brain. In order to achieve these they go to see the Wizard, who directs them to bring back the broom of the wicked witch. They eventually complete this task and return to Oz, expecting the Wizard to endow them with their desired goals, only to discover the Wizard is a fraud. This doesn't matter, though, for they have achieved what they wanted simply by fulfilling the quest he set for them. They had to believe the falsehood—the Wizard—in order to realize they had what it takes to get what they wanted all along. Here we see how the original hypothesis functions as a kind of carrot on a stick, and the attempts to obtain the carrot lead to a higher realization. So also, scientists are led to formulate theories because they believe they are discovering things about the world-as-it-really-is.

The story might have ended with Hegel, except that he had a famous student named Karl Marx (1818-1883). Marx took Hegel's dialectical idealism and applied it more concretely to economics and politics—turning Hegel on his head, as he liked to say. The result was what he called dialectical materialism.

(us) and the known (the world) which is impossible to bridge. Due to our prison of subjectivity, any attempted solution to this problem is doomed to fail, for ultimately all our knowledge is based upon our own self-evidence.

(2) But we do have a method of accessing the world which we have always used and which works marvelously well, if not perfectly, namely, theorizing based on our adequacy guidelines, which I will refer to as Coherence (C'). Granted, we can never know what the world is really like, whether our sentences correctly describe the world-as-it-really-is, but theorizing let's us get as close as possible (Figure 10–3).

(3) But wait. According to (2) we are still defining truth according to the correct description theory; we are still maintaining our sentences are true if and only if they correctly describe the world-as-it-really-is. This means the unbridgeable gap is still in place and we are merely using theorizing (C') as a stopgap measure to make

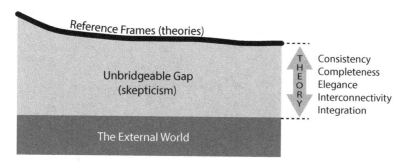

FIGURE 10–3
As we hone our theories, we expect them to better and better describe the external world, but there will always be an unbridgeable gap, guaranteeing we will never know exactly how well our theories match the world.

the best of a bad situation. Why not instead discard the correct description theory of truth altogether and redefine truth simply in terms of (C')? In other words, let's say that our sentences are true if and only if they cohere well with the rest of the sentences (beliefs, hopes, wants, goals, desires) within our conceptual scheme. Call this the coherence theory of truth. We see, then, there are two ways to use (C'):

(a) We can use (C') to match our sentences to the world-as-it-really-is (as best as possible).

(b) We can use (C') to create a coherent set of sentences with no reference to the world-as-it-really is.

Those in (a) are committed to the correct description theory of truth. They believe they must match their sentences to this realm in order to obtain truth (as illustrated in Figure 10–3). As we have pointed out, there is something futile about this view, for you can never really know whether or not your sentences match the external world. We have already seen that certainty won't work here. Those in this position, (a), are stuck within their subjective realm and yet constantly yearn for an objective anchor which they will never have. Those in (b) have given up the search for an anchor and have thus redefined the notion of truth as that which adheres to the adequacy conditions we are referring to as (C') (These adequacy conditions are listed in chapter 4, and illustrated in Figure 10–4).

(4) The behavior of those in (a) is identical to the behavior of those in (b). All those in (b) have given up is an impossible-to-meet standard. Other than that they adhere to the same theories, have the same beliefs, standards of evidence, adequacy conditions, and so on, as those in (a). What they lack is maybe the comfort those in (a) claim to have concerning an absolute external anchor, but this comfort is ill-conceived. It is based on cobwebs they have spun within the prison of their own subjectivity.

⚜

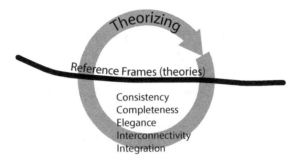

FIGURE 10–4

Here we have dropped the external world as a standard for the truth of our sentences, relying instead only upon theorizing. Our reference frames remain the same (as in Figure 10–3), thus the only difference is that we have lost the unbridgeable gap between our reference frames and the external world, and with it the skepticism.

§3 THE FUNCTION OF THE EXTERNAL WORLD

Is there an external world? In other words, is there a way the world is when we aren't experiencing it? The correct description theory of truth demands that it exist, for according to it our sentences are true if and only if they correctly describe this external world. This, as we have seen, is the common sense way of thinking about the world. Scientists in particular tend to get perturbed when anyone hints that the external world is unreachable, for the explicit goal of science is to describe the way the world really is. Scientific progress is seen as honing our theories in much the same way that nature hones an organism via selection (see Figure 10–5). In both cases the entities are becoming closer and closer equated with the world.

Both goals are, of course, idealizations. No organism will ever be perfectly adapted, first, due to the fact that natural selection builds kluges rather than optimally adapted organisms, and, second, because the environment is continually changing. So also theories, if they approach the god's-eye-view, approach it asymptotically. Our knowledge of the world will always be incomplete for reasons we have seen in chapter 8.

What do we lose if we forget about trying to match our theories to the external world? If we remove the external world from Figure 10–3, the unbridgeable gap necessarily disappears, as does the skepticism inherent within it (Figure 10–4). We are left with only theories, but the function of our theories is no longer to bridge an unbridgeable gap. They have lost their anchor and thus stand alone. The adequacy conditions are no longer used to indicate the fit of our theories to the external world; instead, they do what they always did anyway, they indicate whether or not our theories allow us to function in the world the way we want to function. To revisit our analogies from chapter 6, just as the U.S. abandoned the gold standard, and just as we have abandoned the Platonic forms as the basis of linguistics, so also should we abandon the external world as the standard for the truth of our sentences.

This does not mean we don't think there is an external world. Of course there is an external world. Abandoning the correct description theory is simply a recognition that we can never know exactly what the external world is like and that knowing exactly what it is like doesn't matter—plays no useful role in our life-quest. The

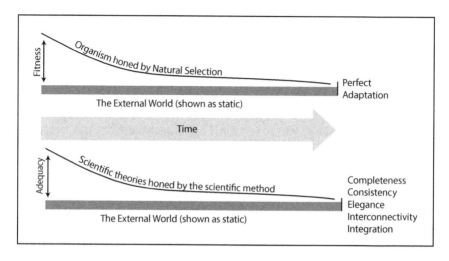

FIGURE 10–5

We have seen that natural selection fine tunes organisms so that they become more and more fit to their environment. In an ideal situation an organism could become perfectly adapted (though this will never occur because the environment itself is continually changing). So also, scientists (among others) often hold that our theories are getting us closer and closer to understanding the way the world really is. This, too, is a pipe dream.

external world is like an old pair of shoes that are now worn out and hurt our feet, but which we cannot bear to part with. So also, reference to the external world as a standard of truth causes us nothing but heartache and anxiety and gives us no benefit.

The fact that there is an external world constitutes a core value within our framework, which means that to deny the existence of such would bring about a seismic disturbance of epic proportions. That is, denying the existence of the world around us would destroy the overall coherence of our frameworks. This coherence means we are justified in believing in its existence. There is no proof for it, though, outside this coherence. We must act as if there is an external world. The world outside our framework may be completely different than we think it is, perhaps totally chaotic, but our theories allow us to turn this chaos into an orderly system, which allows us to get by.

My wife, for example, might be a zombie, might have no inner conscious activity, might simply be an automaton whose external behavior indicates she is a fully functioning conscious human (like me), but instead is completely devoid of consciousness. This is a possibility. Indeed, it may be true of all humans other than me, for I can only be sure of myself. Nonetheless, I must act as if my wife and most other humans are non-zombies, for to seriously contemplate the zombie hypothesis would require too much rearrangement of my conceptual scheme. Thus, I believe my wife is not a zombie, and I am justified in claiming this to be a true belief because it coheres well with all my other beliefs. So also with the external world. I believe there is one and am justified in claiming this belief to be true, for its denial would cause radical seismic damage to my conceptual scheme.

§4 POTENTIAL PROBLEMS

We must now consider several potential problems with the coherence theory. We remember, for instance, that when we asked, of the correct description theory, whether or not it was true, we ran into a problem of circularity. That is, accepting the correct description theory as true meant that the correct description theory itself had to be a correct description of the way the world is, which begged the question. Does the coherence theory also succumb to this kind of self-referential inconsistency? It does not because we need not consider the coherence theory true. Obviously, we will not ask whether the coherence theory is a correct description of the way the world is, for this would be to assume the correct description theory of truth, which we have abandoned. We do not even apply a truth criterion to the coherence theory. It is, instead, what we call a methodological starting point, a constitutive element, the justification of which is whether or not it works. Since we are not interested in matching our theories to an external world, no questions are begged. Yes, the justification of the coherence theory is circular, but it is not a vicious circularity, since everything is based simply on whether or not it does what it is put forward to do, that is, whether or not it works.

Another looming issue is that of relativity. If we have cut the cord to the external world, disallowing it as a touchstone to truth, are we then cast adrift among the detritus of the universe? Can we ever deny the truth of even the craziest theory if it is deemed adequate by an asylum inmate? Do we have to bow to the propounders of astrology, phrenology, fortune-telling, and other mystical arts? Are these of equal value to those theories which depend rigorously upon the scientific method? We already know the answer to this. They are not. No methodology has come close to the success rate of the scientific method when it comes to sorting true facts from false ones. As we have said above, the success rate for all other methodologies is no greater than a throw of the dice or a flip of a coin. We have touched on the answer to this question before, but will now address it more fully. The short answer is "No." Truth is not relative in the sense that it is up to the whim of any individual framework.

Consider a person who believes the earth is flat and that if you travel too close to the edge you will fall off. Let's suppose this person really believes this is true and because of this belief refuses to travel far from home. It is possible that such a person could have a consistent framework with this belief as part of it, though the belief entails the falsehood of many other beliefs people generally hold true. For example, this person would have to explain the existence of the photographs of the earth from space in which the earth appears spherical, but maybe he thinks (as some evidently do of the moon landing) that all such photographs are fraudulent, put together by a power structure trying to impose its views upon us. He would also have to explain away all the travel stories of those who flew or sailed to distant lands and did not fall off the edge of the earth; he would have to deny geological and gravitational theories, cosmological positions, and on and on. But it could be done. Does this mean that his flat-earth belief is true in some significant way?

In reply, we must remember that coherence depends on the five adequacy conditions we set out in chapter 4. These are:

(a) Consistency: internal harmony, absence of internal contradictions.

(b) Simplicity: structural economy, beauty, elegance.

(c) Completeness: comprehensive explanatory power, no major facts left out (ideally, all relevant facts taken into account).

(d) Interconnectivity: robust connections between facts within a theory.

(e) Integration: orderliness, components mesh well with other theories and facts outside of them (conforms to our overall world-view).

Our flat-earth person may succeed in achieving (a), for we humans are really good at rationalizing our beliefs so as to maintain consistency, and even (d) may be achieved because of this, but the other three are problematic. For (b), (c) and especially (e) work together to expand our individual frameworks into social frameworks. A complete theory is also integrated because it must take in data outside of ourselves in order to explain as much as possible about the world around us, and simplicity follows from this because we need not invent extravagant rationalizations to explain away all those other pesky theories that everyone but us holds true. What these three conditions add to coherence is the idea of publicity, and this is, in the end, what disallows the person-relativity of truth. We will talk more about this publicity in §5 below.

We mentioned, when we first set out the above adequacy conditions, that there were other conditions we could have included. This gives rise to a final question, similar to our first, namely, how do we know we have put together the *right* adequacy conditions? But this is an illicit question, for it sneaks the notion of right into the equation once again. On the correct description view, our theories are honed to the way-the-world-really-is and thus become better and better descriptions of the world. But on the coherence view, our theories are honed only to pragmatic considerations—how well they allow us to function—and the belief in the external world is just one aspect of this. We thus add or subtract adequacy conditions based on whether or not they compliment this goal. If we have a condition that turns out to hinder our ability to function as we want to function then that condition would ultimately be dropped. There is general public agreement on the adequacy conditions, but no absolute agreement, especially with respect to which ones are most important (see Figure 10–6).

§5 STAND-ALONE NARRATIVES VERSUS INTEGRATION

The coherence part of the coherence theory stresses integration of theories above all else. In order to be taken seriously, a theory must integrate in a seamless manner with other relevant theories that we hold. In other words, theories should, in the long run, verify each other. Carbon dating can be calibrated by dendrochronology, which can then calculate dates on packrat middens, which can determine the flora and fauna of the area, which can be seen to coordinate with the weather during that specific time and the geography, which is then seen to be consistent

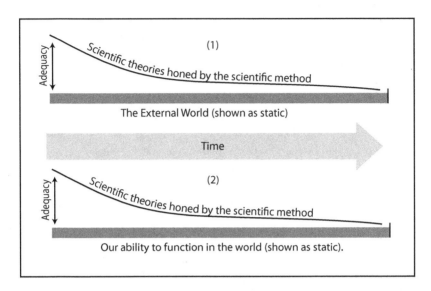

FIGURE 10–6
(1) depicts the correct description use of adequacy conditions: to allow our theories to become better descriptions of the world. (2) depicts the coherence use of adequacy conditions: to insure our theories allow us to function better in the world.

with tectonics, magnetic fields, anthropological investigations, and so on. Without independent corroboration we are left with myth and mumbo-jumbo.

Multiple ties to multiple disciplines and methodologies is what, in the end, justifies our truth claims. In Kant's terminology, this is a reference to a community of believers, or what we might call a community of theorizers. Truth claims are not person-relative; they must pass the test of public verification. Your private views on astrology and fortune-telling might work really well for you and your friends, but you must put them to the publicity test before you start making truth claims concerning them. Thus, when a new discipline or methodology is discovered, it must cohere with the rest of our knowledge or we are not justified in adopting it. For instance, the discovery of spectroscopy allowed us to determine the chemical content of stars based on their light spectrum. If this method had indicated that stars were composed of green cheese we would have thrown out the methodology rather than everything else we knew about stars.

What we end up with on this model is a number of widely accepted theories all closely interrelated, forming a tight circle of justification. Each of these, in turn, is attached to our individual frameworks in various ways. This makes for the possibility of deep connections, of seeing ways in which a seemingly superficial aspect of one theory has deep roots relating it to everything else. The more this happens the more you can be assured that yours is not a standalone viewpoint, that you have tapped into a deep network of knowledge. These multiple and intricate connections to all other theories form the substrate within which a coherence theory of knowledge is anchored, a substrate that is a part of the coherence theory itself and so has no

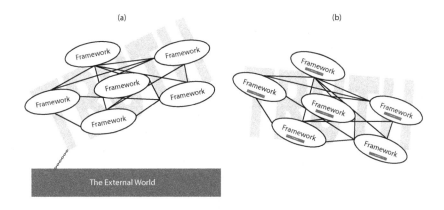

FIGURE 10–7
(a) is a mistaken conception of how one might hold both the coherence theory (to justify the external world) and then resort to the correct description theory, thus maintaining an objective anchor. (b) is the correct conception of the coherence theory, showing the external world as a core value within each framework. There is nothing external to our theorizings to which we can anchor.

inherent skepticism. There is no absolute foundation to our knowledge claims, but rather, a tight circle of justification.

Let me attempt here to clear up one last misunderstanding. Those who cannot quite let go of the correct description theory of truth and yet acknowledge the efficacy of theorizing for getting us close to the world-as-it-really-is, might claim that since the coherence theory admits that the existence of the external world is a core value, doesn't this mean that we are using the coherence theory to justify a version of the correct description theory? Once the coherence theory has given us a solid basis for believing in the external world, then hasn't it also given us a solid basis for the correct description theory of truth (Figure 10–7a)? On this view, it is the coherence theory that plays the Oz wizard who dissipates in the end leaving us with the correct description theory. This view is based on a misunderstanding of the function of the two theories. The problem is that we are dealing with theories of truth, with what makes our sentences true, and you cannot have two mutually exclusive theories doing this simultaneously. The heart of the coherence theory is that it severs the connection between truth and the external world. That's all it does. It does not make the external world go away, but rather incorporates it into each of our frameworks in a more intimate fashion—as a core value constituent (Figure 10–7b). It holds it in place only because it is tied in with everything else. Once you see how this works you will understand that there is no going back to the correct description theory once you have accepted the coherence theory. There is simply nothing left to which you can attach an anchor.

§6   CHAPTER SUMMARY

This has been a crucial chapter, for we have seen how to break our dependence upon the external world. Attempting to tie the truth of our sentences to something firm and abiding is understandable. Such anchors appear to give stability to our theories, something to strive for that does not depend upon the whims of the human operating system. But once we have reified such a safe harbor we realize we can never really get there. As an idealization it is nice to contemplate, but in the real world we have to face the fact that it gives us nothing but a forlorn hope resulting in skepticism. All our knowledge claims are ultimately based on our faith in our own abilities to distinguish truth from falsehood. We can never reach outside of ourselves in a way demanded by the correct description theory. This is the way we process data, and has always been the way we process data. We have always depended upon theorizing for truth, but have only recently (within the last few centuries) come to realize and embrace this. It has been a hard lesson to learn, evidenced by the slow acceptance of the coherence theory. We humans want our anchors to rest on the solid rock of the objective world.

The beauty of the coherence theory is an insight on a par with other enlightenment experiences. Truth is merely the coherence of all our theories, and the more theories we can join within our coherent circle the tighter everything becomes. To paraphrase Ben Franklin, our theories must hang together or they will all hang separately.

NOTES / QUESTIONS

Part 3: Applications

11. Determinism

You will say that I feel free. This is an illusion, which may be compared to that of the fly in the fable, who, upon the pole of a heavy carriage, applauded himself for directing its course.

—Baron d'Holbach

SYNOPSIS

(1) When we reflect upon determinism and free will we often have contradictory intuitions. Our naive understanding makes it seem as if both are plausible, and yet they are supposed to be contradictory. (2) The determinism-free will debate is important because it has ramifications on the extent to which we can be manipulated by others. Even more important is its impact on the concept of responsibility, for if determinism is true, how can we be held responsible for our actions? (3) The Laplacean Super-Calculator is introduced as a hypothetical construct that will help us clarify some of the concepts in the overall debate. (4) Random events are divided into truly random events and those that only appear random, or pseudo-random events. This distinction will have consequences for our view of free will. (5) Free will is redefined in terms of multiple futures and the complexity of causation. The distinction between determinism and free will is redrawn along the lines of the random/pseudo-random distinction. (6) & (7) The ramifications of this redefinition: our deterministic fears are found to be unwarranted even in the face of the truth of determinism. In these sections I show why we need not fear scary deterministic scenarios concerning manipulation or loss of responsibility. (8) Chapter Summary.

CHAPTER OBJECTIVES

- provoke thought concerning causation and its importance
- understand the relation between determinism and responsibility
- contemplate the implications of determinism
- provide insight into the confusions that lie behind the free will discussion
- link the topic of determinism to our previous discussions on anchoring

---

O ur naive understanding of the world tells us that "of course we are free to choose!" After all, you chose to get up this morning rather than stay in bed. You chose to read this paragraph and you can stop at any time. Most people, in other words, do not have to be convinced they have free will. It is a default, though faulty, belief, at least to the extent most understand it. In this chapter we will examine the concept of determinism in hopes that perhaps you, too, will come to have contradictory intuitions. I will then argue for the precedence of determinism, or better, a reinterpretation of our default concept of free will.

Determinism is the claim that there is no free will, and the strongest argument for this is based on the following simple and also intuitive principle, which I will refer to as the Causal Principle:

Every event has a cause.

If you believe this, you are well on your way to becoming a determinist. If you don't, consider the following thought experiment which imagines a case in which it fails:

Your car won't start. Annoyed, you have it towed to your trusted mechanic, who later informs you the car is in perfect working order. Overjoyed, you proclaim, "You fixed it. Great!" But your mechanic hesitates, "No," says he, "I said it is in perfect working order. It still won't start." Puzzled, you ask why it won't start. "No reason," he replies. "It just won't start."

If a mechanic ever said this, you would immediately think he was covering his inability to discover the real reason why the car wouldn't start (and you would be right). We cannot even imagine an event having no cause whatsoever. Remember, our inability to conceive something usually means it is entangled so deeply within the threads of our conceptual scheme we cannot give it up without massive reorganization. This is true of the causal principle. If it were false there would be uncaused events occurring around us, and if this were so, we would lose all predictability and uniformity within nature, and these are the very basis, not only of science in general, but also of our personal world views. Imagine if you could not rely on the air mixture surrounding you to be non-poisonous, or the ground beneath your feet to be stable, or on gravity to hold you to the earth.[1]

Now you see the reasonableness behind the causal principle, for you have never experienced an example of its falseness and cannot conceive of such. If the causal principle is true, then every event has another, prior event or set of events, sufficient for causing it. But these prior events also must have causes and so must those, and those, and those... which means every event has a chain of ancestral causes behind it which determine it completely. You thought you chose freely to get up this morning, but your choice had a cause which had a cause which had a cause... all of which made your choosing to get up this morning inevitable. And yet you feel free. No one denies this. As the quote at the beginning of this chapter says, "this is an illusion." I will claim this feeling of freedom is the simple and often wonderful result of our ignorance, itself a result of the immense complexity of the world.

Another thought experiment to give you a feel for the intuitive correctness of determinism:

Imagine you did something in the past you wish you hadn't done, maybe told a lie which resulted in losing a close friend. Several weeks after this incident you come across a marvelous machine, a time machine of sorts, which allows you to rewind your life like it was a video recorder. You use the machine to rewind your life to a place just before you told the lie, hoping to avert the tragedy.

Most people immediately see this won't help. If your machine is simply a time-rewinder, it will take you back to the time before the lie, but it also takes you back to the exact mental state you were in at the time, which means all the reasons why you told the lie in the first place are intact, which means you will lie once again and everything will play itself out exactly as before. The temptation is to rewind a bit further and then a bit further, for then surely we will eventually be free to deliberate differently. But we always put ourselves back into a mental state which determined our choices. What we want, in this scenario, is a rewinder with a bonus. We want it to rewind and yet retain the lessons we learned in the meantime, which would allow us to make a different decision. Of course, if we had free will then the simple rewind device would suffice, for we would then have a real choice to change the situation. Alas, our intuitions tell us this is not so. The causal principle rules supreme.

If you agree that this seems reasonable, you now have a feel for those contradictory intuitions I began with. We feel certain we are free, but a little reflection makes us certain the causal principle is true, which dictates our determinedness. We will look at several attempts to reconcile these two concepts, but first, we should understand why the topic is important.

---

[1] The claim here is that predictability is a constitutive factor of our world view (our framework). Without it we would not be able to investigate, for example, predictability. In other words, the claim is a methodological presupposition, not a truth claim.

§2 WHY FREE WILL IS IMPORTANT

THE LOSS OF RESPONSIBILITY

Many people think that without free will we cannot have responsibility. How can you be held responsible for something if it was caused by forces beyond your control? This is a reasonable fear: if we can hold no one responsible for their actions, then we cannot rightly punish them, and if we cannot punish them, society will crumble.

Let's use a few scenarios to establish the boundaries of our concepts:

(1) Mild mannered Alfred has a brain tumor of which he is completely unaware. One day he is involved in an argument with one of his friends and, in a sudden rage caused solely by the tumor in his brain, he kills his friend.

(2) Zandra is having an affair with Zeke. The two are deeply in love, but Zandra's husband is a rich and powerful man who will make it very difficult for Zandra to get a divorce. Therefore, Zandra and Zeke decide to murder him, an event which Zandra successfully carries out after weeks of careful planning.

We can now construct a continuum showing Alfred's case on the far left and Zandra's on the far right (Figure 11–1). These two extremes define the bounds of our concept of responsibility.

Alfred Zandra

Not Responsible Responsible

FIGURE 11–1
Responsibility continuum: on the left, Alfred is not held responsible for his actions, while, on the right, Zandra is held completely responsible for hers. Most real-life examples fall somewhere in between, though advances in neuroscience are continually pushing the line to the left.

Most people agree we wouldn't hold Alfred responsible for his actions; he was not in control of his mental faculties, and this lack was not due to anything he could have controlled. Therefore, even though we might not want him on the street until the tumor is removed, we do not punish him. Punishment is reserved for people who are responsible. On the other hand, there is no question Zandra should be punished, for she knew exactly what she was doing.

We have established the outer boundaries of our concept of responsibility. Most scenarios fall somewhere in between these extremes. Consider two more examples:

(3) Marvin grew up in an abusive family and later went on to become an alcoholic. One day, while binge drinking in a bar, he got into a heated

---

The Butterfly Effect & Arbitrary Causation

One of the consequences of the causal principle is that any one event can potentially cause an indefinite series of following events. This is referred to as the butterfly effect: seemingly insignificant events can have massive consequences in the future. (The label "butterfly effect" is taken from chaos theory, where the claim was once made that the turbulence resulting from the fluttering of a butterfly's wings could affect weather patterns throughout the world.) The butterfly effect, while interesting to consider, muddies the waters when trying to establish past events as causes of present events. For example, suppose a friend of mine is in the hospital because he was in an accident while taking his wife to see a psychologist, whom she was seeing in order to deal with her mother's Alzheimer's disease, which ran in her family. If I call in sick in order to visit him in the hospital, should I put down, as my excuse for calling in sick, his wife's mother's genetic propensity for Alzheimer's?

As we trace a present event backward in time, the causes multiply exponentially and the path we choose to follow will necessarily be arbitrary. For example, suppose you begin tracing your own family history. You have to make a choice immediately—your father's or your mother's; and for each generation you have to make another set of (arbitrary) choices concerning which lines to explore. Suppose you decide to trace them all. There are sixteen choices by the time you get to your great great grand parents—are you the consequence of each and every one of them? Individuals interested in tracing their family tree are often guilty of cherry picking, arbitrarily switching lines until they are led back to an important ancestor.

---

argument with a fellow drinker and, in a fit of alcohol-induced rage, stabbed the man to death.

(4) Nancy was a gun collector. Proud of her newest acquisition, a German pistol from World War I, she was showing it to her friend when it accidentally discharged, killing the friend.

Should we punish Marvin? or was he damaged in his childhood sufficiently to say he was not in control of his actions? What about his alcoholism? And what about Nancy, who did not intentionally kill her friend? Notice the subtleties involved in our decisions concerning culpability in such cases. By considering various scenarios in this manner we can map our views on responsibility.

Fear of Manipulation

Responsibility is not the only factor that gives teeth to the determinism debate. Consider the following conversation between Morpheus and Neo from the movie *The Matrix*:

> Morpheus: Do you believe in fate, Neo?
> Neo: No.
> Morpheus: Why not?
> Neo: Because I don't like the idea that I'm not in control of my life.
> Morpheus: I know exactly what you mean.[2]

---

[2] We will ignore that this is a very bad argument for believing or not believing in fate (or anything else). It doesn't follow from the fact you don't like not being in control of your life that determinism is false or that you should believe it false. The world need not conforming to our desires.

When we think of ourselves as completely determined by previous events this might engender scary scenarios of mad scientists and robot-like zombies. But we don't have to go to these extremes. There are fixed-action patterns of behavior all living things exhibit which render us robot-like at times. Consider, for example, the mother turkey, whose maternal instincts are triggered, not by the fluffy cuteness of her chicks or by their smell or closeness, but rather by their cheep-cheeping sound, and by that alone. If a chick won't (or cannot) cheep, it won't be fed. Once we understand the cause and effect relationship involved between mother and chick, we can exploit it.

> For a mother turkey, a polecat is a natural enemy whose approach is to be greeted with squawking, pecking, clawing rage. Indeed, the experimenters found that even a stuffed model of a polecat, when drawn by a string toward a mother turkey, received an immediate and furious attack. When, however, the same stuffed replica carried inside it a small recorder that played the "cheep-cheep" sound of baby turkeys, the mother not only accepted the oncoming polecat but gathered it underneath her. When the machine was turned off, the polecat model again drew a vicious attack. (Cialdini 2)

Maybe this is what worries us about determinism: if determinism is true then maybe someone will discover such traits about us and control us in a similar way, and we don't like to be controlled in this manner (as Neo says). There is something to this. Several years ago I was car shopping and found exactly what I was looking for, except the price I was willing to pay was less than the sticker price of the car. I was thus escorted into a back room and introduced to the sales manager. We haggled for a while, shrinking the gap a bit, but it soon became obvious we weren't going to agree on a price. Then the sales manager seemed to give up. With a sigh and a shrug he leaned back in his chair and asked about my family and our plans for the summer. After a few minutes of conversation he returned to business and asked what we should do about the car. I thought, "What the heck, it's only slightly more than I wanted to pay," so I caved and bought the car at his price. Several months later, I was reading a book on contract negotiations, and the author explained how to close a deal when two parties seem unable to reach an agreement. He described the strategy as follows: "When you and the buyer are at loggerheads, sit back, relax, and change the subject. Start talking about something trivial, a picture on the wall, your kids, doesn't matter. When you return to the deal, nine times out of ten the buyer will close." I stared in amazement; I had been manipulated! I was a mother turkey with a polecat under its wing.

We can all be manipulated because we all have fixed action patterns in our repertoire. Anyone who knows human behavior well enough can use these behavioral patterns to exploit us. (Is this why we are often uncomfortable around psychiatrists and psychologists?) We don't want to become robots, programmed to do our master's bidding, and one of the fears of determinism is rooted in this distaste for being controlled.

FATALISM

There is a distinction between fatalism and determinism. Fatalism is the view that a person's fate has already been foreordained, written in the book, spelled out, before he or she was born. It is captured in song lines and sayings, such as "*que sera sera*" and "everything always works out for the best." W. Somerset Maugham gives us a fine example of fatalism in the following story:

[Death is speaking.] There was a merchant in Bagdad who sent his servant to market to buy provisions and in a little while the servant came back, white and trembling, and said, Master, just now when I was in the marketplace I was jostled by a woman in the crowd and when I turned I saw it was Death that jostled me. She looked at me and made a threatening gesture, now, lend me your horse, and I will ride away from this city and avoid my fate. I will go to Samarra and there Death will not find me. The merchant lent him his horse, and the servant mounted it, and he dug his spurs in its flanks and as fast as the horse could gallop he went. Then the merchant went down to the marketplace and he saw me standing in the crowd and he came to me and said, Why did you make a threatening gesture to my servant when you saw him this morning? That was not a threatening gesture, I said, it was only a start of surprise. I was astonished to see him in Bagdad, for I had an appointment with him tonight in Samarra.

Fatalism says: Necessarily, event A will happen, and then event B will happen, while determinism says: Event A will happen, and then, necessarily, event B will happen. Notice the importance of the change in the location of the necessity operator. All determinism says is that if A happens, then B will definitely happen, but there is no necessity attached to A. The distinction is slight, and the two positions may be indistinguishable with respect to what finally happens, but fatalism's positing of a god's-eye-view reference frame changes everything from our human perspective.

§3   A GOD'S-EYE-VIEW: THE LAPLACEAN SUPER-CALCULATOR

We can look deeper into the concept of determinism by considering a super-calculator (or god-like calculator) as described by the French astronomer Pierre-Simon Laplace (1902):

Given for one instant an intelligence which could comprehend all the forces by which nature is animated and the respective situation of the beings who compose it—an intelligence sufficiently vast to submit these data to analysis—it would embrace in the same formula the movement of the greatest bodies in the universe and those of the lightest atom; for it, nothing would be uncertain and the future, as the past, would be present to its eyes. (4)

If determinism is true, then a being who knew everything about the present would automatically know everything about the future simply by calculating causes and effects.

We humans have this predictive power on a very small scale. For example, if we know (1) the exact position of a car traveling on an interstate highway, and (2) exactly how fast it is going, then we can predict exactly where the car will be in fifteen minutes. We make similar calculations throughout our day, but our knowledge of the factors involved is usually relegated to probabilities rather than exactitudes. If a friend of yours is coming over for dinner and calls to say he is on his way, you might make a similar calculation: you know where he lives and approximately how far away; you know the route—how many stoplights, and so on, he will have to navigate on the way; you can estimate his speed; and you might take into account (from prior knowledge) that he often doesn't mean "now" when he says he is leaving now. There is also a chance he will get in an accident on the way or have a flat tire. We take all of these probabilities into account and calculate an ETA, and so might begin to worry if our calculation is twenty minutes and forty-five minutes have passed.

Notice the difference in our finite calculative abilities and that of the Laplacean super-calculator (LSC). In this scenario, at the moment the friend calls, the LSC knows the entire state of the universe and can calculate everything accordingly. She knows all the traffic patterns and how they will affect the route; she knows the exact state of every mechanical component of your friend's car, so she also knows whether or not it will affect his travel time; she knows everything about your friend and the neural processes within his brain and thus knows exactly when he will actually leave and also knows all decisions he will make in route; she also knows the neural states of every other person in the universe and their decisions and how these might relate to your friend's planned route. In short, everything is known with absolute exactitude and the calculations are made that your friend will arrive in exactly seventeen minutes, twenty-three seconds—and he does. In fact, he must. Either that or the LSC has made an error in her calculation or did not know something, but this is impossible by our definition of the LSC. So, if the LSC says your friend will arrive in seventeen minutes, twenty-three seconds, he will.

This gives us another way to formulate the traditional determinist position, for it doesn't matter at what point the LSC calculates. Once she has calculated the future, she will never have to calculate again, for there is only one possible future. For example, suppose she gathered her data 3.5 billion years ago and made her calculations of the future based upon that data, and one thing she sees will happen in the future is that on July 13, 2020, you will be sitting poolside at a resort in Miami Beach sipping piña coladas and reading this book. Two billion years later she once again gathers her data and recalculates. Sure enough, there you are, on July 13, 2020, sitting poolside in Miami. Nothing has changed. In a determined universe the future is entirely transparent to the LSC (see Figure 11–2A).

§4 Random Events

We can now use our concept of the LSC to help us understand the concept of randomness and how it impacts the determinism debate. There are two interpretations of random event. A truly random event (TRE) is an event that has no cause, that is, an event that violates the causal principle. Our LSC would be completely stymied by such an event. Since she calculates based on causal connections and a random event has no cause (but does have effects), it throws off all calculations. To use our previous example, when the LSC first calculated 3.5 billion years ago she saw you sitting poolside in 2020, but now let's intersperse a TRE between her calculation and 2020. This TRE will change everything, which means (as per the

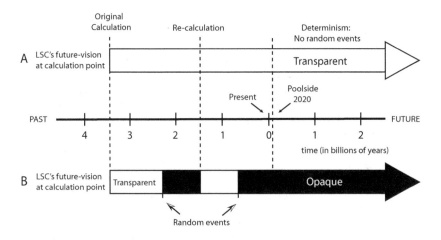

FIGURE 11–2

The god's-eye-view of the LSC. (A) illustrates that in a completely determined universe the entire future is transparent to the LSC, no matter when she calculates. If she performs a calculation and millions of years later recalculates, nothing will change. (B) illustrates what happens when the universe is not completely determined, that is, when truly random events are introduced. Truly random events have no cause, but do have effects, thus the LSC cannot see through them.

butterfly effect) you may no longer be poolside, and thus the LSC will not be able to see past the TRE. She must recalculate if she wants to know what you will be doing in 2020 (see Figure 11–2B)

Another way to put this: if the LSC is ever surprised by an outcome, there is a random event involved. If she is playing roulette at the local casino, loses, and is surprised at having lost, then a TRE has occurred between her last calculation and the spin of the roulette wheel. We have already seen that TREs are inconceivable in our every day life. In fact, the only known candidate for a TRE occurs in the quantum realm with the decay of radioactive isotopes. We might be tempted to disregard these events because they only occur in the world of the very small, but since subatomic events do, or could, have an impact on our world we cannot completely disallow them. Nor should we treat quantum physics as Einstein was wont to do (which is the same way we treated our car mechanic who claimed there was no reason why our car wouldn't start) by saying they *are* caused, we just don't know yet what the causes are (note the future-pleading ploy when confronted with an anomaly). The quantum theory is the best explanation for a number of phenomena and we don't want our denial of random events to hang on proving it wrong. Thus, we must admit, in light of the presumed existence of TREs in the quantum world, that traditional determinism is false, for it maintains there is only one future, while the existence of TREs implies there are many. Every time a TRE occurs there is a branch in possibilities. If we look at the LSC's calculating abilities as a way to see the future, then random events are barriers to this sight; the LSC cannot see through them (they are inscrutable). She would have to recalculate in order to know what was going to happen after a TRE occurred.

COIN FLIPS, DICE ROLLS & OTHER PSEUDO-RANDOM PROBABILITIES

Suppose an urn has 100 marbles in it, sixty of which are white, forty of which are black. If these are well-mixed, what is the probability that we will reach in blindly and pull out a white marble. The answer is 60%. This is, of course the same question as: what is the probability that we will roll a six using a standard dice? The answer is 1/6, but how does this translate into the real world? What does it mean to say there is a 1/6 chance that I will roll a six? It means we should expect a six at least once every six rolls. Try it. You'll be disappointed. I just rolled a dice eighteen times, which means I should have seen three sixes, but I only got one. I also should have seen three fives, but I saw five. What's going on?

The Law of Large Numbers (first formulated by Bernoulli as the Golden Theorem) states that the probability will converge on the ideal as the number of rolls increases. Thus, with eighteen dice rolls I only saw one six, but according to the law of large numbers, the larger my total number of dice rolls, the more consistently I will see a six 1/6 of the time. The same is true of coin flips. Most people who have flipped coins have noticed they don't consistently get heads or tails 50% of the time. So what does it mean to say that the odds are 50% that heads will come up on a particular flip? It means that if you plotted your coin flips, over time you would see the ratio converging on 50%. Bernoulli's theorem shows that a large enough sample will adequately represent the underlying probability. This is important, for it led to the discovery that we need not sample an entire population in order to represent it. The question is: how large a sample is sufficient? Bernoulli, rather impractically, had a very strict standard, requiring "that he get the wrong answer (an answer that differed no more than 2% from the true one) less than 1 time in 1,000." (Mlodinow 98) Interestingly, he referred to this standard as one of "moral certainty." As Mlodinow points out, we moderns have "abandoned moral certainty in favor of statistical significance, meaning that your answer will be wrong less than 1 time in 20. We can attain 90% certainty (+- 2%) with a sample of 1,000." (98)

Many people intuitively grasp this with respect to coins and dice, but sadly, we don't incorporate it well in our everyday lives. The law of large numbers demands we be very careful assigning causality with respect to our actions when dealing with complex situations, and yet one of our fondest shortcomings is using too small a sample size when making decisions. Kahnemann and Tversky have dubbed this human bias "the Law of Small Numbers." Think about it. When a Wall Street fund manager has a few good years he is called brilliant, and is promptly dumped when he has a few bad. In fact, it has been shown that picking stocks by correlating them to winning sports teams is as successful in the long run as any other method touted by professionals. Statistically, everyone will have streaks of good and bad picks. It would take a large sample to ferret out a truly gifted analyst (if there is such a thing). The same is true, of course, in all walks of life, from CEOs to presidents of the United States, we all make large decisions based on samples that are too small.

Some events appear random, but upon closer examination aren't. We will call these events "pseudo-random events" (PRE). These include most of the events we usually call random: coin flips, die rolls, roulette wheels, and so on. Here, again, we can invoke our LSC. If she knew all the complex factors involved in, say, rolling a die: the air pressure, the exact molecular makeup and structure of the die and the table, the spin, the trajectory, the angles, she could compute instantaneously and precisely what number would turn up. The LSC is thus a good test for determining whether an event is a TRE or a PRE: if she is ever surprised by a result, the event is a TRE. If not, the event is a PRE. It goes without saying, then, she would be surprised by the decay of an isotope but not by the results of a roulette wheel or the random number generator within a computer.

§5 WHAT DETERMINISM IS (AND ISN'T)

It's important to understand what we mean when we say we have free will. We obviously do not mean that our choices are random. That is, it seems that free will cannot be defined in terms of TREs—doing so gives us a free will not worth having. Consider the following:

> Suppose you are at the checkout counter of a store and there are two boxes in front of you. One of them is from a charity organization and its banner asks you to use your change to help feed a starving child. The other contains mints available for purchase. You receive a quarter back from your purchase and think about what to do: should you buy a mint or feed a child? After a moment during which you debate the issue internally, you make a decision: to help feed a child, but as you reach out your hand you watch in amazement as you deposit your quarter into the mint box.

What happened? You just made a free choice, interpreted as a TRE. You deliberated over which box to put money in and even decided to help feed a child, and then, at the crucial moment, your brain randomized the choice process (assuming this is possible) and you "chose" the mints, despite your deliberation. This is what made the action free. It was completely uncaused. But who would want this sort of free will? We want to be able to predict what we are going to do; we want our deliberations to determine our actions, and true randomness doesn't allow for determination of any kind. This is a problem, for an event is either random or it isn't—there's no in between.

In fact, given the probability of the existence of random events in the universe, we have to redefine traditional determinism and allow it to be punctuated by random events. Call this punctuated determinism. TREs within the subatomic world have little practical effect on the deterministic world view.[3] Granted, they destroy the far-sightedness of our LSC, and insist we no longer define determinism in terms of one future, but what are such things to us mortals?

---

[3] We can say this because predictability, uniformity, and so on, remain constant throughout history even on the hypothesis of random events in the subatomic world. This seems to indicate that random subatomic interaction with the macro-world is not widespread.

COMPATIBILISM

Compatibilism redefines the concept of free will so it no longer excludes determinism. Compatibilists usually distinguish between two types of causation, internal (mental) and external (physical). The former is said to allow free actions, the latter does not. There are several problems with the compatibilist position, not the least of which is this distinction between types of causation. Does this depend on a dualist view of mind and body? If so, the position is severely weakened. If not, where do we draw the line between mental and physical, between brain and the mind?

This latter problem plagues the compatibilist, causing him to juggle the mental causes in order to avoid having them tainted by the physical. John Locke, for example, tells a story about a man who is locked in a room with another man whom he has always wanted to spend time with. He enjoys his time with the man immensely and chooses to stay with him. Is his choice to stay a free choice? Locke says no, for though he is in the room by his own volition, he could not leave if he wanted. Here, the physical overrides the mental. But another type of compatibilism, hierarchical compatibilism, claims the man is free. As the name implies, a hierarchical compatibilist claims there are different levels of desires. First there is the desire for something or to do something, what the compatibilist calls a first-order desire. These desires can be determined by physical forces. But there is another type of desire which is entirely mental, namely, second-order desires. These are desires concerning your desires. What makes us free is acting on our second-order desires. Desiring to stay in the room is not enough to make a person free because of the possibility of external constraint. What makes the man free is that he desires to desire to remain in the room. Thus the hierarchical compatibilist tries to prevent the crucial mental state from being tainted by moving it up a level of consciousness. But why can't this level, too, be tainted by the physical, maybe by a hypnotist who implants a second order desire of the correct sort? We may then have to move to third-order or fourth-order desires, and so on, in order to avoid the encroaching causation. (The main proponent of hierarchical compatibilism, Frankfurt (1988), claims we need not go past the second-order desires, since we cannot identify with any higher sort. Thus you are free, on his account, if you act on second-order desires that you can identify with.)

There is an intuition here concerning mental states that has some merit, but overall such compatibilist accounts are unsatisfying. The more we learn about mental states, the harder it is to make definitive distinctions between them and physical states, and this is a problem if making such a distinction is the basis for distinguishing between determinism and free will.

The more we know about how the world works, the fewer the events we can label TREs. (This was the basis of Einstein's future-pleading ploy concerning quantum theory, that in the future we will see there were causes to the events, we just did not know what they were at the time.) My proposal is to define free will along the same lines as our distinction between TREs and PREs. We will call an event free if we are, at present, unable to know what caused it, understanding that at some point in the future more knowledge may mean we will have to change the status of the action from free to determined. Free will, then, technically means pseudo-free will, for there are no (interestingly concrete) truly free actions, and determinism reigns supreme.

Why so much confusion over free will and determinism? I think the answer lies in the human propensity to seek out the god's-eye-view. This peculiarly human failing is the result of our self-consciousness, for self-consciousness allows us to contemplate the future from both our own relative point of view (as ours) and from the hypothetical god's-eye-view (the absolute reference frame). I will spend the next few pages elaborating upon this claim.

For billions of years the universe did what it does without us humans. Matter formed and expanded rapidly into nothingness, while gravitational pockets gathered pieces of the elemental stuff and squeezed it ever tighter, ever hotter, kick-starting the fusion engines of dark star cores into shining magnitudes, while occasional explosions populated surrounding space with new creations. Even after life emerged from the demi-chemurgic tender, it was born into blindness until animal eyes first perceived the heretofore sensed but unseen world, initially seen as spots of bokeh-broken lightness, later focusing into multi-dimensional depth. Thus did the gears of causation grind, effect following relentlessly upon cause, all subject to the uncaring laws of physics and chemistry.

And then, at some point in the near past, in years-ago measured merely in the tens of thousands, humans became more than dogs or cats or cows, more than great apes even; their consciousness, instead of sensing just the world, bent back upon itself, saw a reflection, and called it good, lifting their viewpoint from the mudhole of their dull animal dreams, allowing them to contemplate and then control those consequential chains, which had, for so long, held life enslaved.

We have already seen that this higher order knowledge, this consciousness, changes things. Consider:

> You are in a room with a person you trust completely. This person tells you he is leaving and is locking you in the room and you will remain there for 24 hours. There are no windows or other doors that would allow you egress. The person leaves the room and you hear the lock click as they leave. There you sit, imprisoned. But let's suppose, on a whim, you decide to check the door, having nothing better to do. You turn the knob, the door opens. You're free to leave; your trusted friend deceived you.

In this scenario, you were free to leave all along—the door was never locked—but, even though the door was unlocked, in a sense you were imprisoned as long as you believed you were. Knowledge of your situation changes your status. Imagine a being, from a god's-eye-view, watching you as you sit in the room, waiting for someone to come rescue you. This being sees clearly that you are free to leave. You were always free, but now that you know (and only now that you know) are you truly free.[4]

Placing someone (or thing) with a god's-eye-view looking down on us from an absolute reference frame skews our judgment of how our knowledge works, for such observers are not interfering with the plan—they are not involved. They either

---

[4] This example should sound familiar on several levels. First, from our original discussion of reference frames in chapter 7; second, from our discussion of the multiple uses of Kant's categorical imperative, upon which this notion of freedom was developed.

made the plan (god) or they are calculating its connections in order to see it like a map from above (LSC). They are anchors to an objective reference frame. But we humans are involved in our futures; they mean something to us. The fact that we reflect upon our future causal chains changes them. If we see ill consequences in the future we will want to adjust our actions accordingly. Consider the cigarette smoker who becomes aware of the consequences of smoking, to the extent that he is certain cigarette smoking will affect him in a negative way he will take actions to prevent these negative consequences.

Imagine we have the LSC's amazing calculating abilities, and we calculate our future from the present facts. The result of our calculations will be a Future Map (FM_1), but once we have this map in hand it will necessarily be inaccurate because there will be an additional fact that it has not incorporated, namely, that we now know what FM_1 predicts.[5] Our becoming conscious of FM_1 will change FM_1, so we must recompute, incorporating the fact that we know FM_1 and all the changes we would make because of this knowledge. But this recomputation leads to a second future map (FM_2), which will similarly be inaccurate as soon as we look at it. We can thus never capture our future.

An example may help to clarify this. Suppose I gain this amazing calculating ability and at 3 PM I perform my first calculation, which results in a future map (FM_1) of my future from 3 PM today, extending out as far as I want to calculate. As I peruse FM_1, my future, I see my life laid out before me: going to the grocery store, getting gas, eating dinner; I see I will be burglarized, will be in a skiing accident, will catch pneumonia; I see I will meet new friends, enjoy music, go to dinner with my wife. But wait, according to FM_1, at 3:05 I will be getting in my car to go to the store. I look at my watch—it's already 3:07. The map is incorrect. How can this be? It is incorrect because it was calculated before I became aware of my future, but my becoming aware changed everything. Remember the butterfly effect: the smallest change in the present can have a massive influence on the future. So now I have to recalculate, which gives me FM_2, which will likewise be flawed as soon as I become aware of it.

When I look at FM_1 and see that I will be in a car accident, I will attempt to avoid this. So let's suppose I decide to stay home. I then run another set of calculations to see what will happen. Sure enough, when I look at FM_2, I see I have avoided the accident. This map is also already incorrect, of course, since I am looking at it, but it does indicate that I have avoided the car accident (Figure 11–3).

To overcome this problem, the temptation is to say that FM_1 includes the fact that we will look at FM_1 and act according to it. But this is to put ourselves into the god's-eye-view. The LSC's knowledge (or god's knowledge) of what we will do in the future does not affect what we will do. Our own knowledge of what we will do in the future does. We might think, even if we can't use our future map to reliably predict what we will do in the future, at least we can use it to see what other people will do. But even this won't work. While I am looking at my map my thought processes change and this is all it takes to change everything from that point on. Because I was looking at the map I didn't get in my car to go to the store, but my car now no longer influences traffic at 3:30 as it would have before, which causes other

---

[5] Technically, we would see that we read the map and changed our life accordingly, but I will leave out this complication. The point remains the same nonetheless: becoming conscious of the future changes the future.

Future Maps Calculated by Me

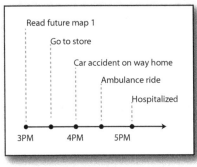

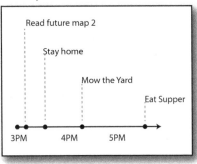

Future Map 01
Run @ 2:55 PM

Future Map 02
Run @ 3:05 PM

FIGURE 11–3

When I calculate my future, looking at the results will change that future, for I am immersed within a relative reference frame. In Future Map 01 I see I will be in a car accident and this knowledge changes my future, for based on this I decide to stay home. My recomputed Future Map 02 shows me that staying home will indeed keep me from having a car accident.

people's futures to vary slightly which causes all their connections to vary, causing massive changes that ripple throughout the future of the world. And all this assumes I am the only person in the world that has this amazing calculating ability. If there are two people, then as soon as either of them calculates the future, everything changes. (Imagine if I printed out my future map and put it in my pocket without looking at it. Nothing would change until I looked at it.)

Figure 11–4 illustrates our above calculation example from the god's-eye-view (the LSC). She does see that our actions take into account the fact that we have looked at our future map, and from her viewpoint we have fatalism, for there is only one future (we are ignoring the possibility of TREs for this example). Note that her future maps don't change our actions because she does not use them to attempt to change the future.

This is all very well, you might be saying, but we are not LSCs. We do not have the amazing calculating abilities that would allow us to gain a map of the future, so all of this is merely speculation. And yet we do have a map of the future. It is not absolutely accurate like the LSC's map, but we all have the ability to see the future with a certain probability, and this probability is all we need. Every time I think about the consequences of an action and adjust my actions accordingly, I rewrite my future. When I realize that smoking causes cancer and that I am vulnerable, I stop smoking. When I lie in bed thinking about whether to go to work today, I am analyzing the future consequences of my action. If I decide not to go, I make massive changes in everyone's future-map. And my map is likewise being rewritten continually by others. But if our maps are continually changing, this means that there is not one future, but myriad possible futures, and this is what we mean when we say we have free will.

Our talk of absolute reference frames (the god's-eye-view) confuses us, for they are purely speculative. It doesn't matter whether or not they exist because even if

Future Maps Calculated by the LSC (assume no TREs)

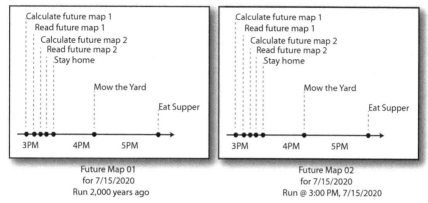

Future Map 01
for 7/15/2020
Run 2,000 years ago

Future Map 02
for 7/15/2020
Run @ 3:00 PM, 7/15/2020

FIGURE 11–4

Future maps computed by the LSC (or as seen by god). The LSC, being in a higher reference frame than I am, sees only one future (we are assuming no TREs in order to make this point clear), no matter when she calculates. I, on the other hand, as illustrated in Figure 11–3, change my future when I look at my map.

they did we could not access them. Furthermore, if there is a mapmaker (like the LSC or god) she cannot use her map to interfere with us humans, for if she did her own map would change—she would have lost her absolute reference frame. She would have become as one of us. Even though we have multiple futures, we are just as determined as before in the sense that the causal principle remains unchanged. Every effect still has a cause. But two factors allay fatalism:

(1) We can map the future, albeit imprecisely, which means our futures are continually being revised as we become conscious of new possibilities.

(2) This guarantees an overwhelming complexity which makes our future opaque in any exact sense.

We are completely determined to make our imprecise future maps and we are completely determined to become conscious of them and thus we are determined to change our future. But changing our future is what we mean by freedom. Thus, we are determined to be free.

§6 MANIPULATION & CONTROL

What are the consequences of embracing determinism? One worry we have already mentioned has to do with our fear of manipulation. If we are determined then we inevitably act according to causal sequences. If we inevitably act according to causal sequences, then we are open to manipulation should someone discover these sequences. It's true; we can be manipulated, witness my example concerning the car salesman (page 249). But this is nothing new; people have been manipulated by salesmen and politicians for centuries. The kind of manipulation we are afraid of is the serious manipulation of someone being able to control our thoughts and actions in a rigorous and systematic fashion. A fixed action behavior is a simple reflex—given a stimulus there is a specific response. Based on knowledge of this cause and effect relationship, given the cause we can predict the effect, which means we can sometimes provide the cause ourselves and thus elicit the effect.

Another sort of control is through brainwashing. If we can invoke certainty we can control other people, for we have seen that certainty and action are intimately related. This is why so many religious cults think it so important to have access to childhood education. Children are, in general, more gullible than adults, so if you can inculcate belief systems into them as core values so that they become certain of them when they are children, this will make contrary belief systems harder to accept as they grow older. Anomalies will be resisted and intolerance promoted. By far the most powerful manipulative tool in our arsenal is the manipulation of certainty. But this is not a deterministic fear. This is a tool available whether or not determinism is true.

This is the extent to which we can control the actions of others (without resorting to drugs or surgery). There is a vast gulf between these types of manipulation and the manipulation of neurons themselves which would enable us to truly control another human. The kind of knowledge, then, that would be required for serious manipulation to take place is far beyond our current abilities. When you add to this the complexities created by multiple persons continually drawing and redrawing their future maps and acting on them in order to change their futures and the butterfly effect of all these inscrutable calculations, there is no need to fear determinism on this account.

A related worry: if determinism is true then, for any action, we could not have done otherwise. This is true on the single future interpretation of determinism (fatalism), but we have seen this interpretation to be implausible. We are afraid we have no opportunities if determinism is true, but if you consider the time-rewind example given earlier (page 246), in many cases we don't really think we have opportunities anyway. When you rewound your life back to before the lie you told in the past, you placed yourself in the exact same mental state you were in the first time, which meant you would do the exact same thing once again. This is our intuition, and if so, then we had no opportunity to do something different. We regret this when things go bad, but not when things go well. We lose an opportunity only if we know it was an opportunity to begin with. The dumpster you walked past on your way to work may have had a bag of diamonds in it, mistakenly thrown away by a senile heiress, but you had no real opportunity to find these.[6] The LSC may know about such things, but our lack of knowledge erases any sadness we might have about our lost opportunities in such cases.

§7 RESPONSIBILITY

The most feared consequence of accepting determinism has to do with the loss of responsibility. I want to argue that the fear of the loss of responsibility is due to a confusion between determinism and fatalism, but first we must give some background on exculpation and punishment.

---

[6] The dumpster diamonds example and the concept of creeping exculpation (below) are both from Dennett (1984).

CREEPING EXCULPATION

From our brief look at several hypothetical cases (in §2) we can understand the subtleties involved in discriminating between degrees of responsibility. Our judicial system goes through this process continually, often exculpating those who have committed crimes based on mitigating circumstances that seem absurd, for example, the infamous Twinkie defense (see box on page 262). These extreme scenarios would not have occurred one hundred years ago, and if we go back even farther, there was a time when no exculpation would have occurred. In ancient times, if you accidentally killed a coworker with an ax, you would be tried for murder, and maybe the ax would be tried as well—animals and inanimate objects were often tried and condemned in the same way—because intentions were not taken into account when deciding punishments. As humans became more sophisticated, though, we realized that, at times, there are mitigating circumstances. Thus, if you did not intend to kill a person, you are not held as culpable as someone who did. Our continuum using Alfred and Zandra (page 247) illustrates the gradations of this notion.

> **EXCULPATE**
> To free from blame or guilt; vindicate or exonerate.

In modern times, as we understand more about the brain processes involved in decision making, we realize sometimes an event can occur in the brain, such as a brain tumor, that renders us less culpable, even if we are unconscious of it. But if brain tumors and mental incapacities can lessen culpability, then so also can other things, for example, the fact that a person's parents were abusive or addicted to drugs or alcohol. Or maybe alcohol dependency itself makes us less culpable, since it may not be our fault we became addicted. We may have turned to drink or drugs because of our genetics, or our upbringing or abuse. If we accept this, then maybe we have to agree excessive sugar intake can also cause temporary insanity in the same way as youth, passion, abuse, depression and brain damage. That we even consider such defenses, much less invoke them successfully, indicates a profound change throughout the years. We allow more and more factors to count as mitigating when meting out punishment. This is what is known as creeping exculpation. The creep in creeping exculpation is caused by increased knowledge. The more we know about the causal situation involved, the less responsible we tend to hold a person. Does this mean that one day, when we thoroughly understand how the brain works, no one will be held responsible for anything?[7]

PUNISHMENT

The punishments we mete out in society are based on cost-benefit analyses, which give us some leeway in how we punish for a particular crime. The speed limit, in most towns throughout the country, is twenty-five miles per hour. We could have made it twenty-three or thirty-one or forty, but twenty-five works well. Any faster and we might endanger people crossing the street; any slower and we might cause traffic congestion. Why do we go faster than twenty-five miles per hour despite

---

[7] In the movie *Minority Reports,* "precogs" can see the future, and inform the police (precrime division) of crimes that are going to happen in the future. The police arrest people in the present for crimes they were going to commit in the future. This scenario gives rise to some wonderful speculations concerning the relation of knowledge, action, punishments, and so on.

knowing we might get caught and have to pay a fine? Because we are rational creatures, continually doing cost-benefit analyses on such situations, and the speed limit situation is this: we know there aren't enough police to enforce the law with any reliability, and even if we do get caught occasionally, we can afford it. Thus, governments allow their citizens to speed. They don't have to, though; they could always decrease the number of speeders by increasing either one or both of the following factors:

1. The level of enforcement.
2. The harshness of the punishment.

For example, we could hire 1,000 more policemen, station them at every intersection in town, and give them all the equipment they need to stop and ticket speeders. The number of speeders would dwindle accordingly. The city budget would skyrocket, but at least there would be fewer speeders. Or, because of the prohibitive cost of hiring more policemen, we could go with the second option and increase the harshness of the punishment for speeding. Instead of that $50 fine, we could make the penalty death by firing squad. Once again, we guarantee a drop in the number of speeders, but everyone realizes this is too extreme, so maybe we just raise the fine to $500. Again, the number of speeders dwindles.

The reasoning behind all this analysis has to do with deterrence. There is a lot of disagreement on the amount of deterrence that can be effected by any particular punishment, but everyone agrees punishment deters to some extent, and (all things being equal) the harsher the punishment the greater the deterrence. The important point here is: there is no reason to punish if there is no deterrence value in the punishment. Consider our example from the beginning of this chapter: there is no reason to punish Alfred for killing his friend, because he had no control over his actions due to his undiagnosed brain tumor. No matter how harsh the penalty, it will not deter someone who could not have been deterred. This is why we don't punish Alfred.

DESIGNER DEFENSES

In 1978, Dan White, a former San Francisco city supervisor, murdered the Mayor, George Moscone, and one of his supervisors, Harvey Milk. In court, White's lawyers mounted a successful defense based on the fact he had been depressed of late, citing, as evidence of his depression, the health conscious former athlete's consumption of Coca Cola and Twinkies. The judge was convinced, and ruled White acted with diminished capacity and the charge was downgraded from first degree murder to manslaughter. (White was paroled after serving five years of a seven year, eight month sentence. He committed suicide within two years of his release.) Although the claim was never made that the sugar content of Twinkies and Coke caused White's diminished capacity, the defense has come to be known as the Twinkie Defense, and cynics claim it may very well have worked even if Twinkies had been invoked as the cause of the diminished capacity. There are other types of designer defenses that seem no less absurd to the ordinary person, including claims of PMS, black rage, homosexual panic, battered spouse syndrome, and so on. Cases like these are interesting for our purpose for they illustrate the extremes to which modern courts take the concept of diminished capacity. The question should be raised: are these cases in which deterrence loses its effectiveness? The fact that it does not indicates a misuse of the insanity defense.

The rules governing the insanity defense were designed along these lines. The M'Naughton Rule, for instance, is a test of a person's ability to be deterred. Nothing more. If you cannot be deterred there is no reason to punish you. This doesn't mean you will go free. If you are a danger to society, we might put you in a hospital or demand treatment of some sort, but we won't punish you.[8]

Responsibility is tied to the notion of deterrence in this way: if you can be deterred, we say you are responsible, and that's all 'responsible' means in this context. In the late twentieth century it has become misinterpreted as relating to the causal factors involved in the case, but it's not the causal factors that are important. What is important is the mental state of the individual. As Steven Pinker puts it (2003):

> The insanity defense achieved its present notoriety, with dueling rent-a-shrinks and ingenious abuse excuses, when it was expanded from a practical test of whether the cognitive system responding to deterrence is working to the more nebulous tests of what can be said to have produced the behavior. (184)

What about creeping exculpation? Doesn't this phenomenon indicate that as we learn more about the causes of our actions we become less responsible, less able to be deterred, so even Zandra will not be punished for the premeditated murder of her husband? No, because determinism and responsibility are disconnected. Determinism, unlike fatalism, does not say you were fated to do what you did. This is a confusion based on making a hypothetical construct (the fatalism of the LSC or god) into a reality. The fatalist has to admit we are, all of us, undeterrable, for we will always do what it is our fate to do no matter what. There is but one future-map available in the god's-eye-view, and this map says Zandra will murder her husband, so she cannot help but do so. The determinist, though, believes you *can* be deterred. As long as we cannot read causal chains like god or the LSC, that is, as long as we can neither trace back complex causal chains nor use them to see into the future, then we humans will be deterrable, barring brain damage, insanity, youth and other such circumstances. Our lack of knowledge guarantees our actions will always remain, for the most part, inscrutable, and this inscrutability guarantees we can be deterred.

Ironically, our free will is tied to both knowledge and ignorance. As we learn about the world around us and compute our possible futures, knowledge insures our survival, opens up opportunities and allows us to actualize our potential and experience ecstatic moments of discovery. But there comes a point (a point we will never reach) when, as knowledge begins to bump against omniscience, it becomes a curse, shutting down opportunities rather than opening them up. Too much knowledge of the future (as with the LSC) would deny us goals to strive for, meaning in life, and the joys of anticipation. It is our ignorance of complex causal chains that gives us all of this, including our freedom. Rolling a die is not random, but acting

---

[8] Putting someone in a mental hospital might seem like punishment, but it isn't, for the same reason rehabilitation is not punishment. Punishment occurs when the primary intention of the government is to harm the law-breaker in response to their breaking the law. In the case of Alfred, when we put him in the hospital, our primary intention is not to harm, but to help him. A secondary consequence of his being in the hospital might be that he suffers in some way, but this is not the main intention.

as if it is allows us to solve decision-making problems in a fair manner. So also deciding to go to work in the morning is not really a free choice, but our thinking it is, our acting as if it is, our ignorance of the vastly complex mental machinery at work behind the scenes, gives us all the wonder and excitement of a new day. Ensconced within the inscrutability of the world, like a diamond in a dumpster, lies our freedom.

§8 CHAPTER SUMMARY

Free will is an illusion based on the inscrutable nature of the world. To say that an event is random is simply to say that it is too complex for us to calculate given our current state of technology. We will never be able to comprehend causal chains in a god-like manner and because of this the human situation is one in which we see randomness at every turn. There may very well be randomness in the universe on the subatomic level, but on our everyday human explanatory level we understand that randomness is equivalent to our ignorance. All the so-called random events we encounter in our everyday life are pseudo-random—they merely appear random. This appearance of randomness is sufficient for everything we need free will for.

We think we're free because we contemplate the god's-eye-view and imagine a causal plan of which we are a part. We see choice nodes at every turn—places where we could choose one thing over another and all the consequences stemming from each of those choices. God surely knows all these possibilities. But in fact, the only way this can work is if god doesn't interact with the world. Anyone who sees their future has already changed it just by knowing it, and by changing theirs has changed many others as well. In this way we have myriad futures, even though we are determined. The processes within the brain that map our future are completely determined, and yet, in generating a future-map which we become conscious of, this consciousness generates something new, a change of plan. This completely determined process is what we mean by free will.

Insisting on a god's-eye-view is like insisting on matching our sentences to an external world. The inherent problem in the correct description theory of truth was skepticism. The inherent problem in insisting on a god's-eye-view is fatalism. Just as we can never overcome the skepticism of the correct description theory, so also we can never overcome fatalism; we can never live our lives in a fatalistic way, as if none of our actions could ever make a difference. The solution to such problems is to cast away our objective anchors, for they only cause needless problems. We have nothing to lose but our chains.

NOTES / QUESTIONS

12. God

The philosophy of the common man is an old wife that gives him no pleasure, yet he cannot live without her, and resents any aspersions that strangers may cast on her character... Of this homely philosophy, the tender cuticle is religious belief...

-George Santayana

SYNOPSIS

(1) The concept of god is examined. God is no different from other objects when trying to determine how we know. We are all imprisoned in our subjectivity. (2) Religious (mystical) experience is one method some tout as overcoming the prison-of-subjectivity problem. It is unsuccessful. (3) A brief look at why we believe in god. Is there a god-gene? Does belief in god have survival value? (4) Religions evolve (as do their gods) as cultures evolve. We would expect this to happen in a system of theorizing, for new anomalies are constantly arising. (5) God is defined as having particular attributes which must be consistent with one another. This is the job of theology proper, but the very nature of god gives rise to rather large anomalies. (6) The attribute of omnipotence, applied to the Judeao-Christian-Islamic god, is looked at in more detail. In particular, we look at the derivations of William of Occam and see how all the various doctrines of a religious position are intertwined. (7) Pascal's Wager, a persuasive argument rather than an argument for god's existence, is briefly considered. (8) An examination of what has become a popular argument for god based on the anthropic principle. (9) A look at the evolution-creation debate in light of theorizing. Why the creationist position is inadequate. (10) Chapter summary.

CHAPTER OBJECTIVES

- to illustrate that religious thinking as just another form of theorizing, subject to all the rules of such
- to become aware of the presence of selection biases that can easily skew our theorizing without constant vigilance.

§1 THE CONCEPT OF GOD

he concepts in this text so far may seem to indicate a resistance to the belief in god, but this is not necessarily the case. If I personally happen to think that the hypothesis is unnecessary, it does not follow that it might not be necessary for others, and to the extent that such a belief does not impinge on my well-being or the well-being of others, it matters not in the least to me whether people believe in god. The problem is that since belief in god is connected to all the important strands within our conceptual schemes, believers often feel obligated to "help" other humans by attempting to convert them. We have seen that this can lead to great cruelty, even with the best of intentions. Nor does it help that many religious memes contain within them commands to disseminate themselves, a simple and extremely effective meme-replication device.

This chapter is not meant to be a detailed consideration of the philosophy of religion, which would traditionally examine all the various proofs for and against the existence of god, and so on. Instead, we will be examining the concept of god and religion in light of what we know about the process of theorizing. My thesis throughout this book has been that we approach all aspects of life by means of theorizing, and I have specifically advocated theorizing by means of the adequacy conditions collectively referred to as coherence. Theists (believers in god) often resist speaking of their beliefs in terms of theorizing because of the loss of certainty necessitated by this methodology. Theorizing can never result in conclusions that follow with absolute necessity—they will always only follow with a degree of probability—and this uncertainty, no matter how small, destroys the absolute certainty many theists are so fond of embracing.

The concept we have referred to as the prison of subjectivity has profound consequences for most theistic positions. The prison of subjectivity refers to the fact that I can never get outside of my self in order to justify the truth of a belief (or

> **THEIST**
> One who believes in god.
>
> **ATHEIST**
> One who believes god does not exist.
>
> **AGNOSTIC**
> One who believes there is insufficient evidence to decide whether or not god exists.

sentence). When you are certain that a particular belief of yours is true, what you are really certain of is that you have the ability to distinguish true beliefs from false ones. When you say you have faith that god exists, what you really have is faith in your own ability to distinguish truths from falsehoods with respect to god. There must be a way in which you come to know god. This might be via nature (seeing the beauty of the world), the Bible, god speaking or appearing to you directly, your experiencing a miracle, or some other method. But for any of these sources you can always ask yourself, "Can I trust this source?" If you believe because god spoke to you, then you must ask how you know it was god; if you believe because you experienced a miracle, you have to ask how you know it was a miracle; if you believe because an authority figure convinced you to believe, you have to ask how you know the authority is correct. As Robert Nozick points out:

> Any particular signal announcing god's existence—writing in the sky, or a big booming voice saying he exists, or more sophisticated tricks even—could have been produced by the technology of advanced beings from another star or galaxy, and later generations would doubt it happened anyway. (49)

Even if god entered your mind and made you feel his presence, you would still wonder whether you were being tricked in some way.[1] Ultimately, the answer to such questions will be, "I just know"—self-evidence. This is the prison of subjectivity. We explained, in chapter 9, that such talk reduces to the fact that it is inconceivable to you that the belief in question be false; the belief is so important in relation to the rest of the beliefs in your conceptual scheme (it is a core belief) that you cannot give it up without incurring significant seismic damage.

This is one of the main reasons why proofs for the existence of god do not work, and why we need not spend time on each proof. All proofs for the existence of god, like proofs for the existence of the external world, and so on, ultimately rest on the coherence of our overall system. The touchstone of a coherent system is the public agreement demanded by the integration condition and made manifest in the scientific method where experimental results, in order to be accepted, must be publicly repeatable. Used consistently, this method guarantees beliefs will be fully integrated with other publicly verified beliefs, all of which hang together in a coherent system.

To free ourselves from the prison of subjectivity using the concept of public verifiability, our beliefs must take one of two forms:

(1) The belief is constitutive of our experience, that is, it must form the basis of our experience so that we could not even progress without presupposing it; or

(2) The belief must be publicly verifiable via repeatable experiment.

These two may reduce to the same point, but show different aspects of publicly agreed upon behavior. We use (1) to satisfy ourselves that there really is an external world. We wouldn't even know how to proceed without assuming this, for we would have no common ground with any other person. We use (2) for theories that

---

[1] God could, of course, make disbelief in himself appear to be inconceivable in the sense that we would realize we had to believe in him in order to make sense of our experience (making the concept of god like the concept of the external world). But he has not done so.

are susceptible to empirically repeatable experiments. For example, we believe germs exist because this belief (along with its interconnected beliefs) has been verified independently many times.

But the belief in god is neither a constitutive belief (since many people in fact do not believe in god and can still function) nor is it susceptible to empirical verification in a manner that is publicly repeatable. Thus, belief in god cannot fulfill all the adequacy conditions required for a coherent theory (in particular, the integration condition). This does not mean, of course, that the belief is false, but rather that the only evidence you can muster for it comes from within your own prison of subjectivity. Theories that don't fulfill the integration condition are a dime a dozen. Fictional novels proclaiming to be true accounts of the world are a good example—they might be internally consistent, elegantly written, and so on, but since they don't integrate with the real world we can eventually determine they are fictitious.[2]

"No problem," the theist may respond, "I believe on faith." But this response is misguided. All merely consistent theories can be said to be believed on faith, but the faith is in your own ability to determine truth from falsehood. The integration condition is what moves you outside of this prison. It changes a standalone theory into one that is publicly verified.

But doesn't the fact that there are many people who believe in god constitute public verification?" No, it constitutes only public belief, since there is no experiment that has been run that would count as verification.[3] Witches were once believed to cast spells, demons were thought to cause diseases, and the earth was thought to be the center of the universe. All of these were publicly believed. Thus, a publicly held belief, by itself, does not meet the integration condition. At the risk of being repetitive, let's apply this to one source of evidence for the existence of god: religious experience.

§2 RELIGIOUS EXPERIENCE

I'm not interested here in indirect communication by god. Most people today don't claim that god speaks directly to them, but rather that he spoke directly to someone at some time in the past who wrote his words down and that god can speak to a person indirectly through the written word. This is still problematic. Words enter our senses in the same way objects do. The fact that we give these words special status as god's words simply puts off the problem, for now we need evidence for believing this (and it cannot come from the words themselves). This is handled by means of a coherent theory like all our other evidence. What interests me in this section is the claim that a person believes because god or one of his minions appeared directly to them, or a person close to them, or that they had an experience (near-death, out-of-body) that can "only be explained" in terms of god, and this is their evidence for believing.

---

[2] I'm reminded of the famous Orson Welles rendition of "War of the Worlds" as a live radio broadcast (October 30, 1938). Many of those tuning in thought Martians had actually invaded, causing widespread panic. An ideal hermit tuning in to this broadcast, who came to believe it was real, may have taken that belief to his grave.

[3] This raises the interesting question: what would such an experiment be like?

To believe in the existence of god is to believe there is a being that exists outside of you. There may be some definitions in which god is merely a figment of a person's imagination, but this is a poor god, one not worthy of the title. No, if god exists then he must exist extra-mentally, and the only way we gain knowledge of extra-mental reality is by means of our senses. God is just one object among many that we must collect evidence for in order to believe (we only believe when we have what we take to be sufficient evidence to warrant belief). God's speaking to you or appearing to you, then, is no different than the light waves from a chair entering your eyes or sound waves from a person speaking entering your ears. These objects are known via their impact upon our senses, which transmit information to the brain, which processes the information and eventually relays a version of it to our consciousness. This seems uncontroversial.

The problem is that god is not publicly verifiable as are chairs and the spoken words of other people. We cannot use a video camera and capture the words and images of god as we can other extra-mental objects; nor can we use electron microscopes, spectrometers, telescopes, and so on. So how do we know that the experiences in our consciousness are connected to (caused by) an extra-mental object we call god? This is the question, and the answer is: you cannot based simply upon the experience. Every conceivable type of internal religious experience can be duplicated via drugs or other forms of stimulation. To requote d'Aquili:

> Electrical stimulation of the right amygdala has been found to produce vivid visual hallucinations, out-of-body sensations, déjà vu, and numerous types of illusions. Stimulation of the right hippocampus has been associated with the production of the sensation of déjà vu, automatic memory recall, and dreamlike hallucinations... Overall, it appears that the amygdala, hippocampus, and neocortex of the temporal lobe are highly involved in the production of vivid hallucinatory experiences. (43-44)

Prior to our modern knowledge of neurology, if I had a non-drug-induced out-of-body experience, this may very well have constituted evidence for god or a non-physical realm in which god would comfortably fit, but no longer. We are trapped in our subjective prison even with respect to so-called mystical experiences. These personal experiences are now no better than crying statues, wall stains that look like Jesus or chocolate drops that look like the Virgin Mary—they are ambiguous experiences that can be interpreted in a multitude of ways—and the only reason you would interpret them as evidence for an extra-mental god is if you already believed in such a god.

I am not claiming that your mystical chat with god or your chocolate Virgin Mary sighting cannot function as evidence for belief in god. Of course it can (and does for many). I am claiming that such experiences no longer have any special status as evidence for the existence of god.[4] My claim is thus a reiteration of my overall thesis that theorizing is the only way we reason about the world. These religious experiences function as a strand in a web of beliefs, goals, hopes and desires that are different for every person.

---

[4] Those who have not incorporated the scientific method into their evidential methodologies are particularly prone to taking such highly ambiguous sightings as evidence. This is because they are not adhering to the demand of publicity which is the hallmark of the scientific method.

⤜⤚⥛

§3 ORIGINS

Voltaire once said, "If god did not exist it would have been necessary to create him." Whether this is true or not, there has been increasing interest in the topic of god's origins in modern times. This endeavor is often spoke of in light of evolution theory, which would have to show some survival benefit to believing in god in order for the belief to flourish as it has. We have to be careful here, though, for biological evolution would only enter into the discussion if believing in god was a biological (rather than a cultural) adaptation. What would have evolved would have been a propensity to believe in god. This is a search for the god-gene. Dean Hamer wrote a book in 2004, called *The God Gene*, in which he claimed to have found such a gene, but his conclusions were both careless and premature. Carl Zimmer (2004) criticized the book as follows:

> *The God Gene* might have been a fascinating, enlightening book if Hamer had written it 10 years from now—after his link between VMAT2 and self-transcendence had been confirmed by others and after he had seriously tested its importance to our species. Instead the book we have today would be better titled: *A Gene That Accounts for Less Than One Percent of the Variance Found in Scores on Psychological Questionnaires Designed to Measure a Factor Called Self-Transcendence, Which Can Signify Everything from Belonging to the Green Party to Believing in ESP, According to One Unpublished, Unreplicated Study.*

A propensity to believe in god would be difficult to prove, for of what would such a propensity consist? Hamer attempted to define this as a propensity for spirituality (self-transcendence), but this concept is notoriously ambiguous. If you define the propensity too broadly it becomes merely a propensity for happiness in general, or well-being, which all humans strive for without the need for a god.

The god-meme is a more interesting topic. Anyone who believes in god could be said to embrace the god-meme, though this may be misleading. First, there is not one god-meme, but rather many different god-memes; one at least for every major religion, but maybe one for every sect, and maybe one for every different aspect of a god. There are no identity criteria for memes (the same is true for genes), so it is difficult to say what we are looking for. But let's suppose there is such a thing, and let's limit it to the Christian religion. We have already said that such a meme is obviously highly successful, since it has replicated copiously since it was first conceived over two thousand years ago. Part of its success lies in the following:

(a) A threat of everlasting punishment for those who don't believe, and a reward of everlasting bliss for those who do.
(b) A command to believe it without regard to normal evidentiary collection procedures.
(c) A command to disregard any and all evidence that might subsequently appear to falsify it.
(d) A command to spread it to all nations.
(e) A command to give part of your earnings to help spread it.

Together, these factors helped the Christian (and also the Islamic) meme spread like wildfire, and when combined with the powers of the state, these became even more powerful. Only when more sophisticated methods of reasoning were developed (the scientific method), was the meme's replication ability impaired.

But once believed, there must be some bang for the buck. In other words, every religion must in some way convince humans that believing their dogma will in some way contribute to their well-being. Suppose, for instance, we decided to start a new religion (which, oddly, would not be that difficult). We begin to proselytize, and our description of our religion is as follows:

> Once you become a member you will immediately be required to undergo almost unbearable physical and mental suffering, including beatings, starvation, burns, exposure, and so on, until you die. When you join you will be blinded and your tongue will be cut out, and you will be required to commit suicide (by drinking sulphuric acid) exactly five years after you join. When you die you will go to the only afterlife available, a hell hundreds of times more fearsome than anyone can imagine.

Any takers? Probably not. People believe in god for a reason, and that reason is connected, either directly or indirectly, to well-being. Religions must provide some kind of well-being for their members that cannot otherwise be obtained. Early Christianity gave solace to millions of slaves, who could look forward to an afterlife of everlasting happiness following a life of enslavement and abuse. Even if this belief was false, once believed, it would have contributed to their well-being; and if true—all the better.

This raises yet another question: Is religion beneficial? This is an odd question, for it obviously is if it is true, especially if there is an afterlife involved. But it becomes more interesting when we put it in a hypothetical scenario. Suppose that, in the future, we come to realize there never really was a god, but we are interested in the history of the illusion. The question we ask is: was religion beneficial to humanity? That is, did it increase or decrease our ability to attain well-being?

Again, the answer is purely speculative, but the arguments go both ways. On the positive side we could say that it gave solace to those who, like the slaves, suffered during their lifetime. It provided meaning to those who felt their lives would otherwise be meaningless. It bonded people together and so pushed the evolution of consciousness and freedom in a way that would not otherwise have taken place. On the negative side, it caused suffering on a massive scale for those who did not belong (from heretics and witches to unbelievers like the Mayans). It promoted the subjugation of women. It slowed the development of science and technology and so contributed to our belief in falsehoods. It made us dependent on external power structures rather than our own selves.

All in all we probably have to admit that there was, at least at one time, survival value in the belief in god. This does not mean it contributed to the well-being of individual humans, but rather that it contributed to their survival overall. Remember that tasting-good-to-humans was the best thing that ever happened to pigs, though pigs themselves might disagree. The debate is endless, but interesting.

§4 EVOLVING GODS

The concept of god is not static. It seems so only to those unfamiliar with history. Cultures change continually, are redefined by technological innovation, immigration, subjugation, and as the needs of the humans within a culture change, so also will their concept of god. This fact was largely unnoticed in the past because the pace of cultural change was slow, but this pace has increased exponentially in the last century with the spread of digital communications. More sophisticated methods of anthropological discovery have also uncovered how pliable ancient cultures were in adding and subtracting the gods within their pantheons, as well as giving us new information concerning their religious practices.

Ancient gods were tribal affairs. Yahweh, for example, the god of the Old Testament, never aspired to be the only god, he merely demanded to be the only god worshipped by the Israelites. When challenged he might show he was stronger than a rival, say, Baal, but he wasn't the only god on the block. His close kin, Zeus, another paternalistic sky god, probably imported from Mesopotamia, was also a tribal god. Both gods began their career as merely large-scale humans. Zeus and the other Greek Olympians, for example, had to eat and drink, they lusted and desired, deceived and cheated, desired human praise and were bound by eternal laws of fate. So also, Yahweh, the Jewish god, described himself as jealous, enjoyed the sweet smell of sacrifices, got angry when disobeyed, and loved those who were faithful to him. As humans developed the ability to form more abstract concepts, though, their gods also became more abstract. Yahweh, for instance, was no longer identified with a particular icon or human form; he became ephemeral, taking on different, non-human, forms: a burning bush, a pillar of smoke. This was true of Zeus as well, for when Semele, who was having an affair with a human-like Zeus, was tricked by Hera into asking him to reveal himself in his true glory, she was burnt to a crisp. Thus did the gods evolve in stride with their subjects. Figure 12–1 illustrates this movement in history, from the earliest, most anthropomorphic concepts of god, to the highly abstract modern concepts.

Abstraction demanded more complex attributes. Gods must be more powerful than their subjects, but reflection expanded this concept beyond mere physical strength. Power itself became abstract, but the more powerful you desire your god to be (and humans always seem to want to promote the power of their gods), the less you will be able to understand him, for the the less you will be able to attribute human motives and reasonings to him. Priests are then needed as intercessors, and suddenly the ordinary person is completely dependent upon the priests for understanding the most important issues of life, a situation which lends itself to an abusive power structure. It is this distance (alienation), this human powerlessness (resulting from dependence upon priests which resulted from god's otherness) that Martin Luther was resisting when he nailed his ninety-five theses to the door of the Wittenberg chapel. Luther not only wanted his cake, but wanted to eat it, too.[5]

Another factor in the evolution of the concept of god arose as human knowledge increased, for the attributes that were once exclusively god's came to be transferred

---

[5] Catholicism is more unified than Protestantism because only the Pope has the ear of god, allowing for a single interpretation of the most important tenets of the church. Those who disagree and break away are no longer Catholic. All Protestants, on the other hand, claim the privilege of being able to interpret god's will. If you don't accept the interpretation of the group you're in, then you break away and start your own (still Protestant) group.

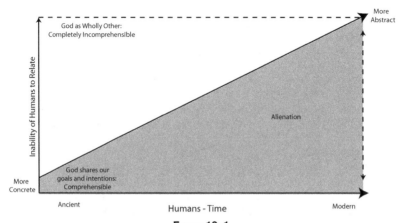

FIGURE 12–1

A graph showing that, as time progressed, the human conception of god became more abstract. The move toward abstraction creates a gulf (alienation) between humans and god that must somehow be crossed. The paradox here is that we want our god to be the greatest, most powerful being, yet the greater your god, the less you are able to relate to him.

to the physical universe. Infinity, for example, was once attributed solely to god, and Giordano Bruno was burned at the stake in 1600 for attributing it to the universe as well. In the mind of the church, ascribing infinity to the universe was tantamount to endorsing pantheism, the claim that god is in everything, a position meriting death. Alexander Koyre sums up this movement as follows:

> The infinite Universe of the New Cosmology, infinite in duration as well as in Extension, in which eternal matter in accordance with eternal and necessary laws moves endlessly and aimlessly in eternal space, inherited all the ontological attributes of Divinity. Yet only those—all the others the departed god took away with Him. (276)

A final aspect of this movement toward abstraction pertains to the afterlife, a concept intertwined with the concept of a deity. Ancient religions, lacking a complex abstract notion of soul, did not have a well-developed afterlife concept. The Old Testament, for example, interpreted immortality in terms of offspring. There was no developed idea that you would live on after death except through your children. So also with the Greeks, whose concept of an afterlife consisted of a shadowy remnant of yourself which travelled to Hades upon death. Hades was originally not a place of reward and punishment but rather a place where all people went, whether good or bad, when they died. When Odysseus visits Hades in *The Odyssey*, he meets Achilles and tries to compliment him on his status in the underworld. Achilles replies that he would rather be a lowly servant on earth than a king in the underworld. As the concepts of god and the human soul became more abstract, though, a more robust concept of the afterlife developed accordingly.

The concepts of the human soul and the afterlife are linked to a concept of god who creates and maintains both, judging those who die, meting out their just rewards. In proper theorizing methodology, these concepts must maintain consistency, and so change hand in hand. For instance, as human society has become less violent we have seen a corresponding transformation of god (at least among the theologians) in which his loving nature is emphasized over his vindictiveness. This, in turn, demands a transformation in the concept of afterlife: less emphasis on the horrors of hell and more talk of universal salvation. As women take their rightful place in society, their subjugation is suppressed, and they are given the right to become priests themselves. As the gay and lesbian movements become more widespread, their members are accepted into the mainstream church, homosexual marriages become sanctioned by the church, and so on. Religions, like any other organism, must evolve or die. The concepts constituting the core of religious belief are all intertwined and must maintain their coherence within a theoretical framework.

§5 DEFINING GOD

"The fool has said in his heart that there is no god," says the Psalmist (14:1). In trying to explain this verse, Anselm (1033-1109) suggested the person denying god's existence is a fool because if he had the correct concept of god he could not rationally deny god's existence. Anselm defines god as "that than which no greater can be conceived." If you have this proper concept of god and yet deny his existence, then you haven't really grasped the concept, for your god is not that than which no greater can be conceived, because I'm conceiving of a greater one right now, namely, one that exists in reality rather than merely in my mind. Thus, if you accept this definition of god and yet deny his existence you are a fool, for you are contradicting yourself.

This little word game, which has come to be known as the ontological argument for the existence of god, has provoked discussion for over a thousand years. In its subtlest form, I think it might be a failed hermeneutic attempt to show god as the ground of our existence, otherwise it is nothing more than an attempt to define him into existence. As Gaunilon, one of Anselm's contemporaries, argued, if this is an argument for god's existence, it is also an argument for the existence of an island than which no greater can be conceived, or the most perfect human, or the most perfect coconut.

How then shall we define god in the Christian tradition? This is the job of the theologian: to put together a concept of god, listing his attributes and making sure there are no contradictions involved. In other words, the theologian puts together a theory using the consistency condition as his fundamental guideline. This is not so easy a task as it might seem, for the attributes you assign god are extremes: we humans know things, but god knows everything; we are powerful, but god is all-powerful; we are here, but god is everywhere. These extreme concepts can easily entangle.

Take, for instance, the concept of omnipotence—the idea that god is all-powerful (which we will consider in more detail in §6). This attribute leads one to ask, "Can god create a rock so heavy he can't lift it?" which seems like just a silly question, but points out an apparent anomaly in the concept of an omnipotent being. If god cannot create such a rock he must not be all-powerful, while if he can then he cannot lift it, which means he is not all-powerful. Therefore, there is no being that is all-powerful. The standard answer to this conundrum, that god can create the rock, but it is no limitation on his power that he cannot then lift it (for to lift a rock too heavy for him to lift would be contradictory), is singularly unsatisfying.[6]

This is not unlike Bertrand Russell's barber, who had the attribute that he shaved all and only those who did not shave themselves. When we ask if the barber shaved himself, we see that a barber with this description is a contradiction, for he does if he doesn't and doesn't if he does. What this proves is that there could be no such barber, for a barber (or anything else) with contradictory attributes is impossible. This is the issue with the rock question: a god with the attribute of omnipotence can no more exist than a barber who shaves all and only those who do not shave themselves.

Omnipotence is not only contradictory in itself, it also clashes with other attributes that theologians want to assign to god. All-goodness, for example, is a common attribute attached to god, but all-goodness together with all-powerfulness generates an anomaly—one form of the problem of evil. The argument goes like this:

(1) If god is all-powerful then he could do away with evil.
(2) If god is all-good then he would do away with evil.
(3) But evil exists.

---

(4) Therefore, god is either not all-powerful or not all-good.

This argument attempts to show that a contradiction arises between the two attributes, that a being cannot possess both. There is an easy solution to this anomaly: simply drop one of the two attributes. The Gnostics, an extremely influential early Christian sect, did just that—they did not include omnipotence in their attributes and the problem of evil did not arise—but the Roman church insisted on omnipotence. So how to handle the anomaly?

One response is to appeal to the concept of the invisible hand. "God works in strange ways," is the saying, "turning what appears to us as evil into eventual good." We humans have a limited intellect and can only understand a small portion of the workings of the world. God, though, has infinite intellect, and understands everything at a glance. The German philosopher Gottfried Leibniz (1646-1716) believed that when god looks out at the universe (the god's-eye-view) he sees all truths as necessary truths, while we, bogged down in our humanity, see mostly contingent ones. Thus, when we have a headache we complain of the pain, which seems quite meaningless to us, but when god looks down on us he sees that our headache in fact plays an extremely important role in the scheme of the universe. Because of this, everything is exactly as it should be, despite appearances.

> **THEODICY**
>
> A vindication of god's goodness and just-ness in the face of the existence of evil in the world.

Voltaire (1694-1778) parodies this position mercilessly in his novel *Candide*, where a Leibnizian character named Doctor Pangloss continually spouts his famous phrase: "Everything is as it should be in this, the best of all possible worlds"

---

[6] Unsatisfying because it allows an omnipotent god to create an impossible thing (a rock too heavy for an omnipotent god to lift), which at least seems odd. It doesn't seem to be a limitation on god's omnipotence that he cannot, for example, create a square circle, for such things don't exist.

whenever anyone complains of evil in the world. Is this the best of all possible worlds? You may think there could be better ones. For example, a better world might be one in which last night's headache went away maybe five minutes before it did, for there would have been five minutes less suffering in the world. But here's the catch: God, being all-good, must necessarily create the best world. If he created less than the best it would tarnish his all-goodness, so this present world must be the best of all the possible worlds he could have created, which means there must be a reason for the extra suffering in this world—a reason we cannot comprehend due to our finitude, but is there nonetheless. This is the notion of god's providence at work behind the scenes turning apparent evil into good.[7]

This response may seem like a ruse, appealing as it does to our ignorance of the larger order of the world, but we've seen this to be a standard way to handle anomalies —what we referred to as the future-pleading ploy. If a theory is working for us at the moment, then we will often put off the solution of anomalies that arise to the future. But the problem of evil is not the only anomaly that arises when we take the attribute of omnipotence seriously.

⌘

§6 OCCAM & OMNIPOTENCE

Omnipotence seems to be the most important attribute of the Judeo-Christian god. I have heard it argued that all other attributes follow from it alone, which may be useful if you prefer a minimalist god, or if you like your god to be Euclidean in his geometric simplicity. Whatever the reason for such contortions, omnipotence looms large, and, as we have already seen, it always leads to trouble. Leibniz's ploy, his theodicy, invoked omnipotence by appealing to the beyondness of god in order to eliminate contradiction. He dressed omnipotence in resplendent goodness so it didn't appear to be a stark power play, but it is what it is, a dangerous hand to play, with insidious consequences lurking within its depths. William of Occam (1288-1348) discovered these when he began to push the concept.

Occam wasn't the first to emphasize god's omnipotence. Anselm, in his *Proslogium*, was already feeling his way toward Occam's conclusions two hundred years earlier, claiming god was not only "that than which no greater can be conceived" (as we saw above), but was also "that which is greater than can be conceived." The first phrase says that god is the limiting factor of our conceptions, while the second pushes him beyond our conception altogether—into the unknown. Occam saw this clearly. God is so wholly other in his omnipotence, we cannot even properly conceive of him. Herein lies a second edge to the omnipotence sword, for omnipotence is an all-engulfing concept: if god is so big we cannot even conceive of him, how can we even speak of him? Once you play this card, it's hard to take it back. In what follows I want to examine a few of the consequences that follow when

---

[7] Hans Blumenberg (1985) notes cryptically that "Docetism is the perfection of Western theodicy." Docetism was the heresy that proclaimed Jesus only appeared to be human, and as such is a response to an anomaly which claims that if Jesus were fully god he would be sullied by being human.

omnipotence is included in one's concept of god; consequences that Occam both traced and embraced.

NOMINALISM

Realism is a philosophical position which maintains that abstract general terms, such as 'cow', terms that cover a number of actual entities, are real things. I won't delve into this except to say that this is a Platonic concept. Realism was the generally accepted position in the middle ages, where it was often held that these terms were real concepts in god's mind, concepts he used as archetypes or patterns when he created the world. Occam, insisting on god's omnipotence, claimed that to say that god used archetypes in his creation limited his abilities. An omnipotent god doesn't need archetypes, he can create spontaneously whatever he wishes. Thus, Occam downgraded the status of such concepts to mere names. This position is called nominalism, and is the position most often held today. When we use the word 'cow' we don't mean that there is an existent thing called cowness in which all cows must participate in order to be cows, we simply mean that 'cow' is an abstract general term we use to refer to all cow-like objects.

This doesn't seem like a particularly radical move, but it affected the very hierarchy of the world. Christianity claimed that the taxonomic categories used to divide the world into explainable parts (family, genus, species, and so on) were real things. This explained, among other things, why evolution could not occur— the categories have been fixed from the beginning of time.[8] Removing these fixed barriers threatened explanatory chaos.

THE RAZOR

There is a famous principle known as Occam's razor which dictates that you should always accept the simplest of theories when trying to explain a phenomenon. "Never multiply entities beyond necessity" is the way Occam formulated it. We saw this in chapter 4: if two computer programs both produce the same results, but one does so with twenty lines of code while the other has three hundred, Occam's razor demands we should embrace the former, simpler, program. The simplest solution is the best solution. How does this follow from his view of omnipotence?

For the medieval thinker, god guaranteed the truth of our view of the world. How do we know that what we are seeing is a reflection of the world? Answer: god, being good, would never deceive us about such things.[9] Thus, god was used as a guarantor, insuring that our sense perceptions were not radically mistaken. Occam takes issue with this position. Requiring god do anything is a limit upon his omnipotence; in particular, we cannot require that he not deceive us with respect to our perceptions of the world. Occam, then, relegates our world view to the status of a theory, one that is on par with every other theory, none of which we can rely upon god to vouchsafe. Why then, accept one theory over another? There is no reason,

---

[8] This position also made the discovery of dinosaur bones an anomaly, for it was thought that the categories could not be empty. God would never allow a species to go extinct. Arthur Lovejoy discusses this under the concept of the plenum in his *Great Chain of Being* (1998).

[9] Many of Descartes' positions came directly from Occam's line of thought. Remember this is how he justified deducing the existence of an external world. The concept of the evil genius is intimately related to this.

according to Occam, other than the arbitrary criterion of simplicity. When confronted with a number of theories, each of which is used to explain a certain amount of data, we should accept the simplest one—this is what the razor dictates. This is a desperate move on Occam's part. He does not use his razor as a criterion of truth, for we mere humans can never, ever know the truth. We are completely blind. We use the razor in despair as an arbitrary method for determining which theory we should accept. Arbitrary, because how do we know that the world conforms to the simplest theory? What if the creator had a taste for the rococo?

We today don't think this is a radical move, but as we have seen, in Occam's time theory was despised as a method for determining truth. The truth was known with absolute certainty, having been given to us by god himself. Theory was relegated to the world of intellectual play, for those putting together alternative world views as an intellectual exercise. Since these exercises were often seen as the result of curiosity, and often led to heresy, they were generally looked down on by the more serious thinkers. The limits of truth were clearly defined in fixed categories given to us by god. According to Occam, though, all of our truth claims about the world are relegated to the status of theory.

INFINITE WORLDS

Christian theology maintained that this world was the only habitable world in the universe. Not only did it have a privileged position as the center of the universe, but it had this position because it was blessed by god—he sent his son here to offer salvation to humans. This obviously won't work for Occam. We can never say of god that he could not do something, so we cannot limit his creation to just this one world. We cannot even hold god to his promises. An omnipotent god can do anything he pleases. Anything.

Giordano Bruno, mentioned above, may be seen as simply expanding the concept of god consistent with Occam's notion when he attributed infinity to the universe. His argument was similar: if god is omnipotent there must be an infinity of worlds like ours, but if the world is infinite and this is god's attribute, then the world must be god in some sense. Ironically, it was this line of thought that eventually led to infinity being detached from god altogether (see Koyre quote above).

PROVIDENCE

Providence is the view that god cares for humanity. He looks out for us, has our best interests in mind. Providence is the fine dressing that Leibniz used in his talk of the best of all possible worlds. But Occam claimed that providence was not consistent with god's omnipotence. When you appreciate the true magnitude of god in all his glory, you will see that the only object worthy of god's attention is god himself. To contemplate something lesser than himself would be to sully himself.

We humans, then, are nothing to an omnipotent god. To think that such a god would spend his days answering our petty prayers, or considering our well-being in any way, is absurd. Providence must go. But what is our status then? Why were we created? Anselm, in contemplating this question, developed his own myth: god has a heavenly choir of angels that perpetually sings his glory, a choir that was depleted when Satan and his followers rebelled and were expelled from heaven. We humans, the best among us, will be used as replacements in this choir. No doubt this selection process has been relegated to a lesser angel-bureaucrat, for god would never concern himself with such details. We are mere servants to an unspeakably majestic god.

This means, of course, that we can never interact with god. Our prayers have no affect on him; we should ask nothing of him, for he will give us nothing. We are but dust designed to serve him. The gap between finite humans and an infinite god is so great it can never be bridged.

Note what is going on here: Occam, when considering the nature of god, decided that his glory and majesty must be promoted and saw that the concept of omnipotence must therefore be applied to him. Omnipotence had always been attributed to him by Christian thinkers, but no one had seriously considered the implications of doing so in a systematic fashion. Occam took it upon himself to do this. What is interesting from our perspective is how this process proceeds. Medieval theologians may have disdained theorizing, but they were all constantly engaged in it—the history of medieval thought is a history of constantly arranging and rearranging data into data sets that tried to make sense of god while remaining internally consistent. These are all interpretations of god using the Bible as a touchstone. Occam's is just one more attempt, but every deduction he makes from omnipotence demands other changes in theology, and ultimately demands a radical reinterpretation of all the basic doctrines. We might even go so far as to say that Occam is arguing against the concept of omnipotence as an attribute of god by showing that a consistent working out of that concept leads to a destruction of Christianity itself. This was not his intent, of course, but one wonders at his conclusions.

CHRISTOLOGY

What about "for god so loved the world that he gave his only begotten son"? (John 3:16) Occam's notion of omnipotence demands a complete reformulation of Christology—the role of Christ in theology. On the standard view, Christ is a theological construct acting as intercessor between humans and a god too wonderful to understand, allowing us a chance at salvation. The problem of a perfect god creating and interacting with an imperfect world was always problematic for theologians. This is the origin of the problem of evil. It is also the reason behind the odd concept of the trinity in Christian thought,[10] and became one of the most fertile sources of heresy. For example, if Jesus was really god, then how could he have suffered and died? The Gnostics position known as Docetism (which claimed Jesus only *appeared* to have a physical body and only *appeared* to die) seems like a decent enough explanation of a difficult concept, but it had to be rejected in order to retain other aspects of Christianity that were held to be essential (transubstantiation, for example). All these intellectual maneuverings are fascinating from the standpoint of theorizing; they are all desperate attempts to maintain consistency.

The idea of an intercessor worked well for Occam, but the concept of the trinity, which demanded that Christ was also god, had to go. Based on what we have seen above, we know this could not be, for this assumes that god actually gives a damn about humans. Occam, then, must take god out of Christ, for the two cannot be seen as equal.

---

[10] The concept of the trinity was not made concrete in theology until the fourth century. It is considered a mystery of the church, something beyond human understanding.

ELECTION OF THE SAINTS

One of the five points set forth by John Calvin after the Protestant rebellion against Catholicism was the election of the saints. This is the idea that god knew, before the foundations of the world, who would go to heaven and who would go to hell. Occam claimed that election was a necessary consequence of the omnipotence of god. He took very seriously the biblical idea that salvation is by the grace of god alone, "not of works, lest any man should boast." (Ephesians 2:9) There is nothing you can do, you measly human, to warrant the grace of an omnipotent god. If you think that you could earn the right to be with such a god, then you are sadly underestimating his glory. Because no human could possibly earn the right to be with god, salvation is by grace alone, which means god randomly determines who will be with him. Here's the gist of Occam's position:

Before he created the world, God made a list of all the humans who would ever exist in the world. He put all these names in a hat, mixed them up, and then drew out a handful at random. The names drawn (constituting only a small portion of the total number) are those who get into heaven. And the rest? To hell with them.

This is the concept of grace, bald and bare. But wait. Why would you devote your life to serving god if such service means nothing to him? If a Hitler has the same chance of going to heaven as a saint, why waste your time? In response to this view of election you might be tempted to say that god would never allow such a thing, but Occam's response would be: who are you to demand of god that he should or shouldn't do anything? If you demand anything of god then you don't fully appreciate the concept of omnipotence. And he would be right. Omnipotence is transcendental in its ramifications. It changes everything when rigorously appreciated.

There are many more ramifications of omnipotence, but these will suffice for our purpose. Occam believed that a true contemplation of omnipotence would bolster faith and make better Christians of us all. Instead, not surprisingly, his teachings had the opposite effect. Instead of making people more godly, it made them turn inward. If you cannot depend on god to help you in this life, you must fend for yourself as best you can. Humans thus had to work to bring in the kingdom of god all by themselves, for an omnipotent god doesn't care. The result of Occam's speculations, then, instead of increasing faith in god, forced people to rely more upon themselves. This movement led directly to the Italian Renaissance, which led to the Enlightenment.

I have spent time on the concept of omnipotence and Occam's interpretation of it in order to to illustrate my point that theologizing is theorizing, whether it is you trying to decide on your own what god is like or whether it is done by theologians attempting to set doctrinal standards for a religion. Your god-theory must be consistent. When you introduce an attribute it must cohere with other aspects of your theory; you must continually adjust and readjust the strands of your god-theory as you see the ramifications unfold. Interconnectivity demands that a change in one concept will lead to changes in many others. This is what happened with Occam and omnipotence.

As an aside, we might ask why omnipotence is held to be so important. Is it really a worship-worthy attribute? Suppose we discovered that a god we worshipped was not, after all, omnipotent. Would this negate our respect for him? or would it maybe make him more endearing? I can imagine a god who says, "Listen, I'm trying the best I can to eliminate suffering, but I can't do everything." This seems better than a muscle beach kind of god who could eliminate suffering but doesn't. In our human relationships we don't love a person because of the power they wield. Many people are attracted to powerful people, but this often equates more to fear than love. The fact that a husband can beat his wife doesn't make her want to worship him, even if he insists the pain is for her own good. Why would it be different with respect to a god?

∽ಱ∾

§7 PASCAL'S WAGER

We have seen that all arguments either for or against the existence of god fall prey to the prison of subjectivity objection. Beside this objection, there are usually other rather obvious problems with such arguments that render them unacceptable unless one is already a believer (or unbeliever). For example, the so-called first cause argument (the cosmological argument) accepts the causal principle we mentioned in the previous chapter, that every effect has a cause, and uses it to trace existing things back to a first cause, which is then called god. But if we consistently use the causal principle, shouldn't it apply to god as well? And even if we can stop at god, why would a Christian think that the first cause would be the Christian god? A Muslim would claim it was the god of Islam; a Jew the god of Judaism, and so on. Thus, the first cause argument only gets you where you want to go because you have preplanned the route. Because of these types of failures, rather than give an exhaustive overview of various arguments for the existence of god, I will mention only two that are most instructive based on the themes of this text: Pascal's wager-argument, which we will discuss in this section, and the argument from the anthropic principle which we will discuss in §8.

Arguments can be formulated for two purposes: they can be used in an attempt to obtain truth (as in science) or they can be used in an attempt to persuade (as in law). Pascal's wager, formulated by Blaise Pascal (1623-1662) in his work *Pensées,* is an argument of the second ilk; it is not an argument for the existence of god (though it is often propounded as such), but rather an argument designed to persuade you to believe in god. We can set up the argument by agreeing that everyone must either believe in god or not believe in god (the agnostic is thrown into the atheist camp, for to withhold belief is to choose not to believe), and, no matter whether you believe or not, you will either be right or wrong. This allows us to display the argument in a decision matrix as indicated in Figure 12–2, which gives us the following solutions:

(1) You believe in god and god exists.
(2) You believe in god and god does not exist.
(3) You do not believe in god and god exists.
(4) You do not believe in god and god does not exist.

If you are in (1), then, when you die, you will go to heaven and enjoy eternal bliss. If (2) you have believed falsely, but the belief comforted you and gave meaning to your life, so nothing was lost. If (3), when you die you will go to hell and suffer eternally. If (4), you have gained nothing and when you die you will turn to dust. According to Pascal, then, if you choose to believe you have everything to gain and

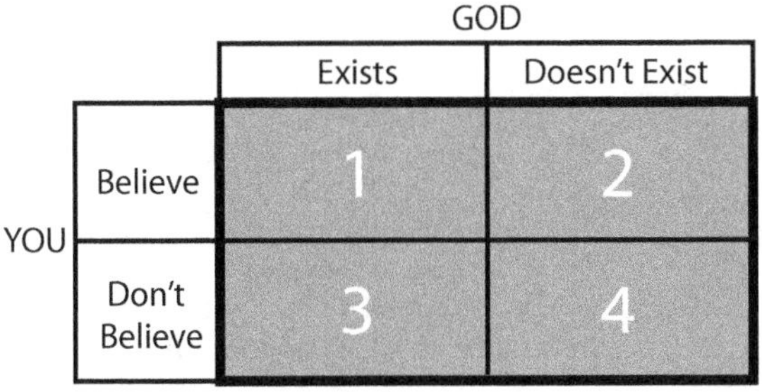

FIGURE 12–2

A decision tree for Pascal's Wager: If you believe and your belief is correct (1) then you experience eternal bliss, while if your belief is incorrect you have lost nothing. On the other hand, if you choose not to believe and your belief is incorrect (3) then you will suffer eternal damnation, while if your belief is correct, nothing is gained. Thus, by believing in god you have nothing to lose and everything to gain; by not believing you have everything to lose and nothing to gain.

nothing to lose, while if you choose not to believe you have everything to lose and nothing to gain. His conclusion: "take the holy water; have the masses said."

As a purely persuasive argument, Pascal's wager gives us no evidence to believe in god, but only tries to show the advantages of believing. This, of course, assumes there is convincing evidence available, for we cannot believe just any-thing, even if we try—even if we have strong motivation. Suppose I give you a wager-type argument for believing in the Pillsbury Doughboy. You must truly believe this seemingly fictional character is god in order to experience eternal bliss when you die. No matter how hard you might want to get to heaven, it will probably be impossible to believe that the Pillsbury Doughboy can get you there (unless you are really gullible). We are also assuming you cannot gain the benefits of the wager by mere ritual, by accepting last rites, or merely professing belief. A friend of mine once related to me a visit with his father, who was in the hospital dying of cancer. His father had always been a devout atheist and my friend was surprised to find him praying with a priest. His father looked up sheepishly at his son and muttered, "Just hedging my bets." If mere ritual would work, then Pascal's wager makes more sense, but most would agree that this is not the necessary requirement for salvation under the Christian doctrine. You must really believe in god (and possibly do other things as well) in order to get to heaven.

This raises an interesting question, namely, how many people would believe in a Christian god (or any other god) if there was no heavenly reward attached? No one escapes death, and all modern religions offer some kind of comfort for it, whether it is eternal bliss in heaven or a merging with the oneness of being itself. This gives rise to yet another interesting question: What constitutes a proper motivation for belief in god? The pious want to hold that believing in god simply as fire insurance is not sufficient, but a more realistic approach recognizes that we all seek well-being, and to deny this as a motivation for believing in god may be unrealistic.[11]

---

[11] Maybe god rewards those who reflect seriously on his existence, even if they conclude he does not exist. This gives rise to another interpretation of the wager-argument, in which those who are persuaded by it are sent to hell rather than heaven.

§8 THE ANTHROPIC PRINCIPLE

The anthropic principle is a formula that draws conclusions from the simple fact that we humans exist. Our observations of the world must be compatible with the fact that we, as conscious beings, exist. This principle has two forms, the weak and the strong.

The weak principle says that the fact that we, conscious humans, exist restricts the characteristics of the universe. This is obviously true. If, for example, the earth had formed beyond the orbit of Jupiter instead of where it in fact did form (within the so-called Goldilocks zone, see Figure 12–3), then life, including us, would never have arisen. As Hawking (2010) says, "Obviously, when the beings on a planet that supports life examine the world around them, they are bound to find that their environment satisfies the conditions they require to exist." (153) Hawking continues by noting that the anthropic principle would be better called a selection principle, since our existence determines what characteristics we allow our universe to have. This is a complex topic and one fraught with recursive confusion, for it involves our becoming conscious of an unconscious selection bias concerning our origins. The weak anthropic principle merely acknowledges this bias and is not dangerous in itself, but the strong anthropic principle adds an entirely new dimension.

The strong anthropic principle says that the fact that we, conscious humans, exist, puts necessary parameters on the universe so that we *had* to exist. In other words, if we look at the number of parameters that had to be "just right" in order for us to be here, the odds are overwhelming (they could not have just happened);

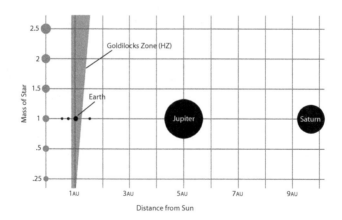

FIGURE 12–3

An illustration (not to scale) of the Goldilocks, or habitable, zone. Within any solar system, the mass of the central star will determine the zone within which human-like life could occur. This is one example of a broader phenomenon known as the fine-tuning of the universe.

therefore, there must be a designer, and this designer we call god.[12] The strong anthropic principle has been intellectually seductive, especially to (but not limited to) those who have a theological ax to grind.[13] But no matter its sultry powers, I will argue that it is based on a failure to take seriously the impact of selection biases on the conclusions we draw from our premises.

SELECTION BIASES

In March 1979 the core of the nuclear reactor at the Three Mile Island plant in Pennsylvania suffered a partial meltdown. The reactor was cooled by a steam turbine system, the water from which was filtered by sophisticated polishers, which would routinely become clogged. Workers were clearing such a blockage when the pumps feeding water to the polishers stopped. A bypass valve, which should have rerouted water to the steam turbine then failed, which stopped water flowing to the pumps, which then automatically shut down, which in turn shut down the steam turbine. When the primary pumps stopped, three secondary backup pumps were activated, but due to maintenance all three valves had been turned off, so there was no water to pump. With the primary cooling system shut down, the reactor automatically performed an emergency shutdown. This stopped the core reactions, but residual heat from isotope decay continued to accumulate,

GOLDILOCKS ZONE

Also known as the habitable zone (HZ), this is the region in a star-centered orbit where an Earth-like planet can maintain liquid water on its surface and thus give rise to Earth-like life forms.

FINE-TUNED UNIVERSE

The assertion that a small change in several of the fundamental physical constants of the universe would have produced a universe radically different from the one we now inhabit.

which was no longer being removed via the steam turbine. This caused a pressure buildup, which activated a pressure release valve. The pressure was released but the valve was faulty and failed to close when the pressure decreased, thus allowing coolant water to escape from the core, which increased the heat buildup, which eventually melted the reactor rods. Mlodinow, in *The Drunkard's Walk*, comments on this chain of events:

Viewed separately, each of the failures was of a type considered both commonplace and acceptable. Polisher problems were not unusual at the plant,

---

[12] A listing of these parameters would include (but not be limited to) the ratio of the strength of electromagnetism to that of gravity; the strength of the force binding nucleons into nuclei; the relative importance of gravity and expansion energy in the universe; the cosmological constant; the ratio of the gravitational energy required to pull a large galaxy apart to the energy equivalent of its mass; and the number of spatial dimensions in spacetime.

[13] Stephen Hawking (2010) is the most recent candidate (among the big intellectual guns of our time) to toy with the strong anthropic principle. He seems to think that by multiplying examples of fine-tuning beyond our solar system the principle becomes stronger, which is like insisting that since one leaky bucket won't hold water, then maybe ten will (as Anthony Flew once said). Instead of deducing god from the anthropic principle, Hawking deduces the multi-verse, which seems to be the new god of the cosmologists.

nor were they normally very serious; with hundreds of valves regularly being opened or closed in a nuclear power plant, leaving some valves in the wrong position was not considered rare or alarming and the pressure relief valve was known to be somewhat unreliable and had failed at times without major consequences in at least eleven other power plants. Yet strung together, these failures make the plant seem as if it had been run by the Keystone Kops. (203)

Investigations followed, blame was attached, heads rolled, laws were legislated, and yet, from a purely mathematical analysis, the series of events was not unexpected. As Mlodinow concludes, "in complex systems (among which I count our lives) we should expect that minor facts we can usually ignore will by chance sometimes cause major incidents." (204) But this is not the main point I want to draw from the Three Mile Island example. My point is that hindsight introduces a selection bias into our organization of events that can distort our perceptions of the probabilities involved.

We humans are extremely susceptible to this kind of bias.[14] For example, take any situation in life and imagine the complex set of events that "had" to occur in order for that event to happen at that very moment. As we saw in the previous chapter, if even a single parameter had changed (one other person deciding to do something different) then the entire future of humanity might change. So when you meet that special person in the crowded bar and later marry him, it might be tempting to say that it was meant to be—for he almost didn't go that night and she had just broken up with her longtime boyfriend, and if these had not occurred along with all the events that led up to them... Now apply this to your parents and you get a situation closer to the anthropic principle. When you calculate the odds it's amazing that they met and conceived you, which makes you nothing short of a miracle. But instead of being amazed at this, you should instead realize that if one of those factors had been different (so that they did not meet) then you simply wouldn't be here thinking about it. This is exactly analogous to the way the anthropic principle is posed. You are not here of necessity or by design, and from the fact of your existence (or the existence of humans in general), nothing follows except that the past state of the universe produced the present.

§9 THE EVOLUTION DEBATE

As one final exercise in theorizing differences we will consider briefly (and broadly) the difference between religious and scientific theories on the origins of humans, namely, evolution versus creation as competing theories. Most people, even those believing in creation, agree that selection occurs, not only artificially

---

[14] Bayesian analyses are designed to counteract aspects of this bias. A classic example of the selection bias at work: pickpockets, when caught, were hung in medieval England. These hangings were public, and during these events pickpockets regularly worked the crowds. It was thus concluded that hanging was not a deterrent to pickpockets. What this reasoning fails to take into account, though, is how many pickpockets were *not* working the crowd because they were deterred by the hangings.

BLACK SWAN EVENTS

We have touched before on the concept of the black swan, but there is a technical usage of the phrase that signifies the fragility of human cognitive systems. Nassim Taleb, in his book, *The Black Swan*, emphasizes this interpretation. According to Taleb, a black swan event is a rare, extremely improbable, and thus unpredictable event which has massive consequences. Extremely improbable events occur all the time—these are events that are considered outliers on a bell curve of probable events. These events are going to occur and some of them are bound to be dramatic. Examples of such include the meltdown at Three Mile Island and the Japanese attack on Pearl Harbor; Taleb adds to this list the events leading up to World War I, the rise of the internet and the personal computer, the September 11 terrorist attacks on the U.S., and the financial collapse of 2008. In his book, Taleb emphasizes the three features of a black swan event:

1. unpredictability
2. major impact
3. retrospective justification

There are various biases and fallacies attached to black swan events. The most obvious is the retrospective belief that the events could have been foreseen with more conscientious and thorough observations. This is useful for assigning blame, but the fact is, black swan events are unforeseeable by their very nature. We tend to think that events we have to worry about fall on the high shoulders of a bell curve, while the tails, the outliers, are so improbable they won't happen, which makes them easy to dismiss. To protect ourselves as best we can against these high impact events, we must develop robust, redundant systems, and approach them with the attitude, not that they might fail, but that they will.

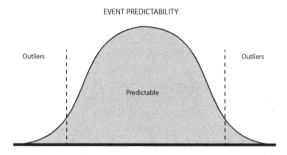

EVENT PREDICTABILITY

Outliers   Predictable   Outliers

(as when we breed dogs for a specific trait), but naturally (those with beneficial mutations pass their genes on and become better adapted to their environment), a phenomenon impossible to deny. But creationists balk at allowing the creation of new species by means of evolution, even though allowing that evolution occurs. Why? Because this denies a central tenet (a core value) in their religious theory, that god created all species in the beginning when he was creating everything else. Why believe this? Because the Bible says this is the way things happened. But why believe the Bible? (You shouldn't believe the Bible just because the Bible says you should believe in it. We don't believe a person is telling the truth just because he says he is.)

There have been many attempts to justify the truths of the Bible, but in the end you believe it because you want to believe it, which means it fits in well with your other beliefs. In other words, you believe it because it coheres well with the rest of the beliefs you hold important. This is theorizing. You hold fast to the creationist interpretation because giving it up would mean other parts of your religious theory would have to be questioned, which maybe you are unwilling to do. There is even a community of believers who hold the same beliefs you do. Thus, it may seem that creationism and evolution theory are on par as theories: they both have anomalies that are handled in various ways common to theorizing (including the future-pleading ploy), they both have an objectified group of people they can refer to, and so on. Creationists themselves attempt to make this point. But there is a major difference. Creation theory is not testable. It is a black box explanation. It posits the creation of the universe (and thus of humans) by a hypothetical entity called god, but there the explanation ends—with a mystery beyond which you cannot travel, and there is no way to test this hypothesis in a public fashion (and publicity is the only methodology that allows us to escape our subjective prison). Where did this god come from and how did it create stuff from nothing and who created it and… Thus creation theory brings up more questions, none of which are answerable, even in principle. Another problem with creation theory is that it seems to dictate that some well verified and quite beautiful theories are false. These are all problems with integration. Thus, creation theory must be classified as what we have called a standalone theory.

If you are committed to believing that the universe is only six thousand years old, you will have problems integrating your theory just as would someone believing in the flat earth. First you must deny the efficacy of carbon dating, despite the fact that it can be calibrated with other means (as we saw in dendrochonology). Plate tectonics must also be false—the idea that the plates making up the crust of the earth have shifted over the years. This would involve denying theories explaining the formation of mountains not to mention the occurrence of earthquakes and so on.

One solution to these anomalies is to assert that god made the earth with the appearance of being billions of years old in order to lead thinking people astray. But then we would have to explain why god would perpetrate such an elaborate deception, one that leads reflective people astray (but not non-reflective people). This is akin to giving a starving person a purposefully inaccurate map showing how to find a food cache. So also god gave us reason, which enables us to find truth, but not the truth about him, which he makes available only to those who refuse to use his gift. This solution thus begins to erode god's character.

The evolution-creation debate is not unlike the earlier debate between Copernican and Ptolemaic systems. As knowledge accumulated, the Ptolemaic system became a standalone theory, one that contradicted too many other well-accepted theories and eventually had to be modified into the Copernican system. This will eventually happen with creationism; it will eventually be modified so as to incorporate evolution theory. The lesson that should have been learned from the Ptolemaic fiasco is that you should not base your belief in god on theories that dispute current well-accepted scientific theories. In other words, respect the integration condition.

Note that everything depends on the valuation structure each person places upon the individual parts of their religious theory. The person who is absolutely committed to the literal interpretation of the Bible in all its aspects will have a much more difficult time integrating his theory than someone who is willing to give up certain aspects of the interpretation argument. Everything is give and take. Occam is a good example of this. Theories are malleable entities, and their malleability is limited only by the dogmatism of our value structure.

✌︎✿❦︎

§10 CHAPTER SUMMARY

In this chapter we have seen that theology, whether corporate or personal, uses theorizing to form its concepts. We mold our concept of god and our lives around this concept based on our conceptual schemes, which function like theories. We must, above all else, maintain the consistency of our theoretical outlook or suffer cognitive dissonance, but it is a mistake to think that, having solved anomalies and rid ourselves of dissonance, that our theories are adequate in the fullest sense. We are far too good at self-deception.

Our modern reflective attitude is continually fine-tuning our adequacy conditions, with the integration condition being the latest addition. This condition itself is subject to numerous fallacies, prominent among them the selection biases we humans so easily fall prey to. Proper reflection on our conceptual schemes is a difficult and complex task, but one worth the effort in the end, for the better we get at determining overall coherence, the more likely we are to live fulfilling lives.

It may be that belief in god, even if he doesn't exist (as Pascal maintained) is the most probable route to well-being. No doubt it is for some, though this strategy may be less and less successful insofar as it depends on consistency alone. Modern society, with worldwide digital communication, puts more and more stress on integration which, hopefully, will bring about more tolerance for differing world views (a position I develop more fully in chapter 14). Imagine all the people…

13. Self

· ·

What kind of sycophant would you like me to be?

— *Butler to Cruella, 101 Dalmations (movie)*

SYNOPSIS

(1) We begin with a hint at the strangeness of the concept of self and then argue that this concept is constitutive in the sense that a self must be pre-supposed in order to even think about the world in a reflective manner. In this way the concept of self is likened to the concept of the external world. (2) How the abstraction fallacy is responsible for our concept of a self that is separate from our body, when in fact the two are inseparable. (3) We are teleological systems. An explanation of what this means and how it applies to our everyday experience. (4) We begin our examination of the self using the analogy of a literary work, which includes the concepts of author, characters, and audience. This works well since we humans are storytellers by nature. The self is a story we tell our self. (5) We have seen before how interpretations of literary works are like theories. We now show that the same is true of the literary work we refer to as our self. (6) An examination of some of the disanalogies between self and author, none of which turn out to be sufficient to undermine the overall analogy. (7) More detail on our life story and its formulation. How self-deception is kept in check by means of publicly verifiable touchstones. (8) The roles we play and whether this can lead to claims of inauthenticity or false con-sciousness. These judgments are seen to be unfounded. (9) We turn to a discussion of the importance of memory for our concept of self. Memory is necessary (though not sufficient) for this concept. (10) An extension of memory to the public realm. Our extended memories connect us, in an ever-widening circle, to everything. (11) Chapter Summary.

CHAPTER OBJECTIVES

- think about what we are as individuals: who is the "I" we continu-ally refer to
- understand the structure of our lives as teleological, and how this affects the meaning of our life
- give impetus to reflection as a means of improving our life
- instill an appreciation of the complexities of our relationships with others and how these are interconnected

§1 T<small>HE</small> S<small>TRANGENESS OF</small> S<small>ELF</small>

t some point in the future we may be offered a new travel option: transporters like those in Star Trek. There are two types of transporters, both of which work on similar principles. The earlier models scanned your molecular structure, took you apart molecule by molecule, and transported these molecules along with your scanned instruction set to the destination where you were reconstructed. But these were unnecessarily cumbersome; they had to keep track of individual molecules, and it all got very complicated. To solve these problems a new type was designed that scans your molecular structure, but does not send the individual molecules to the destination. After all, a molecule is a molecule; it doesn't matter whether the exact same molecules are used to reconstruct you. So now only the information concerning your molecular structure is sent to the destination where you are reconstructed from new molecules while your original body is deconstructed.

What is your experience of a trip by transporter? You pay for your ticket, step into the transporter, there is a moment of blackness, you open your eyes and you are at your destination, thousands of miles distant. "Cool," you say. "No more waiting in airports, no more discomfort, no more delays. This is the way to travel." Yes it is. Transporters have been in operation for ten years and have a 100% safety record. Nothing serious has ever gone wrong. Would you use one?

My recommendation? Never, ever travel via transporter. Never. That person who arrives at the destination is not the same person who departed. Let me illustrate. Suppose you decide to travel to Paris, France. You step into the transporter, there is a moment of blackness… and nothing happens. You are still at your point of origin. Two burly officials appear and politely ask you to follow them into a back room. "What's going on?" you ask. "No big deal," says one. "The deconstructor sometimes doesn't work, so we have to do it by hand." He takes a pistol from his belt and points it at your head. "Wait!" you cry. "You can't do this." The official smiles. "Not to worry. This is not you. You arrived in Paris a few moments ago. Everything is fine." And he pulls the trigger. Meanwhile, in Paris, you open your eyes and smile. "Cool. No more waiting in airports, no more discomfort, no more delays. This is the way to travel."

The person in Paris thinks he is you, thinks transporters are the way to travel, but he is not you.[1] What just happened? He has all your memories stored in his head, he has a body just like yours, he has your habits and your quirks, but he isn't you. If the continuity of our consciousness is broken, even momentarily, we are undone, and we can be completely unaware of the disaster. What a strange thing—this notion of our self.

HOW TO PROCEED

I am the only firm ground on which to stand. I am the one reflecting on my life and its meaning, on my freedom, on my death. These are my reflections. The prison of my subjectivity is my prison. Everything I know is filtered through my brain. Information bubbles up from nerve ending portals, is processed and reprocessed, and eventually results in sensations, consciousness and self-consciousness. But who or what is this "I" that I keep referring to? You would think I would know who I am, and yet it's not surprising I don't since I don't even know what I'm looking for when I try to find me. When I look for my self, all I find are memories of my past and expectations of my future. I am able to give these a semblance of chronological order and assume they are connected to the body I see when I gaze into a mirror. When I look for a pencil, I know what I am looking for and when I see it I know I have found it, but when I look for my self, I am looking for the very thing that is doing the looking. This recursive oddness has given rise to a plethora of conundrums. Self-consciousness is the result of our self moving to a higher reference frame so that it can see itself as an object. We may be able to draw an analogy to the way the brain functions with respect to pain. Pain occurs in the brain, yet we feel it as projected to various body parts. This is what the self is: a projection of the brain that stitches our various bits and pieces of experience together into a whole.

Maybe you think this entire discussion is absurd. But what do you really know about you? Yes, you have memories, but we know memories are fallibly fragile. Even if you can trust your memories, how do you know the person appearing in them is you? The more you reflect the more you realize, as David Hume did long ago, that what we call our self is nothing more than a bundle of perceptions we collect into a whole. The self might be a projection, but it is a necessary projection. Even knowing this, as Hume once said, "we cannot long sustain our philosophy, or take off this bias from the imagination." (I,iv,6) The bias is that we are one thing that remains the same through time, even though we don't have a single molecule within us that was part of us ten years ago. These reflections constitute a serious anomaly to our view of our self as one person existing throughout time.

I want to argue that we should handle this anomaly as we handled the anomaly that we are unable to prove conclusively the existence of an external world. The belief that we experience a world outside our own minds, that we are not creating all of reality within our heads, is a core value, a constitutive belief, one that forms the very basis of our ability to function in the world. To give up this belief is unthinkable, inconceivable. So also with our concept of a single self existing through time. Neuroscience indicates that our selves are mental constructs, picture shows on a

---

[1] Understanding this point is crucial for appreciating the passion of the magician in the movie *The Prestige*. He is willing to die in order to perform the perfect trick.

wall in Plato's cave, but we must act as if these are real in the same way that we must act as if there is an external world and as if our actions are free.

In other words, we posit our self as an independent and continually existing entity. This is a fundamental axiom of our entire framework; indeed, it is the very scaffolding upon which our framework is built, one we cannot even conceive as false, for if we think it is false there must be someone who is thinking it false. All our theorizing is about us; everything we know is from our point of view. In a point that harks back to Descartes' *Cogito, ergo sum*: I theorize, therefore I exist. Theories are interpretations, but someone has to be doing the interpreting. To even think about ourselves as theorizing we must assume a theorizer, namely, us. The ultimate justification of this axiom is its coherence within our framework—that it works. The self is the basis of all we are and know; it is the fundament, the omphalos, the very core of our universe.

§2 DETACHABLE SELVES

The abstraction fallacy, in which we reify mental constructs, turning them into things, lies at the heart of our concept of our self. When we reflect upon the self we have constructed, we place it in a position equivalent to a god's-eye-view and give it a life of its own. From the god's-eye-view we look down on our bodies, making them appear dispensable. This leads to a view I call the detachable-self, a conception of our selves as things separate from our bodies. On this view my body is not essential to who I am; it is merely a container, and a disposable and interchangeable container at that. Consider the following:

> You go into the hospital for minor surgery, but there is a mix-up and you are mistaken for a person slated for a brain transplant. Your brain is, accordingly, transplanted into someone else's body. After the operation, you awaken in a darkened room. You feel groggy, but okay; you're still alive. You're glad you made it through the surgery and can't wait to see your family, get back to work, and so on. Imagine your surprise when a contingent of administrators and doctors comes into your room to explain that there has been a terrible mistake. When the lights come up you look down and do not recognize your hands. You demand a mirror. When provided, the face staring back at you is not yours.

This is standard philosophical fare, which has been taken to illustrate that my body cannot be essential to who I am because I can imagine myself in a different body, or even without a body, and still be me. This gives rise to futuristic scenarios in which I could download the contents of my brain to a computer hard drive and then, when I die, could simply upload the contents into a different body or even a sophisticated machine and continue on as I was.[2] If the body is not essential then it

---

[2] This assumption seems to underlie those cryogenic facilities that offer the service of freezing only your head. The idea seems to be that in the future technology will be available that will allow the transfer of your self to some other object, animate or inanimate. You will wake up as if from a deep sleep and simply pick up your life where you left off. As with transporter travel, the break in continuity here is a problem.

is at least plausible that the mind can exist alone, and since we understand mind-functions to be located in the brain... It all makes sense: the mind gets separated from the body and enjoys an existence all by itself. The further beauty of the detachable-self theory is that I need not decay as my body does; I might even live on after it dies, whether this be in another unworldly place (heaven or hell) or in another body (reincarnation).

It is impossible to find evidence that would confirm such a view, which means it can only be held as part of another, larger theory, and these are usually of the standalone sort. This doesn't mean we don't have motivations to believe them. Our all-too-human fear of death gives us a large incentive to believe in the detachable-self. If we don't want to consider that we might some day disappear completely from the universe, resolving into the dust from which we came, we obviously have a problem, because bodies rot. We know this—moldering corpses are anomalies to our immortal aspirations. So if we want to maintain our belief in a continued exis-tence we must pin our hopes elsewhere, and the detachable-self is the only place to pin them.

This separation of self from body seems to me to be a fundamental flaw, which relies upon a version of the same abstraction fallacy which gave us, among other things, the god's-eye-view as a real place from which to view the world, which (in chapter 11) became the basis for the fatalistic viewpoint (see Figure 13–1). I can easily project my self as something separate from my body, but it does not follow from this that I *am* separate from my body, just as the fact that I can project color on to the object of my perceptions in the world does not mean that these objects are themselves colored. We are integrated wholes, body and self, and should maybe take a lesson from physics and refer to our body-self as we speak of space-time. These are not two separate entities. Our minds and hence our selves are the causal result of our brains, but they are not reducible merely to that gray matter resting within our cranium. There is an inseparable connection between our brain and the spinal cord which is further connected to the entire nervous system which is itself a set of sensors that branch throughout our bodies from toes to fingertips, from eyes to anus. That nerve ending that hurts when you stick a pin in your finger—that is an extension of your brain. And is not, too, the flesh it is embedded in?

The fact that you can sever the spinal cord from the brain does not mitigate this fact. Cutting off a limb destroys a section of our nervous system, but it still functions. The spinal column merely connects the nerves from various body parts and channels them to the processor. But remember an earlier point: processing occurs even in the spinal cord. The brain, though, has access to all inputs including the processed inputs from the spinal cord. No one doubts that the brain is the control center, but once you realize how dependent it is upon the rest of the body—how inseparable it really is—you cannot blithely distinguish between the two as between an apple and an orange. We are a mind-body amalgam, a complex system of cells that is more than its parts. This isn't granting all that much, and it doesn't change the fact that the conundrums confronting us are complex. We are creatures interested in leading meaningful lives, searching for well-being. How are we to look at ourselves in such a way as to further our ability to achieve our life-goals?

ঙ৳ঢ়

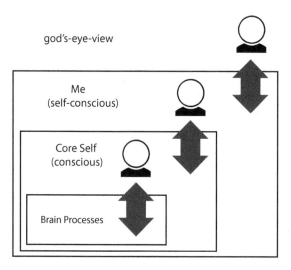

god's-eye-view

Me
(self-conscious)

Core Self
(conscious)

Brain Processes

FIGURE 13–1

A simplistic view of our projections (and reifications). Multiple brain processes give rise to the emergent core self. This is the level of pure animal consciousness. This core self has the further capacity to then look for itself as an object, which means it must project a looker, which gives rise to self-consciousness. The self-conscious entity can then imagine other points of view outside of itself, that is, it projects a hypothetical viewer of itself (and others). When we use this to take in everything, this becomes the god's-eye-view.

§3 TELEOLOGY AND THE TEMPORAL STRUCTURE OF OUR EXPERIENCE

A teleological system is a system with a purpose, and we humans are teleological systems. Teleology is built into our experience of the world, a constitutive structure of our experience—it is the way we necessarily experience the world.[3] We can experience the world in either a non-reflective or a reflective manner (and all the gradations in between), and we can switch back and forth between these. Consider your experience of listening to a melody. You put on your headphones, press the play button, and enjoy your favorite song, immersing yourself in the music. You are not analyzing it for errors or hoping to play it yourself or trying to memorize lyrics; you are simply enjoying it. This experience of musical immersion is not a reflective experience (since we are not analyzing); we are conscious of the song, but not self-conscious. This immersion is also how we experience the world when we are not fully self-conscious. In order to analyze we have to step back (or up) to a higher reference frame, and when we do this we can break our experience into pieces, the units of which are arbitrary: for music, we could use notes, measures, lines or any other grouping, but let's consider a song from the level of its individual notes. Any note you consider within a melody, especially a melody you are familiar with, presupposes both the note before it and the note after it—your experience of it contains the memory of what came before and the anticipation of what is to come.

---

[3] My treatment here is heavily dependent upon the concepts utilized by Edmund Husserl, Martin Heidegger, and especially Wilhelm Dilthey.

Without this, you would experience just a note like any other note, but your melody is a conjunction of notes put together in a sequence, which means the notes are ordered in time.[4]

To put this in more general temporal terms, the present moment always includes within it both a retrospective and a prospective aspect. Neither the past nor the future exists, except as constructs of our reflection. We often structure our thought using various metaphors that reify time as something that flows past us or as something we can move past, but these are merely metaphors that allow us to take a higher reference frame with respect to time and our experience. Only the present exists, but our memories of what came before (retrospection) and our expectation of what should come after (anticipation) always condition our experience of this present. This tripartite structure of our temporal experience is a structure that, not surprisingly, also holds true for actions and events (see Carr 1991). As I type this sentence, each word I type (or each letter or each phrase, however you want to arbitrarily group the units) has the same retrospective/prospective structure. So also when you play a song on the piano, or throw a ball, or drive a car.

We can label these structural parts as beginning, middle, and end, noting that these are relative terms. For example, whether I am typing a letter or a word or a sentence, each of these, as a unit, takes into account what came before and what will come after. This is now beginning to smack of teleology, for the end is where we want to be (in the future), our goal or purpose, and the middle is the means to this end (temporally, it must be achieved in order to reach the end—it is what I am doing now), and we are doing this now because of what we did or decided to do before (in the past). The interesting aspect of applying the notion of teleology to our experiences, actions and events is that these are seen to contain the ending, the goal, within their beginning. When I act intentionally, I have a future goal in mind, and as I go about striving to reach this goal I am constantly presupposing both this future goal and my past actions that led me here. This is what I mean when I say that we humans are teleological systems. I am not implying that every random action has this structure, but rather that this structure is constitutive of our experience of the world. We cannot experience the world without imposing this structure upon it.[5] We will call this structure the narrative structure, for this is how narratives are constructed (beginning, middle and end), and will approach the topic of the self by way of this narrative metaphor.

---

[4] There's an old advertising gimmick that utilizes this feature of a song. As a child I remember a catchy jingle for Salem cigarettes: "You can take Salem out of the country, but... you can't take the country out of Salem." The commercial ended with only the first part: "You can take Salem out of the country, but..." which leaves the listener with a feeling of incompleteness. The idea is to make you, the listener, want to finish the jingle yourself, which sets the brand more thoroughly in your psyche. There are many techniques used by musicians that also exploit this temporal notion of our experience. (Huron 2006)

[5] This is a loaded sentence. There are complex philosophical issues embedded in this claim that I wish to avoid. My point is that our experience is really not reducible to mere moments of sensation even if this is how it happens in the world-as-it-really-is. We don't know the world-as-it-really-is, we only know the world-as-we-experience-it, and our experience always has this structure due to the way our brains process information.

§4 THE AUTOBIOGRAPHICAL SELF

The narrative structure which is constitutive of our experience is the same structure found in stories, and it is a basic cognitive fact that we are story-tellers. When we want an explanation for something in the world, we tell a story that explains it. In ancient times humans told stories to explain events they could not otherwise explain. For instance, the Icelander Snorri Sturluson (1179-1241) tells of Loki's punishment for causing Baldr's death. He was imprisoned in a cave beneath the earth, bound so that he could not move. A poisonous snake was fastened above him

so that the venom from it should drop on to his face. His wife Signyn, however, sits by him holding a basin under the poison drops. When the basin becomes full she goes away to empty it, but in the meantime the venom drips onto his face and then he shudders. (Barber & Barber 20)

This story explains why there are earthquakes, just as the story of Demeter in Greek mythology explains why we have the seasons. The method is ubiquitous in the mythologies of all cultures. We humans must make sense of our world and stories of this sort relieve the cognitive dissonance inherent in our inability to understand what is happening around us. There are forces we know not and telling stories resolves the tensions caused by these, giving us comfort. These ancient stories were theories we now refer to as myths. A myth is the epitome of a standalone narrative. It demands consistency, but is formulated without reference to the more sophisticated aspects of coherence. Science still tells stories, but scientific stories are more firmly based on evidence and use a more self-conscious methodology, which allows us to predict the future much more accurately. This is why we prefer science to myth.

Even today we are constantly engaged in the practice of storytelling. If you are asked why you are late to a meeting, how you broke your arm, why you aren't coming to the party, you tell a story. If you want to entertain, you tell a story, write a novel, produce a film. Add a moral and we can use stories to teach. As explanations, we expect stories to be true, but they need not be. We can make up stories either for entertainment or to mislead. We sometimes construct stories as explanations when we have no idea what the real explanation might be, a phenomenon that seems to be embedded within our cognitive functioning. Michael Gazzaniga (2009) investigated this phenomenon by testing subjects whose connection between the two hemispheres of their brain (the corpus callosum) had been surgically severed. This procedure (used to reduce seizure activity) isolates the hemispheres so they cannot communicate with each other.

With special equipment, you can tell the right hemisphere to do something by giving a visual command to one eye, such as "pick up a banana." The right hemisphere controls the motor movement on the left side of the body, so the left hand will pick up the banana. Then if you ask the person, "Why did you pick up the banana?" the left brain's speech center answers, but it doesn't know why the left hand picked up the banana, because the right hemisphere can't tell it that it read a command to do so. The left hemisphere gets the visual input that there is indeed a banana in the left hand. Does it say, "Gosh, I don't know?" Hardly! It will say, "I like bananas," or "I was hungry," or "I didn't want it to fall on the floor." I call this the interpreter module. The intuitive judgment comes out automatically, and when asked to explain, out pops the interpreter to make a rational explanation, keeping everything neat and tidy. (118)

The "keeping everything neat and tidy" is a reference to our inner urge toward coherence. Our inner story must make sense both to us and to others, and we will make up reasons for our actions in order to make it so. This phenomenon is not relegated only to the dysfunctional. Part of my insistence that I just know a fact to be true when I cannot come up with a good reason why might be at work here.

I want to take this notion of storytelling seriously as a description of who we are. This is not implausible, for neuroscientists use the same language. The self is described as autobiographical, because our brains are constantly mapping and remapping our processed inputs in light of our relation to the world. We continually weave and reweave the story of our self, and tell these stories, not just to our self, but to others. Indeed, my point will be that I am such a story. I am first and foremost a construct my brain puts together from a collection of inputs, sensorial images, imagination, memories and as-if calculations. As Antonio Damasio (2010) puts it:

> Conscious minds result from the smoothly articulated operation of several, often many, brain sites ... and not in one site in particular, much as the performance of a symphonic piece does not come from the work of a single musician or even from a whole section of an orchestra. The oddest thing about the upper reaches of a consciousness performance is the conspicuous absence of a conductor before the performance begins, although, as the performance unfolds, a conductor comes into being. For all intents and purposes, a conductor is now leading the orchestra, although the performance has created the conductor—the self—not the other way around. The conductor is cobbled together by feelings and by a narrative brain device, although this fact does not make the conductor any less real. The conductor undeniably exists in our minds, and nothing is gained by dismissing it as an illusion. (23-4)

This self is an emergent process. But the self, as conductor, then takes control and (this time on a self-conscious level) embellishes the story. This self-conscious conductor is the one who authors the story we call our lives.

Given, then, that we are storytellers at our very core, I want to use this storyteller metaphor to enlarge upon our concept of self and how we relate to the world. In order to do this we will further develop the concept of the narrative, and see how this relates to our self. I will proceed, then, by first discussing (in §5) various types of stories and how they function. In §6, I will relate this to the self using the storytelling metaphor. Using a literary analogy, we will see our autobiographical selves as literary works put together by means of an author. This is not a new approach; indeed, literary criticism has spent much (maybe too much) time analyzing these concepts, but hopefully our use of these metaphors will allow us to understand what we are and how we relate to the world.

> ### ON EXACTITUDE IN SCIENCE
>
> Jorges Borges' (extremely) short story is a comment on the impossibility of a complete description (Borges 1999:325):
>
> > … In that Empire, the Art of Cartography attained such Perfection that the map of a single Province occupied the entirety of a City, and the map of the Empire, the entirety of a Province. In time, those Unconscionable Maps no longer satisfied, and the Cartographers Guilds struck a Map of the Empire whose size was that of the Empire, and which coincided point for point with it. The following Generations, who were not so fond of the Study of Cartography as their Forebears had been, saw that that vast Map was Useless, and not without some Pitilessness was it, that they delivered it up to the Inclemencies of Sun and Winters. In the Deserts of the West, still today, there are Tattered Ruins of that Map, inhabited by Animals and Beggars; in all the Land there is no other Relic of the Disciplines of Geography.
> >
> > - Suarez Miranda,Viajes de varones prudentes,
> > Libro IV,Cap. XLV, Lerida, 1658

§5 STORIES AND THEORIES

In chapter 4 I used various interpretations of the "cry wolf" story as examples of theorizing. The events within the story constituted the data in need of a thesis, the thesis provided was the theory. The thesis of a story must cohere in the same ways that any theory coheres. Our tendency is to employ a version of the correct description theory and claim that a thesis (or interpretation) of a work is true if and only if it correctly describes the author's intent. Many authors think this way and are insulted when literary critics make either too much or too little of their work. The story is told of Ernest Hemingway who, upon hearing the elaborate interpretations applied to *The Old Man and the Sea*, supposedly responded with, "sometimes a fish is just a fish." This seems to indicate he thought he knew the correct interpretation of his story and the critics were mistaken.[6] I prefer to apply the coherence theory to literary works. If an interpretation adheres to the adequacy conditions, then it will be deemed a correct interpretation no matter how much it diverges from the author's intent. Sometimes, of course, diverging from the author's intent is impossible. Our latitude in doing so depends partly upon the type of work, and partly upon the author. Let's examine some different types of writing and see how these interrelate.

CHRONICLES & NARRATIVES

Joshua Foer (2010) relates his meeting with a man named Gordon Bell, who calls himself a life-logger. Bell uses technology to extend his senses in order to capture the experiences around him.

---

[6] But, in fairness, he also said, "No good book has ever been written that has in it symbols arrived at beforehand and stuck in. … I tried to make a real old man, a real boy, a real sea and a real fish and real sharks. But if I made them good and true enough they would mean many things."

A miniature digital camera, called a SenseCam, dangles around his neck and records every sight that passes before his eyes. A digital recorder captures every sound he hears. Every phone call placed through his landline gets taped and every piece of paper Bell reads is immediately scanned into his computer. (156)

In attempting to capture every detail of his life, Bell is involving himself in a project not unlike the fictional cartographers described by Borges (above), whose attempt to create an exact map resulted in a map drawn on a 1:1 scale with the surrounding terrain. This is an extreme example of a chronicle, for a chronicle gives an account like a play-by-play announcer at a baseball game: "Casey steps up to bat. Here comes the pitch. It's low and inside. Casey swings. He misses. Strike one..." This is a linear tale that flows past the present point of view. The perfect chronicle would have an emphasis on completeness, and therein lies the obsessiveness of Gordon Bell, whose intent is to give a complete account of his life. But completeness is a goal impossible to achieve. For one thing, Bell's chronicle is told from only one point of view; to know Bell, or anything else in the universe in the most complete sense, we would have to know everything about everything.

Given the impossibility of the perfect-chronicle-project, we settle for less. We purposefully leave information out, that is, we filter, and our filters depend upon our purpose (our intent). If our purpose is to give a complete account of our lives, we are doomed to failure, so we restrict our ambitions. The result of such filtering is a narrative rather than a chronicle (see Figure 13–2). A narrative does not attempt to take in every detail, but rather to tell an interesting, informative story. The boredom factor of a chronicle increases with its emphasis on detail, and the author of a narrative is thus more cognizant of his audience and will pick and choose from a store of facts to tell the best story possible. Again, a story is like a map and the author can scale it according to the detail he wants to include.

FICTION & NON-FICTION: FILTERING

Chronicles and narratives need not be factual. There are science fiction and fantasy stories that can be told as if they were describing reality, but we require the same coherence within fiction as we do within factual accounts. Blatant contradictions or obvious gaps within a plot are always problematic. For example,

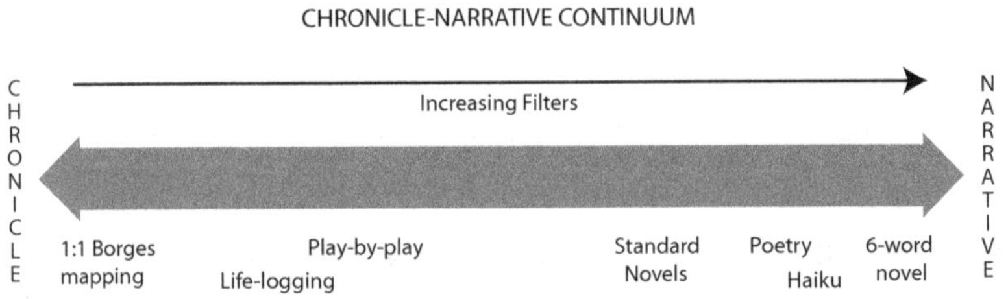

CHRONICLE-NARRATIVE CONTINUUM

FIGURE 13–2
An unfiltered 1:1 scale account of any event is an extreme chronicle, which is an impossible-to-produce work. Because of this, filters are invoked, and the more they are invoked the more condensed the narrative. Filters necessitate leaving out (sometimes huge) chunks of data.

in the movie *Thank You for Smoking*, Nick Naylor is trying to get cigarette product placement into movies. The publicist (Jeff Megall) suggests a futuristic movie set in a space station. Nick is skeptical:

Nick: So cigarettes in space?

Jeff: It's the final frontier, Nick.

Nick: But wouldn't they blow up in an all-oxygen environment?

Jeff: Uh... Probably. But it's an easy fix. One line of dialogue: "Thank God we invented the..." you know, whatever device.

We view the fictive worlds created by authors as coherent wholes, demanding consistency, simplicity, completeness, interconnectivity, and integration. As mentioned in chapter 8, the difference between the factual world and any fictional world will be the unlimited depth of the factual world. This by itself guarantees that completeness, interconnectivity and integration will be inherently compromised in the fictional.[7]

The unlimited depth of the factual world indicates that an exhaustive account of any subject, whether coffee or cars, will result in a veritable history of the universe. This means we must filter: for one thing, we must rise above the minutia of a situation and see the bigger picture. But, having seen this, we must then delve back into the dirt, though exactly which details we include in our account will be somewhat arbitrary: some must be included while others will have no business whatsoever within our account; but some will be marginal, and on these margins the real choices must be made. This is why two accounts written about the history of the automobile, published simultaneously by different authors, could be completely different. There are no doubt details each must include: Model T's, Henry Ford, and so on, but the focus of a work will determine the marginalia included. (This self-conscious filtering is a mimic of our unconscious filtering.) In true teleological form, the end or goal of our project determines the means, or filtering methods, used to achieve it.

Authorial intent has what we might call informational mass, which acts as a data attractor. Filtering is an attempt to control this by limiting the data based on topic relevance. All data may ultimately be relevant, but this would lead to a Borges type mapping, so we take practical considerations into account and prune our data tree. A history of the automobile will probably never mention Kant or the cost of coffee, though there are relations between these that a more exhaustive project might bring to light. Each project will have a set of values, determined by the author's intent (goal), which determine the filtering process. This is true of both fiction and non-fiction.

BIOGRAPHY & AUTOBIOGRAPHY

Filtering is obviously at work in both biography and autobiography. We usually think of an autobiography as an account, by the author, of her past, told from the standpoint of the present. But in most cases the author is attempting to portray

---

[7] This is true of all types of fiction, including lying. The difficulty in being a consistent liar lies in one's inability to keep all the various stories straight. This is a problem of interconnectivity and integration.

SPARSE FICTION: FILTER FORMATS

There are several genres in fiction that limit the number of words to a relatively small number. Some trace the roots of this movement to Hemingway's (apocryphal) 6-word-novel:

For sale: baby shoes, never worn.

There is usually no specific word length, though a size continuum (in wordiness) would run something like this:

novel, novella, novellete, short story, sudden fiction, flash fiction, micro fiction, drabble, dribble, hint fiction

All boundaries between these categories suffer from the pebble-rock syndrome, except drabble (100 words) and dribble (50 words) which are tightly defined in terms of length. Hemingway's six lines would probably best fit in the final category of hint fiction, which has limits variously based on Twitter's 140 character limit or a more arbitrary 25-word limit imposed by some. Most short-form fiction emphasizes pithiness and elegance, moving it more toward poetry. Indeed, we might say that brief-fiction is to the novel what haiku is to poetry. (Pound's "In a Station of the Metro" comes to mind.)

Swartmore (2010) claims that hint fiction truly engages the reader by only suggesting a storyline which the reader must use her imagination to complete. Two more examples (note how the title plays an interesting interpretive role in the story):

The Return (Joe R. Lansdale)
They buried him deep. Again.

The Golden Years (Edith Pearlman)
He: Macular. She: Parkinson's. She pushing, he directing, they get down the ramp, across the grass, through the gate. The wheels roll riverwards.

---

herself in a very specific way, usually to a very specific audience, including herself. In other words she is using the autobiography as a means of explaining the present in terms of the past by attempting to construct a coherent narrative of her life.

The biographer is at a disadvantage, since the autobiographer has privileged access to information concerning her own life—information not available to the biographer. The biographer collects data, which consists of accounts of the subject's behavior from various sources, and attempts to put all of this information into a coherent whole, speculating on the motives and intentions of the subject. The subject might then read the biography and smile knowingly (or become enraged) at the errors made in attributing motives that were not there. If the explanations given by the biographer fulfill the adequacy conditions, then the author is justified in reaching these conclusions, even if the subject denies their truth, and to rebut the charges made she would have to give a contrary account that was at least as coherent as that of the biographer in order to be believed. This would entail making information public which, had the biographer been aware of, would have been incorporated within the biography. In other words, both author and subject have to explain the subject's external behavior, but the subject has access to more information than the biographer and so might be able to give a more complete account, in which the known behavior is shown to be consistent.

It is not as obvious as we might think that a subject's point of view will be privileged. Confabulation must be taken into account, for we are not always the best interpreters of our own actions. For instance, my wife will sometimes question why I behaved in a certain unflattering way, and will attribute a motive to my actions as an explanation. My immediate response is to deny the motive and provide a different, more flattering, explanation. I am often completely convinced of my account, and sometimes I remain convinced, but there are times when, upon further reflection, I realize that her account is more accurate than my own. We can always rationalize our behavior in order to make ourselves appear in the best possible light, and if you choose to never delve deeper into your motivations that may become the standard story you tell yourself and others, but it does not follow that it is true simply from the fact that it's your story. We all have an ax to grind.

§6 THE SELF AS AUTHOR

As storytellers, we compose narratives continually to explain our actions, not only to others but to ourselves. These narratives are then nested within larger narratives which are nested within still larger narratives, until we reach our highest possible reference frame, from which vantage point we look down at our lives as a whole. Each of these narratives must cohere internally (interconnectedness) as well as with each other (integration). This is true on many levels. For example, each sentence I type has to have an internal coherence; it has to make sense in itself. I watched enrapt while my deep-sleeping pet chased dream-rabbits through endless fields of bliss. But it also must make sense within the paragraph, which the previous sentence failed to do. The sentence about my pet, inserted within this particular paragraph, causes immediate dissonance. By itself it is well-formed and thus coheres on the sentence level, but fails to cohere on the paragraph level (until I explain it is an example, at which time its very incoherence contributes to its coherence). So also, paragraphs must cohere within chapters which must cohere with the overall project of the book. From an even higher viewpoint, the book project must cohere within my life-story. Each progressively higher reference frame imbues the levels beneath it with meaning. The meaning I want to portray using a particular sentence gives meaning to the collection of words, which is to say, the words are the means I use to reach the goal of writing a meaningful sentence. So also, the sentence only makes sense in light of the meaning-goal of the paragraph, and is a means to reach this. And on and on. The sentence I am writing now is ultimately meaningful because it contributes to my overall well-being (my highest life-goal).

We can thus view ourselves as authors of our lives, as autobiographers, but the cogency of this analogy is immediately threatened by some obvious disanalogies. I want to explore several of these in order to further explicate the concept of self I have in mind.

THERE IS NO CLEAR DISTINCTION BETWEEN AUTHOR AND AUDIENCE IN MY LIFE-STORY.

This is important, for the storyteller molds his story to the interests of the audience, that is, the audience dictates the structure of the story to a large extent. Who am I trying to impress with my autobiography: myself or others? Or do I write separate versions: one for my own consumption, one for my friends, one for the general public, and so on? And if this is what I do, which one is really me? Or is there another, higher and always unknowable me controlling the whole project? Asking these authorial questions is analogous to asking deep questions of meaning about my self and my relationship to others. This is what we want to explore with the authorial metaphor.

We will explain this using the following sequence (Figure 13–3):

(1) Various brain-mapping feedback processes give rise spontaneously to a core self that is conscious of the world, as something separate from the world that experiences the world.

(2) This self becomes self-conscious as it experiences itself as an object in time, as having a narrative structure. It builds a picture of itself as existing on a timeline from birth to present and projects itself as existing into the future. This portrayal of the self by the self is the persona: how I see myself as a person. This persona is a theory of me, of who I am, and thus must cohere. We can identify the persona with what we have earlier called the conceptual scheme.

(3) The persona does not exist by itself. We are social animals who must present ourselves to others. These others might be friendly or unfriendly. Because of this we portray ourselves to others in various ways. These public projections of our private self are masks.

The three different aspects of our self are continually interacting by means of feedback loops. My persona is continually being updated based on my present experiences, which affect my projects (goals), all of which have to be made to cohere with my persona. So also with my public projections (masks). These performances of mine are seen by others who react to them in various ways, and these reactions are fed back into the self which adjusts both them and the persona as needed. This takes place continuously as we interact with the world, and can be either unconscious or conscious.

To answer the question, then, of who is the author and who is the audience: the core self is both the author and audience of the persona, from which it cannot be separated. This complex entity is then the author of our masks, the audience of which is the public. There is no unknowable self behind the curtains controlling our actions as a puppet-master controls his puppets. The self just is the persona trying to make sense of itself in the world.

WE DO NOT EXPERIENCE EITHER THE BEGINNING OR THE END OF OUR OWN STORIES.

While true, this fact doesn't seem to present a problem. This is an aspect in which our overall narratives (from our authorial reference frame) differ from the narratives nested within it. This feature does not negate the narrative structure of our lives, though, for we are assured that we were born at some point and that we will die. In the absence of living relatives or records, our birth is still a fact guaranteed by our present existence, and though we will never experience our own death, it, too, is inexorable in its approach. Our authorial point of view takes in our life up to the present, and projects our future life as anticipation.

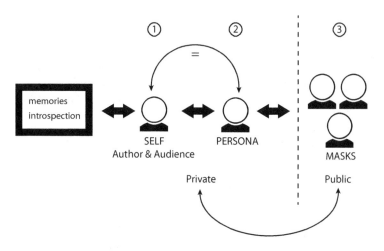

FIGURE 13–3

Self as Author and Audience. The Core Self arises from brain processes. "I" become conscious of myself and thus construct a narrative (a Persona) to explain my life. This "I" must also relate to others and in order to do so projects masks in order to portray itself in the correct light depending on those it is interacting with.

WE ARE NOT IN CONTROL OF OUR NARRATIVE.

Another disanalogy between our life-story and a fictional story is that we do not know what to expect in the future; we do not have control over our lives in the way an author controls the lives of his characters. We may not know, but we plan, we anticipate, and based on these we formulate future-maps of what our life will be like. These future projections must cohere with our life-story up to the present. For instance, you may have recently graduated from nursing school and are looking for an entry level job as a nurse. If you generate a future-map in which you will land a job with a six-figure salary within your first year, this will not cohere well with the reality of your life-story to date. Such future-maps will lead to frustration (cognitive dissonance) and will have to be adjusted when the actual salary does not match expectations. The world is our touchstone to reality. Our stories cannot stray too far from the facts without running afoul of coherence just as the thesis of a story cannot stray too far from the facts of the story.[8]

A related issue arises because it seems that an author has complete control of his story, while we do not have complete control over our lives. We do not, for instance, choose our parents or the social milieu into which we are born, while an author seems to have complete control over the details. You cannot accuse the fiction-author of inaccuracies in the way in which we could be guilty in our own life story. Though true, this is not an important disanalogy, for authors must adhere to coherence when spinning their stories as much as we do ourselves in spinning our

---

[8] To say that the world is our touchstone does not imply an absolute, external anchor. Remember, our view of the world itself is a theory determined by our adequacy conditions. Thus the demand for consistency between our life-story and the world at large, is simply the demand for overall coherence within our world view.

own. The importance of the analogy between author and self lies in the way in which stories are constructed, and all stories ultimately rely on coherence.

As an author writes a fictional narrative his options narrow as he progresses. Each detail used to flesh out a character or a situation delimits that character's future; each plot construction sets boundaries on where the story can and cannot go. This is likewise true of our lives. Our genetics and social situation set limits on what we can accomplish, but in youth there are a myriad of options to choose from. To put this another way, consistent with our talk in chapter 11, in youth there are many possible future-maps which can be actualized, but as you grow older these possibilities dwindle.

OUR LIVES ARE NOT CONSTRUCTED FROM AN AUTHORIAL POINT OF VIEW.

This is true. We do not, for the most part, contemplate our lives as an author does his characters. This is the same point made when we discussed the narrative structure of experience. You can move to a higher reference frame and contemplate a melody note by note or word by word, but you are usually just listening to the song—living through the experience rather than analyzing it. So also with life. Another way to put this would be to say we are more invested in our protagonist than is an author of a fictional work. And yet we do plan our lives as an author plans a story, and this is the relevant point of the overall author-narrative analogy. We are teleological beings, so our meaning is often determined much more by our future plans than our past actions, and if those past actions do give us meaning it is usually because they were once future goals that have now been accomplished.

§7 TOUCHSTONES & COHERENCE

How creative can I be as author of my life-story? As a prisoner within my subjectivity I might think I have unlimited freedom to create myself however I see fit, manipulating memories at will to conform to an image I construct. But we have already seen this view is mistaken. My core values dictate that there is a world outside of me, and my concept of self must cohere with this world at the cost of severe cognitive dissonance. This takes several forms.

Every fact about my life (my ontogeny) available outside of my memory is a restriction upon my persona. My birth certificate, for example, filed in the county clerk's office, is a fact I have to incorporate within my persona. If I want to portray myself to myself as younger than my birth certificate indicates, then I will have to solve the anomaly this project presents. I might claim it is a forgery, but what is my evidence? This is not an insurmountable problem, for our powers of self-deception are great, but there are other larger problems lurking. My school records, from elementary to high school to college, interconnect robustly with my birth certificate, which means all of these will have to be manipulated. Then there are those photographs of me as a newborn in my mother's arms, the date on which also corresponds with the birth certificate. It would be difficult to ignore these facts, but not impossible. As long as I don't have contact with childhood friends and family, I could probably maintain a running self-deception concerning my age.

A more difficult self-deception would be one that clashed with my physical characteristics. For example, suppose I wanted to portray myself as trim and athletic when in fact I am neither. Looking at myself in the mirror might be a dead giveaway, so maybe I don't look in the mirror, but such a delusion is going to be harder to maintain publicly. So also if I wanted to portray myself as a genius, or as having an excellent singing voice, and so on. The common thread here is that we could customize our self image however we wanted except for those pesky public facts, which tend to keep us in line. We have seen this restriction before with respect to truth, which is why the integration condition is so important to overall coherence. Without integration, we develop standalone narratives that appear completely consistent and interconnected; but integration demands that our narratives also cohere with the wider public realm, a fact which often prevents us from committing the more egregious self-deceptions.

This still allows us considerable leeway with respect to mask construction. I may not be able to deceive others that I am thin or tall when I am not, but the less publicly obvious a characteristic is, the more susceptible it is to deception. If you don't know me I might convince you I am a bit older or younger than I really am. I can take on the accoutrements of a physician or a lawyer or a teacher as long as I am not put in the position of having to prove myself. Most of us have no need for such elaborate deceptions, though we perpetrate countless smaller deceptions throughout our daily lives: we dye our hair, shave, and paint our nails; we wear makeup, hairpieces, slimming outfits, clothes of a certain cut; we put on deodorant, cologne, perfume, lipstick, and jewelry; we get face-lifts, breast implants, false teeth, tans, and botox injections; we withhold information, talk in ambiguous vagaries; we fake smiles, tears and orgasms; and of course we outright lie.

Every time I come in contact with other people I involve myself in a strategic game of theorizing, for not only do I have to maintain my performance before them, I also must judge their performances. This results in a delicate and sometimes fragile dance in which we are slipping in and out of performances depending on our social circumstances, adjusting our roles to the contingencies of life and evaluating them in light of the roles of others. William James (1992) says, of a person's social interactions, that

> ... we may practically say that he has as many different social selves as there are distinct groups of persons about whose opinion he cares. He generally shows a different side of himself to each of these different groups. Many a youth who is demure enough before his parents and teachers, swears and swaggers like a pirate among his "tough" young friends. We do not show ourselves to our children as to our club companions, to our customers as to the laborers we employ, to our own masters and employers as to our intimate friends. (177)

Dissonance is constantly experienced, evaluated and handled. The causes can range from social indiscretions (a public belch), to bold-faced lies. Some we might politely ignore, others publicly deride, but all are grist for our theorizing mills. Job interviews and police interrogations are blatant forms of this, in which I present myself before a person who is suspicious of my claims, and tries to see behind my appearance. These interviewers will be judging my performance, looking for telltale inconsistencies that might indicate a deeper truth. In these cases I attempt to put on the mask of innocence or efficiency, characteristics that maybe my persona lacks. First dates are not unlike job interviews, though the evaluation is more reciprocal, for both parties are being interviewed.

A persona is my view of myself as a character within my life-story. A mask is a public projection of my persona which need not be an accurate representation of my persona. You might say it is a projection of my theory of myself in light of my theory of you. A mask is a response as is an emotion. I can choose carefully which characteristics to emphasize to the public, giving rise to multiple characters which are all me, but represent different aspects of myself. This projection is how I want others to see me and so results in a distorted image in the minds of others concerning who I am. Distorted because I may be acting a part beyond my abilities. For instance, I might want to see myself as an athlete and portray myself publicly in this light; but I may not be able to pull it off well, and so am labeled (by some) as a poser. To the extent that my persona is all show I will tend to be exposed as a poser the more I am in contact with those who really are athletes.

There is a difference in seeing myself as an athlete, wanting others to see me as an athlete, and how they actually see me. If I see myself as an athlete then I really think I am one and my athlete-mask is an undistorted image of my persona. I could be mistaken—my athlete-persona might be a case of wishful thinking—which means I might be portrayed as a poser by those not taken in by my performance. (One method of testing your athlete-persona is to mix with real athletes; if you are left in their dust, you may have to reconstruct your persona.)[9] I might want others to see me as an athlete regardless of whether I really am an athlete or see myself as one. In other words, my masks (public personas) may differ from my private persona.

Notice the possible layers of deception here (indicated in Figure 13–4). (1) My persona (my portrayal of myself to myself) might be mistaken (I might see myself as an athlete when I am not one). This is usually self-deception. (2) My mask does not match my persona. This becomes complex because I might be projecting what I think is a true picture of myself, but I am involved in self-deception. Thus, I may think I am an athlete when I am not and thus sincerely project an athletic mask. (3) Regardless of the truth or falseness of personas and masks, other people might misinterpret my performance, leading to a public perception of me that is quite different than what I want to project.

§8 ROLES

As characters within our own life-story we must accept certain roles throughout the course of our lives, most of which are ready-made by society. If you are a physician, for example, you incorporate aspects of this socially defined role into your persona. As a physician you must give lip service to at least some of these norms even if you don't believe in them yourself. The structure of these roles is complex. For example, there is a very public set of procedures for physicians prescribed by

---

[9] But not necessarily. Remember the American Idol Effect, which just goes to show: our powers of self-deception are amazing.

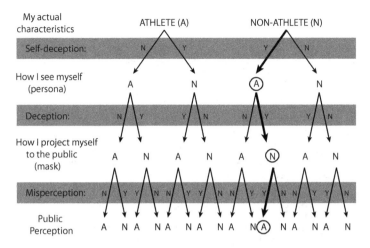

FIGURE 13–4

The possibilities of distortion with respect to one characteristic that could be applied to a person. Suppose, for instance, I am not athletic, but see myself as athletic. In this case I am deceiving myself. Suppose I want to hustle someone (I might bet them I could run a four minute mile), then I would want to deceive them concerning my supposed athleticism. Finally, they may fail to be taken in by my mask, that is, they misperceive my performance, think I am an athlete, and thus refuse to bet. In this case I am a non-athlete who thinks he is athletic, but portrays himself as non-athletic, but is perceived as athletic.

the AMA, which constitute part of the physician-role. Not abiding by these can result in loss of one's ability to practice medicine. A more subjective set of physician-role-characteristics is attached to this—that which is shown to the public by each physician, surgeon, and so on. These are a part of the life-stories authored, often with vast amounts of improvisation, by the individuals. Each subjective persona is different, but together they form a publicly-perceived role. A homeless person has a less complex role, at least to the extent there is no governing body from which he can be excluded. The individual homeless person, to the extent that he identifies with the homeless role, has his own interpretation of what this means, and again these collected roles, viewed by the public, constitute our public conception of a homeless person. There is obviously no one collective role we must adhere to when considering either a doctor or a homeless person, but there is a general perception (a stereotype) which we may agree with to some extent. We use these stereotypes as a standard from which we judge individual instances. For example, a general perception of doctors might be that they are intelligent, wealthy, well-dressed, and so on, while a general perception of the homeless might be that they are handicapped, poor, and dirty.

A non-reflective person might accept a societal role without question, molding himself to what is expected of him, while a more reflective person might question these and act in ways inconsistent with expectations. To some extent, if you automatically conform to societal norms you are controlled by what others think of you. There are those who claim that the essence of being human is to be free, and people who conform unthinkingly to societal standards are inauthentic individuals,

VITAL LIES

Ernest Becker published an influential book entitled *The Denial of Death* in which he argued that the concept of our own death is too terrible to contemplate. So we consistently deceive ourselves with respect to our mortal status, choosing to believe that we are immortal gods. This is a vital lie we must tell ourselves in order to function day by day. We are, he says, "gods that shit," for we are continually confronted with anomalies that belie our immortal status, yet we refuse to take account of these. We live, says he, in a world in which organisms are routinely

> ... tearing others apart with teeth of all types—biting, grinding flesh, plant stalks, bones between molars, pushing the pulp greedily down the gullet with delight, incorporating its essence into one's own organization, and then excreting with foul stench and gasses the residue. (282)

The concept that we are continually living by means of vital lies is interesting, though I tend to think it is false. On this view, those we label abnormal, (schizophrenic, psychotic, and so on) are those who lack the defense mechanisms most of us have that allow us to lie about reality—to make reality livable and often charming when in fact it is terrifying. On Becker's view, ignorance really is bliss, but we have to make ourselves ignorant and actively work to keep ourselves in that state.

But is this view really necessary? Even if we accept that we do in fact deceive ourselves in various ways and that the world can be a vicious place, why should we emphasize these particular aspects and pick them out as reality?

living in bad faith (Sartre) or suffering from a false consciousness (Marx). We have learned to be leery of talk of essences, though, for these are themselves projections of others proclaiming what all humans should be. We have instead, in these pages, opted for a more pragmatic approach. What sorts of behavior are consistent with achieving what we most want out of life? What sorts of behavior will contribute to our overall goal of well-being? We have already noted that being able to differentiate true sentences from false sentences contributes to our ability to achieve these goals. That is, truth is usually conducive to our well-being. It further follows from this that, since the scientific method is the best method for consistently sorting truth from falsehood, using this (carefully reflective) method throughout our life is our best bet for achieving well-being. We have identified the scientific method with the use of theorizing according to a set of adequacy conditions we refer to as coherence.

Active use of coherence in molding your life in order to obtain well-being presupposes a reflective rather than a non-reflective attitude. Again, those who examine their lives by means of theorizing via the scientific method are more apt to reach the goals they set for themselves. This is all we are saying. We are not proclaiming any overriding goal for humans that is not justified by lived experience. This is why I have chosen well-being, which is a goal we can agree that humans seek, in the same way we seek coherence—a goal we can all identify with. In fact, coherence and well-being may be one to some extent. These are not imposed upon humans from without—they are simply what we are; they are conditions of our existence and thus conditions we share with all other living things, conditions that can be empirically verified. (I will argue this point in more detail in the final chapter.)

Unconscious organisms cohere or they die. So also with self-conscious organisms, but our self-consciousness gives us more control by allowing us a higher reference frame from which to view our situation. The results (the goal) of our use of the coherence methodology (the means) justifies its use (see Figure 13–5).

It might be said that, in many cases, ignorance is bliss. There is certainly evidence for this position: we can easily point out those who flow through their lives with little or no analysis and die happy, having lived a life no one would deny was a life of well-being. These are the exceptions, however, that prove the general rule. The rule is not absolute. You certainly may happen upon a life-path that gives you everything you want without a moment of contemplation concerning the meaning of life or how to achieve well-being. But such lives are rare. Do you want to risk the one life you have on the small chance that maybe you will achieve happiness by luck or coincidence rather than by planning? On the other hand, the complexity of life guarantees that our best-laid plans will go awry. Our plans must be flexible, with emphasis on improvisation.

Even the most unreflective person is continually constructing a narrative that explains her life to herself; she merely takes a less self-conscious role in its formation. In a sense the unreflective person's life-story (the story she tells herself about who she is) is more like a biography than an autobiography, for she is not utilizing all the information and methodologies available in order to sort truth from falsehood. What should we say about such a person? Should we label them inauthentic? No. The fact is, the examined life is not for everyone. Some people may attain well-being through consistent self-deception. We cannot make any universal judgments concerning what people ought to do with their lives, or look down upon them because they choose not to examine their lives as we do.

It doesn't follow from the fact that we cannot judge a person's level of reflection that everyone's life story is equally successful. I can imagine both highly reflective and completely unreflective people who were never able to put their lives together

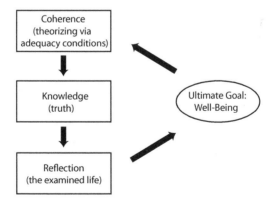

FIGURE 13–5

A reiteration of the circle of justification in the coherence theory. The axioms which form the starting point include the notion of coherence. Using coherence gives rise to theories that contain core values such as the self and the external world. Ultimately, theorizing turns out to work well to further our life-goals (coherence "works"), which is the justification for using coherence in the first place.

in a manner they (or others) would deem satisfactory. The larger question concerns those who write their life story (whether reflective or unreflective) based upon the suffering of others. In other words, I can imagine a highly reflective person who puts together a completely coherent life-story consisting of his life as a pursuit of pleasure at the expense of the suffering of others. We will address this topic in the next chapter.

♂♀

§9 THE IMPORTANCE OF MEMORY

Years ago I read about a woman who had been assaulted and was found in a park having no recollection of who she was or what had happened to her. The memorable part of this story was that, when she was interviewed while recovering, she insisted that her attacker, when caught, be tried for murder, for he had killed her. I don't know how the story turned out—whether or not her memory eventually returned (it usually does in such cases)—but her claim is interesting. She had been murdered, for her attacker had taken her memories and the person she was now was no longer the same person. Same body. Different person.

It is impossible to over-emphasizes the importance of memory in our everyday life, particularly short-term memory. If you can't store anything in short-term memory, you are always living in the present moment. This is called anterograde amnesia, as opposed to retrograde amnesia in which you cannot remember the past. There are actual cases in which people suffer radical anterograde amnesia. EP, for example, (initials are used to protect his privacy) contracted herpes simplex, which usually causes only cold sores, but in his case attacked the brain, destroying the medial termporal lobes, including the hippocampus, which is responsible for moving memories into long-term storage. He completely lost the ability to create new long-term memories (and lost much of his long-term memory as well). He cannot remember that he cannot remember, which his wife refers to as a blessing. He has momentary emotional states, but,

> without the ability to compare today's feelings to yesterday's, he cannot tell any cohesive narrative about himself, or about those around him, which makes him incapable of providing even the most basic psychological sustenance to his family and friends. After all, EP can only remain truly interested in anyone or anything for as long as he can maintain his attention. Any rogue thought that distracts him effectively resets conversation. A meaningful relationship between two people cannot sustain itself only in the present tense. (Foer 73-74)

His family describes him as "very happy" and he thinks his memory is "pretty good." EP is the ultimate argument for the blissfulness of ignorance.

Memories are not sufficient for making us who we are—we are more than a mere collection of memories—but they do seem to be necessary. Consider the following thought experiment:

> Suppose that, on your deathbed, an angel appears and tells you that you must make a choice with respect to your afterlife. When you die you can

either (1) go to heaven or (2) turn to dust. If you want (1), then you must leave all of your (substantial) assets to the church. If you want (2), you need do nothing. One final piece of information. If you opt for (1), when you get to heaven (which is truly a wonderful place), all your memories concerning your life here on earth will be wiped clean. All of them. Gone.

Which option would you choose? I find that the final piece of information about wiping my memories changes everything. In a sense, that person enjoying heaven is no longer me, so why should I give up control of my wealth (depriving my children or pets or favorite charities of my wealth)? At first glance, the options (1) and (2) seem radically different, but are they?

In today's world we depend on our memories less and less because we have developed sophisticated technologies to store information externally. When you jot down a note, write in a journal, take a picture or video, you have created an external memory. We suffer a loss if these external memories are destroyed. People who have had their homes destroyed by fire or natural disaster often most regret having lost their family pictures. Memories are not just stored on media of various sorts; they can be inter-related with objects. These are mementos: objects that are important to us because they are associated with memories we hold dear. People, too, are mementos, objectified memories.

§10 THE EXTENDED SELF

Why do we think of our self as existing in our head? Maybe because our eyes are our visual source, our portal to the world. But my self is the coherent life-story I have constructed based on my memories and my future projections, and at least some of these memories are objective (public). Our natural tendency is to bound the self as an object, a tidy category contained within our cranial vault. But I want to suggest we should expand this outside of our bodies (as we expanded the phenotype in chapters 1 and 6). Our bodies give us locomotion, but they are not all there is to us. Objects, both animate and inanimate are also, in a very real sense, a part of us. Other people are particularly important, for, unlike other things, we can share our memories with them. Thus, rather than seeing my self as this discrete bag of blood and organs bounded by skin, I think a better representation might be, say, a cloud-like object with tendrils extending out into the world. I like the cloud analogy on several levels, for it fits well with the idea that we are complex adaptive systems and thus reminds us that our various aspects are not discrete, but interactive. (I will revisit the cloud analogy in chapter 15.) These aspects are the result of multiple feedback loops that create more feedback loops, and so on. This mirrors our relations to other people and objects in the world. We do not simply relate to them. Our performances change people's way of seeing us, which changes their performance, which changes ours... We attach importance (meaning) to both objects and people, and these relationships become embedded within our conceptual schemes and so become a part of us. My self, then, can be seen as an extended network of people and objects (see Figure 13–6), all of which are interconnected.

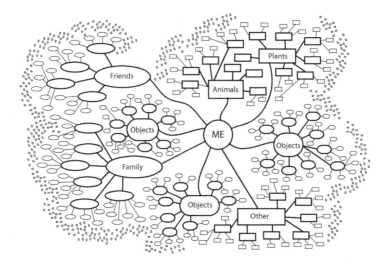

Figure 13–6

A vastly oversimplified diagram of my relationships. Each of my friends, for example, has relations to others, which are related to others, and so on, forming a matrix of connections throughout the world. So also are we related to other living things—if only in our shared DNA, and these things are all interrelated in a variety of manners. This holds true of objects as well. The bottom line, which is impossible to illustrate in a finite diagram, is that everything is connected in some way to everything else.

The only part of our self we can be untrue to is that part that is publicly available, and even this is unimportant. So what if I convince myself that I am artistic or athletic when I am not? And who cares if my masks are many? Two-faced you say. Amenable to circumstances, say I. Are not masks lies? and are we not, then, perpetually lying? To say that we are constantly evaluating our own theory of self and those of others and revamping them in light of each other is to say that our selves are dynamic entities. We transfigure ourselves daily. We are, as Nietzsche once pointed out, much more artistic than we realize.

Masks are essential to the task of maintaining ourselves as individuals, with boundaries intact against the world. Santayana (1923) puts it this way:

> Living things in contact with the air must acquire a cuticle, and it is not urged against cuticles that they are not hearts; yet some philosophers seem to be angry with images for not being things, and with words for not being feelings. Words and images are like shells, no less integral parts of nature than are the substances they cover, but better addressed to the eye and more open to observation. (131)

So also with our masks. They, like shells and skin and cellular membranes, are no less integral than that which they protect. Yet we tend to judge masks as mere appearances, wanting to know the person underneath, but we cannot make this distinction. With our distinctions between personas and masks and diagrams illustrating their relationship, it is easy to forget that there really is no distinction. My mask, the one you see right now, is my persona reflected off your mask. Am I deceiving you? Only to the extent that I see the deception as a necessary means for dealing with you given my life-projects. Con artists are professional mask-makers bent on causing harm. Their mask is their means to achieve this deception, but it is no less a part of their persona.

And then the final step. I would not need a mask if I were alone in the world, which means my mask and the masks of others are intimately related, since your mask depends on mine and others as well. This is the same inter-reliance we saw in chapter 11 when we noted that your actions are inextricably intertwined with those of everyone else, for one person's actions change everyone else's. No man is an island, and the bell, when it tolls, tolls for us all.

§11 CHAPTER SUMMARY

We have seen that our concept of self is a theory subject to adequacy conditions (coherence), and we have used the analogy of a narrative to throw some light on the terms within this relationship. Not only is our experience and our life conditioned by the narrative structure, but our reflection upon our lives also takes this story-form. This allowed us to compare our autobiographical self to an author, raising points about the meaning and structure of our lives. As we see the importance not only of interconnectivity but also of integration into a world of others, we lay important groundwork for our next chapter on morality, for morality is founded upon our relationships to others.

The hermit is an interesting concept within the context of self and morality, for a hermit is a person (ideally) with no connections whatsoever with anyone outside of himself. We have seen that this is an impossible situation. There are no true hermits. We humans are social animals and our very concept of self is bound up with those of others. The more closely we bind ourselves to other people and objects (creating core values) the more meaning we create for ourselves. Other people are of overriding importance in establishing these meaning relationships, for they are reciprocal in a way objects are not, and in this reciprocity lies all the wonder and tragedy of the human condition.

14. Morality

It is vain to talk of the interest of the community, without understanding what is the interest of the individual.

- Jeremy Bentham

SYNOPSIS

(1) This chapter is an articulation of morality based on our coherence position; it is not a general discussion of moral theory, though some theories will be briefly touched upon. (2) The differences in an egoistic point of view versus an altruistic point of view. On an individual level egoism may be preferable, but we are never really on an individual level. On a social level, altruism is the preferable point of view. (3) The only viable form of altruism is reciprocal altruism and this gives rise to the real problem of morality: free-riders, those who use the benefits of social cooperation for their own advantage. Moral rules arise to protect ourselves from such people. (4) Empathy is described as a phenomenon that expands reciprocal altruism, allowing us to expand our moral circles to include more and more people (and maybe even those outside humanity). Empathy gives rise to our own formulation of the golden rule, from which can be derived the core moral rules within all societies. (5) We are now in a position to explain morality and how it functions: it is that set of rules that protect our most important (core or constitutive) values. (6) The relativist position is outlined. Here we mention competing, non-relative moral theories, in particular formalist theories based on god or natural law and utilitarian theories. Both are shown to have the same flaw. (7) Why the relativist is undeterred by the moral reproach of others, unless such reproaches are warnings of dire consequences. (8) The coherence approach is applied to moral theory. Core moral rules are shown to be constitutive in the same way we have accepted other beliefs as constitutive. As such, these are judged in terms of how well they contribute to our overall goal of well-being. (9) Chapter Summary.

CHAPTER OBJECTIVES

- understand the nature of morality and moral reasoning, i.e., why some actions are said to be "immoral"
- see how a morality might be justified in terms of coherence

§1 INTRODUCTION TO MORALITY

In the last chapter we developed the analogy between self and author and argued that the self can be viewed as extending beyond the bounds of our bodies. The important connecting point to this chapter comes when we realize that our own character is merely one character, though the protagonist, in the sprawling historical novel we call our life-story. Ours is a wiki-novel, a true-life example of participatory quasi-fiction, in which the story is continually being edited in real time by billions of people, every one of which is a character who believes his own is the protagonist. We are somewhat in charge of our own character, but are constantly forced to revise it as we read and are otherwise affected by those written by others, most of whom we do not even know.

Our public (published) version of our life story is available to others and it is important to most of us that our version cohere with theirs at least with respect to how they see us (depending on how important they are to us). Not surprisingly, this depends upon core values. An atheist might not care whether the theist sees his story as coherent, but may still care that he himself not come across as a complete poser. That is, we generally care, at least to some extent, what other people take us to be (again, to varying degrees). If the image you portray of yourself is that of a kind and caring altruistic individual while everyone else's portrayal of you is as a backstabbing, self-centered monster, there is a problem. You may not care, but you won't get as many benefits from this portrayal, so you may work on your public image to make it more amenable. You may end up with multiple images (we all do). You may realize yourself to be self-centered and unscrupulous—this is how you see yourself—but you may purposefully portray yourself as kind and caring to the world at large.

As we will see, morality is the connecting point between our self and others. Moral rules are the rules I use to get along with you and other people. In their simplest form, they are the rules I use to further my own well-being in a world in which others are always seen as either a threat or an aid to the attainment of my most important life-goals. This is often taken only in a negative sense: we are looking out for number one; but there is a positive sense as well. We have evolved as empathetic organisms and this ability to imagine what others are feeling can greatly affect our well-being. In this sense others are a threat or aid to our well-being insofar as they demand or we offer assistance. The true hermit, as a person who has abso-lutely no connections to anyone else, is the limiting case of the completely isolated individual, and as such does not exist. We talk of a personal morality, which often refers to the rules that we as individuals stipulate for ourselves (or agree to accept from another source) in order to achieve our own well-being, but these are rules that help us function in a world in which we cannot separate ourselves from others.

Since this chapter is an application of what we have articulated in previous sec-tions it will obviously make use of the notion of our development. In other words, we must understand our moral concepts in terms of our evolutionary development, particularly with respect to the development of our brains. I will argue that morality has two foundations: empathy, which is the ability to feel what others are feeling and react to this accordingly; and reciprocal altruism, which puts our empathetic experience into action and demands the same from others. Furthermore, we have seen that our conscious processing of experience is only the tip of the iceberg with respect to our overall cognitive output; the vast majority of our processing is unconscious, and because of this we (as con-scious beings) do not always understand why we do what we do. In morality this often mani-fests itself in the form of moral conundrums or an inability to understand why we feel the way we do. Finally we will turn to look at the concept of relativism in light of two major theories of morality. I will argue, not unexpectedly, that coherence is at work throughout these processes.

> **ALTRUISM:**
>
> Acting in consideration of the interests of others, without ulterior motives.
>
> **EGOISM:**
>
> Acting in consideration of your own interests.

This is not a treatise on morality as might be found in an introduction to philoso-phy. I am not interested in setting out detailed explanations of the various theories of morality and giving arguments pro and con for each. Rather, I am attempting to show how the moral point of view fits into the overall life view of theorizing as put forth in this text.

§2 EGOISM & ALTRUISM

We have seen that living organisms diverged at one point in their evolutionary development depending on their survival strategy. Plants are those that remained fixed and depended upon their food coming to them. Animals developed locomo-tion so that they could go to their food rather than depending on it coming to them. Humans have evolved as particularly social animals, and they, too, have survival options available to them analogous to the plant-animal option. The difference is that our options are, to some extent, conscious choices—ones that we can, at least in part, change, barring damage to our brain caused by injury, genetics, or abuse during formative years. One option is: whether or not you will tie your search for well-being to others or go it alone. This is never a black and white choice, for no one ever goes it alone completely. On the other extreme, no one can tie their own life story completely to everyone else's. The person who attempts to go it alone will have what we have called a standalone narrative—one which has less chance of

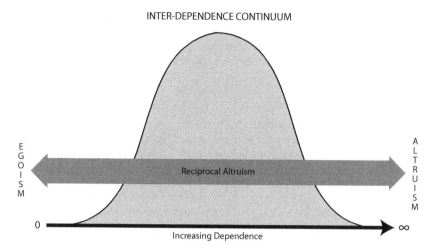

INTER-DEPENDENCE CONTINUUM

FIGURE 14–1

The bell curve here indicates that most people are neither pure egoists, always seeking their own benefit, nor pure altruists, always seeking to benefit others. The middle road is that of reciprocal altruism in which we help others in exchange for their helping us. This is linked to dependence, for the further a person moves to the left, the more selfish, the less he can be depended upon to reciprocate. He will, in other words become a free-rider. It is always in the egoist's best interest to appear altruistic.

success than those who allow others to help. I will return to this idea in §8 below, but this option is related to a second. Allowing others to help entails that we will in turn help them, and we can, again with certain stipulations, choose the extent to which we will participate in the give and take of society. Figure 14–1 shows how this choice can be set up on a continuum, where the left side is the taker (which we will call the egoist), and the right side is the giver (the altruist). Most of us fall somewhere in the middle, and there is a good reason for this: our chances of attaining well-being drop off precipitously as we approach the extremes. Consider the following thought experiments:

(1) Suppose two people are stranded on a desert island, one of whom is an egoist, the other an altruist. There are limited resources and no hope for a quick rescue. Who will be most likely to survive? Probably the egoist, for he will not give up resources to help the altruist, while the altruist will give up resources to help him.

(2) Suppose there are two islands. On one island a group of egoists are stranded; on the other a group of altruists. There are limited resources and no hope for a quick rescue. Which group will be most likely to prosper? In this case, I would put my money on the altruists, for they will help each other while the egoists are in every-man-for-himself mode. This scenario may play out so that the egoists will reduce their numbers to a very few prosperous survivors, while the altruists will prosper as a group.

(3) Suppose again there are two islands, one of altruists and one of egoists. One of the egoists constructs a boat and makes the perilous journey over to the altruist island, where, of course, he is taken into the
group. What will be the result? The egoist is the wolf within the sheep-
fold, a free-rider, which is a best-case scenario for an egoist. He can
take and take and all he has to do in return is give the appearance of
giving back. He will prosper at the expense of the others in the group.

Even a limited altruism is a wonderful thing, for it allows for cooperation instead
of constantly battling others to achieve one's own goals.[1] Cooperating organisms
can rise to heights unattainable by single organisms. Indeed, much of our own
technological progress is probably due to increased cooperation produced by con-
gregating large numbers of humans together within civilizations. The temptation,
though, within a group of cooperators, is for one individual to take advantage of the
group. This is the free-rider problem we have encountered before.

§3 RECIPROCAL ALTRUISM & THE PROBLEM OF FREE-RIDERS

Reciprocal altruism is a mechanism in which I help you in return for your help at
some time in the future. This means I must be able to keep track of you to insure
you pay back what you owe; if I don't, then I am expending precious resources for
nought. This personal accounting is not difficult in a small primordial band of hunter-
gatherers, but it becomes more difficult as the population increases, especially
when we may be giving up goods for the pleasure of unknown people (via taxation,
for example). Anonymity in any form makes it easy for free-riders to flourish.

Free-riders constitute a threat to our well-being. In civil society we label them
selfish, criminal, immoral, or some combination of these. The murderer or embez-
zler or rapist all attempt to take advantage of others in some way; they take from
individuals without an implicit or explicit reciprocal agreement. This has no doubt
contributed to our concept of fairness, which lies at the heart of morality. We attempt
to prevent free-riders by means of the threat to inflict suffering upon them or by
withholding goods from them as the behavior is discovered or persists. We also
attempt preemptive measures by means of various forms of indoctrination, which
are related to the notion of punishment via deterrence. We inflict suffering upon
free-riders in order to send a message to others that such behavior will not be tolerated. Other, less obvious but no less powerful mechanisms, the moral emotions,
may also have arisen from the existence of free-riders. If you can make a person
feel guilt or remorse for acting in a non-reciprocal manner, this will also function as
a deterrent.

Even with free-riders, reciprocal altruism leads to an equilibrium, for the negative effects of the free-riders will increase until the system crashes, which makes
it less hospitable for them, and their subsequent disappearance allows the system to return to prosperity, thereby attracting free-riders once again. This negative

---

[1] Studies have shown that, even given equal resources, when individuals are pitted against
each other in constant competition stress levels are increased and this leads to a decline in the
potential to achieve well-being.

feedback system is illustrated in Figure 14–2. One example of this might be corruption in government, which is tolerated on a small scale, but eventually increases beyond the bounds of acceptability, at which time laws are passed and government officials are censured, lowering corruption temporarily. The equilibrium maintained here is an overall acceptable level of corruption. We could take another example from the financial crisis of 2008. For years, banks, insurance companies, and investment houses involved themselves in very profitable but very risky ventures. When the housing market crashed, they were unprepared, and many faced financial ruin. The government infused their businesses with the public's money, claiming they were "too big to fail." We can view this as a case in which free-riders took risks that should not have been taken for their own profit. The collapse brought about new government regulations as well as public fury. Under close government scrutiny these companies will no doubt be well-behaved for some time to come, but eventually, when attention is focused elsewhere, the free-riders will return.

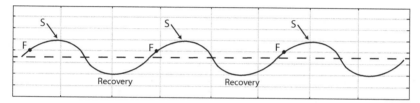

FIGURE 14–2

The system of feedback produced by the introduction of free-riders (F), which eventually causes a system collapse (S), which is no longer amenable to the free-riders. Once recovery has begun, however, the free-riders return, and the cycle begins again.

§4 EMPATHY

Empathy is the ability to put yourself into the mind of others and imagine the world from their point of view, and to some extent this must underlie reciprocal behavior within humans (we reserve the term 'empathy' for those creatures with minds). If we are to share food, for example, we must be able to understand that another creature is hungry when they go without food as we are hungry when we go without food. This is an amazing ability, and it is not only humans who possess it. Monkeys and apes can read emotional expressions from others via facial or vocal expressions or body language, and consolation is often shown to the loser of a fight by other group members. Even rats will attempt to help other rats, who are suspended above them, by pressing a bar, and rhesus monkeys will refuse to pull a chain to get food when pulling it also results in another monkey getting shocked. (Baron-Cohen 143f) On the other hand, human empathy has in many ways surpassed that of other species, as Baron-Cohen relates:

whereas even toddlers will use their index fingers to point to things, to share attention with another person, pointing is not seen in other species. Nor do other animals convincingly engage in deception, suggesting they do not think about another animal's thoughts, even if they can respond to that animal's emotions.

And in a striking example from vervet monkeys, mother monkeys who are swimming across a flooded rice field to get to dry land might have their infant monkeys clinging to their furry underbelly. Even though each mother's head is above water, many are blissfully unaware that their infant's head is underwater, so that when the mother arrives safely at the other side of the field, tragically their baby has drowned... Clearly, whatever glimmerings of empathy we can discern (or imagine we discern) in other species, the level of empathy that humans show is qualitatively different from that seen in any other species. (144-45)

There are two aspects to empathy that must be considered: the cognitive aspect, which is the ability to think about the thoughts of others including how they are feeling, and the affective aspect, the ability to respond to the emotions of others. I will refer to these as recognition and reaction, respectively. The majority of people, when given empathy questionnaires, have a great deal of both aspects. Figure 14–3 plots the empirical results of these tests. What this indicates is that there is no simple black and white distinction between those with high levels of empathy and those with none—all are gradations. The shoulders and tails of the bell curve are particularly interesting. On the left, those with decreasing or no empathetic abilities,

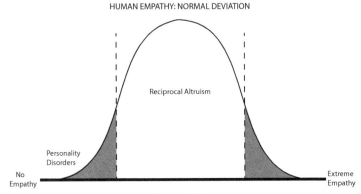

HUMAN EMPATHY: NORMAL DEVIATION

Reciprocal Altruism

Personality Disorders

No Empathy

Extreme Empathy

FIGURE 14–3

A bell curve indicating that reciprocal altruism is functioning throughout the spectrum of human behavior. This is strongly correlated with the existence of empathy. Even those with a degree of empathy impairment can still participate in reciprocal altruism, though the more severely impaired, the more likely the person will become a free-rider should the opportunity present itself. In the most extreme cases there is no attempt at reciprocity. Though not free-riders, those on the opposite extreme can also cause harm if, for example, their giving to one cause leads to neglect of another deemed more important by some.

are the free-riders. They fail to see their actions as affecting other people or, if they do see this, don't care (or both).

Figure 14–4 breaks this down according to the empathetic aspects, the circle on the left containing all those with some empathetic recognition ability, the circle on the right containing all those with some empathetic reaction ability. Their union, in the middle, contains all those who have both abilities. The normal deviation is plotted indicating that most people fit into this union section. Psychopaths are shown to have recognition ability, but no reaction ability. They recognize that others are suffering, for example, but do not care, or may even enjoy this experience. On the other side, those with Asbergers are unable to recognize the social cues and emotional states of others, but they have reaction ability; they have no desire to hurt anyone, and will attempt to help if the cues are made explicit. In this diagram, the bottom curved triangles on either side represent those who have no empathetic abilities whatsoever.

Empathy plays two roles in morality. First, a lack of empathy may explain why people become free-riders. They fail to recognize that their actions are hurting others, or they just don't care. Bernie Madoff, for example, was an investment advisor whose Ponzi scheme defrauded his clients of over $65 billion. He used the life savings of both wealthy and middle class families to buy homes, jewelry and other luxuries for his own benefit. Madoff apologized to his investors after being sentenced to 150 years in prison, which seems to indicate that he may have had some concept of empathy. Madoff undoubtedly caused much suffering, and yet his behavior pales in comparison to members of Nazi death units, whose job was to systematically murder those found to be genetically inferior under the Nazi ideology. There are, unfortunately, numerous examples of this sort of behavior.

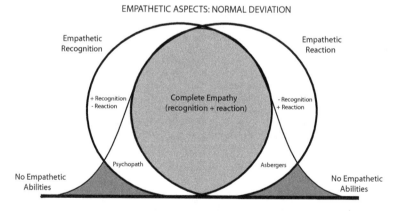

EMPATHETIC ASPECTS: NORMAL DEVIATION

FIGURE 14–4

In this Venn diagram, the left circle represents empathetic recognition, the right circle empathetic reaction. When we overlay the bell-curve plot of empathy in the general population of humans we see that personality disorders (psychopathy, borderline, narcissism, Asbergers, and so on) fall in the low ranges on either side. Psychopaths, for example, have recognition ability, but have no ability to react in acceptable ways to what they see, while Asberger patients have no ability to recognize the social cues most of us take for granted.

MORAL MONSTERS

Adolf Eichmann, responsible for the deaths of millions, once claimed himself to be "...merely a little cog in the machinery that carried out the directives and orders of the German Reich. I am neither a murderer nor a mass-murderer. I am a man of average character, with good qualities and many faults..." (Eichmann, 1999: 19) The philosopher Hannah Arendt (2006), who attended his trial, said that "Except for an extraordinary diligence in looking out for his personal advancement, he had no motives at all... He merely, to put the matter colloquially, never realized what he was doing." (287)

Moral monsters is a phrase often applied to those who commit such atrocities, implying they are somehow special, lacking what we well-adjusted humans have an overabundance of. I disagree. The Eichmanns and Hitlers are not extraordinary examples of evil personified, but rather extreme examples of an unfortunately common problem Arendt has characterized as the banality of evil, a condition brought about by a lack of critical reflection, which allows others to decide for us in areas that are most important. If this is true, then the person next to you or even you, should you let down your guard, could become an Eichmann. Is this possible? Can ordinary people do extraordinarily evil things? The evidence seems to indicate they can.

In 1963 Stanley Milgram conducted an experiment in which research subjects, ordinary people off the street, were assigned the role of teacher and told by an authority figure to deliver electrical shocks to a learner every time the learner made a wrong response to a question. The learner could not be seen by the teacher, though the teacher could hear the response of the learner to the shocks. Unknown to the teacher, the learner was not really being shocked, but was an actor trained to give the proper responses based on the strength of the electrical shock. Each time the learner missed a question the teacher would increase the voltage, from a minimal amount to a maximum of 450 volts—enough to kill. The psychiatrists involved in the test predicted that only the rare sadistic sociopath would go all the way to 450 volts. In fact, 62 percent of the teachers continued escalating the voltage of the shocks until the lethal level had been attained.

Milgram (2004), in his analysis of the experiment, claimed the teachers did not feel responsible for what they were doing because they had given up their decision making role to an authority figure. In other words, they failed to reflect adequately upon what they were doing. We often think really horrible events must be the result of moral monsters whose intentions are evil through and through, yet horrific events are often brought about by ordinary people with banal motivations who just never stop to think reflectively about what they are doing. The motives of these people would not be considered evil at all in a different context, which may account for how they can remain oblivious to the broad ramifications of their actions.

Nor are we, who live for the most part on the upper reaches of the bell curve, exempt from non-empathetic behavior. Even those with high-level empathy can put their empathy on hold if need be by means of rationalizations (sometimes as a result of some form of temporary insanity, whether rage-induced or artificially stimulated by alcohol, drugs, love, and so on). Milgram's obedience to authority experiment in which ordinary people were induced to give lethal shocks to other humans seems to indicate that a large number of us are capable, under certain conditions, of turning off our empathy.

But free-riders are not the only ones in need of explanation. Reciprocal altruism is a way of life; it entails neither the badness of humans nor their goodness. For all the stories we can tell of cruelty, violence and hate, there are likewise stories we can tell of sacrifice, giving and love. Reciprocal altruism is an egoistic altruism, but as Figure 14–3 indicates, as you approach the right tail of the bell curve something wonderful happens. There we find total strangers helping each other. Herein lies the impetus behind the money sent to tsunami, earthquake and flood victims who live tens of thousands of miles away. The cynic will argue there are selfish reasons for acting this way (ulterior motives), and he may be right, which is why I change the shades on the extreme lower shoulders of the graph. Yes, you may get a dopamine rush for sending part of your paycheck to help flood victims you will never know and who will never know from whom their help came, but that is not what reciprocal altruism says. Reciprocal altruism developed in order to combat the selfishness of organisms which hinders their ability to survive, and it is a truly magnificent mechanism. But where is the reciprocity in this kind of giving? To say that there is a selfish basis is not to explain it in terms of reciprocal altruism, nor does it negate the goodness of the act, for we may have derived the same rush from buying something for ourselves with our money. Herein lies the second role of empathy, for empathy seems to be what pushes human behavior past mere reciprocity toward a purer type of altruism.

If everyone had a fully functioning empathetic system so that we all fell somewhere on the right side of the bell curve in Figure 14–3, would the world be a better place? Possibly. Though it's also possible that the bell curve indicates an equilibrium, a mean between a world red in tooth and claw and a world in which we suffer constantly because we feel the suffering of others too much. Even without free-riders there will still be suffering, not only from natural disasters like floods and earthquakes, but also from our own fallible calculations, and to take this suffering into ourselves as our own (which the increasingly empathetic person must) would surely inhibit our ability to achieve well-being. If we could develop an empathy pill we could run an empirical study to see the actual effects of an overload of empathy, but for now we must be satisfied with our unscientific observations. But these observations are compelling. I have watched families fall apart because several members become so involved in helping others they no longer care for themselves and their family members. I have also seen people become so involved in the suffering of others that it interferes with their own ability to function in the world and actually inhibits their ability to exhibit altruistic behavior to others.

Rather than a futile wish for more empathy, my own suggestion is that we work on pushing the empathy levels we have to include more organisms. This is the gist of Peter Singer's concept of the expanding moral circle (Singer 2011, see Figure 14-5). The tendency is to wish that we could expand our empathetic abilities to new heights, while my suggestion is to expand the empathetic abilities we have to more and more people.

W.D. Hamilton argued, in his influential theory of kin selection, that treating those closest to you in altruistic ways is a evolutionarily stable strategy for passing on your genes (hence the "unselfish love" of parents is a form of reciprocal altruism). This explains why we tend to treat family members better than non-family members. We tend to treat people better (are more apt to act altruistically toward them) to the extent that we perceive (even if falsely) that they are closely related to us. Most people feel this intuitively. Given the choice of feeding your own hungry children or a stranger's, you will put the needs of your own children first (*ceterus paribus*). In the same way, we tend to extend our altruism to our neighbors before those in another country. When we look at the broad history of the human species, this circle

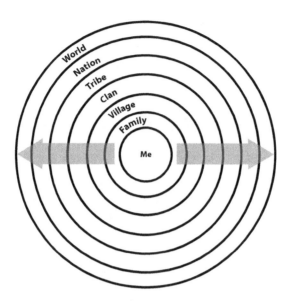

FIGURE 14–5

The expanding moral circle seems to indicate that we humans are making moral progress. This is best explained as expanding our empathetic abilities outward and is no doubt related to the modern revolution in communications which allows us to see the suffering of others in a way we never could in the past. The diagram above shows only political entities, but we might also show species. We have already expanded the moral circle to include bans on cruelty to animals based on the similarities of their neurology. Would we do the same to similarly designed aliens?

is expanding. The ancient Greeks were typical of ancient cultures in regarding those outside their own culture as barbarians, who should be treated as enemies. It is only in more recent times that we have expanded our moral circle to include other races and nations. This was the impetus, for example, behind the abolition of slavery. The notion that slavery was justified because the slaves were less than human was a last ditch effort to keep the circle's expansion at bay. Is this not due to our ability to see others as more like ourselves? And, in so seeing, treating them in a more humane fashion?

Empathy, then, seems to be the foundation of a kinder, gentler world. The rule that it dictates is a rule upheld in some form by every known culture:

ER: Treat others the way you would have them treat you.

I call this the empathy rule (ER), though it may be more familiar as the golden rule. I want to argue that this rule is constitutive of the way we (most of us) view the world. I have no proof for this rule, no anchor, other than the fact that it is inconceivable that it be false in a world in which we want to achieve well-being. Thus, this fundamental axiom is proved in terms of the adequacy conditions of our framework as a whole. We can derive all the important moral rules from this one: we don't want others to kill us: Don't murder; we don't want others to inflict unwarranted suffering on us: Don't hurt others unnecessarily; we don't want others to take what is ours: Don't steal; we don't want others to feed us falsehoods: Don't lie, and so on. I will return to a discussion of the ER and how it functions within a coherent system in §8 below, but first we must clarify the concept of morality and see how this fits within our world view.

❦

§5   WHAT IS MORALITY?

So far we have assumed that everyone knows what we mean when we speak of moral and immoral. My claim is that moral judgments (sentences, beliefs) are valuation sentences that we apply to our beliefs and the actions that result from those beliefs. We make these sorts of value judgments continually on matters both important and trivial. Valuing assumes a higher reference frame, a judging. We reflect on a belief and prioritize it within the scheme of our system of beliefs. My contention is that those beliefs or rules that we see as most important for achieving our overall goal of well-being, are what we deem our moral rules, or our morality.

The same problem that plagued the concept of the self (over-abstraction, which we have referred to as the abstraction fallacy) also plagues morality. We continue to push the level of abstraction (the reference frame) upward toward the god's-eye-view, which results in moral rules that become disconnected from the beliefs and actions within our everyday lives in the same way that the self becomes disconnected from the body. Put in terms we have used before, this upward movement is an attempt to anchor human behavior (or the rules of human behavior) in something outside of humanity, whether this be in god's commands or the laws of nature.

In what follows I want to disengage ethics from external anchors (as we have done with everything else), and use society itself as our touchstone. How will this work? First, we have to see that morality is simply a set of core values made public—an external expression of a group's core values. These are reflected in the laws of a society, though through a glass darkly. If there were a completely cohesive group of people who all held exactly the same core values, then law would equal morality. Laws work like the strands within a conceptual scheme: the more connections, the more important. Thus, if we could posit a social person that stood for all the people in a society (an impossible task as we will see), this social person would have a conceptual scheme of connected hopes, wants, beliefs, goals, desires, that would match every individual person's conceptual scheme. The values inherent in this social conceptual scheme would be the laws on the books of that society.

THE UTOPIA

Let's develop a thought experiment to explore this using a simple three-person society. Suppose the three people are identical triplets (making them genetically equal) who grew up together and have only the slightest differences between their frameworks. In fact, they are so similar that all their values are exactly the same (an obviously impossible but theoretically interesting situation). Maybe they became fed up with their current society and went into the wilderness and started their own. For whatever reason, they are isolated, they form a society of three, and they are in perfect agreement on all their values. Since one of the values they share is the notion of equality, they form a government that is democratic, agreeing (unanimously of course) that decisions should be unanimous. In a society this small there is no need to write out a set of laws or create a bureaucracy for their government, but let's suppose they do so anyway. These legal rules will include such things as: you shouldn't kill, you shouldn't steal, and so on. An exhaustive set of laws for the three members of the society will exactly reflect the values of the three individuals. The degree to which the laws match each of the three is an indication of how closely their values are shared. Even with just three members we can imagine discrepancies occurring, but we have stipulated an ideal situation in which these three share *exactly* the same values, from trivial to core. The laws, then, that they formulate for their society will be an exact duplication of their individual frameworks, from most important to least important, in a hierarchical system. Another way to put this would be to say that the social person (the state) they have created has a conceptual scheme that exactly matches each of the three individuals of which it is composed (Figure 14–6).

There may be some seemingly arbitrary laws on the books, like the speed limit set at 25 MPH, but these are stipulations that are attached to other values that are more important. The speed limit law is on the outer fringes of a web of values, and so has few attachments itself, and is thus considered rather trivial. But it is attached to other values which are more important and these are attached to others until eventually a core value is reached (this is why some might say it is immoral to exceed the speed limit). If this were not so, the law would not be on the books. There would be no reason for it. So, on this small idealized level, my claim is that an exhaustive set of laws (legal rules) would map 1:1 to the conceptual schemes of each individual within the society. Our conceptual schemes have core values that we have defined as those strands having the most interconnections, but there is no specific number of connections that must occur in order to be considered core, that

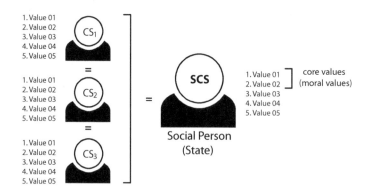

FIGURE 14–6

Each of the three members in our utopia have exactly the same value set (1-5), prioritized in the exact same way, that is, their conceptual schemes are identical. Their newly created state will mirror this with its laws (1-5). The core values, those given the highest priority, constitute the morality of both the individuals and the state. This is a utopia since there is no alienation whatsoever between the individual citizens and the state.

is, the notion of a core value is a pebble-rock concept. We have a somewhat fuzzy set of core values that grades off into non-core values. This hierarchy will also be reflected in the laws of our small society, and the core values of both the individuals and the society will be considered moral values.

Let's call the publicly agreed conceptual scheme, which is made manifest in the rules of the state, the social conceptual scheme (SCS), in order to distinguish it from the group of individual conceptual schemes (ICS) of which it is composed. All nations (states, communities) larger that the smallest hunter-gatherer society are social constructs, that is, imagined entities, since members never know or even see all the members of a community. This SCS will include more than merely legal rules, but also morays and customs which dictate actions in a non-legal way. To simplify, we will consider all of these as part of the SCS. My claim is that, in this artificially composed situation, SCS = ICS. This idealized situation is the strongest, most coherent, political entity possible, and as such is a situation towards which all modern nations strive, for if all individuals are in complete agreement there is no dissension. All individuals will agree on all values and thus on all decisions made for the body politic. This kind of cohesion can never be achieved in a modern state, though it is a goal toward which all states strive, and which is met only in various imperfect ways. It is stronger to the extent that individual members of the community feel they have a say in the workings of the government, weaker when they do not. We will call (with Marx and others) the separation of the SCS from the ICS alienation. An individual is thus alienated from the state to the extent that his ICS differs from the SCS.

ALIENATION

Now let's grow our idealized society. Enter an outsider, who wishes to join. She is allowed to join on the condition that she agrees to abide by the laws of the land, which she does. She thus becomes a citizen, but since she was not among the original group, she has a slightly different ICS, which means there is now a slight mismatch between the SCS and the ICS. It won't be a large discrepancy, for otherwise the person would not join the group, or would not stay, but it might be enough to cause some disagreement.[2] For instance, when a new law is proposed and voted on, it might not now get unanimous approval, so the legislative procedures will have to be changed, maybe to a majority rule. The three original members will be concerned to protect their original values against intruders, and thus will cast a negative light on immigrants who might dilute their value pool. Obviously, the more people who join the society the less the SCS will match the ICS. To the extent that an ICS differs from the SCS, an individual is alienated from society, that is, she will not feel she completely belongs. This is illustrated in Figure 14–7, where the newcomer, CS4, holds a slightly different set of values than the original members. Since the majority sets the laws, the newcomer's values will not be reflected in the SCS, causing her to be somewhat alienated.

---

[2] Unless of course the person is forced to conform. This is what happened in the United States, for example, with the indigenous populations who occupied the land before the Western Europeans arrived, and also with slaves who were brought in from outside.

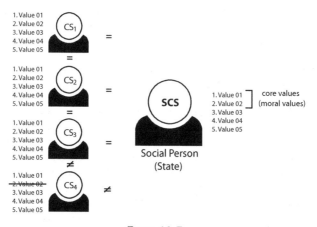

FIGURE 14–7
The new citizen has a slightly different conceptual scheme than the previous three, and because of this there is a mismatch between this person's ICS and the SCS. Since one of these differences concerns a core value, the morality of the state will not match the morality of the new citizen.

As more people join and gain a majority they can begin to change the laws in ways that vary from that of the founders.[3] The SCS becomes an amorphous mix of values, and its solidarity, as an SCS that represents all individuals equally, becomes more and more imaginary. There will still be a core set of values that most members of the society will adhere to, but there will be many others that members will disagree with. For instance, the core group may have originally had a law on the books banning abortion, but in time, with new members added, this law is amended to allow abortions in the first trimester. Abortion is still felt to be universally wrong (as a core value) by some, even though it is no longer banned universally. This is how we come to have a distinction between what is legal and what is moral, for those who made the law originally will claim that the amendment allowing abortion in the first trimester is immoral. But, at least in a democracy, the set of laws on the books will most accurately reflect the ICSs of merely a majority of members, and will perfectly

---

[3] There is often great resistance to changes in the SCS from those who first founded it. The founders will see the changes as weakening the fabric of "their" society, since they are becoming alienated from the SCS. Nationalism, in its explicit forms, is a means to combat this by maintaining a sense of national unity. Note, though, that there may already be unity, but not the type of unity the founders want. The United States, for example, is famously called a melting pot because it incorporates many different cultures under its own umbrella, and its cohesion remains strong regardless. The founders, however, might see the public values shifting away from their own and thus institute movements to curtail the shift. This accounts for anti-immigration movements, which in their most extreme form, can become xenophobic. All individuals who have a stake in their nation fear dissension to some extent. Dissension is to a political system what cognitive dissonance is to individuals. Before the modern era, those who felt so threatened either moved and started a new community (Puritans, Quakers), or stayed and banded together with a singular purpose to maintain their purity (Jews). Anti-semitic feelings have often arisen as anger against those who refuse to accept the national values of a state or hold their own to be superior.

ROUSSEAU AND THE GENERAL WILL

Rousseau, in his *Social Contract*, distinguished between the general will and the will-of-all in a manner similar to our distinction between the ICSs and the SCS. His concept of the general will, though, was an idealized projection of a different sort. The general will, for Rousseau, is the actual best course of action for a nation, whether we know what that course of action is or not. This is opposed to the will of all, which was what the people as a whole think is the best course of action. This is an interesting distinction, which leads to its own kind of alienation. We all agree this happens continually—that what we think is best for the nation often turns out not to be the best course of action.

Rousseau thought that an enlightened legislator was a better judge of the general will than the ignorant, unscrubbed masses, so his problem was how to bring the general will (as seen by the enlightened legislator) in line with the will of all. His answer: deceive the masses. The enlightened legislator should convince them that he has had a vision from god, who told him the correct course of action for the ship of state. The people will then believe him and the will of all will conform to the general will, which makes for a stable state.

In my opinion, this is where Kant got his idea of the as-if movement of the categorical imperative in which an ideal is posited as a necessary fiction in order to achieve a higher state. In Rousseau's case the enlightened legislator is like the Wizard of Oz, who lies to his subjects, but only in order to bring about what is best for them. Marx also reflects this attitude (Lenin seems to have missed this point)—the thousand year reign of the proletariat was merely a goal to push the workers to unite and overthrow their masters. It was not an end in itself.

reflect the ICSs of none. This is illustrated in Figure 14–8, in which we can let each individual on the left represent groups of individuals, none of which have the same values as those held by other groups.

SUMMARY

We have used this scenario of an original situation, beginning with three members and then growing into a large society, to make several points:

(1) SCS = ICS is always an idealization. All nations (and all communities within the nation and groups within these communities) are imaginary constructs which deviate to varying degrees (are alienated) from the ICSs which compose them (whether it's your local bike club, a national service club, or the Republican Party). In other words, the legal rules and social morays of a nation as a whole are manifestations of the SCS, but will never match any one ICS.

(2) The rules formulated by an individual to protect his core values (which are themselves core values) are referred to as moral rules. These shade into non-moral rules in a pebble-rock fashion. This is also true within the SCS, where the most important laws will, for the most part, also be considered moral rules.

(3) This distinction between the individual ICSs and the SCS gives rise to a two-tiered concept of morality. The public morality is that manifested

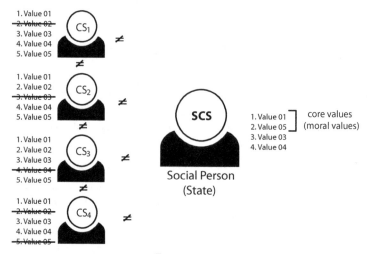

FIGURE 14–8

A more realistic portrayal of the relationship between individuals and the state to which they belong shows each individual (or we can imagine each figure on the left representing a group of individuals) with a different set of values so that the SCS does not perfectly reflect anyone's ICS. So also, since the core values differ, what are considered moral rules by some will not be deemed moral by others. The differences between ICSs and the SCS of a nation explain why the legal is out of synch with the moral.

by the SCS in the laws of the land, while the private morality is that manifested by each ICS. This distinction is often overlooked.

(4) Private moralities always trump public moralities. This is because a public morality is more ephemeral (less real) to an individual than their own private morality. Public morality is an abstraction like 'dog' or 'cat,' which cannot be applied specifically to any one dog or cat, yet covers them all.

(5) Public morality does not really exist (hence its ephemeral nature). It is reified as a useful fiction based upon the SCS which manifests itself in the laws of the land. Private moralities, on the other hand, are very real. They just are the action-rules related to the core values of each person's ICS.

Those who believe that a god is the author of our moral rules move their own private morality to a reference frame above the social—to the god's-eye-view. In this case god's rules are an ICS (like a dictator's) imposed top-down upon us humans. Since each individual's beliefs concerning god and his rules are different (again divided into groups based on similarities), the individual's private morality (reified into god's morality) trumps the public morality. This because a person does not join or remain within a group if the group's point of view goes against their own to any significant degree. If you belong to a fundamentalist church, you do so because

---

AUTOCRACY

An autocracy is any form of government in which the few impose their will upon the many. The most exclusive form is the dictator, whose ICS, and his alone, constitutes the SCS. Such a government, in which rules are imposed on a community from the top down based on the ICS of the leader (or small group of leaders) are the least cohesive (unless the dictator is a benevolent despot, which means he strives to match his ICS, and thus the SCS to the ICSs of the many), for he is trying to impose his own hopes, wants, goals, and desires upon the many. Democracies tend to be more cohesive for this same reason, at least until the members of the society begin to feel they have no say in the government. This alienation leads to a weakening of the cohesiveness of the nation.

All nations, whether dictatorships or democracies, strive to inculcate this kind of cohesion by means of various forms of indoctrination. Democracies tend to be more subtle, making education mandatory and including civics and history classes within the educational requirements. Giving the members of a nation a shared knowledge of culture and history increases their cohesion. Dictatorships, on the other hand, might opt for more explicit methods such as propaganda or re-education classes. If a person is forced to adhere to a set of values that he would not otherwise hold, he will give them up at the first viable opportunity. For this reason, to the extent that an individual is alienated from the SCS to that same extent will the nation be weakened.

---

your individual core beliefs match the core beliefs of the group to a greater or lesser extent. As you move toward the lesser extent you will be tempted to move to a different community of believers.

Some individuals are much less specific in their rule-set than others. An unreflective individual, for example, might only know that he wants to be comfortable and that a certain community provides this comfort. Such an individual will be more susceptible to the influence of the community (or cult). That is, since they are only interested in the most abstract sense of well-being they will allow themselves to be easily led. Those who are more reflective, on the other hand, will have more specific ideas on what their values are and will not be so easily led. These more reflective people are those who will move to a different group if there is a small, but important, doctrinal shift in ideas away from what they think is important.

A nation is an entity like a cell or a human; an entity that must maintain a boundary against the world outside itself. Without constant care it will disintegrate. This constant care is the demand of coherence. When coherence fails, a society begins its slide toward decay and death.[4] A nation must handle threats to its coherence whether these be external (invasion by a foreign nation) or internal (the national debt). These are anomalies, and can be handled using adequate means (funding a standing army, instituting fiscal limits on spending) or inadequate self-deceptive means (failing to take action by claiming the threat is not real or that the enemy has been placated). We modern humans are a fractious race, and when we appreciate this point we will begin to see the ultimate fragility of a nation. There is an unseen and undetermined tipping point at which governments can no longer sustain themselves as a viable entity.

---

[4] Edward Gibbon's *Decline and Fall of the Roman Empire* is a masterful picture of this process of disintegration at work.

§6 MORAL THEORIES

The subjectivist has always been the whipping boy of morality. The traditional question plaguing morality has been: how do we anchor our moral rules so they do not depend only upon individuals? The subjectivist claims there is no such anchor; morality is based upon the individual or a group of individuals (a culture). To this the anchor advocate (the objectivist) responds: we cannot, then, call a serial killer immoral because he chose his own path as one that leads to his personal well-being. What we need, say the god's-eye-view moralists, is some set of rules that transcends individual desires so that we can deem some people (who perform heinous actions) immoral in an absolute sense. Attempts to set up these transcendent rules have divided moral theory into two large camps, the utilitarians and the formalists. We will look at each of these briefly. My point will be that both are axiomatic systems that profess to anchor their axioms on solid rock, but in fact have no anchor at all other than their own subjectivity.

CONSEQUENTIALISM / UTILITARIANISM

Consequentialism attempts to anchor the rightness or wrongness of our actions in their consequences. If the sum total of good in the consequences of an action outweighs the bad, then the action is the right thing to do, otherwise it is wrong. I think this has to be correct on some level. I have ascribed to it myself in claiming that our goals imbue the means to reach them with meaning. In this sense we ultimately judge all our actions in terms of well-being. We judge our actions in terms of how successful they are in bringing about the consequences we intend. The obvious problem with such a system is that it shifts all importance to the goals of our actions. We do not have foresight, however, which means that unintended consequences often occur that can ruin our good intentions.

Consequentialist calculations give rise to the question: Whose good should we strive to maximize. Utilitarianism answers this question with "the greatest number." Hence the utilitarian claims that an act is right if and only if it promotes the greatest amount of good for the greatest number of people. The benefit of the utilitarian approach is that it takes empathy seriously, but from an empirical standpoint it gets things backwards. Utilitarians claim that our life-goal should be to bring about the greatest good for the greatest number, but note the "should be" in that claim. This is the utilitarian's illicit jump to a higher reference frame. To rephrase this correctly, without making an unjustified pronouncement about what everyone should do, they would have to say instead "our life-goal as humans is to bring about the greatest good for the greatest number," but as an empirical pronouncement this is just false. We do not, as humans, strive to bring about the greatest good for the greatest number. The rightness of what Bentham says about happiness (see chapter 1) is sullied by this switch. We humans naturally strive for our own well-being. Our altruism is only of the reciprocal sort. Our empathy might extend this, but only so far as we judge it feasible in light of our own well-being. Why would I do anything, for myself or for others, if I knew it would detract from the quality of my own life, when all is said and done? People do make hard choices in which they choose to suffer rather than see someone else suffer, say, for their children. We might argue that even these choices are made because a person is more comfortable suffering herself than seeing her children suffer. But we don't have to go there. We can admit that maybe at times people make absolutely altruistic decisions, but this is the exception rather than the rule. It does not detract from the fact that, empirically, we humans act in terms of our own well-being.

FORMALISM

Formalist moral theories are non-consequentialist. They generally look to the source of the rules as a means of anchoring them, a source which often transcends humanity. God functions as one such guarantor. But, as we have seen, the problem with gods is that they must speak through humans, and how do we know these humans are really in touch with the being they claim to be speaking for? After all, if you wanted to control people's actions it would be convenient for a controller to tell people that there is an invisible power of some sort which only the controller could see, and whose rules, as proscribed by the controller, everyone must follow (this was the strategy of Rousseau's enlightened legislator). This is a large problem, especially if the god tells different people different things, or speaks so ambiguously as to lead to multiple, contradictory interpretations, or demands that his people commit atrocities in his name (which actions would then no longer be deemed atrocities). The size of this problem is indicated by the number of different sects within any religion—there are tens of thousands of Christian sects alone—all of which claim to have a better grasp on the Christian god's words than any other group. This is why I have made the claim that private morality trumps public morality, since you will ultimately be the one who decides the moral rules you will adhere to; you will be the one who decides who speaks truly concerning your god's moral pronouncements.

Another potential non-human guarantor (anchor) for moral rules is natural law. This is a time-honored tradition, to invoke natural law when you don't know where else to go. This is the idea that the rules of morality are somehow etched in the fabric of the universe, and we connect to these laws by means of our intuition or our reason. Jefferson invoked natural law when he claimed certain truths to be self-evident in his justification that all men are created equal. All talk of objective rules of any sort, whether founded on gods or on nature, will ultimately reduce to a claim that I just know my rules are correct—to faith in my own ability to distinguish correct from incorrect rules. This was the same problem that faced the correct description theory of truth, and all moral theories that depend on objective rules fall prey to it.

We see, then, that the formalist error is one with the utilitarian error: both attempt to install a reference frame beyond human experience, one that judges human experience rather than using it as a basis. These moves can only be justified by dogmatic assertion, and all dogmatic assertions are ultimately justified only in terms of the claim "I just know."

§7 THE FAILURE OF THE MORAL REPROACH

Let's suppose I decide that I should cheat on my next exam. I might do this because I am lazy or unprepared or both, but the justification behind these is that I should cheat because it will further my life-goals as I see them. Suppose also that I tell you of my plan to cheat on the exam and you respond: "Oh no. You can't. That would be immoral." There are two responses the relativist might make to this:

(1) No it's not. I determine what's moral for me.

This isn't enough for most people. They want the cheater or the murderer to be wrong from more than just his own point of view; they want him to be immoral from all points of view, including his own. This gives rise to the second relativist response:

(2) So what?

It is this latter response that will interest us in this section.

To be swayed by someone's claim that an action I want to perform is immoral I would have to already hold the value of the person condemning me (namely, that something higher determines my morality) as a core value and give it priority over the action I want to perform. But usually I will already have performed this calculation. I know you have a rule against cheating, and I may even often hold this to be a core value of my own, but by deciding to cheat on my next exam I have given priority to another value, namely, my passing the exam. So maybe your moral reproach is a reminder to me that cheating usually goes against one of my often held core values, but it's not like I didn't know this. In this case, then, your reproach has no force.

Maybe, though, your moral reproach was a warning that I will be punished for my action. This punishment might be threatened from different levels:

(a) by a higher reference frame (god or karma)

(b) by the school (a higher authority)

(c) by a soiled reputation (others)

(d) by guilt (myself)

Each of these depends upon a set of rules: (a) depends on a set of rules transcending humanity; (b) on a set within the school I am attending; (c) on a set within a societal group I am interested in maintaining relations with; and (d) on a set I myself accept and wish to adhere to. (a) and (d) are similar in that my act of breaking the rule is completely transparent to both god (or whatever constitutes the higher reference frame) and myself. There is no chance of hiding the fact that I committed the act, as I can attempt to do with (b) and (c). This same fact negates the force of (b) and (c), for if these are important values for me, then I will only act if I think I can keep knowledge of my cheating from them, and since I have already decided to cheat I obviously think I can. I did tell you I was going to cheat, though, which may mean your opinion doesn't really matter that much to me or that I trust you will not rat me out or that it will not affect your view of me. Or maybe my response will be, "Oh, right. It would be immoral. Thanks for reminding me. I won't cheat after all." After which I cheat without your knowledge. (d) falls in the same manner, for as we have seen, if I have decided to cheat, then I value passing the exam over the rule that I shouldn't cheat. This leaves (a). Maybe your admonition is that my cheating will come back to haunt me later, that is, that what goes around will come around in some mystically fatalistic fashion, but I would already have taken this into account as well and deemed it not worth worrying about (maybe by means of rationalization). The point here is that a moral reproach has no special force other than a reminder that bad consequences might follow from breaking the rule in question.

This is the truth behind the consequentialist position, and to the extent that a formalist agrees, they, too, are, at base, consequentialists.

Rule valuation, then, is all important within morality. In order to have force a rule must have some relevance to one of your core values. Both formalists and utilitarians claim there are some values which all humans "should" consider core, but this claim only has force if we make *it* a core value, that is, if we already adhere to their system. As much as some people would like to dictate their rules to us and have us obey them, we only need do so if we value their overall project.

§8   APPEAL TO COHERENCE

Goals give meaning to the processes by which we attain them. This process is one of valuation. In other words, when we have a goal or a project we want to reach, certain beliefs and actions of ours become valuable as a means to fulfilling that goal or project. The more important the project, the more valuable the means. This gives us the basis for understanding morality. Our most important project in life is our quest to achieve well-being, which presupposes not only our continued existence, but also an existence not marred by horrible suffering. As we have seen, these needs are reflected in the empathy rule:

ER: Treat others the way you would have them treat you,

From this rule we can derive many of the rules that help us in our life-quest. These rules are our most important rules because they protect our most important life-goals, our core beliefs. These are the rules we call moral rules. They are not rules that I alone value, for despite our many differences we humans are similar in many ways. We have a similar anatomy with similar brain functions, and so on. We are all capable of being killed or of suffering terrible pain. This means there are values most humans accept as core no matter their culture, no matter their race. Our desire to live (when we could easily end it all with a bare bodkin) is a valuation of life, but, as we pointed out in chapter 1, merely staying alive isn't enough; we humans want to thrive. We want well-being, a life with pleasure and meaning. This is the core value behind most, if not all, of our beliefs and subsequent actions based upon them. Figure 14–9 illustrates this human solidarity with a schematic representation of an individual conceptual scheme. We all, barring those damaged either genetically or environmentally, share Level 1 beliefs, and many of us share most Level 2 beliefs as well. These levels contain the (constitutive) beliefs that are necessary conditions for achieving our life-goal of well-being. Level 1 beliefs are protected by ER, which forms the core of our morality, in the sense that all other moral rules must (at some point) relate to this rule, which in turn relates to our life-goal. As you move to the right, the levels become less commonly held and less important.

Level 1 and most of Level 2 beliefs are covered by moral rules, but somewhere between two and three we fade into non-moral rules, morays, customs, and so on, and further down the levels the rules become less and less important to the extent that they are less crucial to our achieving well-being. Still, every rule will eventually be traced back to well-being (which is its justification). For example, we might, in our culture, have a rule of etiquette stating that it is impolite to belch loudly in public

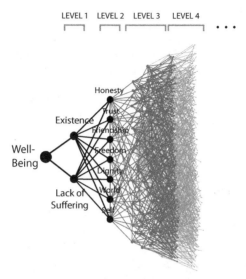

FIGURE 14–9

A view of a human conceptual scheme organized in terms of value dependence. The most important goal is well-being; level 1 goals (values) are the necessary conditions for achieving this, and so are considered essential (most valuable). Level 2 goals are those necessary to attain level 1 goals, level 3 goals are those necessary to attain level 2 goals, and so on. The rules we formulate to insure we achieve the goals we consider most important we label as moral rules, these rules would normally include level 1 goals and many level 2 goals.

during dinner. This may seem like a rather arbitrary rule, for in other cultures or subcultures it may be perfectly acceptable, yet for all its triviality it is nonetheless connected to well-being. If you are in a culture where the no-belching rule is in place, you will be subtly (or not so subtly) punished if you break it. You will lose face in the eyes of a group whose values are similar to your own, which will impinge on your comfort level, which will affect your well-being. The farther we move to the right in Figure 14–9, the less important the beliefs, so that at some point we won't even bother having rules to cover the beliefs. These beliefs exist on the outer fringes of our conceptual scheme and can be given up with little or no damage to our core values.

There are core beliefs we hold that I have called constitutive. These include not only our goal of well-being, but also our belief that there is an external world, that theorizing via adequacy conditions is a means of attaining truth, that we have a self, and that self is free to choose different life-paths. These are beliefs we cannot prove with absolute certainty, yet giving them up is inconceivable, for they constitute the very ground upon which we talk about the world and live our lives. We use these beliefs as our foundation; they are fundamental axioms in our framework, to which the rest of our beliefs must conform. Their justification lies in the fact that presupposing them allows us to live the kind of life we want to live. Thus are we justified in maintaining these beliefs, not because a god proclaimed them good or because they are etched in the fabric of the universe, but because, by doing so, we are better able to reach the goals we want in life—in particular we are better able to achieve well-being. We don't need to ground our beliefs on some rock-solid entity outside of ourselves that we "just know" is solid and immovable. This is a parlor trick that comes back to bite—our attempts to transcend our humanity are always ultimately grounded in our humanity. We must build and rebuild our lives while living them, like Neurath's boat which must be rebuilt while at sea. Some planks cannot be removed without sinking the entire project. These (constitutive) planks warrant protection with rules we call moral.

Our morality, then, is composed of these core beliefs and those most closely related, and that's all morality is. As humans, most of us (remember the bell curve) have a working empathetic sense that makes in inconceivable for us not to see all other humans as sharing our most basic goal of well-being, that is, as accepting ER. Those who do not hold this view are a threat to us and our well-being. We call them immoral, but this does not mean they have transgressed a universal law or will burn in hell. It means only that I think they have a faulty means of achieving their goals in life and that faulty view endangers my own as well.

We are inextricably bound to others, some by choice, others by circumstances beyond our control. This is what we mean when we say that humans are social animals, and this is also the truth behind the utilitarian admiration of the great-est good for the greatest number principle. It behooves us, as social animals, to take this principle into account, not because we "should" on some higher level, but because taking it into account is necessary in order to insure our own well-being. This is the force of ER. As our futures become more and more attached to the lives of others throughout the world, we must expand our moral circle accordingly. Figure 14–10 illustrates our prior point that at some level all humans share core values. As you expand outward to include more individuals the number of shared values decreases, but, as humans, we will always share a core set.

Let's return to the serial killer problem. Can we, as moral relativists, make any claims against those who lack what we would call a basic moral point of view? To answer this, consider an analogy with our belief in an external world. Is there an external world? Of course there is. I could not function (I could not attain well-being, since none of my other theories would work) if I didn't presuppose there was an external world. Is what a serial killer does immoral? Of course it is. I could not function if I didn't presuppose his actions immoral. Does he disagree? He might. If so, who is right? Here is the crux of the matter. In a relative world, a world in which coherence rules, there is no absolute answer to this question. The very question assumes there is a god's-eye-view from which to judge, but we have already denied that there is such. All I can say is that from my point of view, and from the point of view of the vast majority of humans, he is immoral. My claim is that my system in which he is immoral, is a system that works better to produce well-being. He might claim the same, of course, but his is a standalone theory. He can certainly maintain it, but, from my point of view it will never provide the kind of well-being I, and those I am connected to, desire.

This is analogous to the person who maintains that the earth is flat. When push comes to shove, there may be no way that I can convince him that he is wrong. I might tell him to look at the horizon and see ships appear and disappear in the distance, but he merely replies that it is an illusion like seeing water on a hot high-way. I reference the pictures of the earth taken from space, but he replies that the space race is a conspiracy perpetrated by those in power to use our tax dollars for

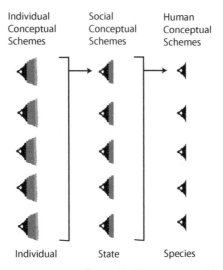

Individual   Social   Human
Conceptual   Conceptual   Conceptual
Schemes   Schemes   Schemes

Individual   State   Species

FIGURE 14–10

Individual conceptual schemes within a culture will share a core set of values. As we widen the group to include more individuals in different cultures or different states, the number of shared values will decrease. If we widen the group to include all humans, the only shared values will be those core (constitutive) values used to insure our ability to attain well-being. Since these are our core, our moral, values, we can say that humans, at base, share a common morality. How these core moral values are interpreted from culture to culture will vary widely.

nefarious purposes, and so on. In the end, I let him be. I believe my theory will, ultimately, allow me to get around in the world better than his, but I may never be able to prove it to him. My claim is that my theory is a better theory because it adheres to the adequacy conditions which means it is not only consistent with my other beliefs, but is well-integrated with other publicly accepted and well-verified theories. I do not have to rely on *ad hoc* explanations for my beliefs as he does. All of this means that I am justified in thinking my theory will cohere better as an explanation of the world.

So also with the serial killer. His is also a standalone theory, for he lacks connections that would be essential for most people in finding well-being. Thus I claim his theory is inadequate, and since it has to do with core values, this makes it an inadequate moral theory, which translates to immoral. And here arises an important disanalogy between the flat earth theory and the serial killer's theory. The flat earth theorist does not endanger me or others in any significant sense (this is why the flat earth theory, though inadequate, is not immoral). But the serial killer does. His theory is immoral, and, since this endangers my own project as well as that of others around me (which is what we mean by 'immoral'), he must be made to stop doing whatever he is doing that endangers the well-being of the rest of us. He is a free-rider endangering the system that sustains us. Stopping him is no different than plugging a leak in a sinking boat. We may stop him in as humane a way as possible, but he must be stopped.

Let's take just a moment and compare ER to the Categorical Imperative (CI) we discussed in chapter 10. Kant believed that if everyone used the CI they would arrive at the same set of rules, since all humans are rational in the same way (according to Kant). Our ER is more elegant, for it is derived empirically, from watching humans and determining what they need in order to attain well-being. We don't make the assumption that all humans are rational in the same way. All we need is to assume that certain things are essential for all humans in order to reach the goal of well-being: existence, freedom from suffering, and so on. As means to our most important goals, these will form our core values, our moral rules.

§9   CHAPTER SUMMARY

I have now briefly sketched a moral theory based on our coherence approach. The result is that we see the moral realm is not a special realm that applies, by virtue of a god's-eye-view, to all humans. We don't have to worry about whether we have interpreted a book of rules or whether we will be punished in hell, but this doesn't mean that everything is crystal clear and that we can break any rule we please without consequences.

Everyone has a different ICS, and even if we assume a core set of constitutive values, how these are applied is a different matter. Take our abortion example from earlier in the chapter. The basis of this rule is the Don't murder! rule derived from ER. Yes, everyone agrees that we should not murder, but murder means that unjustified killing is frowned upon. Unjustified. And therein lies the rub, for what constitutes justified? Here we begin splitting into sects faster than Protestants after the Reformation. Is abortion moral? What about killing in war? Should drunk drivers who kill people be treated like serial killers? Can I help kill Grandpa if he is suffering and begs me to help him end his life? We are also faced with the sorts of problems that utilitarians face: when do the rights of individuals override the rights of the many? Should we feed Christians to the lions if it brings about a greater overall good (and thus contributes to my achieving personal well-being)? All these are valid questions. How do we go about solving them?

The way we solve these moral problems is the way we solve all our problems— we theorize. We put together a theory that adheres to our adequacy conditions. When attempting to solve anomalies, the differences in moral statements are handled in the same way as differences concerning whether or not the earth is flat. We try to come up with a position that coheres with the rest of our world-view.

We cannot blithely break rules we don't agree with; at least not without consequences. The SCS which is manifested in the laws of a society guarantees we cannot. The fact that you may not agree with a particular law on the books doesn't matter, even if it is a moral disagreement. You may feel you cannot obey the law on moral grounds, that it is an immoral law, but as long as it remains on the books as a law within the society it is a reflection of the ICSs of the people making up the nation and you will be punished for disobedience. (Even in a dictatorship, the laws are a reflection of the dictator's ICS which is, by a combination of fiat and force, standing in for the SCS.) If your well-being is threatened by adherence to what you consider immoral laws, then you are obligated to break them. Consequences will follow, but we are never guaranteed an easy life.

15. Extending Coherence

In my beginning is my end.

— T.S. Eliot, East Coker

SYNOPSIS

(1) This chapter is an attempt to tie the concept of a coherence system to an expanded concept of homeostasis. This will bring together several different strands of our argument. (2) Organisms that are alive are one example of a coherent system. What this means and how it is related to other systems. (3) Life is one of the many thresholds crossed in an exploration of the development of the human condition. (4) Feedback loops are an important ingredient within a complex system. (5) A very brief discussion of entropy, which not only breaks down systems and establishes the arrow of time, but is also the most basic state of coherence. Entropy is a tendency toward equilibrium achieved by dissolving all other equilibriums. (6) A discussion of teleological systems—purposeful systems which counteract the entropic tendency toward decay. We humans act with purpose and, in turn, tend to impose this purposive structure on everything else. Teleology imbues a system with meaning. (7) How systems give us a point of view and why this is important. (8) The teleological nature of our actions helps explain why rewards and punishments work the way they do. An expansion of these concepts. (9) We can now return to homeostasis and equilibrium, relating these to coherence and how we theorize. (10) Chapter Summary.

CHAPTER OBJECTIVES

• expand the concept of coherence, showing it to be ubiquitous
• relate coherence to our search for meaning

§1 WHY COHERENCE?

tthe very core of our theorizing lies our set of adequacy conditions, which, when taken together we have called coherence. Coherence, in turn, makes sense only in reference to a system that maintains itself in various ways. But the discerning reader may have already asked, "Why coherence?" Why should this concept have some special value? We have already outlined an answer to this question by saying that our adequacy conditions are the axiomatic starting points from which we deduce our world view—a view that works well for us on a very practical level, which in turn justifies the selection of our axioms. Thus, coherence is sufficient for what we want to accomplish, but is it necessary? Why these particular adequacy conditions rather than some other arbitrary set? Or are they arbitrary? Could they be different? Could we change our entire view of the world if we could but construct a non-coherent view of theorizing?

In this chapter I want to accomplish two things. First, I will sketch the idea that coherence is not arbitrary; that its basis lies in the fundamental laws of nature. This is not an attempt to anchor coherence outside of itself; such a project would be futile. We can only discuss nature in terms of a theory which we demand to be coherent. Rather, it is to add another plank to the self-justifying platform we are already using. Second, I want to expand the concept of coherence in order to show how we, as complex systems, are related in various ways to other systems throughout our world. I will do this by relating it to the concepts of equilibrium and homeostasis, which will hopefully allow us to see interconnections within the complexities of nested systems.

Coherence presupposes that things hang together in various ways; it brings to mind a force of sorts, an attractor, turning a disparate number of objects into a system. This grouping can be natural (as with the gravitational force) or artificial (as with the concept of a set in mathematics). But whether natural or artificial, if a part of a group doesn't fit well within the group, the tendency is toward exclusion. Attraction itself, though, doesn't fully capture the scope of coherence, which includes the idea of an equilibrium. However we ultimately characterize them, these concepts are at the very heart of our cognitive processing, incorporating the ideas of theorizing, consistency, anomalies, reference frames, points of view, and conceptual schemes.

§2   LIFE (AGAIN)

Let's begin our discussion of coherence by extending it to something we are intimately familiar with: life. We have described life as a constant battle to maintain integrity against a hostile environment. Before self-conscious (reflective) creatures arose, this battle was not personal. Nature is subtle, but not nefarious. The lion doesn't eat the gazelle because it has a grudge against gazelles; it eats the gazelle because it's hungry. The lion maintains its integrity at the expense of the gazelle. Unpacking this concept of integrity, as we have seen, leads to the concept of homeostasis.

Each human being is a discrete system, which is composed of smaller discrete systems (cells) which are composed of smaller discrete systems (nuclei, organelles, mitochondria), which are composed of smaller discrete systems (molecules, atoms, subatomic particles), and so on. Each system is nested within another like Russian babushka dolls. We don't know how far down this nesting goes. If we go the other way, when humans group together they form systems (societies), these groups of humans must interact not only with each other, but with their environment and this gives us more systems (ecosystems), while the sum of all ecosystems is still another system (the earth), which is part of a solar system, which is part of a galaxy, and so on. We don't know how far up this nesting goes, continuing through multiverses and maybe multi-multiverses. If we put these nested systems on a continuum (as in Figure 15–1) we will have the usual problem of making hard distinctions between them. We will also notice that what we call life constitutes a very small window within this continuum. The extremes of the continuum are of interest, for on the hypothetical extreme left we would have the elusive elementary particle, the basic stuff of life, of which everything else is composed. From ancient times humans have claimed to have discovered this basic substance,

> **HOMEOSTASIS**
>
> The ability or tendency of an organism, cell, person or social group to maintain internal equilibrium by constantly adjusting its systemic processes.

SYSTEM-SIZE CONTINUUM
(# of nestings)

LESS ← ? Life ? → MORE

| Quarks | Molecules | | Organisms | | Galaxies | Universes |
| Atoms | | | Cells | Ecosystems | | Clusters |

FIGURE 15–1

A continuum depicting a number of nestings. On the extremes all we can say is less and more because we have no idea how small or how large systems get. On the (hypothetical) far left would be the elementary particles; on the (hypothetical) far right, the all-encompassing god's-eye-view.

whether it be water (Thales), air (Anaximenes), fire (Heraclitus), or atoms in the void (Democritus), but something more basic always lurks beneath. On the hypothetical extreme right we would have the highest possible reference frame, the god's-eye-view, the system incorporating all systems. Life is in the middle of this continuum only because we are the one's making the continuum. We have no idea of the true scales of the extremes.

Life is, at the minimum, the ability to maintain individual integrity against the wiles of the rest of the world; to have a delineating boundary which separates the organism from others. Maintenance of the boundary demands a delicate interplay of forces, an equilibrium we have identified as homeostasis. To qualify as living an organism must have the ability to input nutrients to a power plant which generates the energy used to maintain its discreteness—its boundary conditions, its force-field against the world. That is all. This is what distinguishes a cell from a solar system. The latter has an equilibrium imposed upon it from without (gravity, or the topology of space-time), while cells take energy and use it to maintain themselves.[1] Even if such an organism never developed the ability to replicate, it would be alive. On the simplest level this may have been a clumping together of molecules whose felicitous conjunction suddenly and wonderfully produced a new form of energy via solar power.

Inevitably there were many failed attempts to come to life, not just on this planet but on other worlds in other galaxies. We usually don't get to see evolutionary failures;[2] they don't exist, because they are naturally selected out before they can leave a trace. The success story is the organism that was sufficiently adapted to its environment so that it lived long enough to make copies of itself. Originally this would have been something like an archaebacteria—a simple version of a prokary-ote. I picture the original primal soup scenario as one in which life was continually occurring. We often think of life beginning with a random lightning bolt striking a fecund matter mass at just the right instant, giving life to one creature who then spawned all other life forms. More likely, though, there was a window of opportunity in which organisms continually came to life, sputtered, and then expired, like a two-stroke engine trying to catch and continue. An analogy is crystal formation: crystals can form spontaneously in a very specific environment, giving rise to beautiful

---

[1] The orderliness of a solar system occurs when the individual constituents follow the space-time paths of least resistance and, once in orbit will continue until the space-time paths change, which they will as the mass of the star around which they orbit eventually changes. This system is not taking in energy and using it to maintain its integrity. It is slowly using up its original store of energy, and thus is in a constant state of unending decay according to the law of entropy. Life, on the other hand, defies entropy momentarily, as we will see below. This is why we will classify the beginning of life as a threshold.

[2] Failure, of course, is relative. The failures we never see are the genetic mutations that led to the death of an organism before it could reproduce and pass on those mutations. Extinctions, in this sense, are simply system failures of a larger bent. We see some of these failures in the fossil record, though only a miniscule portion. For example, as a mountain biker, I often wonder why a trail over flat terrain twists and turns. One day, while stopped for a water break on such a twist, I noticed the vestigial remains of a fallen tree in the crook of the curve, almost invisible. The fallen tree explained why the path meandered, but once the tree rotted away, this explana-tion was lost. This is also true of the development of species: many of the developmental stages have been lost and all we see is the meandering result. Extinction, by the way, is a failure to which all species will eventually succumb.

specimens which in turn promote further formations.[3] If the environment changes, the creation process stops abruptly. Crystals did not develop the ability to adapt and so they stop forming when the environment changes. The earth's environment, containing original life forms, changed as well, but by the time it did, ending the creative window, there were organisms in existence that had gained the ability to metabolize and this gave rise to selection, which led to adaptation.

§3 THRESHOLDS OF CHANGE

There are, in our ever-developing world, what we might call thresholds of change, also known as tipping points. These occur when a system reaches a critical point which sparks an innovation after which everything changes (see Figure 15–2). A threshold occurs when the proverbial straw breaks the camel's back. This can be likened to the change that occurs in water with temperature changes. At 32° Fahrenheit something marvelous occurs—a liquid transforms into a solid. The molecular structure is unchanged, but the temperature causes a rearrangement, and what you could once wallow in you now can walk upon. If we move in the other direction, heating water instead of cooling it, another amazing phase shift occurs: liquid water becomes a gas. This is an example of how thresholds work, though the thresholds we are interested in are thresholds of increasing complexity.

Our universe has never been a homogeneous place, a place where all its simple elements were evenly spread throughout space-time. Gravity would not allow this. Early in the history of the universe, the structure of space-time caused bits of matter to cluster, forming simple elements (hydrogen and helium). These elements further constellated into great clouds. Gravity changed things. Once a group of elements comes together, their combined mass has more influence (more pull) than a single passing element, which is then drawn toward it, becoming part of the group. This, in turn, increases the mass of the group, which gives it more pull. This same systematizing phenomena occurred elsewhere and eventually there were great clumps of matter spread throughout the universe. This gravitational pull brought together a volatile mix that invoked more interactions between the particles, increasing heat and sparking fusion generators that became stars. A star is a discrete, complex system of elements interacting with each other. It is more than its parts. It is an entity in itself, having both a beginning and a predictable end. Within its hot fusion core new combinations of particles are occurring, new elements are continually being formed.

The method of a star's death depends upon many various facts and events, but one particularly violent end is of interest. When a supernova occurs the ejected material from its core is spewed into surrounding space in vast dust clouds upon

---

[3] In the crystallization process, molecules first begin to spontaneously gather into clusters according to their atomic structure. This usually occurs when a temperature threshold is passed (cooling), causing a phase-transition. These clusters will attain stability or not depending on whether they can reach a critical size. Whether or not they reach this depends on the environmental conditions at the time: temperature, supersaturation, and so on. Unstable clusters redissolve and crystals never form; stable clusters form nuclei which can then begin to grow. (Examples of this type of crystallization range from gemstone formation to honey and snowflake crystallization.)

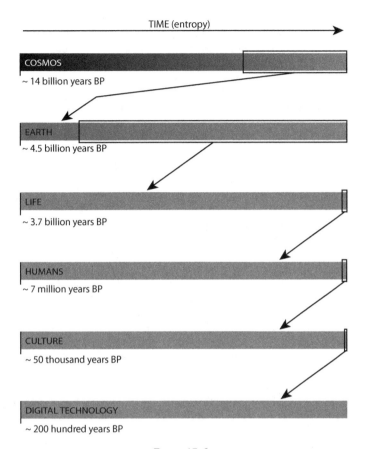

FIGURE 15–2

Six thresholds: (1) The formation of the cosmos; the bang that started our universe. (2) The earth, in its Goldilocks zone, becomes a planet ripe for experimentation. (3) Life. Though it would be odd if our planet had the only existing life forms, life, wherever it appears, seems destined to change everything. (4) Humans, which gave rise to (5) Culture, with its own evolution. From this point on humans take control of their biological evolution. (6) Digital technology. 0's and 1's revolutionize communication technology.

which gravity works its congealing magic once again. But the result is now more than the original mix of mere hydrogen and helium, for star-cores are the origin of all our more complex elements, and these now come together, drawn into the gravitational fields of yet other stars, orbiting aimlessly, collecting cosmic debris and maybe eventually gaining enough mass to become a planet. Planets are parasites on their sun's energy source—they have no fusion generator of their own, but are themselves systems which become a part of the solar system which is a part of a galaxy...

Gravity compresses dust into stars, sparking fusion generators that infuse their planetary systems with energy. Planets, also formed from gravitational forces, themselves become ever-changing systems, going from volatile volcanic reactions (if the environment is conducive to forming solids), cooling into rocky formations of crust-plates which move and shift about, forming and reforming continents. Thus planets, too, like stars, are born and die. Yet every planet is different: composed of different combinations of elements, different masses, different orbits determining how much energy they receive from their sun.

Gravity is a basic attractor; it brings diverse elements together to make a complex system. This complexity leads to further interactions which, in turn, change the nature of the collection. Such systems are often referred to as complex adaptive systems. The philosopher Karl Popper once made a distinction between clocks and clouds that illustrates this concept.[4] When you understand how a mechanical clock works, how all the gears connect, how the spring moves them, resulting in the hands displaying the time on the clock face, you then know all there is to know about the clock-system. Nothing surprising will ever happen; a clock is simply the sum of its parts, all of which work in coordination. A cloud is different, for there is much more at work within a cloud; there is a complex interaction between the molecules that cannot be captured in a mechanical diagram. The gears of a clock have a simple causal connection, but when the molecules within a cloud interact they change each other, and these changes then cascade through the system in what is known as a feedback loop, which leads to effects that cannot be foreseen in a simple mechanical analysis. A cloud, then, is more than the sum of its parts; its parts lead to emergent properties, completely new properties over and above the properties that caused them. Lightning and thunder, for example, are emergent properties of clouds.

In the case of our own planet, Earth, this complexity brought forth life. Life is a threshold, the result of a tipping point, and once it emerged everything changed. It is not for nothing the atmosphere of the earth is radically different from the atmospheres of all the other planets in our solar system. The earliest organisms, sucking in a volatile methane mixture, excreted their own volatile mix of oxygen, at first poisonous to all life forms. These excretions changed the earth's atmosphere, and other organisms evolved to take advantage of the change, which further changed the atmosphere. This is the ongoing dance we expect within a complex system. We have referred to it before as dialectic. Nothing exists in isolation. One thing affects another which in turn affects it and its ability to affect the other, and on and on. (It is only by means of abstraction that humans can even begin to separate themselves from this process.) This interconnection is important enough to formulate into a rule:

Rule$_1$: Everything is connected.

What follows from this rule is another:

Rule$_2$: You can never do just one thing.

---

[4] Popper was illustrating a different point, but the analogy remains useful. In particular it explains the difference between the modern uses of 'complex' as opposed to 'complicated.' A clock may be complicated, but it is not complex. A cloud, on the other hand, may be complicated, but it is also complex.

For if everything is connected, manipulating one thing will necessarily lead to changes in others, which will lead to changes in others, and so on. Another way of stating Rule$_2$ which I will state as another rule, is this:

Rule$_3$: There is no free lunch.[5]

I separate these because Rule$_2$ tells us there are consequences to everything we do while Rule$_3$ says something about those consequences, namely, that they are not always what they appear. These are the unintended consequences that plague so many of our manipulations. Rule$_3$ generalizes the notion that you cannot get something for nothing. As such, it is a core principle, not only of economics, but also as an informal statement of the law of entropy, which we will discuss in §5 below.

§4 FEEDBACK LOOPS

Feedback loops occur when the consequences of an event within a system are fed back into the system that caused them. There are two types of feedback, negative and positive. A negative loop shuts down the processes that brought it about while a positive loop multiplies the processes that brought it about. Put in our terms, both positive and negative feedback are a system's attempt to restore coherence gone awry.

POSITIVE FEEDBACK

Positive feedback loops are the most dangerous of the two types, for they smack of recklessness—a system out of control. In childbirth, for example, a contraction causes the release of the chemical oxytocin which in turn causes more contractions, which releases more oxytocin, which causes still more contractions, and so on. Blood clotting is another example, in which injured tissue releases chemicals that activate platelets in the blood, and these platelets in turn release more chemicals that activate more platelets.

A graph of an exponential curve (Figure 15–3) illustrates how a system exhibiting positive feedback can get out of control very quickly, since its growth is exponential. There is an ancient story that illustrates exponential growth.

The man who invented the game of chess once presented it as a gift to his king. The king was enthralled with the game and told the man to name his reward. He responded that, as a humble man, all he wished was for the king to place a single grain of wheat on the first square of the chessboard, two on the second square, four on the third, and so on, doubling the amount on each square until each square had its complement. He would then take either the grain or its monetary equivalent as his reward. The king resisted, saying it was too modest a demand, but eventually consented. When the reward was being tallied, however, the king became aware of his mistake,

---

[5] To the best of my knowledge Garrett Hardin was the first to connect these rules in this manner.

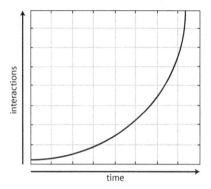

FIGURE 15–3
A graph plotting the exponential growth of a system. The explosive growth here can be illustrated as follows. Imagine a lily pad in a pond that doubles in size every day. It covers the entire pond in ten days. On what day does it cover exactly half of the pond?

for the number of grains of wheat on the last square alone was 2^{63} (nine million trillion grains).

Positive feedback is the hallmark of a complex system (a cloud-like system), for it produces effects that go far beyond it—small perturbations that can lead to large-scale effects. If the effects are drastic enough they may lead to what we have called a threshold, a point at which everything within the system is affected. The danger of an exponential curve within a system is obvious—if not stopped it will destroy the system. To allay this destruction, positive feedback loops usually result in a negative feedback loop, as in the above examples of birth contractions and clotting, but sometimes the worst case occurs and systems crash. Positive feedback also occurs in an evolutionary context, giving rise to phenomena such as the widowbird's wondrously long tail (discussed below, page 371). This process is also eventually controlled by negative feedback, for birds with tails that are too long cannot fly and thus perish.

NEGATIVE FEEDBACK

As we have indicated, negative feedback occurs when the consequences of events within a system feed back into the system and suppress the events that caused them. A governor on a mechanical steam engine is a good example of a negative feedback loop—one in which the effects are fed back into the system by design in order to control it. As water is heated and turns to steam, pressure in the boiler increases. This pressure can do work when released—push pistons and turn turbines. The problem is, if this pressure is not controlled it will destroy the entire system. To keep this from happening a governor is introduced—a method of using the very pressure generated within the boiler to maintain that pressure at a safe level. As the pressure increases it activates a switch which opens a release valve, letting off excess steam, lowering the pressure. As the pressure is lowered, the switch closes, allowing the pressure to build up once again. On average, the pressure is maintained at a specific level, or equilibrium, much like you might maintain the temperature of your home with a thermostat. These are all clock-like systems. Gears and turbines, flanges and switches are what they are—they do not interact with each other in surprising ways.

Figure 15–4 is a graph of the effects of a negative feedback loop. Note the state of equilibrium (E) that is maintained by the negative feedback. We can use population growth as an example of a potentially positive feedback loop controlled by negative feedback. In its simplest state, population growth is exponential. If two parents have two children, and each of those children have two children, and all of those children have two children, and so on, the result is a population explosion, which would be plotted on a graph like that in Figure 15–3 above. This is positive feedback at work. The natural limits on population are environmental, that is, negative feedback kicks in at some point in order to restore the system's coherence (equilibrium). In the graph below, with abundant resources, the population within a closed system (say, deer living on an island) will increase until it exceeds (E), at which point the system can no longer comfortably support the population. This is the point of equilibrium, known in ecological circles as the carrying capacity of the land.[6] As the population continues to rise, at some point (F) the system will fail (there will not be enough food for the deer), which results in a drastic reduction in the deer population, reducing it to a level below the carrying capacity. At this new level there is once again an abundant supply of food and the deer population will again begin to rise. An appreciation of negative feedback loops in the context of populations led to Darwin's insight that those who survive the die-off at (F) will be better adapted to their environment. Thus are negative feedback loops also connected to adaptation.

The peaks within a negative feedback loop, when applied to sensate systems, indicate suffering, and the higher the peaks, the greater the suffering. This same structure can be seen in economics, where changes in supply and demand lead to cycles of boom and bust. In the U.S. the Federal Reserve attempts to flatten the peaks of the graph by controlling the money supply, thereby reducing the overall suffering which occurs within the natural feedback cycles. The point to note, for our

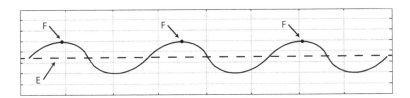

FIGURE 15–4

Graph of negative feedback within a system. This could graph the pressure within a steam engine, the thermostat setting within your home, population level in nature, business cycles, and so on. (E) represents the point at which the system is at an equilibrium. (F) represents the point of system failure. The height and depth of the peaks and valleys are indications of damage done.

---

[6] Carrying capacity is vague to the point of being almost useless. It differs for every organism and is impossible to designate as applying to a specific land area. This vagueness is no doubt due to the complexity of a system and is complicated further by Rule$_1$ above.

purposes, is that systems strive to reach an equilibrium. A financial depression, like mass starvation, is a method of reaching an equilibrium, one that occurs naturally if no one interferes with the feedback loops.

Another aspect of the economic model is brought out by Adam Smith who, in his *Wealth of Nations*, used the metaphor of an invisible hand to explain the unseen workings of systems with a tendency toward equilibrium. Smith was impressed by the fact that an individual with completely selfish motivations could bring about a greater good for the system as a whole:

> he intends only his own security; and by directing that industry in such a manner as its produce may be of the greatest value, he intends only his own gain, and he is in this, as in many other cases, led by an invisible hand to promote an end which was no part of his intention. (IV,2,ix)

In striving only to accumulate his own personal wealth he forms business ventures which employ people who can then increase their own wealth. This is the same non-zero-sum game we saw take place with respect to reciprocal altruism in evolution theory.

These are reasons why complex systems become more than merely a sum of their parts. The tendency toward coherence brings about seemingly magical side effects—magical, that is, until we understand how such systems work. It is often our failure to understand the function of complexity that leads to the reification of a higher cause (like an invisible hand) as an explanation for the beauty and effects seen within the functioning of a complex system.

§5 ENTROPY

Every living thing dies. Or, more generally, everything decays. Dying is just one step in the process. At some level you would think there might be a basic maintenance, something that does not decay, but it is not to be. Everything falls apart, eventually attaining a maximum state of dispersal. This is a fundamental feature of matter as we know it, for everything is subject to the laws of thermodynamics.

The first law demands the conservation of energy: the total amount of energy in the universe never changes (energy is neither created nor destroyed). The total amount doesn't change, but the quality is constantly changing and this is the crux of the second law, the law of entropy: the quality of the energy within a system is continually being degraded. When high quality energy is input into a system it allows the system to do work. We eat food, and the resulting energy allows our bodies to function, keeping our barriers intact. Most energy on earth is originally input from the sun.[7] This is the highest grade energy available—itself a waste product of the fusion process deep within the sun's core. This solar energy drives the power within plants via that all important biomolecule, chlorophyll,[8] and this energy is transferred

---

[7] The other source is from the earth's core, which is the result of gravity (again). There are creatures who live off the energy emerging from the earth's core in vents far beneath the surface of the sea. Some scientists maintain this is where life began. Verlinde (2011) has recently proposed a theory (entropic gravity) in which gravity itself is reducible to entropy.

[8] Plants absorb electromagnetic radiation (light) from the sun, but almost exclusively from

FORESEEN & UNFORESEEN CONSEQUENCES

Foreseen consequences are those we have in fact predicted will follow from an idea with some degree of probability. Unforeseen consequences are those which we did not predict. The degree of probability involved is based on the knowledge we have at the moment. For example, if my idea to build a piece of furniture spurred me to learn carpentry, then the consequences of that idea were foreseen, that is, I could have predicted I would probably be learning carpentry in the future. On the other hand, if I had an idea to go to the store and, while backing out of the driveway collided with another car, the collision was an unforeseen consequence of backing out of the driveway. I had no way of predicting such an event (even though a little thought would have led me to agree it was possible).

There are also foreseen consequences that are ignored. These might be ignored for a variety of reasons. The most obvious reason for ignoring a foreseen consequence is personal gain. The Ford Motor Company may have foreseen that the Pinto had a propensity to explode when hit in the rear due to a faulty gas tank, but since the car was already in production it was too expensive to recall. Another reason for ignoring a foreseen consequence is the probability of the consequence actually occurring, which might be deemed too small to be considered.

As finite creatures, there is only so much we are expected to know, which means there is always the possibility of unforeseen consequences for any manifestation of an idea, no matter how trite. For example, several states passed luxury taxes on boats in the 1970s to raise revenue. The consequences of these laws were supposed to include increased revenue. In fact, what happened was that people stopped buying boats, which put many boat manufacturers out of business, laying off individuals who could then no longer afford to purchase other commodities such as cars, which caused a general economic slump.

Note that unforeseen is not equal to unforeseeable, for there are unforeseen consequences that should have been foreseen, but were not due to a lack of imagination, the complexity of the issues, carelessness, and so on. This raises an important question: to what extent are we responsible for foreseeable but unforeseen consequences? For example, the drug thalidomide was developed as a sedative in the 1950s, but was pulled in 1961 after it was found to cause severe birth defects when taken during pregnancy. In the 1950s it was "thought unlikely" that the effects of a drug could pass through the placental barrier and harm the fetus. What probability would constitute immoral behavior? 1%? 30%?

Once we take these considerations seriously it might give us pause in proceeding with unknown technologies, particularly if they are already suspected to be dangerous in some way. History has given us good reasons for caution.

---

to organisms that eat the plants and breath their waste product (oxygen). Other organisms gain their energy from eating the plant-eaters (or other meat-eaters) and they, too, expel waste which is used as food by yet other organisms. (All living things, it seems, eat shit and die.) This entire process is a degradation of energy. Oxygen is a degraded form of sun-energy that helps power us humans, and our waste is grist for yet another mill. We generate electricity, turning turbines by means of water, which itself was raised to a height capable of work by the process of evaporation. When this water reaches sea level, it is at equilibrium—where there is no more work within. Thus entropy, which appears as a destroyer of coherence, is also a striving for such.

---

the red and blue parts of the spectrum, which is why they appear green to us—the green is reflected.

We humans are insatiable energy users, using our technology to pull the sun-energy stored not only in water, but also in plants that died hundreds of millions of years ago in the form of coal, oil and natural gas. Eventually this energy, once high in quality, can do no more work for any organism. The second law says this is the eventual fate of all energy. When all the fusion engines in all the stars have sputtered down and stopped, then has a universe died. Death occurs naturally, whether for universes or planets or humans or amoebas, when energy can no longer be made to produce work within a system. For living things, this translates into the inability to maintain one's integrity against the world as an individual organism. We must maintain our force-fields or disperse back to the dust from which we came. We must maintain our engines (allowing for ATP synthase) so that our parts continue to cohere.

A further by-product of the law of entropy is that it allows us to specify the arrow of time (Hawking 1998). Entropy is the engine of change, which is the essence of time. Within any system, time is measured by change, which is fueled by decay. Decay is not the result of time; rather, time is the result of decay. Death is inherent within time, whose measurement in our world corresponds loosely to the rot rate of road kill on a sun-baked tarmac.

§6 TELEOLOGICAL SYSTEMS

So far, we have been speaking of systems as they are nested on a horizontal scale, as illustrated in Figure 15–1, but we can also view systems as nested on a vertical scale in terms of what we have referred to (in chapter 7) as reference frames. Reference frames are a function of the reflective capabilities of self-conscious humans, and are coherent systems in themselves. They are the result of a creature having a point of view. There are different ways we could describe these systems, but I will use the notion of teleology, for we humans are teleological animals through and through—we talk about and impose purpose on everything, especially upon ourselves. For example, the purpose of something we make is its function: a chair is made for the purpose of sitting. We then take the fact that manufactured things have a purpose and apply this to non-manufactured things, including, again, ourselves.

Machines do what they are programmed to do. If we want a robot to vacuum the carpet, we program it to move in certain ways. As it traverses the floor it formulates a map of where it's been. When it encounters an obstacle it attempts to move around it and remembers its position on the map so it knows to avoid it in the future. It's goal is to vacuum all accessible parts of the floor. An obstacle is an anomaly which it must solve. We could say that a core value for a vacuum robot is "I must vacuum all relevant floor space." Given its purpose, then, it follows that judgments will have to be made concerning what is deemed relevant with respect to meeting its goal. As it traverses the floor, it senses an object. Is this a permanent mappable item (a sofa), or a temporary obstruction (the family pet)? This is a valuable distinction for the vacuum, for the sofa will always be there, but the pet won't. Thus, the purpose of a thing determines its values, which in turn determine its actions in the world as it endeavors to accomplish its goals. One difference between a machine and a human being is that the machine is externally driven. We program it. It has no feeling of fear or hope for success, and because of this we can neither reward nor punish it. If it continually failed to reach its primary goal it would not be here (a different, better suited model would be built). In a sense, then, its reward for success is its existence; its punishment for failure would be non-existence. The machine that fails to achieve its goal has failed to adapt properly to its environment, and is artificially selected out of the machine pool. You never see these failures, for the designer fixes the flaws and makes a better model. You only see the relative successes. But don't be fooled. A vacuum in itself has no purpose other than that imposed upon it by humans. In a world bereft of humans, a vacuum would merely be a collection of decaying parts. This is what I mean by an external teleological system—its teleology is imposed upon it from without.

A purpose can only be bestowed upon something from a higher reference frame. We humans bestow purpose upon ourselves in this way—by means of reflection. This is how we differ from machines; our teleology is internal, self-generated. The pretended difference is that we act as if our purpose is permanently installed and all we are doing is looking for it. We reify the purpose as something existing in itself. We act as if we have a purpose bestowed from above (from a god's-eye-view) or inherent within us (which is the same thing). All purpose depends upon a point of view, and points of view depend upon a sophisticated sort of self-consciousness, which only humans (and possibly a few other mammals) possess. We are the purpose-makers of the world, bestowing them like a king bestows titles, based on our wants and wishes (Figure 15–5).

What is the purpose of humans? Or, what have we humans decided upon as our purpose? The question of purpose is important, for the purpose of a thing determines its values. The purpose of a vacuum is to clean the floor; so what is valuable for a vacuum cleaner is what helps it perform this function. So also for humans—whatever we deem our purpose will determine our core values, which will determine

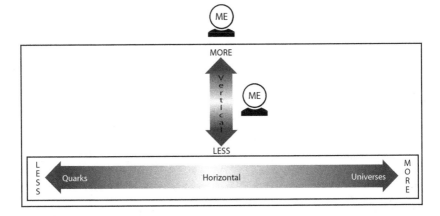

FIGURE 15–5

We have the ability to reflect upon not only the world outside us (shown here as nested horizontal systems), but also upon ourselves and our projects. We can even imagine ourselves outside our own nested systems. The higher reference frames bestow meaning upon everything beneath them.

how we act, including how we treat other people. This is why discovering our purpose was primarily an ethical investigation for the ancient Greeks—you must know what goal you are seeking in order to discover what is valuable to help you get there. These values are then called virtues. Virtues are means to help you achieve your purpose as a human.

You may remember we broached the question of our purpose in chapter 1, where we talked about life goals and how to reach them. My position was that we humans, in a general sense, all strive for the goal of well-being, and in order to reach this we must be able to reflect upon our situation in a thoughtful manner. In other words, reflection is a virtue, for it helps us reach our purpose (well-being). Reflection helps us understand who we are by showing us how we developed and how we think about the world. Without knowing these things we are easily misled by our inborn biases and so are less likely to reach our goal. Any technique we have that helps us achieve our goal is a virtue. For example, I have indicated that the scientific method is a virtue because it tends to help us sort true sentences from false sentences more efficiently than any other known method, and this kind of truth-sorting is helpful in reaching our goals.[9]

External teleology is a by-product of self-consciousness, that is, it depends upon a higher reference frame. For billions of years, bacteria interacted with each other without reference to teleology. One can only invoke the teleological perspective of a system more encompassing than your own by positing a conscious entity above the process who created it for a specific purpose. This overriding purpose, then, gives meaning to the individual existing organisms, for they then play a part in a larger scheme of things. Evolutionary systems have only internal teleology. Each organism strives for its own goal of survival (coherence). Self-conscious organisms have expanded this to well-being.

§7 POINTS OF VIEW

We first talked about reference frames in chapter 7, during our first discussion of truth and enlightenment. A reference frame is a conscious point of view, which is why, when we speak of enlightenment we speak of moving to a higher reference frame—we become conscious of something we were not aware of before. Horizontally nested systems, as we have discussed them in this chapter, do not have points of view. On the molecular level, for example, molecules are not conscious

---

[9] Those who believe humans are creations of god believe that we have a program instilled in us from without, much like the robotic vacuum. God constitutes the higher reference frame that imbues us with purpose as we do vacuums. C.S. Lewis once said that humans have a "god-shaped void" within them, meaning (I think) that god has programmed us to seek him and not be satisfied until we find him. This goal, then, is what gives meaning to our lives. On the traditional Judeo-Christian-Islamic view, there were no faulty models that never made it to the showroom floor. Since god is perfect, his creation was just the way he wanted it from the start (which is problematic in itself). God has given us our value system, and this anchors us firmly—we know what to hold important because god created us with a function. So also, on this view not just individual humans, but all of human history can be seen as moving toward the completion of an external goal given to us from without.

entities, so there is no point of view. A point of view is an abstract mental vantage point from which you view other things. We have the ability to vary our points of view from place to place. For example, we can look at ourselves and our own life as if from the outside (as was illustrated in Figure 15–5). This is a self-conscious point of view, different from our normal immersed-in-the-details-of-life point of view. We can also entertain imaginary points of view. I can, for example, imagine myself or another person on the moon, looking at the earth, or in a fictional setting.

Not only do we have a point of view, we can also imagine other systems as having a point of view (anthropomorphism). This is the essence of the god's-eye-view, in which we hypothesize a highest possible point of view and survey everything else from that system. The god's-eye-view is posited as a reflective system higher than ours (Figure 15–6). We impose our purposes on anything we like. Imposing a purpose imposes goals and proper ways to reach those goals, and this implies imposing values. We have seen this is not just true of our creations (vacuum cleaners), which are obviously made for a specific purpose, or even for random objects we hijack for a purpose (a rock we might use to prop open a door), but is inherent within our very experience of the world. Furthermore, we look at (horizontal) systems larger than our own and ask: what is their purpose? Why is there a universe? or, for that matter, Why is there anything at all? One way to answer this is to treat the universe as we would treat a vacuum cleaner: posit a creator, and once there is a creator there is purpose. Thus purpose gets reified upon systems other than our own. Positing a god's-eye-view creator necessarily imbues everything with purpose, and hence meaning. Without a god's-eye-view the purpose of a system is determined by its own internal strivings. My point in this chapter is to illustrate that all systems have similar strivings, namely toward coherence. We self-conscious

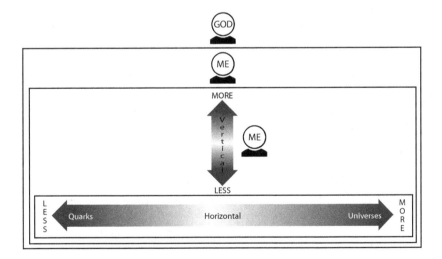

FIGURE 15–6

Not only can we humans posit ourselves outside of ourselves in order to view our entire life, we can also posit a point-of-view beyond our self. For example, we can view our self from the viewpoint of others. Taken to the extreme, we can posit a god's-eye-view, which is the highest possible point-of-view.

creatures call this well-being; living organisms might call it survival, non-living things equilibrium.

Our experience has an internal temporal structure, but as we weave these together the structures get more and more complex: I am rewriting this sentence at this moment. This action has a temporal (retrospective/prospective) structure. But it, and the one I am now engaged in are part of a larger whole: writing this chapter, which is part of a larger whole: writing this book, which is part of a larger whole: providing a coherent world view that I can share with others, which is part of a larger whole: achieving my goals as a teacher, which is part of a large whole: living a fulfilling life and achieving well-being (Figure 15–7). But typing these sentences is not all I will do today. I will also go mountain biking, shop at the grocery store, cook and eat meals, brush my teeth, read a novel, and go to sleep. All of these are nested within my teleological framework. Consider just one of these: grocery shopping is part of several larger wholes. I go to the grocery store in order to get ingredients so I can cook dinner, which I do because I enjoy cooking, which enjoyment adds to my well-being; but I also cook so that I can have dinner with my wife, which I enjoy on several levels: both the food and the company, and dinner, of course, also inevitably keeps me alive and functioning. Furthermore, when I go to the store, I usually get several items for my mother since she can't get out herself. So going to the store is also part of the larger whole of taking care of my mother, which itself is part of a larger whole, and so on. You can easily see how complex these nestings can become.

Even at the simplest of levels, the meaning of any one thing depends on a larger nesting. Typing this sentence is meaningless unless I know what I want it to say and how it is to fit into a paragraph. This is how teleology imbues meaning. Even at this level there is structure: a beginning, a middle and an end. Before I even start typing I have a goal in mind: what the sentence will say. Typing is the means I use to convey this goal, but the end is in place before I even start, as anticipation of the goal—it moves me to use the means and gives coherence to what I am doing. The moment before I begin typing the sentence is packed with anticipation: for it also has within it the goal of every nested project of which typing this sentence is a part. And the typed sentence, as a coherent project itself, is also a means to a higher project (finishing the paragraph), which itself is a means to a higher project, and so on. Each project instills meaning on whatever is contained within its nestings. The higher echelons of nestings are what we consider core values (Figure 15–7). Note, then, that our notion of project nestings is just another way of talking about interconnectivity. When we discussed conceptual schemes we described a core value as one which contained many connections (leading to seismic disturbances if damaged). The same notion is captured here with nesting levels, for nesting implies connection so that the higher the reference frame the more connections and also the more damage if the ordering frame is damaged. Note also the similarity to a formal, or axiomatic system: our core values function as axioms which percolate downward throughout the system. The system itself is only as strong as its grounding axioms, just as the conclusion of an argument is only as strong as its weakest premise.

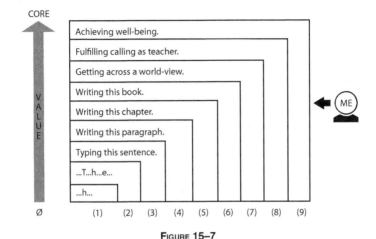

FIGURE 15–7

A nesting of points of view, each with its own narrative structure. The higher (more inclusive) the nesting, the more valuable to me. Each higher level imbues every level beneath it with its meaning because these are considered means to its end.

§8   REWARD & PUNISHMENT

Teleology, containing as it does the notion of an end or goal and the means to achieve the end, gives rise the concepts of reward and punishment, for both can be seen as incentives to reach a goal. A goal is something we want to achieve for whatever reason and because of this it contains the concept of a reward within it, as if it is pulling us toward it. Rewards and punishments are the means used by one system in order to persuade another system to achieve the goals of the first.

Sensations evolved in order to help organisms monitor their bodily states. Our lives depend upon the coordinated operation of different systems within our bodies, some of which we are responsible for as self-conscious individuals. Food and water, for instance, are essential. Living organisms must seek these out in order to survive. The strategy adopted by plants was to remain relatively immobile and let nutrients come to them, but animals developed a different strategy: locomotion. Animals must actively seek nutrients, but why do so? Since gaining nutrients depends upon actions initiated by the organism, incentives have also developed to ensure these actions are performed. This includes the pleasure of taking in food and water, as well as the pain of dehydration and starvation.

So also, if something is gnawing on one of your extremities and this could lead to serious injury, you must be able to determine you are being gnawed upon in order to take evasive action. In sensate organisms this takes the form of pain. Pain occurs within the brain (the periaqueductal gray); it is a function of neurons firing. (Hence phantom limb pain. We have already noted that all pain is hallucinatory, for it is not the body part that hurts.) As much as we dislike pain, it must have evolved as a motivational tool. Pain is to the body what cognitive dissonance is to the mind, and as such it motivates us to fix a problem, whatever that might be. So sensations allow an organism to monitor its bodily states which it must do in order to maintain its integrity or coherence.

In order for a reward (or punishment) to begin to work in a creature with a mind, an organism must be able to make and recall an association between an action and something pleasurable which followed the action. When you command a dog to sit and then give it a treat when it obeys, you are attempting to form this association. This, as we have seen, is operant conditioning. Without (1) associative abilities (basic analogical skills) and (2) memory storage and retrieval, operant conditioning is impossible. But sensations are continually spilling through a dog's brain; why take particular interest in the one between a spoken word and an action? Ah, the reward, which focuses the attention upon the association, making it special—making it valuable. The pleasure makes the dog want to make the association again, and so perform the action that led to it. This is what we mean by reward. If pain was associated with the action, the individual would want to avoid making the association, and so not perform the action that led to it. This is what we mean by punishment. If there were neither pleasure nor pain associated, the dog would neither seek out nor avoid the action.

There is a similarity here between the responses of an organism to incentives and the responses to gene mutations in natural selection. Let's make this explicit. Here are the options:

(1) Associated feeling of pleasure creates a desire to replicate an action.
(2) Associated feeling of pain creates a desire to not replicate an action.
(3) No associated feeling creates no desire or extinguishes a desire.

Now, notice the similarity in these responses and what follows from different types of genetic mutations. On the genetic level we cannot talk of feelings, but the causal response is the important point. On the genetic level the feeling of pleasure (1) is equivalent to a gene that is beneficial to survival (and hence replication); the feeling of pain (2) is equivalent to a gene that is detrimental to survival (and hence replication; and no associated feeling (3) is equivalent to a gene that is neither beneficial nor detrimental to survival. Using this as our basic metaphor, then, we can map the concepts of reward and punishment to non-sensate beings. This makes a reward equivalent to continued existence, and a punishment equivalent to non-existence. Death-before-reproduction is the ultimate punishment for a non-human living organism, for its genes are not passed on (death-after-reproduction is neither here nor there in evolutionary terms). This is different for humans, who, because of our consciousness (giving rise to culture), have created our own non-evolutionary values. For us, death is not tied merely to reproduction. Death is the end of our ability to experience, to enter into relations, to feel pleasures, and so on, and as long as we enjoy these things, death itself is the ultimate punishment.

We humans make plans. Our brains are continually spinning hypothetical scenarios (maps) and we choose between these scenarios based on values we assign them. Once we choose a scenario, a plan, as something we want to accomplish, then the goal takes on value which is then projected back to the means. The means to procure the goal then become valuable in light of that goal; their value is reflected, like moonlight. The chosen plan itself is constantly updated with present data, with changes being made and new hypotheticals run. As the probabilities increase that the plan or goal will be reached, expectation increases accordingly. When an event occurs that threatens a goal of ours, this constitutes an anomaly—it threatens something of value—and the result is cognitive dissonance. The amount of cognitive dissonance suffered is directly correlated to the value placed on the belief.

ADDICTION

Dopamine is a neurotransmitter responsible for rewarding animals with pleasurable feelings. We humans are dopamine addicts. We crave it. It is our reward for reaching goals that we set for ourselves. This is why it feels good to complete a task. We get a dopamine dose when we complete one (and also when we eat or drink certain foods and liquids). Knowledge of this connection can lead to our being controlled by others in certain ways. We have talked before about reciprocity. It feels good to reciprocate—we get a dopamine reward (and also an oxytocin reward) when we do so, and those who want our money know this. They have glommed on to this fact of human nature and use it to try to take our money. This is the origin of the "free" gift (and now you see why there is no such thing as a free lunch) in advertising. Video game manufacturers have perfected a particularly nefarious strategy based on our reward system connected to goal achievement. Anyone who has played a video game knows that most are set up with multiple levels of achievement. The levels must be difficult, but not too difficult to achieve. If they are too easy, our system doesn't see reaching the goal as an achievement and will not reward us; if too hard we get frustration instead of reward. This will insure that mastering a level will result in a feeling of satisfaction (that's the dopamine at work). But of course, achieving one level introduces you to another which promises the same sort of reward, and after a while you begin to crave the reward. This is why video games are addicting. This is no different, really, than a heroin addiction (or any other type of addiction). We humans realized early that we can imitate the effects of dopamine artificially using various methods. The earliest was fermentation, which is still a favorite (this imitation is necessary, for dopamine input externally cannot cross the blood-brain barrier), others include naturally occurring substances that can be ingested (refined or unrefined). These stimulate the production of dopamine and give rise to the same craving. These cravings can become so intense that they are substituted for well-being itself, making the means to satisfy them core values. Families of addicts (whether cocaine, amphetamines, alcohol, sex, gambling, nicotine, work) are often surprised when they find themselves secondary to the addiction in terms of priority. Indeed, we can probably consider all humans addicts because of our various cravings; some addictions are simply considered more socially acceptable than others.

Dopamine is not the only neurotransmitter that makes us feel warm fuzzies: Seratonin is known as the happiness hormone (though it is not a hormone) and contributes to our feelings of well-being; Oxytocin, secreted in the breast milk of females, ensures bonding between mother and child. It is also produced in males during sex. Adenosine makes you feel weary (and is blocked by caffeine); Vasopressin boosts feelings of trust and love and may help learning and memory; GABA/Glycine are both involved in neuron inhibition—they stop those positive feedback loops from getting out of control; and Anandamide is named after the Sanskrit word for bliss—need I say more?

§9   COHERENCE AS HOMEOSTASIS AS EQUILIBRIUM

Equilibrium is always relative to a reference frame. From the cheetah's perspective, its equilibrium has been upset when it fails to catch the gazelle it was pursuing. From the gazelle's perspective its equilibrium was maintained by the same event. But if we step up to a higher reference frame, the whole chase and pursuit scenario, where sometimes the prey is caught and sometimes is not, is all part of a larger equilibrium, which includes not just cheetahs and gazelles but also hyenas and vultures and crocodiles. A higher reference frame yields a view of the Serengeti plain as an ecosystem itself striving for equilibrium, which in turn is part of a larger system, eventually incorporating the entire earth.

From a human perspective, our brains seek coherence; we don't like it when, say, sensory data contradicts a belief we might have, or when two beliefs are contrary. Why? Cognitive dissonance is the feeling that something is wrong or out of balance within our framework. These feelings are based upon value judgments, which in humans is the realm of the emotions. Damasio (2005) has shown that, without emotions, we cannot make decisions. Our reasoning sorts out all the possibilities, but doesn't weight the alternatives and so cannot make a choice. Giving more weight to one alternative than another is a value judgment, and it is our emotions that allow us to do this. As Nozick (1990) has pointed out:

> Emotions inform us of the evaluations we are making, including unconscious ones, since the feelings involved are present to consciousness, we can use them to monitor, reexamine, and perhaps alter our underlying evaluations… Emotions provide a kind of picture of value, I think. They are our internal psychophysiological response to the external value, a response that is specially close by being not only due to that value but an analog representation of it. (91-93)[10]

We also impute value to other organisms. We say the cheetah "wants" to catch the gazelle (the goal), and if she doesn't she is "disappointed." We can even say, of non-living things, that there is a system of sorts: the earth and other planets journey around the sun, and these can be portrayed as teleological in terms of abiding by the laws of science and nature. Cheetahs try to catch prey—they must in order to eat. Planets orbit their sun—they must according to the laws of physics. But things can go awry for the individual object or organism. The cheetah can fail to catch its prey, a planet can be caught in the gravitational pull of a passing massive object and be torn from its orbit. These are both anomalous occurrences with respect to the status quo. If a planet was conscious it might say that its "goal" was to continue traveling around its sun, and when ripped from orbit would consider this anomalous and would suffer cognitive dissonance as a result. This might sound ridiculous, but the point is that systems fall into a pattern of activity which, from the point of view of an observer over time, might be termed normal (hence the status quo). This is the broad state of equilibrium, which we referred to (in living organisms) as homeostasis. This equilibrium is simply the result of the laws of science allowing everything within a system to work in accord with every other thing, in a symbiotic relationship. We might say that any system "strives for" or "desires" equilibrium.

Atomic structure demands an equilibrium between positive and negative charges; subatomic particles and molecules adhere to the same demand. Individual cells seek their own equilibrium, as do individual plants and animals which are composed of cells. Groups of plants and animals also seek an equilibrium with respect to their own members, other groups (species), and the environment. This is what we have referred to as adaptation.

Teleological adaptations are those dependent upon the foresight of the organism involved. Such adaptations are much more complex than the non-teleological variety for the same reason that a clock is different from a cloud. For example, suppose I have a goal and a strategy to reach that goal. You then discover my goal and corresponding strategy and try to keep me from reaching it (since it may conflict with one of your goals). But once I become aware of your goal to waylay my goal,

---

[10] Just as a ship on the ocean's surface might use echo-location to plot the ocean floor, so also emotions might be seen as an analog indicator of our value system.

I will change my strategy, and if you find out I have done so, you will change yours accordingly. Furthermore, once I am aware that you are attempting to waylay my goal, I might try to deceive you with respect to my strategy, as you might me with your response. We go through these complex maneuverings continually throughout our lives.

Non-teleological (non-conscious) adaptations, those that occur to organisms unable to make use of foresight, are discussed in terms of evolutionarily stable strategies (ESS). Take, for example, the tail feathers of the widowbird, which are flamboyantly long. The length of the tail feathers is based on a line of equilibrium, a balance between the length preferred by female widowbirds and the length allowable by flight restrictions. Evolution finds this equilibrium. An extremely long tail might be preferred by females (and this desire for a long tail is passed along genetically to female offspring), but when tail length begins to inhibit the survival of the male (and hence his ability to pass on his genes) it will no longer be selected. So the actual length of the male's tail is a compromise (with many mathematical solutions).[11] This is an ESS with respect to one characteristic of a bird, stemming from sexual selection. Similarly there are ESS's between predators and their prey. There is a balance between how fast a cheetah can run and how fast a gazelle can run. If the cheetah could easily outrun any gazelle, cheetahs would reproduce until the gazelle population disappeared (at which time the cheetah population would also dwindle). This is negative feedback; it is nature maintaining an equilibrium.

Consider Le Chatelier's principle, a chemical principle that has been generalized to many different fields, including economics and evolution theory. A generalized version might be stated as follows:

Any change in the normal state of a system will provoke a response from whatever is affected by the change.

This is merely a statement of the fact that everything will abide by the laws of nature, for it is these that define the equilibrium. We seek to know these laws so that we can understand our life situation in terms of them. Once we know them we see that everything is as it should be. If the world seems contrary, it is because we do not have a perfect understanding of the laws. This, then, is the demand of coherence, that everything acts according to the laws of nature.[12]

Our original question was: why coherence? What is so special about our adequacy conditions that we should strive for these, even when we aren't conscious of so striving? The answer is that there is nothing at all special about coherence. Coherence is just equilibrium, and the individual is a system in itself (composed of many smaller systems) striving for such. Why? Because without it we would not survive. The system would fail and we would cease to exist. The only difference

---

[11] Along the same line, there are many different ways you could keep your home at a constant temperature in the winter: you could run your heater alone, turning it off now and again to maintain the temperature, or you could run the heater full blast and simultaneously run an air conditioning unit to maintain a temperature. Note all the different equilibria available on the heater/air conditioning combination: set the heat at low and the air at low, set them both at medium, set them both at high, and all the combinations in between. So also for the length of the widowbird's tail.

[12] Thus, we have come full circle, for we have now explained coherence in terms of itself, for we only know the laws of nature as part of a coherent system.

between the husband's realization that his spouse is having an affair and a planet being ripped from its original orbit is that the former is conscious of itself as a system, while a planet is not. Equilibrium is that comfort state toward which we strive. It is part and parcel with well-being.

§10 CHAPTER SUMMARY

In this chapter I have sought to expand the concept of coherence beyond its original use as a set of adequacy conditions within theorizing. The analogies I have made take it far beyond this. Analogies, when stretched in this way, begin to break down, but even at the point of breaking (incoherence?) they can be useful. This is how I view my treatment of coherence, for, in applying it to the far realms of the universe, both great and small, we begin to see that there are fundamental ways in which we experience the world and deal with this experience. If coherence is essential to theorizing, and theorizing is ubiquitous with respect to our interaction with the world, then so also is coherence.

Our connections to other people and other things run deep, and ultimately it is these connections that imbue our lives with meaning. Multiple connections create value, and these connections are manifest in the many nestings within our conceptual schemes. We have seen that the number of strands a belief is connected to determines its value in terms of the damage done if the connections are severed. This holds true as well in our interpersonal relations; whether concerning a spouse, a relative, a friend, or an enemy; the connections formed between yourself and another person make that person more important in your life. The same is true with physical objects, for these can act as touchstones for our memory, invoking emotions dependent on connections those objects have to important places or events within our lives. The physical equivalent of a core value is a sacred object. All of these relationships must work for us in practical terms—they must cohere with all our other beliefs and memories. Thus does coherence permeate our lives.

The ancient stoics taught that virtue was attained when a person's will, with which he controls his life choices, is in agreement with nature. This would give him an equanimity that would further promote his overall well-being. There is some truth to this. We, along with everything else in the universe, strive for such agreement. We have called this coherence or equilibrium, but the underlying concept is the same. All sensate systems, whether conscious or self-conscious are most content when they (which includes the parts that make them up) are in equilibrium.

NOTES / QUESTIONS

Afterward

• •

Philosophy, as we have practiced it in these pages, is the most practical of disciplines, for its aim is to contribute to your well-being: reflecting on your life will help you lead a better one. Reflection is hard but worthwhile work, and I urge you to do more of it, for we have barely scratched the surface of a myriad of topics. The more you examine yourself—how you process information, how you reason about the world, how you interact with others—the more you hone your living skills. This text is really nothing more than a hint at the underlying structure of connections awaiting your exploration. Our starting point was the fact that:

(1) We do not have direct access to the world.

Our sensorial input is processed and reprocessed before we become conscious of it. This is the fundamental fact around which everything in this book circles. Acknowledgement of this fact will change your life—it is what separates reflective from non-reflective living. At least two major implications follow: first, we must revamp our ideas of how we come to know; this will lead to a more thorough examination of theorizing and the scientific method in particular; second, the processing that takes place in our brains is not truth-optimized, which should lead to an examination of the biases that cloud our judgment. We have hunter-gatherer brains in a complex modern world. Both of these points warrant much thought beyond the pages of this text. Contemplation on (1), for instance, gives rise to the concept of

The Prison of Subjectivity. This is a direct result of our disconnection with the world. Direct access was our umbilical, supposedly feeding us truth and certainty. But a full appreciation of (1) cuts this cord, leaving us isolated and alone. This was the main thrust of Chapter 9 on certainty: the ultimate ground of all our knowledge is self-evidence—it all boils down to "I just know" at some point, faith in our own ability to distinguish truth from falsehood.

If we don't have direct access and thus are trapped in a subjective prison, how then can we know anything? This leads to the next point:

(2) We theorize.

We always have, though we have only recently come to realize this. As long as we thought we were directly connected to the world, theorizing was seen as the realm of intellectuals who had the luxury of playing mental games, arranging and rearranging their data into different patterns. But once we come to appreciate (1), we see that (2) must follow, for theory is the bridge between our subjective prison and the world.

Theorizing was first used only as a bridge to the external world; it was a move of desperation (as we saw with Occam). It was the last attempt to tie our beliefs to something solid and unchanging. We have referred to these attempts as anchors.

> **Anchors**. We humans have a penchant for anchors, no doubt born in our inherent need for stability. Anchors keep us from drifting; they give us a solid foundation upon which to build our systems of knowledge, politics, morality and self.

Anchors were needed because the acceptance of theorizing meant the loss of certainty. Theorizing only gives us degrees of probability. Hence the desperation. Moving to theorizing was seen as a loss of some sort, a fall from the paradise of direct access. But no one ever had direct access to the world. Those who thought they did in the past were mistaken, which means they were theorizing without knowing it. Because they did not (and could not) acknowledge their methodology, they had no reason to attempt to refine it. Thus the biases that are built into our processors (our brains), led them astray. We mentioned two of these biases in particular:

> **The pebble-rock fallacy** is the result of thinking that we have a direct connection with the stable, eternal divisions of an unchanging world. It is the view that the world really is divided up into nice neat categories and our job is merely to discover what these are. This is a forlorn hope. The world is not stable and unchanging, and we impose our categorical distinctions upon the it in order to make sense of it.

> **The abstraction fallacy** is related, for it occurs when we posit abstractions (entities in our brains) as real things. This occurs on a basic level when our brain reifies pain, placing it at certain parts of our body when it is actually occurring in our head. So also do we posit colors, tastes, smells and so on out into the world when they, too, exist only in our head. Self-consciousness is also an abstraction, as are the reference frames we use when viewing ourselves and the world as if from above.

The abstraction fallacy is only a fallacy when we fall prey to it unawares. It is self-consciousness asserting itself in our lives. When we reflect upon the world, when we see our experience as our experience rather than just experience, we have abstracted from the flow; we have stepped up a level to a higher reference frame, like climbing a tree or viewing a map in an attempt to get an idea of where we are. Our natural tendency is to continually find a higher reference frame, a larger more all-encompassing point of view. This leads to another concept we have utilized continually:

The god's-eye-view, which is the highest possible, or absolute, reference frame, in which we attempt to see the world from a godlike perspective. Misuse of this construct is a result of using the abstraction fallacy, for it is a reification of the highest reference frame as something that actually exists. Once the god's-eye-view is reified, it becomes the stable and unchanging anchor many have always wanted. It is seen as the bastion of our beliefs in god, morality, freedom and our very self.

Alas, it is but an abstraction, useful at times, but an abstraction nonetheless. Realizing this takes us back to the fact that we are alone in the world, imprisoned in our subjectivity. But this is not as bad as it seems. In fact, everyone has always been imprisoned in their subjectivity, they just didn't know it. Appreciating the fact frees us to develop alternate methodologies that improve our ways of getting around in the world, more reflective methods that overcome, to some extent, our inherent biases. The major improvement I am referring to is, of course:

(3)   Coherence.

The coherence theory of truth replaces the correct description theory of truth and cuts our anchor to the external world with respect to truth. The correct description theory was at the heart of our troubles; it tantalized us with a truth we could never obtain. Theorizing was used for centuries as a means to cross this gap, but always left us unfulfilled. Our solution is to cut this useless anchor to the external world and embrace the coherence theory. On this view sentences are true if and only if they cohere well within our framework according to the adequacy conditions we have specified: consistency, simplicity, completeness, interconnectivity and integration.

Again, this is what we humans have been doing for thousands of years without realizing it. The problem is that it seemed to land us back in our subjective prison, for there was no touchstone to the external world. It's ironic that this fear kept us from embracing theorizing which kept us from realizing that better adequacy conditions can help overcome this fear. Mere consistency won't allow us to develop useful theories, but if we add the condition of integration, which demands that our personal beliefs cohere not just internally but also publicly with other coherent theories, we then have a better means of getting about in the world, of sorting true sentences from false ones. The addition of this integration condition to theorizing gave us:

The scientific method, which introduced publicity into our theorizing methodology. Publicity, which we have included in our adequacy conditions under the heading of integration, is manifest in terms of repeatability. One person's experimental result is a standalone theory. If they are to be taken seriously they must be publicly repeatable. This gives us a new touchstone, an external anchoring in publicity.

We drew an analogy with memories. Memories are a good example of our subjective imprisonment, for how do you know that the memory you have of, say, fishing with Dad as a five-year-old is real? Did you really go fishing? From your subjective prison, you will never know, but if you can tie this memory to some other independent sources, you are more justified in believing it. If you have a dated photograph of you and Dad fishing, and Dad himself verifies that, yes, you went fishing together at that time, you have then anchored your subjective belief in the public realm. So also with our other beliefs. The more we can connect them to other publicly verifiable theories, the more we are justified in believing them to be true.

But, of course, the question arises: how can publicity rescue us from our prison? Put another way, this is like asking: how do we know that coherence gives us true sentences? This is an illicit question, for it tries to sneak the correct description theory back into the picture. Coherence is not subject to truth claims. It is a methodological presupposition. Using coherence helps us get around in the world—coherence works—and this is all we need. When you come to appreciate this fact you can then see how you are truly no longer dependent upon an unknowable external world.

The coherence point of view puts an emphasis on connectivity. Everything coheres in one way or another and this gives us deep connections not only to other living things but to non-living things. You have genes within you that are over three billion years old—the genes of archaebacteria and before. You have elements within you from supernovas that brightened a sky no one would see for billions of years. Your self-consciousness is the most wondrous phenomenon you can imagine, allowing you to contemplate the very processes which produced you, giving you the ability to change those processes and create multiple futures. The world is out there, awaiting your explorations. Fare forward, travellers, impress your hand on millennia as on wax:

Why so soft, so pliant and yielding? Why is there so much denial, self-denial in your hearts? So little destiny in your eyes? (Nietzsche 326)

Illustration Credits

All figures are original, with the following exceptions:

Cover illustration: network © Tasosk #4190949 (modified fotolia vector)

Figure 2-9 on page 43 and the figure in the box on page 44 are redrawn from (Armel 2003)

Figures 3-5, 3-6, & 3-7 on pages 56-57 are redrawn from (Ramachandran 2011)

Dilbert comic strip (Figure 5-3, page 114): dt990908dhc0, licensed to David Payne

Figure 8-6 on page 184: architecture © sabri deniz kizil #11421023 (modified fotolia vector)

References

Angier, N. (1999). *Woman: An Intimate Geography.* Houghton Mifflin Harcourt.

Arendt, H. (2006). *Eichmann in Jerusalem: A Report on the Banality of Evil.* Penguin Classics.

Ariely, D. (2008). *Predictably Irrational: The Hidden Forces That Shape Our Decisions.* HarperCollins.

Armel, K. C., & Ramachandran, V. S. (2003). "Projecting Sensations to External Objects: Evidence from Skin Conductance Response". *Proceedings Royal Society London,* 270, 1499-1506.

Baker, R. (2006). *Sperm Wars: Infidelity, Sexual Conflict, and Other Bedroom Battles.* Basic Books.

Barber, E. W., & Barber, P. T. (2006). *When They Severed Earth from Sky: How the Human Mind Shapes Myth.* Princeton University Press.

Baron-Cohen, S. (2011). *The Science of Evil: On Empathy and the Origins of Cruelty.* Basic Books.

Becker, E. (1997). *The Denial of Death.* Free Press.

Bentham, J. (1780). *An Introduction to the Principles of Morals and Legislation.* PDF of original edition.

Blackmore, S. (2000). *The Meme Machine.* Oxford University Press, USA.

Blumenberg, H. (1985). *The Legitimacy of the Modern Age* (Studies in Contemporary German Social Thought). The MIT Press.

Borges, J. L. (2010). *Collected Fictions.* Penguin.

Burton, R. (2009). *On Being Certain: Believing You Are Right Even When You're Not.* St. Martin's Griffin.

Camping, H. (2011). "Another Infallible Proof." http://www.familyradio.com/graphical/literature/proof/proof.html.

Carr, D. (1991). *Time, Narrative, and History* (Studies in Phenomenology and Existential Philosophy). Indiana University Press.

Christian, D., & McNeill, W. H. (2005). *Maps of Time: An Introduction to Big History* (California World History Library). University of California Press.

Cialdini, R. B. (2007). *Influence: The Psychology of Persuasion* (Collins Business Essentials). Harper Paperbacks.

Clausewitz, C. v. (1989). *On War*. Princeton University Press.

Conrad, J. (1994). *Heart of Darkness*. Penguin Classics.

D'Aquili, E., & Newberg, A. B. (1999). *Mystical Mind* (Theology and the Sciences). Fortress Press.

Damasio, A. (2010). *Self Comes to Mind: Constructing the Conscious Brain*. Pantheon.

Dawkins, R. (1979). *The Selfish Gene*. Oxford University Press.

Dawkins, R. (1999). *The Extended Phenotype: The Long Reach of the Gene* (Popular Science). Oxford University Press, USA.

Dennett, D. C. (1984). *Elbow Room: The Varieties of Free Will Worth Wanting*. The MIT Press.

Dennett, D. C. (1996). *Darwin's Dangerous Idea: Evolution and the Meanings of Life*. Simon & Schuster.

Diamond, J. (2005). *Collapse: How Societies Choose to Fail or Succeed*. Penguin (Non-Classics).

Eichmann, A. (1999). *Eichmann Interrogated: Transcripts from the Archives of the Israeli Police*. Da Capo Press.

Festinger, L. (1966). *A Theory of Cognitive Dissonance*. Stanford University Press.

Festinger, L., Riecken, H. W., & Schachter, S. (1956). *When Prophecy Fails: A Social and Psychological Study of A Modern Group that Predicted the Destruction of the World*. Harper-Torchbooks.

Foer, J. (2011). *Moonwalking with Einstein: The Art and Science of Remembering Everything*. Penguin Press HC.

Frankfurt, H. G. (1988). *The Importance of What We Care About: Philosophical Essays*. Cambridge University Press.

Gazzaniga, M. S. (2009). *Human*. HarperCollins e-books.

Gere, C. (2011). *Knossos and the Prophets of Modernism*. University Of Chicago Press.

Gladwell, M. (2011). *Outliers: The Story of Success*. Back Bay Books.

Goffman, E. (1959). *The Presentation of Self in Everyday Life*. Anchor.

Gopnik, A. (2010). *The Philosophical Baby: What Children's Minds Tell Us About Truth, Love, and the Meaning of Life*. Picador.

Gould, S. J. (1988). *An Urchin in the Storm: Essays About Books and Ideas*. W. W. Norton & Company.

Greene, B. (2011). *The Hidden Reality: Parallel Universes and the Deep Laws of the Cosmos*. Knopf.

Haidt, J. (2006). *The Happiness Hypothesis: Finding Modern Truth in Ancient Wisdom*. Basic Books.

Hawking, S. (1998). *A Brief History of Time*. Bantam.

Hawking, S., & Mlodinow, L. (2010). *The Grand Design*. Bantam.

Hofstadter, D. (2001). "Analogy as the Core of Cognition." In D. Gentnor (Ed.), *The Analogical Mind: Perspectives from Cognitive Science* (pp. 499-538). Cambridge: The MIT Press.

Hofstadter, D. & Sander, Emmanuel. (2013). *Surfaces and Essences*. New York: Basic Books.

Hume, D. (1902). *An Enquiry Concerning Human Understanding.* Gutenberg.

Humphrey, N. (2011). *Soul Dust: The Magic of Consciousness.* Princeton University Press.

Huron, D. (2008). *Sweet Anticipation: Music and the Psychology of Expectation* (Bradford Books). The MIT Press.

James, W. (1890). *The Principles of Psychology*, 2 Vols. Henry Holt & Company.

James, W. (1992). *William James : Writings 1878-1899 : Psychology, Briefer Course / The Will to Believe / Talks to Teachers and Students / Essays* (Library of America). Library of America.

Kaku, M. (2009). *Physics of the Impossible: A Scientific Exploration into the World of Phasers, Force Fields, Teleportation, and Time Travel.* Anchor.

Kuhn, T. S. (1996). *The Structure of Scientific Revolutions.* University Of Chicago Press.

Lakoff, G., & Johnson, M. (1999). *Philosophy in the Flesh : The Embodied Mind and Its Challenge to Western Thought.* Basic Books.

Lakoff, G., & Johnson, M. (2003). *Metaphors We Live By.* University Of Chicago Press.

Laplace, P. S. M. d. (2010). *A Philosophical Essay on Probabilities* (1902). Cornell University Library.

Lovejoy, A. (2009). *The Great Chain of Being: A Study of the History of an Idea.* Transaction Publishers.

Marcus, G. (2004). *The Birth of the Mind: How a Tiny Number of Genes Creates The Complexities of Human Thought.* Basic Books.

Marcus, G. (2008). *Kluge: The Haphazard Construction of the Human Mind.* Houghton Mifflin Co.

Maslow, A. H. (1987). *Motivation and Personality.* HarperCollins Publishers.

Milgram, S. (2004). *Obedience to Authority: An Experimental View* (Perennial Classics). Harper Perennial Modern Classics.

Mlodinow, L. (2009). *The Drunkard's Walk: How Randomness Rules Our Lives* (Vintage). Vintage.

Neisser, U., & Harsch, N. (1992). *Phantom Flashbulbs: False Recollections of Hearing the News About Challenger.* New York: Cambridge University Press.

Nietzsche, F. (1977). *The Portable Nietzsche* (Portable Library). Penguin Books.

Nisbett, R. E., & Cohen, D. (1996). *Culture of Honor: The Psychology of Violence in the South.* Westview Press.

Nozick, R. (1990). *The Examined Life: Philosophical Meditations.* Simon & Schuster.

Nunez, P. L. (2010). *Brain, Mind, and the Structure of Reality.* Oxford University Press, USA.

Pinker, S. (2003). *The Blank Slate: The Modern Denial of Human Nature.* Penguin (Non-Classics).

Pinker, S. (2012). *The Better Angels of Our Nature.* New York: Viking.

Plato, Grube, G. M. A., & Reeve, C. D. C. (1992). *Plato: Republic.* Hackett Pub Co.

Ramachandran, V. S. (2011). *The Tell-Tale Brain: A Neuroscientist's Quest for What Makes Us Human.* W. W. Norton & Company.

Rescher, N. (1979). *Cognitive systematization: A systems-theoretic approach to a coherentist theory of knowledge.* Rowman and Littlefield.

Rescher, N. (2006). *Epistemetrics.* Cambridge University Press.

Ridley, M. (2003). *The Red Queen: Sex and the Evolution of Human Nature.* Harper Perennial.

Rosa, M. d. S. (2009). *Colombo Português - Novas Revelações (Portuguese Columbus - New Revelations)*. Esquilo Ediciones y Multimedia.

Santayana, G. (1923). *Soliloquies in England and Later Solilioguies*. Charles Scribner's Sons.

Sartre, J.-P. (2007). *Nausea*. New Directions.

Shattuck, R. (1981). *The Forbidden Experiment: The Story of the Wild Boy of Aveyron*. Pocket.

Singer, P. (2011). *The Expanding Circle: Ethics, Evolution, and Moral Progress*. Princeton University Press.

Smith, A. (2011). *The Wealth of Nations*. Simon & Brown.

Sober, E., & Wilson, D. (1999). *Unto Others: The Evolution and Psychology of Unselfish Behavior*. Harvard University Press.

Swartwood, R. (2010). *Hint Fiction: An Anthology of Stories in 25 Words or Fewer*. W. W. Norton & Company.

Taleb, N. N. (2007). *The Black Swan: The Impact of the Highly Improbable*. Random House.

Taylor, C. (1992). *Sources of the Self: The Making of the Modern Identity*. Harvard University Press.

Veblen, T. (1899). *Theory of the Leisure Class*. Public Domain Books.

Verlinde, E. P. (2011). *On the Origin of Gravity and the Laws of Newton*. Journal of High Energy Physics, 1-26.

Weber, M. (2001). *The Protestant Ethic and the Spirit of Capitalism* (Routledge Classics). Routledge.

Wilson, Edward O. (2012) *The Social Conquest of Earth*. Liveright Publishing.

Wright, R. (2001). *Nonzero: The Logic of Human Destiny*. Vintage.

Zahavi, A., & Zahavi, A. (1997). *The Handicap Principle: A Missing Piece of Darwin's Puzzle*. Oxford University Press, USA.

Zimmer, C. (2004). "Faith-boosting Genes: a search for the genetic basis of spirituality." Scientific American.

Zuk, Marlene. (2013) Paleofantasy. New York: W.W. Norton.

Index

abortion 10, 336, 347
Abraham (Old Testament) 7, 214
absolute reference frame 152, 160, 162-163, 166-167, 256, 258-259
abstract general terms 126, 129, 280
abstraction fallacy 179, 294, 297-298, 333, 376-377
Achilles 276
addiction 139, 369
adequacy conditions (see individual conditions)
ad hoc hypothesis 76, 90-95, 98, 100, 106-107, 114-115, 140-141, 212, 346
afterlife 212, 274, 276-277, 316
agnostic 269, 284
Alexander the Great 188
allegory of the cave (Plato) 109, 162
altruism 124, 141-142, 145-146, 216, 322-326, 330-331, 340-341, 360
American Idol Effect 115, 312
analog vs digital 10
Anaximenes 353
Anselm, St. 277, 279, 282
anthropic principle 268, 284, 286-288
anthropology 62
anti-semitic 336
Aquinas, St. Thomas 189
Aristotle 24, 51, 92, 167, 172, 188-189, 218
artificial selection 67, 363
associative learning 59, 71, 126
Augustine, St. 98, 160
author 35, 81, 249, 294, 302-310, 319, 323, 338
autocracy 339
axiomatic system 167, 185, 189, 206-207, 217-218, 340, 366
bacteria 23, 25-27, 364
barber paradox 278, 301
Bayesian analysis 288

behaviorism 62, 117-118
Bell, Gordon 303-304
benevolent despot 339
Bentham, Jeremy 8, 321, 340
Bernoulli 253
binding problem 13, 23, 53
biography, autobiography 34, 305-307, 315
black swan 182, 289
Bladerunner (movie) 195
blank slate 61-63, 117
blindsight 30-32
Boas, Franz 62
Borges, Jorges 303-305
brain in a vat hypothesis 178
Bruno, Giordano 99, 276, 281
butterfly effect, the 248, 252, 257, 260
Calvin, John 283
Camping, Harold 115
Candide 279
carrying capacity 359
Cathari 167
causal principle 245-246, 248, 251, 259, 284
causation 70, 87, 244, 248, 255-256
Ceres (dwarf planet) 12
Challenger Study 193
Charlemagne 189
Clark, Arthur C. 191
classical conditioning 59-60
clitoris 134
clocks & clouds 127, 160, 165, 183, 200, 215, 354, 356
coherence (theory of truth) 223-224, 229-231, 233-238
Columbus, Christopher 21, 76-79, 82, 84-87, 92
compatibilism 255
completeness 81, 83-85, 88, 91-92, 100, 111, 235, 304-305, 377

complex adaptive system   142, 317, 356
Compte, Auguste   177
condemnation   166-167
consequentialism   340, 343
conservation of energy   360
consolation   97, 167, 327
Conspicuous consumption   145
Copernican   12, 76, 95-96, 98-99, 290-291
Copernicus, Nicolas   89, 92, 95, 99, 104
core self   31, 33-34, 38, 40, 308
core value   36, 39, 104, 111-112, 114,
        116, 139-140, 146, 163, 166-167,
        210, 213, 215, 233, 237, 260, 290,
        296, 310, 319, 323, 333-338, 342-
        347, 362-363, 366, 369, 372
corpus callosum   301
correct description (theory of truth)
        152-153, 166, 169, 219, 224-226,
        229-232, 234, 237-238, 264, 303,
        341, 377-378
cosmological argument   284
cost-benefit analysis   80-81, 106-107,
        111, 144, 261-262
creationism   268, 290-291
creeping exculpation   260-261, 263
crystals   93, 182, 192, 347, 353-354
cultural evolution   70, 124, 135
curiosity   38, 44, 79, 98, 100, 109, 111,
        155-156, 181, 281
Dante   93, 156
Darwin, Charles   167
Declaration of Independence   186
deduction   172, 180, 183-190, 206, 216-
        217, 282
Demeter   301
Democritus   353
dendrochronology   191, 235
Descartes, Rene   178, 217, 280, 297
detachable self   297-298
determinism   9, 243-246, 248-252, 254-
        256, 259-260, 263
deterrence   262-263, 326
dialectic   143, 230, 356
dialectical materialism   230
Dilthey, Wilhelm   299
Dirac, Paul   83
disenchantment   98, 167
dogleg   129-130, 135
Donne, John   92
dopamine   8, 111, 163, 166, 216, 331, 369
dystopia   127
egalitarianism   61-62
ego   116-117
egoism   322, 324-326, 331
Eichmann, Adolf   330
Einstein, Albert   89, 161-162, 164-165,
        186, 215, 252, 255
election of the saints   139, 283
elegance   81-85, 87-88, 110, 160, 163,
        235, 306, 347
Eliot, T.S.   98, 349
embodied perception   131, 179
empathy   142, 146, 322, 324, 327-332,
        340, 343
empathy rule (golden rule)   146, 322, 332,
        343
enlightenment   152, 162-163, 166, 191,

        238, 283, 364
entropy   26, 350, 353, 357, 360-362
equilibrium   12, 26, 89, 326-327, 331,
        350-353, 359-361, 366, 369-372
Euclid   186, 217
evil genius   217, 280
evolution   5, 35, 57, 64, 67-68, 70-71,
        124, 133-135, 138-139, 167,
        273-274, 276, 280, 289-291,
        360, 371
evolutionarily stable strategy (ESS)
        331, 371
Exactitude in Science   303
exaptation   133
exponential growth   357-359
extended phenotype   16-17, 136
extended self   317
exteroception   177
faith   100, 182, 200, 207, 214-215,
        219, 238, 270-271, 283, 314,
        341, 375
fastball problem   71-72
fatalism   9, 250, 258-260, 263-264
Federal Reserve   359
feedback   23, 35, 43, 308, 317, 350,
        356-360, 369
        negative   326, 357-359, 371
        positive   357-359, 369
feral children   124-127
Festinger, Leon   111, 115
fiction   174, 191, 304-306, 337-338
fictional worlds   17
filters   16, 52, 116, 118, 193-194, 206,
        212-213, 217, 225, 287, 296,
        304-306
fixed action behavior   58, 249, 260
flashbulb memories   194
flat earth theory   234-235, 290, 346
fMRI   29-30, 36
fog of war   5
formalism   341
free association   117
free riders   141, 322, 326-327, 329-331
free will   9, 73, 244-247, 254-256, 258,
        263-264
Freud, Sigmund   116
frozen accident   132
Galileo   162
general will   337
genetic drift   37, 133
genome   64, 67, 138
Gilgamesh   125
Gnosticism   97-98, 269, 278, 282, 284
god gene   268, 273
god meme   273
Goldilocks Zone   286-287
gold standard   127, 232
good trick   5
Gould, Stephen J.   133-134, 168-169
gravity   12, 44, 215, 234, 246, 256, 287,
        351, 353-356, 360, 370
Great Disappointment, the   115
gullibility   87, 260, 285
Hamilton, W.D.   331
handicap principle   145
Hawking, Stephen   175, 287, 362
heaven   62, 167, 282-283, 285-286,

298, 317
Hegel, G.W.F.   230
Heidegger, Martin   299
Hemingway, Ernest   303
Heraclitus   353
Hitler, Adolf   283
Holmes, Sherlock   190
homeostasis   25-26, 111, 350-353, 369-370
homunculus fallacy   31-32, 41, 44
House, M.D. (TV show)   151
Hubble space telescope   176
Hume, David   70-71, 296
Husserl, Edmund   299
hydrostatic equilibrium   12
id   116
imagined entities   335
Imitation   136, 369
improvisation   313, 315
inconceivable   208, 252, 270, 296, 332, 344-345
increments   4, 9, 14
induction   172, 180-190, 193
informational mass   305
Inquisition   98, 211
integration   81, 84-88, 100, 111, 120, 160, 192, 220, 235, 270-271, 290-291, 298, 305, 307, 311, 319, 377
integrity   12, 26, 352-353, 362, 367
interconnectivity   13, 81, 84-86, 88, 95, 100, 111-112, 114, 120, 160, 220, 235, 271, 284, 294, 305, 311, 317, 319, 366, 377
interoception   177
Intimations of Immortality (poem)   119
intolerance   211, 260
inverted color spectrum   118
invisible hand   278, 360
James, William   34, 119, 311
Jefferson, Thomas   186, 341
just so stories   133
Kant, Immanuel   116, 161, 224-230, 236, 256, 305, 337, 346-347
kin selection   331
Laplacean Super-Calculator (LSC)   244, 250-252, 254, 257-260, 263
LaPlace, Pierre-Simon   250
large numbers, law of   253
Leibniz, Gottfried   278-279, 281
Lewis, C.S.   364
Libet, Benjamin   71, 73
Locke, John   61-62, 255
Luther, Martin   99, 214, 275
Marxism   63
Marx, Karl   63, 230, 314, 335, 337
masks   143-144, 308, 312, 318-319
Maslow, Abraham   7, 11
Matrix, The (movie)   110, 163, 178, 207, 248
meme   124, 135-138, 140, 146, 195, 269, 273-274, 317
memento   317
Memento (movie)   195
memory   13, 16-17, 23, 33-36, 41, 53, 58, 83, 106, 116, 126, 129, 136, 138, 146, 158, 172, 181, 193-196, 207-209, 217, 272, 294, 296, 299-300,

302, 310, 316-317, 368-369, 372, 377
Mercury's perihelion   215
metabolism   25-26, 29, 177
Michelson, Albert   176
Milgram, Stanley   330
Minority Reports (movie)   261
miracle   270, 288
mirror neurons   180
moral circle   331-332, 345
moral monster   330
multiverse   175, 352
narrative   120, 194-195, 235, 300-304, 306-311, 315-316, 319, 324
NASA   173
Nationalism   137, 336
natural selection   37, 41, 48, 52, 64, 66-67, 135, 167, 169, 232, 368
Neisser, Ulrich   194
nested systems   53, 351-352, 364
neural correlates of consciousness (NCC)   23
neuroscience   23, 53, 116-117, 186, 296
neurotransmitter   369
Newton, Isaac   78, 89, 160
Nietzsche, Friedrich   318, 378
nirvana   166
noble savage   62, 125
non-associative learning   58
non-contradiction, law of   48, 51-52, 77, 82, 90, 109-110
non-Euclidean geometry   186
non-zero-sum game   360
objectification   126
Occam's razor   54, 82, 280-281
Occam, William of   268, 279-284, 291, 376
Odysseus   156, 276
omnipotence   98, 268, 278-284
ontological argument   217, 277
operant conditioning   59-60, 368
oral culture   126, 138
Osiander, Andreas   99
oxytocin   111, 357, 369
packrats   192, 235
pantheism   276
Pascal, Blaise   284-285, 291
Pavlov, Ivan   60
pebble-rock fallacy   9
Penrose Triangle   57
perception   xi, 35, 37, 44, 54, 70, 72-73, 78, 95, 98-100, 127-128, 131, 143, 172-174, 177-180, 208, 211, 225, 312-313
persona   116, 143-144, 308, 310, 312-313, 318-319
phantom limbs   40-41, 44, 178, 367
Philolaus   91
phrenology   116, 234
pillars of Hercules   156
plate tectonics   290
Plato   x, 61-62, 109, 129, 158-160, 162, 166-167, 172, 188-189, 194, 218, 232, 280, 297
pleasure principle   116
plenum   280
Pope (Catholic)   98, 275

Popper, Karl   356
possible world   279, 281
postulate of visibility   98-99
preponderance of evidence   204
Prestige, The (movie)   296
prion   25
prison of subjectivity   38-39, 131, 196,
    225, 230, 256, 268-272, 284,
    290, 301, 316, 375-377
private language   124, 126, 130
probable cause   204
problem of evil   98, 278-279, 282
Prometheus   96-97, 155
propaganda   339
proprioception   177
proto-self   33
providence 95, 97-98, 100, 279, 281-282
psychopath   63, 329
Ptolemy (Ptolemaic universe)   76, 92,
    94-95, 98, 290-291
punctuated determinism   254
punishment   247, 260-263, 273, 276,
    301, 326, 342, 363, 367-368
Pythagoras (Pythagorean)   91, 193
quantum theory   90, 177, 252, 255
Quine, W.V.O.   17
QWERTY keyboard   132
reciprocal altruism   124, 141-142, 146,
    216, 322, 324, 326, 330-331,
    360
reductionism   15, 117
reification   22, 40-41, 43, 129, 166,
    297, 300, 360, 363, 377
relativism   168, 322, 324, 342, 345
relativity theory   90, 162, 164-165, 177,
    186, 215, 234
religious experience   163, 271-272
Renaissance   283
reputation   141, 342
reverse engineering   124, 131-135, 144
Robinson Crusoe   14
Rorschach test   117-118, 157
Rousseau, Jean-Jacques   62, 337
Russell, Bertrand   278
Sagan, Carl   71
Santa Claus   110, 169, 207
Sapir-Whorf hypothesis   118
Sartre, Jean Paul   6, 123, 314
scientific method   88, 172, 180, 182-
    184, 187, 189, 196, 218, 220,
    234, 270, 272, 274, 314, 364,
    375, 377
seismic disturbance   112, 163, 208, 213,
    233, 270, 366
self-deception   114-115, 120, 141-142,
    212, 291, 294, 310-312, 315
self-evidence   61, 167, 186, 196, 200,
    207-208, 218, 230, 270, 375
sentience   22-23, 26-28, 30-33, 37, 41,
    160, 180
serial killer   340, 345-346
sexual reproduction   64
simplicity   24, 54, 81-84, 88, 100, 110,
    235, 279, 281, 305, 377
skepticism   18, 224-226, 232, 237-238,
    264
skin conductance response (SCR) 29, 42

Skinner, B.F.   60
Smith, Adam   360
social group   124, 139-142, 144, 146, 352
Socrates   61
Sophocles   9-10
stand-alone theory   89, 220, 224, 235-
    236, 271, 290, 298, 301, 311,
    324, 345-346, 377
stere-year   17
Stoicism   8-10, 97-98, 218, 372
supernova   17, 71, 173, 354, 378
superstition   71
symbiosis   14, 25, 370
taxonomy   9
teleology   167, 294, 299-300, 305, 310,
    350, 362-364, 366-367, 370
telephone syndrome   28
Thales   353
theodicy   279
theory of relativity   162, 164-165, 186,
    215
thermodynamic   26, 360
Three Mile Island   287-289
threshold   52, 350, 353-354, 356, 358
Tours, battle of   189
tragedy of the commons   142
tragic (Greek)   97
transporter   295-297
Truman Show, the (movie)   109, 163, 174
twinkie defense   261-262
twin paradox   165
twins   63-64, 125-126, 165
uncertainty principle   176
under-determined   78-79, 92, 95, 130
Ussher, Bishop   115
utilitarianism   322, 340-341, 343, 345,
    347
utopia   127, 141, 333
validity   184-185
vampire bat   141
Veblen, Thorstein   145
vegetative state   28, 30
virtue 49, 72, 174, 347, 364, 372
virus   25, 136
Voltaire   273, 279
volvox   163
War of the Worlds (radio broadcast)   271
Watson, John   62
Weber, Max   167
Welles, Orson   271
widow bird   358, 371
wiki-novel   323
wild boy of Aveyron   125
Williams, Robin   68
will of all   337
Wittgenstein, Ludwig   126
Wizard of Oz   62, 73, 132, 192, 230,
    237, 270-271, 337, 370
Wordsworth, William   119
world of the forms (Plato)   129, 166,
    188, 218-219
Zadig   190
Zeus   275
zombie   21-22, 24-30, 35-37, 233, 249